THE GUINNESS
RAILWAY
BOOK

THE GUINNESS
RAILWAY
BOOK

John Marshall

GUINNESS BOOKS

Editor: Beatrice Frei
Design and layout: Christie Archer Design
Picture Editor: Alex Goldberg

Published in Great Britain by Guinness Publishing Ltd,
33 London Road, Enfield, Middlesex

Phototypeset in 9/11 Palatino and 9/11 Optima
by Ace Filmsetting Ltd, Frome, Somerset
Printed and bound in Great Britain by
Butler & Tanner Ltd, Frome, Somerset

British Library Cataloguing in Publication Data

Marshall, John, *1922 May 1–*
    The Guinness railway book—2nd ed.
    1. Railways. Records of achievement.
    I. Title   II. Marshall, John, *1922 May 1–*
385'.09

ISBN 0–85112–359–7

Illustrations:
Half-title page Flying Scotsman
Title page Eastbound 'Super Continental' of the Canadian
National Railways crossing Yellowhead Pass, 1133 m
(3717 ft), the lowest crossing of the Canadian Rockies.

CONTENTS

ACKNOWLEDGEMENTS

No book of this type could be compiled by one person alone, and I am deeply grateful to those individuals and organizations who have supplied information, including numerous correspondents who have written to correct, enlarge or update minor details in *Rail—The Records*. Many who were acknowledged in that book and in the three editions of *Rail Facts and Feats* have continued to supply material and to reply to my queries.

In particular I must mention: Mr C. P. Atkins, Librarian, National Railway Museum, York; and Messrs R. F. Corley, Toronto; W. L. Fletcher; P. M. Kalla Bishop; K. I. MacFarlane; F. Mills; A. M. Moss; A. J. Mullay; R. Olgiati; D. Perriam; N. T. Pitts; P. Rees; R. M. Robbins; R. Russell; B. Smith; R. Weaver; J. P. Wilson. The continued valuable assistance of my sons Simon and Andrew and the tolerance of my wife Ann has made me realize again what a family business is the making of a book such as this.

John Marshall has been fascinated by all aspects of railways since childhood. He has established himself as one of the leading railway historians and has written numerous books and articles on railways in Britain and abroad. Besides a detailed and scholarly history of *The Lancashire & Yorkshire Railway*, in three volumes, he has written a history of *Metre Gauge Railways in South and East Switzerland*, published in 1974 and *A Biographical Dictionary of Railway Engineers* in 1978.

John Marshall is also the author of the best-selling *Rail Facts and Feats* (3 editions) and of *The Rail Factbook*, both published by Guinness Superlatives Ltd.

PICTURE CREDITS

All illustrations by the author except for the following:

Black & White

Altoona Area Public Library: 125
BR Inter City: 136, 137
Brighton Public Libraries: 132, 154
Brush Electrical Machines Ltd: 136
British Railways: 15, 25 (top), 116, 123, 159, 193
Burlington Northern Inc: 95
Canadian National Railways: Title page, 66, 83 (bottom)
Canadian Pacific: 64 (bottom), 65, 93 (bottom), 120, 164
Chinese People's Republic Railways: 98
Dudley Public Libraries: 103 (top)
J. E. Edgington: 115 (top)
French Railways Ltd: 24, 31
From an old CM Poster: 56
Gloucester Railway Carriage & Wagon Co: 155
Greater Manchester Museum of Science & Industry: 118/119
Japan Rail: 90
Ricardo Kelly: 12
Keystone Collection: 6, 36, 54, 58 (bottom), 157, 167, 179, 185, 195
London Regional Transport: 169
Simon Marshall: 175
The Milwaukee Road: 165
National Library of Ireland: 173
National Railway Museum, York: 144, 147
The Photo Source: Half title page
Neil Pitts: 50 (bottom)
The Science Museum, London: 14, 16, 20, 21, 25 (bottom), 33, 102, 103, 105
Simpson Lumber Company: 83 (top)
Smithsonian Institute, Washington: 8
Southern Pacific Transportation: 35, 64 (top)
Brian Stephenson: 129
Victoria & Albert Museum: 192
Western Australian Government Railways: 146
Andreas Zingg: 93 (top)

Colour

Archiv Für Kunst und Geschichte: 1 (top), (middle), 2 (top), 22 (top)
E. T. Archive: 1 (bottom)
Hugh Dady: 19 (top)
Norman Gurley: 4 (bottom left)
Alex Hansen: 4 (bottom right)
Images Colour Library: 4 (middle right), 9 (top), 15 (bottom)
Keystone Collection: 23 (bottom)
Kobal Collection: 21 (top)
Andrew Marshall: 6 (bottom), 7 (bottom), 11 (bottom), 19 (middle)
Mary Evans Picture Library: 11 (top)
The Photo Source: 8, 15 (top), 16 (bottom), 18 (bottom), 21 (bottom), 22 (bottom)
Quadrant Picture Library: Front cover, 6 (top), 12
Spectrum Colour Library: 5 (top), 23 (top)
Vintage Magazine Company: 14, 20

INTRODUCTION

This book presents a broad collection of information on railways, their origins, creation and achievements, ranging throughout the world. It is the successor to *The Guinness Book of Rail Facts and Feats*, published in three editions in 1971, 1975 and 1979, and *Rail – The Records*, 1985. Much new material has been added, and standing matter has been updated, some to within weeks of finalizing the text.

It is a strange paradox that in the two countries which gave birth to the modern railway, Great Britain and the USA, where there is the greatest enthusiasm for railways among lay members of the public, there should be the greatest neglect of this form of transport by the governments. Other countries, as disclosed in this book, are vigorously expanding and improving their rail networks, yet in these countries one finds few enthusiasts.

The importance of rail transport cannot be overstated. Modern railway systems around the world are proving that the railway can handle most of our transport needs. Where in the past it failed, the fault could usually be attributed to human negligence or inefficiency, even downright obstinacy, or to lack of co-operation between neighbouring systems or administrations, not to the railway as a system of transport. The modern railway, evolved over 150 years, is by far the safest and most economically efficient form of transport available.

The Association of American Railroads established that a railway can move an item of freight for a fifth of the fuel, a sixth of the accidents and a tenth of the land that road haulage requires for the same load, and can carry seven times as much freight per employee.

The most practical and best tried solution to future transport problems is railway electrification on both inter-city and urban routes. The electric railway makes the most economical use of energy of all types of mass transport, also it is swift, clean and relatively quiet. By confining pollution hazards to power stations this problem is simplified, though by no means eliminated.

Throughout the world, one country after another is becoming aware of the urgency of railway electrification. British Railways, hampered by government apathy, with only 23.25 per cent of its 16 729 km (10 395 miles) electrified, takes 14th place in the 21 major European networks. Japan, a similar densely populated country, with 21 091 km (13 106 miles) of railway route including the Shinkansen, has electrified 52.8 per cent, more than twice the British percentage.

A modern double-track high-speed electric railway has a greater traffic capacity than a six-lane motorway while occupying only a third of the land. Every year, in Great Britain alone, thousands of acres of good agricultural land are buried beneath new roads. At the present rate of use world oil supplies will dry up in 2019. But as long as governments can enrich themselves from taxes on oil products and road transport they are unlikely to encourage the development of a form of transport which reduces their incomes, however economic it may be in its use of energy resources.

While much of this book is concerned with the history and development of various aspects of railways, and the achievements of the many outstanding engineers, emphasis is constantly placed on the important part which railways play in modern life. The aim has been to maintain complete impartiality and to state facts, both pleasant and unpleasant, without emotion. The reader seeking railway nostalgia will find none of it in this book, but it is hoped that anyone with an intelligent interest in railways will find plenty to satisfy him.

In its compilation only the most authoritative sources have been used, albeit secondary (printed). For up-to-date information on railways throughout the world the best sources are *Janes's World Railways* and the *Railway Directory and Year Book*, both published annually and available at most large reference libraries.

Because of the enormous amount of published material on railways, a bibliography has not been included. Readers requiring bibliographical information should consult *A Bibliography of British Railway History* by George Ottley, first published in 1965. A new edition was published by Her Majesty's Stationery Office in 1983 (ISBN 0–11–290334–7). A supplementary volume bringing the work up to date is just published by HMSO. The updating process is being continued in the *Journal* of the Railway & Canal Historical Society. For American books the reader may find it useful to consult the *Bibliography of railroad literature* published by the Association of American Railroads in Washington. The best British periodicals for keeping abreast with railway developments throughout the world are: *Railway Gazette International* and *Modern Railways*.

ORIGINS

The principle of a railway, a track which guides vehicles travelling along it, dates back to Babylonian times, about 2245 BC. Parallel lines of stone blocks with grooves in the centres, with a gauge of about 1500 mm (5 ft), can still be found.

The ancient Greeks used grooved stone wagonways with a gauge of 1626 mm (5 ft 4 in). Remains of these can be found all over Greece, principally between Athens and Piraeus.

The oldest known illustration of anything resembling a railway is a window high up in the Minster of Freiburg im Breisgau, Germany, dating from about 1350. It was presented by Johann Snewlin der Gresser who owned the Schauinsland Mines, and shows a miner pushing a box-like vehicle.

One of the earliest illustrations of a mine railway is found in a book published by Johan Haselberger of Reichenau in Lower Austria about 1519, with a title beginning *Der Ursprung gemeynner Berckrecht wie die lange Zeit von den Alten erhalten worde. . . .* It shows a man pushing a small truck along a wooden railway.

A Flemish painting, dated 1544, entitled *Les Travaux de la Mine*, on a wood panel 106.7 × 55.9 cm (42 × 22 in) was discovered about 1940. It shows a miner pushing a four-wheeled truck along a railway out of a mine. The painter probably obtained his information from the above book.

The earliest record of a railway in the generally accepted sense is an illustration of a narrow-gauge mine railway at Leberthal in Alsace in *Cosmographiae Universalis* by Sebastian Münster (1489–1552), dated 1550.

Rail wagons were described and illustrated by Georg Bauer (1494–1555), (in English 'George Farmer') who called himself Georgius Agricola, in *De Re Metallica*, first published in 1556.

A mine wagon with flanged wooden wheels, some wooden track with a gauge of 480 mm (1 ft 6⅞ in), and a switch or point with one blade, as used in gold mines in the Siebenbürgen in Transylvania, is stored in the Verkehrs und Baumuseum, Berlin. They are said to date from the late 16th century which, if correct (and this is doubtful) would establish that railways were in general use in central Europe in the late Middle Ages. Transylvania is now part of Romania.

EARLY BRITISH RAILWAYS

The earliest recorded railway in Britain was a line about 3 km (2 miles) long, made of baulks of timber, on which wagons with flanged wheels were drawn by horses, from coal pits at Strelley to Wollaton Lane End about 5 km (3 miles) west of Nottingham. It was built at a cost of £166 between October 1603 and October 1604 by Huntingdon Beaumont (1561–1624), a Leicestershire mining engineer. Beaumont, who had leased pits at Strelley and Wollaton from Sir Francis Willoughby of Wollaton Hall in 1601–3, went on to establish wagonways on Tyneside between 1605 and 1608.

Flanged wooden wheels were used on English wagonways from about 1660 or earlier. They were generally turned with the grain lengthways, that is parallel to the axle. Elm was preferred, but beech, oak and ash and even softwood were used. One example discovered at Broseley, near Ironbridge in Shropshire, probably dates from this period. It measures 241 mm (9½ in) diameter over the flange and 203 mm (8 in) over the tread which is 95 mm (3¾ in) 'wide' (along the grain).

Examples of early rails at the National Railway Museum, York. In the foreground is a section of oak track, mid-18th century, from Groverake Mine near Blanchland, County Durham. The rails are 1.8 m (5 ft 10½ in) long, about 89 mm (3½ in) square and are laid to a gauge of about 457 mm (1 ft 6 in) on sleepers 825 mm (2 ft 8½ in) long. Above it is a piece of 'L' section tramway rail; to the right is a fish-bellied cast-iron rail, and in the top left a length of wrought-iron rail in chairs on stone block sleepers.

The idea for the flanged wheel was a direct outcome of the guide-pin (*Leitnagel*), allowing a much wider gauge to be used with corresponding greater stability and carrying capacity. The guide-pin ran between the rails which had to be close together and on this narrow-gauge wagons were small and easily upset.

The first recorded use of the word 'railway' was in 1681 at Pensnett about 4 km (2½ miles) north-east of Stourbridge, in Staffordshire (now West Midlands).

'Railroad' was first used at Rowton on the Tarbatch Dingle line near Coalport on the River Severn in Shropshire in 1702. The two words were then used indiscriminately in Britain until about 1850 after which 'railway' became standard. In North America this was reversed and 'railroad' became the more widely used term.

The word 'waggonway' [sic] was first recorded at Broseley in Shropshire in 1631. It became widely used on Tyneside where it lasted until about 1800.

The earliest discovered record of the word 'tramroad' was in the Minutes of the Brecon & Abergavenny Canal Company, in South Wales, on 17 October 1798. This generally referred to the L-shaped iron rails or plates and was used in this connection. 'Tramway' usually denoted a light railway or mineral railway.

The word 'tram' is believed to derive from a low German word *traam* meaning beam or shaft, and probably originated with the old wooden railways or with the frame on which baskets of coal were carried.

The most famous of the early British wagonways was the Tanfield Wagonway in County Durham. The first section was built in 1725 and it was extended in 1726. It was a double-track wooden railway with a gauge of 1219 mm (4 ft), and was converted to iron rails in 1839. The Tanfield, or Causey, Arch built in 1727 by mastermason Ralph Wood, has a span of 32 m (105 ft) and is probably **the world's oldest major railway bridge**. It carried the wagonway over the Beckley Burn near Causey at a height of 24.4 m (80 ft) with a semi-elliptical arch 6.9 m (22 ft 7½ in) wide and a rise of 10.5 m (35 ft). The bridge remained in use until the late 1760s. It has recently been fully restored. It was the largest arch in Great Britain until surpassed by the 42.7 m (140 ft) span over the Taff at Pontypridd, built by William Edwards in 1755.

Part of the Tanfield line continued in use for coal traffic until 18 May 1964.

Cast-iron flanged wheels were made at Coalbrookdale in Shropshire from 1729.

Scotland's first railway was the Tranent–Cockenzie Wagonway, about 16 km (10 miles) east of Edinburgh, laid down with wooden rails in 1722. Part of the line was used on 21 September 1745 in the course of a battle with the Young Pretender, Prince Charles Edward. Iron rails were used from 1815. It continued as a horse tramway until after 1880 when part of it was converted into a steam colliery railway.

Ralph Allen's wooden wagonway at Prior Park, Bath, from an engraving by Anthony Walker published in 1752, the first illustration of an English railway and the first railway in Britain known to have used flanged wheels.

A wagonway was constructed for Ralph Allen (1694–1764), the Post Office reformer, at Prior Park, Bath, to connect his quarries on Coombe Down with Dolemeads Wharf on the Avon, about 2.4 km (1½ miles). It was built in 1730 to a design by John Padmore, a Bristol engineer. Rails were of oak scantlings about 150 × 125 mm (6 × 5 in) to a gauge of 1143 mm (3 ft 9 in). It was dismantled soon after Ralph Allen's death in 1764. The engraving by Anthony Walker was the first illustration of an English railway. This was the first railway in Britain on which the use of flanged wheels is positively recorded. It also has the distinction of being the first railway mentioned in English literature. (See chapter 17.)

The first railway authorized by Parliament in Britain was the line from a colliery at Middleton into Leeds, constructed under an Act granted to Charles Brandling, Lord of the Manor of Middleton, on 9 June 1758. It was described in the Act as a 'wagonway' and was **the first on which steam locomotives were commercially used**. It had a gauge of 1254 mm (4 ft 1⅜ in). The first two engines, built by Matthew Murray (1765–1826) of Leeds to an order by John Blenkinsop (1783–1831) first ran on 12 August 1812. Because Blenkinsop believed that smooth wheels would not grip the rails, it was propelled by a toothed wheel engaging on a rack on one of the rails. Two more similar engines were built in 1813. The rack engines continued in service until 1835. The wheels of a similar one from the Kenton & Coxlodge Railway on Tyneside, dating from 1813, are preserved on a section of original track in the National Railway Museum, York.

A portion of the Middleton Railway is still active, preserved by the Middleton Railway Trust, founded in 1959 with the co-operation of the National Trust. Steam locomotives are still at work after 163 years—a world record.

The 'standard gauge' of 1435 mm (4 ft 8½ in) was first established on the Willington Colliery wagonway system near Newcastle upon Tyne. Killingworth Colliery, where George Stephenson began his railway work, was part of this system. The first section of 4.8 km (3 miles), from

Killingworth Moor to Willington Quay on the Tyne, was built in 1764–5. It had wooden rails.

Cast-iron bars on the tops of wooden rails were first recorded in use at Coalbrookdale, Shropshire, in 1767. They served a double function: to protect the rails from wear; and to act as a store for stocks of pig-iron during a period of low prices and at the same time to enable the furnaces to remain in operation. They were 1.5 m (5 ft) long, 102 mm (4 in) wide and 38 mm (1½ in) thick. The men who fixed these were known as 'plate-layers', a term still in use today for permanent-way men.

The first use of a railway as a canal feeder was from Caldon Low Quarries in Staffordshire to Froghall Wharf for which the Trent & Mersey Canal Company obtained an Act on 13 May 1776, the second British Railway Act. The canal was authorized in 1766 and completed at the same time as the railway in 1777. The course of the railway can still be traced.

Iron flanged rails or 'plates' were introduced in England by John Curr of Durham, while he was viewer of the Duke of Norfolk's collieries at Sheffield in 1787. They were first used only underground in Sheffield Park Colliery. The L-shaped rails, laid on wooden sleepers to a gauge of 610 mm (2 ft), were 1.8 m (6 ft) long and weighed 21–22 kg (47–50 lb) each. Their first use on surface lines was in 1788 on the Ketley inclined plane in Shropshire. They were cast at Ketley Ironworks and were laid on longitudinal timber bearers, 356 mm (14 in) square. The rails were 1.8 m (6 ft) long, 203 mm (8 in) wide, 50 mm (2 in) thick and the flange was 76 mm (3 in) high.

The flanged iron plates cast at Coalbrookdale rapidly replaced the cast-iron bars on wooden rails for flanged wheels used around Coalbrookdale since 1767.

Flanged rails were inefficient compared with edge rails and their use was restricted to mineral lines on which wagons were pulled by horses. Their most concentrated use was probably in South Wales, in the Forest of Dean in Gloucestershire and around Coalbrookdale. **The world's first steam locomotive**, Richard Trevithick's of 1803 (see chapter 8) was designed to run on flanged rails but proved too heavy for them. On the Peak Forest Tramroad in Derbyshire they continued in use until the 1920s and in the Forest of Dean until 1952.

The principal advantage of a 'plateway' was that flat-wheeled wagons could make part of their journey by road and part by rail. It was the first 'road-rail' device. Flanged rails formed a side track in the evolution of railways and were not in the direct line of development.

The oldest surviving railway wagon in Britain is a quarry truck of 1797, which ran on flanged rails, from the Peak Forest Canal Company, Derbyshire. It can be seen at the National Railway Museum, York.

Cast-iron edge rails for flanged wheels were first used in South Wales about 1790. They were 1.8 m (6 ft) long, 76 mm (3 in) wide at the bottom, 64 mm (2½ in) at the top and about 50 mm (2 in) thick.

'Fish-bellied' cast-iron rails were designed by William Jessop (1745–1814) in 1792 and were laid in 1793–4 on the railway from Nanpantan to Loughborough in Leicestershire. They had a broad head on a thin web, deepest in the centre. One end had a flat foot which was nailed into a peg in a stone block. The other end had a round lug which fitted into a slot in the foot of the next rail. These were the true ancestors of the modern rail.

The first malleable iron edge rails were used at Walbottle Colliery near Newcastle upon Tyne in 1805. They were faulty, however, and were replaced by cast-iron 'fish-bellied' rails.

Wrought-iron rails were first used on Lord Carlisle's Railway in Cumberland, between 1808 and 1812 when about 5.6 km (3½ miles) were relaid with wrought-iron bars on stone block sleepers.

Lord Carlisle's Railway was built as a wooden railway, begun in 1775 and completed in 1799, but was soon relaid with cast-iron rails. In 1836 the company bought the Stephensons' *Rocket* from the Liverpool & Manchester Railway and used it until 1840.

An improved method of rolling wrought-iron rails was patented by John Birkinshaw (1811–67) at the Bedlington Ironworks, Northumberland, on 23 October 1820. They had a swelled upper edge and were in 5.5 m (18 ft) lengths. The patent even included welding the rail ends.

The first recorded use of flanged wheels in eastern Europe was in 1794 at the Oraviga Mines in the Banat, Hungary. They were wooden rollers, 200–230 mm (8 or 9 in) diameter, with flanges about 355 mm (14 in) diameter between the rails. The rollers were turned with the grain across them and frequently split. They lasted, at best, about a year. The use of flanged wooden wheels in the Banat and Transylvania dates from about 1774, possibly even earlier.

Wagon and length of wrought-iron rails in chairs on stone block sleepers dating from 1836, from the Stratford & Moreton Railway, preserved at Stratford on Avon.

The oldest wagon with flanged wheels in Britain, also at the National Railway Museum, is from the Belvoir Castle Railway in Leicestershire. This was a 1333 mm (4 ft 4½ in) gauge railway with 'fish-bellied' cast-iron rails 914 mm (3 ft) long, laid in 1815 by the Butterley Company of Derbyshire, to carry supplies from the Grantham Canal up to Belvoir Castle. Wagons were pulled by horses, until the line closed in 1918. It was dismantled in 1940, but parts near Belvoir Castle remain *in situ*.

The first railway to carry fare-paying passengers was the Oystermouth Railway, also known as the 'Swansea and Mumbles Railway', incorporated by Act of Parliament on 29 June 1804. It was opened about April 1806 and carried passengers from 25 March 1807. Horse-traction was used at first, and even sail-power was tried.

From about 1826 horse-buses began plying along a turnpike road beside the railway and completely stole the passenger traffic, probably the first instance in the world of a railway succumbing to road competition.

Passenger traffic was resumed in 1860, after the track was relaid. Steam-power was introduced on 16 August 1877 and lasted for 52 years until, on 2 March 1929, electric double-decked cars were put in service. They were the largest electric tramway cars in Britain, seating 106 passengers.

For goods traffic a petrol locomotive was obtained in 1929 and a diesel in 1936, making in all seven forms of motive power on one short railway.

For the second time, on 5 January 1960, the railway succumbed to a bus service. This time, however, it was dismantled.

It was the first railway in the world to celebrate 150 years of passenger services.

The first 'proper' railway in Scotland was the Kilmarnock & Troon Railway, incorporated on 27 May 1808 and opened for horse-drawn traffic on 6 July 1812. Steam-traction was introduced in 1817.

The oldest portion of the former Midland Railway, part of which still survives, was the Mansfield & Pinxton Railway in Nottinghamshire, incorporated on 16 June 1817 and opened on 13 April 1819. It was taken over by the MR in 1848, completely rebuilt, and reopened for steam-traction on 9 October 1849.

The first public railway to use steam from the beginning was the Stockton & Darlington Railway, opened on 27 September 1825. Steam locomotives were used at first only for goods trains, and for passenger trains from 1833.

The Canterbury & Whitstable Railway was opened on 3 May 1830. Stephenson's locomotive *Invicta* was driven by Edward Fletcher (1807–89), later to be locomotive superintendent of the North Eastern Railway. It inaugurated the first regular steam passenger service over a mile of the line between Bogshole Farm and South Street, Whitstable.

Opening of the Liverpool & Manchester Railway at Edge Hill, Liverpool, on 15 September 1830, from a drawing by Isaac Shaw made from the mouth of Wapping Tunnel. The buildings on each side of the 'Moorish Arch' housed the boiler and winding engine for winding trains up and down the incline to the goods station at Wapping.

After years of display in the open at Canterbury, *Invicta* has been restored at the National Railway Museum, York, for display under cover in a museum at Canterbury.

The world's first 'modern' railway was the Liverpool & Manchester. The engineer was George Stephenson (1781–1848). The first of its several Acts received the Royal Assent on 5 May 1826 and the entire railway was opened on 15 September 1830.

It was the first public railway to be operated entirely by locomotives, except for winding engines at Edge Hill, Liverpool, for working traffic to and from the docks, Crown Street, and later Lime Street Station. It was the first to have double track throughout and the first to operate passenger trains to a timetable with freight trains fitted into 'paths' in between. It was also the first to operate all the traffic itself with its own vehicles and locomotives.

It is still a busy main line today, with 15 to 20 passenger trains daily each way between Liverpool and Manchester.

The first railway in Ireland was the Dublin & Kingstown (now Dun Laoghaire) Railway, opened on 17 December 1834. It was standard gauge but was converted to the Irish standard of 1600 mm (5 ft 3 in) in 1857. The first locomotive, the 2–2–0 *Hibernia*, was built by Sharp Roberts & Company, Manchester.

The first section of the Ulster Railway, from Belfast to Lisburn, was opened on 12 August 1839. The gauge was originally 1880 mm (6 ft 2 in). It was converted to the Irish gauge of 1600 mm (5 ft 3 in) (see chapter 2) in 1847.

The first railway in London was the London & Greenwich

Railway incorporated on 17 May 1833, and opened on 8 February 1836 from Spa Road to Deptford, extended to London Bridge on 14 December 1836 and to Greenwich on 24 December 1838. The railway, 6 km (3¾ miles) long, was almost entirely on a brick viaduct of 878 arches.

The first British trunk railway, or railway connecting two other systems, the London & Birmingham and the Liverpool & Manchester, was the Grand Junction Railway, opened on 4 July 1837. Joseph Locke (1805–60) was the engineer. Together with the London & Birmingham (1838) and the Manchester & Birmingham (1842) it became part of the London & North Western Railway on the formation of that company on 16 July 1846 after having already absorbed the Liverpool & Manchester Railway. With the opening, on 17 December 1846, of the Lancaster & Carlisle Railway, of which Locke was again engineer, it formed a section of the main line from London (Euston) to Carlisle.

Birmingham was bypassed by the opening of the 64 km (39¾ mile) Trent Valley line from Rugby to Stafford on 15 September 1847, now part of the West Coast main line.

The opening of the Caledonian Railway from Carlisle to Glasgow and Edinburgh, again engineered by Locke, on 15 February 1848 completed the West Coast route.

The first railway across England was the Newcastle & Carlisle Railway, opened on 18 June 1838. It became part of the North Eastern Railway on 17 July 1862.

Robert Stephenson's High Level Bridge over the Tyne at Newcastle, looking towards Gateshead. When opened in 1849 it formed an essential link in the East Coast Route from London to Edinburgh.

The first section of the Great Western Railway, engineered by I. K. Brunel (1806–59), was opened from London (Paddington) to Maidenhead on 4 June 1838. It had a nominal gauge 2134 mm (7 ft). It was extended to Twyford on 1 June 1839, to Reading on 30 March 1840, and was completed to Bristol on 30 June 1841. Brunel was then only 35 years old. The present Paddington Station was designed by Brunel and opened on 16 January 1854.

The oldest principal section of the 'East Coast Route', the Great North of England Railway from York to Darlington, was opened on 4 January 1841 for goods trains and on 30 March for passengers.

A through railway between London and Aberdeen was completed with the opening of the Scottish North Eastern (later Caledonian) Railway between Perth and Aberdeen on 1 April 1850.

The 'East Coast Route' from London (Euston) to Edinburgh via the Midlands was completed in 1848 with the opening, on 29 August, of a temporary bridge over the Tyne between Gateshead and Newcastle and, on 10 October, a temporary viaduct over the Tweed at Tweedmouth.

The Tyne bridge was replaced by Robert Stephenson's High Level Bridge, opened for rail traffic on the upper deck on 15 August 1849, and for road traffic below on 4 February 1850.

The Royal Border Bridge across the Tweed, also by Robert Stephenson (1803–59) was opened on 29 August 1850.

Great Northern Railway trains reached Doncaster from London via the 'Loop' from Peterborough through Boston and Lincoln on 7 August 1850. From Lincoln to Retford trains ran over the Manchester, Sheffield & Lincolnshire Railway.

King's Cross became the terminus of the East Coast route when the GNR was extended from Maiden Lane on 14 October 1852. The 'Towns Line', Peterborough (Werrington Junction)–Grantham–Newark–Retford, was opened on 1 August 1852.

North of Doncaster the route to York lay over the Lancashire & Yorkshire Railway and the York & North Midland (later North Eastern) Railway. The NER direct line Doncaster–Selby–York was opened on 2 January 1871.

North of Darlington trains ran via Leamside to Newcastle until 1872 when they were routed over a new line via Durham.

The first trans-Pennine railway, the Manchester & Leeds, was opened throughout on 1 March 1841. On 9 July 1847 it became the Lancashire & Yorkshire Railway. It passed beneath the Pennine watershed between Littleborough and Todmorden in the Summit Tunnel, 2638 m (2885 yd) long.

The Chester & Holyhead Railway was completed with the opening of Robert Stephenson's tubular bridge over the Menai Strait on 18 March 1850. It formed the northern part of the main line between London and Dublin.

EARLY FRENCH RAILWAYS

The railway was introduced to France by an Englishman, William Wilkinson (c. 1744–1808), who built a line in 1778–9 at Indret at the mouth of the Loire to serve a new ordnance factory. It was used until about 1800.

The first recorded use of the French term 'chemin de fer' was in 1784 by a Frenchman named de Givry, after a visit to Coalbrookdale in Shropshire.

The first public railway in France, from Saint-Etienne to Andrézieux, was begun in 1824 and formally opened on 1 October 1828. The Concession had been granted on 26 February 1823. The railway was used unofficially from May 1827. Passenger traffic began on 1 March 1832, but horse-traction was used until 1 August 1844. Cast-iron 'fish-bellied' rails were used. It was extended from Saint-Etienne to the Loire in 1828, using wrought-iron rails.

On 7 June 1826 a Concession was granted for the Saint-Etienne–Lyon Railway and the section from Givors to Rive-de-Gier was opened on 25 June 1830.

It was on this line that Marc Séguin (1786–1875) tried out his locomotive on 7 November 1829.

The remainder of the railway was opened from Lyon to Givors on 3 April 1832, and from the Rive-de-Gier to Saint-Etienne for goods on 18 October 1832 and passengers on 25 February 1833.

The first public steam railway in France opened on 26 August 1837, ran from Paris to Le Pecq and was later extended over the Seine to St Germaine-en-Laye. This line is now part of the Regional Métro or Réseau Express Régional (RER), which starts at Auber near the Place de l'Opéra.

EARLY RAILROADS IN THE USA

While in northern Europe the railway had to be fitted into an already highly developed agricultural or industrial environment, and brought into well-established towns, in the USA, except in the older eastern States, and in Canada, the railroad opened up the country. The early railroad-builders were pioneers, often even explorers. In many towns the railroad station was the first building. One can note this pattern, for example, in Denver, Colorado, where the older streets are laid out parallel to or at

Reproduction of the first locomotive to operate in Germany. The original, from contemporary accounts named *Der Adler*, was built by Robert Stephenson & Co., Newcastle-upon-Tyne, in 1835 for the Ludwigsbahn, Nuremberg to Fürth.

First railways in other European Countries

Country	Date of Opening	Route	Distance km	Distance miles	Comments
Austria–Hungary	7.9.1827	Budweis (now České Budejovice, Czechoslovakia) to Trojanov			Used horse-traction. Locomotives were used from 1872. Became part of the Linz–Budejovice line.
Belgium	5.5.1835	Brussels to Malines	23.4	14.5	The first railway to be built and worked as part of a planned national system, by the Belgian Government. The first two loco-motives, inside-cylinder 2–2–2s, *La Fleche* and *Stephenson*, were built by Robert Stephenson & Co. at Newcastle upon Tyne.
Germany	7.12.1835	Nuremberg to Fürth	8	5	The Ludwigsbahn. Robert Stephenson & Co. built the first locomotive *Der Adler*, similar to the Belgian.
Russia	30.10.1837	St Petersburg to Tsarskoe Selo	3.2	2	1829 mm (6 ft) gauge; changed to 1524 mm (5ft) in 1902. Provisional opening with horse traction 9 Oct 1836. Extended to Pavlovsk 1838.
Austria	23.11.1837	Vienna to Floridsdorf & Deutsch Wagram	17.7	11	Kaiser Ferdinands Nordbahn.
Netherlands	24.9.1839	Amsterdam to Haarlem	19	12	The first locomotive, *Arend* (Eagle), was built by R. B. Longridge & Company at Bedlington, Northumberland (Works No. 119), and was scrapped in 1857. A full-size replica stands in the Netherlands Railway Museum Utrecht.
Italy	4.10.1839	Naples to Portici	8	5	
Switzerland	15.6.1844	Basel to St Ludwig (now Saint-Louis, France)	6.4	4	The Zurich–Baden Railway (opened on 9 August 1847) was the first railway entirely in Switzerland.
Hungary	15.7.1846	Pest to Vacz	33	20½	An early line from Pest to Kobanya was opened in August 1827.
Denmark	26.6.1847	Copenhagen–Roskilde	31	19½	The Altona–Kiel Railway, opened in 1844, was afterwards annexed with its territory by Prussia.
Spain	28.10.1848	Barcelona to Mataro	27	17	The first locomotive was named *Mataro*.
Norway	1.9.1854	Christiania (later Oslo) to Eidsvoll	67.6	42	Known as the Hovedjernbanen (main railway). Robert Stephenson was one of the consultant engineers.
Portugal	28.10.1856	Lisbon to Carregado	37	23	
Sweden	1.12.1856	Gothenburg to Jonsered and Malmö to Lund	15 17	9 10½	A narrow-gauge horse-operated line from Fryksta to Klarälven in Värmland, 8 km (5 miles), was opened in 1849.
Greece	1869	Piraeus to Athens	8.8	5½	

right angles to the railroad, and only the later portion of the city is planned on a north–south axis. Thus railroad history in the USA and Canada is much more bound up with the growth of the country than it is in Europe.

The first railway in North America was a short length of wooden track laid on Beacon Hill, Boston, Massachusetts, in 1795 to carry building material for the State House. A railway was laid on the same hill in 1807 to carry bricks. It was operated by Silas Whitney.

In 1811 a railway was built at Falling Creek near Rich-mond, Virginia, to serve a powder-mill. Another was built at Bear Creek Furnace, near Pittsburgh, Pennsylvania, in 1818.

The first American railroad charter was obtained on 6 February 1815 by Col. John Stevens (1749–1838) of Hoboken, New Jersey, to build and operate a railroad between the Delaware and Raritan rivers near Trenton and New Brunswick. Lack of financial backing prevented construction.

The first steam locomotive in North America was built by John Stevens in February 1825 and was tested on a circu-

Tom Thumb, the first steam locomotive on the Baltimore & Ohio Railroad, built by Peter Cooper in 1829.

lar track at his home at Hoboken. It had four flat-tyred wheels guided by four vertical rollers running against the insides of the rails, and it was propelled by a central toothed rack.

John Stevens was granted another railroad charter on 21 March 1823 for a steam-powered railroad from Philadelphia to Columbia, Pennsylvania. The company was incorporated under the title of the 'Pennsylvania Railroad' which established that name as the oldest among the numerous railroad companies of the USA. It was partly opened in 1829 and wholly on 16 April 1834.

The Delaware & Hudson Canal Company obtained one of the first USA railroad charters on 23 April 1823 for a line from Carbondale to the canal at Honesdale in the Lackawanna Valley. The railroad was built by John Bloomfield Jervis (1795–1885) and was opened on 9 October 1829, with a gauge of 1295 mm (4 ft 3 in).

For this railroad a steam locomotive named *Stourbridge Lion* was obtained from Foster, Rastrick & Company, Stourbridge, England, and it was tried on the line on 8 August 1829, driven by Horatio Allen (1802–90). It was too heavy for the wooden rails covered with iron strips, and for many years afterwards the line was worked as a gravity railroad. It later became part of the present Delaware & Hudson system.

Steam operation was resumed in 1860. The *Stourbridge Lion* was unquestionably **the first sub-standard-gauge locomotive in the western hemisphere**. It weighed 8 tons and was 4.572 m (15 ft) high and 2.311 m (7 ft 7 in) wide. It ran only a few trial trips. About 1845 the boiler and one cylinder were sold to a foundry for use as a stationary engine and the boiler worked until 1871. This and a few other parts are preserved in the Smithsonian Institution, Washington DC. A full-size operating replica built by the Delaware & Hudson Railroad in 1932 is exhibited at Honesdale, Pennsylvania.

The first railroad in the USA to offer a regular service as a public carrier was the Baltimore & Ohio Railroad. This was chartered on 28 February 1827. The first stone was laid on 4 July (Independence Day) 1828, and the first 21 km (13 miles) between Baltimore and Ellicott's Mills, Maryland, were opened for passenger and freight traffic on 24 May 1830. It was the first double-track railroad in America. The first fare-paying passengers were carried on 7 January 1830 from Pratt Street, Baltimore, to the Carrollton Viaduct. Horse-traction was used until July 1834. This line was closed to passengers on 31 December 1949.

The first steam locomotive on the Baltimore & Ohio Railroad, *Tom Thumb*, was built in 1829 by Peter Cooper (1791–1883) and was first run on 25 August 1830 from Baltimore to Ellicott's Mills and back. It had a vertical boiler, and one cylinder 89 mm diameter × 356 mm stroke (3½ × 14 in).

The first train into Washington was run by the Baltimore & Ohio on 24 August 1835. In 1842, shortly after Charles Dickens had travelled on it, the railroad was extended to Cumberland, Maryland.

Washington became linked with New York in January 1838 by a chain of railways with ferries across major rivers and stage-coaches between stations in cities.

The first successful steam locomotive to be built in the USA, *Best Friend of Charleston*, was built by West Point Foundry, New York, for the South Carolina Railroad in 1830 and was first tested with passengers on 14 December. It entered service on Christmas Day. It had a vertical boiler, weighed under 4 tons and developed about 6 hp. On 17 June 1831, while it was being turned on the 'revolving platform', the fireman held down the safety-valve to stop the steam escaping. In a few minutes the boiler blew up, injuring the fireman and several others including Mr Darrell, the engineer. This was the first locomotive boiler explosion in the USA.

The first steam train in New York State was pulled by the *De Witt Clinton* on the Mohawk & Hudson Railroad from Albany to Schenectady on 9 August 1831. This engine was also built at the West Point Foundry. It was a 0-4-0 with cylinders 140 × 460 mm (5½ × 16 in), 1371 mm (54 in) wheels, and it weighed 4 tons.

One of the earliest constituents of the Pennsylvania Railroad, the Newcastle & Frenchtown Turnpike & Railway Company, was opened in July 1831; it was 27.8 km (16.2 miles) long. Steam-power was used from October 1832.

US mail was first carried by rail on the South Carolina Railroad (now part of the Southern Railway) in November 1831, and on the Baltimore & Ohio in January 1832.

The first American railroad tunnel was Staple Bend Tunnel, 275 m (901 ft) long, 6 km (4 miles) east of Johnstown,

Pennsylvania, on the Allegheny Portage Railroad, opened on 7 October 1834. Work on the tunnel began in 1829 and it was built by J. & E. Appleton at a cost of $37 498.84. It is 6 m (20 ft) wide, 5.9 m (19 ft) high, and it is lined with cut stone for 46 m (150 ft) at each end.

This section of the Pennsylvania Railroad, linking canals between Johnstown and Hollidaysburg, formed part of the route between Philadelphia and Pittsburgh. It was abandoned when the Pennsylvania Railroad opened its new route across the mountains, including the famous Horseshoe Bend, on 15 February 1854.

Charles Dickens travelled over the Portage Railroad in 1842 and described the journey in his *American Notes*.

By 1835, over 200 railway charters had been granted in eleven States and over 1600 km (1000 miles) of railway were open.

The Great Lakes were first joined by rail to the Atlantic seaboard in December 1842 when, except for the crossing of the Hudson River at Albany, New York, there were continuous rails from Boston to Buffalo on Lake Erie.

The first unbroken line of rails between the Atlantic and the Great Lakes was the New York & Erie (now Erie Lackawanna), completed from Piermont, New York, on the Hudson River to Dunkirk, New York, on Lake Erie and formally opened to through traffic in May 1851.

The first locomotive in Chicago was the *Pioneer*, weighing 10 tons, built by Matthias Baldwin (1795–1866) of Philadelphia. It arrived by sailing-ship on 10 October 1848 and made its first run out of Chicago, pulling two cars, on 25 October.

Chicago became linked by rail to the eastern cities on 24 January 1854, but several changes of trains were necessary.

The first locomotive west of the Mississippi, *The Pacific*, ran the 8 km (5 miles) from St Louis to Cheltenham on 9 December 1852.

The first railroad to reach the Mississippi was the Chicago & Rock Island (now Chicago, Rock Island & Pacific), completed to Rock Island, Illinois, on 22 February 1854, opening up through rail communication to the eastern seaboard.

The first railroad bridge across the Mississippi, at Davenport, Iowa, was opened on 21 April 1856. It was partly burned down on 6 May after a collision by the steamer *Effie Afton*, but was rebuilt and reopened on 8 September 1856.

The first railroad in the Pacific coast region was opened on 22 February 1856, when the locomotives *Sacramento* and *Nevada*, which had arrived by sailing-ship round Cape Horn, ran from Sacramento to Folsom, California, 35.4 km (22 miles).

The first southern rail route between the Atlantic seaboard and the Mississippi, from Charleston to Memphis, was completed on 1 April 1857.

Rail traffic first reached the Missouri River at St Joseph on 14 February 1859. The first bridge across the Missouri, at Kansas City, was opened on 4 July 1869, establishing a through route from Chicago.

The first locomotive in the Pacific North-west, the *Oregon Pony*, arrived at Portland, Oregon, on 31 March 1862.

The first American transcontinental railroad, from the Missouri River to the Pacific, was authorized by an Act signed by President Lincoln on 1 July 1862 and was completed in 1869. (See 'Transcontinental Railways', p. 62.)

The first railroad bridge in the USA with an all-steel superstructure was completed in 1879 at Glasgow, Missouri, on the Chicago & Alton Railroad, now part of the Illinois Central Gulf RR.

EARLY RAILWAYS IN CANADA

The first railway in Canada about which there is any positive information was a double-track balanced incline 152 m (500 ft) long built at a cost of £695 by the Royal Engineers in 1823 to carry stone from a wharf on the St Lawrence to the top of the escarpment at Quebec during construction of the Citadel. It was worked by a horse gin, but later references to boiler repairs suggest that the gin may have been replaced by a steam engine, and that it lasted into the 1830s.

Coal-carrying railways were built in Nova Scotia at Pictou in 1827 and North Sydney in 1828. Both used horses. They were standard, 1435 mm (4 ft 8½ in) gauge and were probably the first in North America to use iron rails, which were cast in 1.5 m (5 ft) lengths.

Canada's first steam railway was a standard gauge line 26.5 km (16½ miles) long, operated by 'The Company of Proprietors of the Champlain & Saint Lawrence Rail Road', chartered in 1832. It was opened from Laprairie on the St Lawrence to St John on the Richelieu on 21 July 1836.

The first locomotive was ordered from Robert Stephenson & Company, Newcastle upon Tyne, on 26 October 1835. During trials before the railway was opened the water in the boiler was allowed to get so low that several tubes were burnt out and had to be temporarily plugged so that the engine was unable to produce its maximum power on the opening day. It was named *Dorchester* after the delivery of a second locomotive in 1837. It worked until it blew up in 1867 when it was scrapped. Compartment-type cars were used, built at Troy, New York, in 1836.

The first coal-burning locomotives in Canada, *Samson*, *Hercules* and *John Buddle* worked on a 9.7 km (6 miles) railway built in 1839 to carry coal from the Albion Mines to

Pictou Harbour, Nova Scotia. *Samson* is preserved at New Glasgow, Nova Scotia.

The Erie & Ontario Railway, built in 1839, was the first railway in Upper Canada. It ran round Niagara Falls from Queenston to Chippawa. The original gradients were too steep for locomotives, and horses were used. It was later rebuilt with easier grades and in 1854 was reopened with locomotive operation. It was thus the third railway in Upper Canada to use locomotives. The Great Western and the Ontario, Simcoe & Huron Union Railway, both opened in 1853, used steam locomotives from the start.

The Montreal & Lachine Railway was opened in 1847, using an 18 ton American locomotive which took 21 min to cover the 13 km (8 mile) journey. The gauge was officially 1448 mm (4 ft 9 in).

The oldest operating constituent of the Canadian Pacific Railway was La Compagnie du Chemin à Rails du Saint Laurent et du Village d'Industrie, 19 km (12 miles) long from Village d'Industrie (now Joliette, Quebec) to Lanoraie on the St Lawrence about 56 km (35 miles) north-east of Montreal. Regular services began on 6 May 1850. It came into the possession of what is now CP Rail with the purchase of the Eastern Division of the Quebec, Montreal, Ottawa & Occidental Railway in September 1885, and part of it is still in use.

The first international railway link in North America was opened from Laprairie, Quebec, to Rouses Point, New York, on 16 August 1851. By international agreement, **the first of its kind in the world**, rolling stock of a foreign railway was given free entry into Canada or the USA. This arrangement still operates.

The first steam train in Upper Canada ran from Toronto to Aurora, 48 km (30 miles), on 16 May 1853. This was the first section of the Ontario, Simcoe & Huron Union Railway (later Northern Railway) from Toronto to Collingwood on Georgian Bay, Lake Huron, completed in 1855. It is now part of the Canadian National system.

The railways of Canada grew from 83 km (52 miles) in 1847 to 103 km (64 miles) in 1850 and to 3026 km (1882 miles) by 1860.

Canada's first sub-standard-gauge steam-operated railway was the 1067 mm (3 ft 6 in) gauge Lingan Colliery Tramway on the island of Cape Breton, built in 1861. The first locomotive was a 0-4-0 saddle tank built by Black Hawthorn & Co. at Gateshead, County Durham, in 1866.

The Glasgow & Cape Breton Coal & Railway Company operated the first steam-worked narrow-gauge railway in Canada. The 914 mm (3 ft) gauge line was opened in May 1871, using a Fox, Walker 0-4-0 tank engine, built in Bristol.

The first locomotive to be built in Canada, at the foundry of James Good, Toronto, was named *Toronto*. It made its first run on 16 May 1853 on the Ontario, Simcoe & Huron Union Railway, later renamed the Northern Railway.

Through trains were inaugurated between Montreal and Toronto on 27 October 1856 by the Grand Trunk Railway, later part of the Canadian National Railways.

Canada's first railway tunnel was opened by the Brockville & Ottawa Railway on 31 December 1860. It was about 540 m (1/3 mile) long, passing beneath the town of Brockville, and was used by Canadian Pacific Rail until abandoned in 1974.

The first railway in British Columbia was built in 1861 at Seton Portage, 225 km (140 miles) north of Vancouver. It had wooden rails, and cars were drawn by mules.

The first railway in Newfoundland, from St John's to Hall Bay, was begun on 9 August 1881, against much local opposition and violence. The 870 km (547 miles) of 1067 mm (3 ft 6 in) gauge line, from St John's to Port aux Basque, were completed in 1896. The first passenger trains ran on 29 June 1898.

FIRST RAILWAYS IN AUSTRALASIA

The Australian Agriculture Company constructed an inclined tramway of iron rails to carry coal from its mines at Newcastle to Port Hunter in 1827, and another there in 1830. These were the first railways in Australasia.

In Tasmania a wooden railway 8 km (5 miles) long was laid across a peninsula in 1836. Passengers paid a shilling to ride in trucks pushed by convicts to avoid a stormy sea journey.

Australia's first steam-operated railway was the 4 km (2½ miles) long 1600 mm (5 ft 3 in) gauge Melbourne & Hobson's Bay Railway, opened from Flinders Street, Melbourne, to Sandridge, Victoria, on 12 September 1854. The first passenger railway was the 11 km (7 miles) Port Elliot & Goolwa Railway in South Australia, also 1600 mm gauge, opened with horse traction on 18 May 1854.

In New South Wales standard gauge was adopted for the first railway opened from Sydney to Panamatta Junction, now Granville, on 26 September 1855. It was built by the Sydney Railway Company, but was taken over by the New South Wales Government before opening.

The first locomotive in NSW was Class 1 0-4-2 No. 1, built by Robert Stephenson & Co. at Newcastle upon Tyne for the Sydney & Golburn Railway in 1854, to a design by J. E. McConnell. It weighed 45 tons 5 cwt, and worked the first train from Sydney, where it is now preserved.

As in the neighbouring state of Victoria, **South Australia** adopted the 1600 mm gauge for its first railway from Adelaide to Port Adelaide, 12 km (7½ miles), opened on 21 April 1856. It was built and worked by the South Australian Government. Although the 1600 mm gauge was adopted as standard, a considerable length of secondary route was built to 1067 mm gauge and its position between New South Wales and Western Australia resulted in South Australia being crossed by the standard, 1435 mm, gauge transcontinental line. Thus South Australia is the only state in Australia to have all three gauges. Adelaide was the last of the mainland state capitals to be reached by the standard gauge, on 8 December 1982.

Queensland adopted the gauge of 1067 mm, because of its lower construction cost, for its first railway opened in July 1865 between Ipswich and Grandchester, 33 km (21 miles), in the Southern Division. Queensland was the first railway authority in the world to adopt a sub-standard gauge for main lines.

The railways of NSW and Victoria met at Albury on 14 June 1883, after the completion of the bridge over the Murray River.

The first ordinary railway in Tasmania, to a gauge of 1600 mm (5 ft 3 in) as in South Australia, was opened in 1871 between Launceston and Deloraine, 72 km (45 miles). It was taken over by the Government in 1872 as was the later Launceston–Hobart line, opened in 1876. The lines were converted to 1067 mm, adopted as the Tasmanian standard, in 1888. The first line to be built to 1067 mm gauge was opened in 1885.

In Western Australia the first railway was a 1067 mm gauge private timber-carrying line from Yoganup to Luckeville, 19 km (12 miles), opened on 6 June 1871. It was worked by horses until August when the locomotive *Ballarat* arrived from Ballarat, Victoria, where it was built. In 1879 the Geraldton–Northampton line was opened, 55 km (34 miles). The first railway to Perth, from Fremantle 33 km (20 miles), was opened in 1881. These early lines were acquired by the Western Australian Government in 1896.

The first railway in New Zealand was the horse-operated Dun Mountain Railway, 21.7 km (13½ miles) long to Nelson in the north-west of the South Island. It was opened on 3 February 1862 with 30 lb/yd iron rails laid to a gauge of 914 mm (3 ft). It ran from a chrome ore mine at a height of 610 m (2000 ft) down to Nelson on a gradient of 1 in 23. It worked for only four years.

On 1 December 1863 the first steam-operated railway was opened from Christchurch to Ferrymead, also in the South Island. It was built to a gauge of 1600 mm (5 ft 3 in). The line to Ferrymead was only temporary while a tunnel was being built. On 9 December 1867 the permanent line was opened to Lyttleton and the short section to Ferrymead was abandoned.

On 5 February 1867 a standard-gauge line had been opened from Invercargill to Bluff, the farthest south reached by a railway in Australasia. To avoid the confusion of different gauges, already bedevilling Australia, it was decided in 1870 to adopt a gauge of 1067 mm (3 ft 6 in). In 1876 the Christchurch–Lyttleton section was converted to 1067 mm gauge.

In the North Island the Bay of Islands Coal Mining Company built the first railway, standard gauge, to carry coal from mines at Kawakawa; it was completed in 1870.

The first section of the North Island's 1067 mm gauge system was opened from Auckland to the port of Onehunga on 24 December 1873.

FIRST RAILWAYS IN ASIA

The first railway in India, part of the Great Indian Peninsula Railway, was opened on 18 April 1853 from Bombay to Thana, 40 km (25 miles). The 1676 mm (5 ft 6 in) gauge was decided upon by Lord Dalhousie (1812–60), then Governor General of India, and it became the Indian standard.

The first railway in what is now Pakistan was the 169 km (105 miles) line from Karachi to Kochi, 1676 mm gauge, opened on 13 May 1861.

In Sri Lanka (Ceylon) the 1676 mm gauge was again adopted for the first railway from Colombo to Ambepussa, 93 km (58 miles), opened on 2 October 1865.

Burma adopted the metre gauge as standard. The first railway, Rangoon to Prome, 257 km (160 miles), was opened on 1 May 1877.

In Japan the 1067 mm (3 ft 6 in) gauge became the standard, used on the first railway from Yokohama to Sinagawa, opened on 12 June 1872. It was completed to Tokyo on 14 October. In the 10 years from 1880 to 1890, Japanese railways grew from 158 km (98 miles) to 2348 km (1459 miles). By 1986 the total was 21 091 km (13 105 miles).

China had no railway until 1876 when a 726 mm (2 ft 6 in) gauge line was opened from Shanghai to Woosung, about 32 km (20 miles). It was operated by two 0–4–0 saddle and side tanks, built by Ransomes & Rapier, Ipswich. They had 203 × 254 mm (8 × 10 in) cylinders, 686 mm (2 ft 3 in) coupled wheels, and they were named *Celestial Empire* and *Flowery Land*. The engineer was John Dixon (1835–91), nephew of John Dixon of the Stockton & Darlington Railway.

The Chinese were hostile and suspicious and, following a fatal accident, as soon as the redemption money was paid in October 1877, the railway was bought by the Government, dismantled, and dumped in Taiwan (Formosa).

The first permanent railway in China was the standard-gauge Tongshan–Hsukuchuang line, opened in 1880, extended to Lutai in 1886 and Tientsin in 1888. It now forms part of the Beijing (Peking)–Mukden section of the

Chinese People's Republic Railways. Steam traction was introduced in 1883.

By 1900 there were 2346 km (1458 miles) of railway, mostly in isolated sections, built to exploit rather than to develop the country. At the time of the 'liberation' in 1949 there were about 22 000 km (13 700 miles) of route of which only about half was usable. By 1980 China had 50 000 km (31 000 miles) of high-grade railway. The Chinese are building about 1000 km (over 600 miles) of new railway a year and hope to have about 80 000 km (50 000 miles) by the year 2000.

FIRST RAILWAYS IN AFRICA

The first railway in Africa was the standard-gauge main line from Alexandria to Cairo, 208 km (129 miles), opened in January 1856.

In Algeria the first railway, Algiers to Blida, 48 km (30 miles), was opened on 15 August 1862. It had a gauge of 1445 mm (4 ft 8⅞ in). (See 'Gauges', chapter 3.)

The first railway in South Africa, from Durban to The Point, about 3 km (2 miles), standard gauge, was opened by the Natal Railway on 26 June 1860. It was acquired by the Natal Government on 1 January 1877. Cape Province's first railway, also standard gauge, was opened to Eerste River on 13 February 1862 and extended to Wellington in 1863.

For economy of construction it was decided in 1873 that further railways should be built to a gauge of 1067 mm (3 ft 6 in). This became the main South African gauge and by 1882 the standard-gauge lines had been converted to it.

FIRST RAILWAYS IN SOUTH AMERICA

The first railway in South America was opened on 3 November 1848. It ran from Georgetown to Plaisance, 8 km (5 miles), in British Guyana. It formed part of the standard-gauge East Coast line, 98 km (61 miles), and was closed on 30 June 1972.

The first railway in Chile ran from the port of Caldera to Copiapo 396 m (1300 ft) above sea-level, a distance of 80.5 km (50¼ miles). The company was formed locally in October 1849; the line was laid out by William Wheelwright (1798–1873) and built by Allan and Alexander Campbell of Albany, New York, and was opened on 25 December 1851. Locomotive No. 1 *Copiapo*, built by Norris Brothers of Philadelphia, in 1850 is **the oldest steam locomotive in South America**. It was standard gauge and worked until 1891. The railway was taken over by the Chilean Government in 1911 and later converted to metre gauge.

Copiapo is unique in being the only surviving American 4–4–0 of the 1850 period and, unlike other preserved early American locomotives, all of which have been extensively rebuilt, it is almost in its original form. The

engine had about 60 m² (645 ft²) heating surface, cylinders 330 × 660 mm (13 × 26 in), coupled wheels 1524 mm (5 ft), and weighed 19 tons in working order.

The first railway in Brazil was the 1676 mm (5 ft 6 in) gauge line, 16 km (10 miles), from Maua at the end of the Bay of Rio to the foot of the Petropolis Serra. It was opened on 30 April 1854 and was later converted to metre gauge. On its extension to Petropolis it climbed the Sierra de Estrella for 6.4 km (4 miles) with a Riggenbach rack. In 1897 it became part of the Leopoldina Railway.

From 1862 the Dom Pedro II Railway (later Central of Brazil) established 1600 mm (5 ft 3 in) as the Brazilian broad gauge.

The first sub-standard-gauge railway in South America and probably the first steam-operated sub-standard-gauge public railway in the western hemisphere was the 1067 mm (3 ft 6 in) gauge União Valenciana Railway in Brazil. Baldwin Locomotive Works of Philadelphia built three locomotives for this line in 1869.

The first railway in Argentina from Plaza del Parque in Buenos Aires to the suburb of Floresta, 9.9 km (6.2 miles), was opened on 30 August 1857. It was built to 1676 mm (5 ft 6 in) gauge because its first locomotive, named *La Portena* (built in 1856 by E. B. Wilson & Company, Leeds), was originally intended for India, and this established the 5 ft 6 in gauge in Argentina.

The oldest steam locomotive in South America, Caldera & Copiapo Railway No. 1 built in 1850, now preserved at Copiapo, about 1000 km (621 miles) north of Santiago, Chile.

2

PIONEERS

William Jessop (1745–1814) was one of the leading early British civil engineers who, although mainly concerned with the construction of canals, was responsible for several important early railways. He was one of the founders, in 1790, of the Butterley Company in Derbyshire, close to the great tunnel on his Cromford Canal, a company which became responsible for many early iron railway bridges. He was the designer of the 'fish-bellied' cast-iron rail. After constructing several short lines of railway in connection with canals, he engineered the Surrey Iron Railway, the first public railway in Britain to be sanctioned by Parliament (1801). It was followed by a line from Croydon to Merstham in 1805. In this he was assisted by his son Josias Jessop (1781–1826) who laid out the Cromford & High Peak Railway in Derbyshire in 1825.

John Stevens (1749–1838), pioneer of mechanical transport in the USA. After graduating in 1766 he studied law for three years and then joined the army, serving under General Washington. In 1784 he bought a large estate in New Jersey, including most of what is now Hoboken. About 1788 he became interested in the work of Fitsch and Rumsey in the development of the steamboat and from then to the end of his life he devoted himself to the development of mechanical transport by land and water. In 1791 he became one of the first United States citizens to take out patents, for an improved boiler and a steamboat engine. In 1803 he patented a multi-tubular boiler, 26 years before the Stephensons' *Rocket*, and in 1804 built a steamboat with two screw propellers. In 1809 his *Phoenix* became the first sea-going steamship in the world. In 1810 he turned his attention to railways and pioneered some of the earliest in Pennsylvania. In 1825, at the age of 76, he designed and built a steam locomotive and a circular track on his estate at Hoboken. This was the first steam locomotive to be built in America.

Matthew Murray (1765–1826) was one of the earliest steam locomotive engineers. After training as a blacksmith he worked on flax-spinning machinery until 1795 when he entered into partnership with James Fenton and David Wood at Leeds. Murray took out a number of patents for steam engines from 1799. In 1811–13 he was engaged by Blenkinsop (qv) to build engines for the 1254 mm (4 ft 1⅜ in) gauge rack railway from Middleton Colliery to Leeds. Four engines were built and they ran for 20 years. They had two double-acting cylinders, and the piston rods worked in vertical guides with connecting rods to the spur wheels which drove the 965 mm (3 ft 2 in)

diameter cog driving wheels. Murray can claim to have built the first commercially successful locomotive. From about 1813 he also built engines for boats.

Edward Pease (1767–1858), promoter of early railways, friend and supporter of George and Robert Stephenson. In 1818 he first projected the Stockton & Darlington Railway and in 1821 became acquainted with George Stephenson whom he appointed engineer, also financing the construction of *Locomotion*, the first locomotive on the railway. The first rail of the S & D was laid in 1823 and the railway was opened in 1815. Also in 1823, with George Stephenson and Thomas Richardson, he established the firm of Robert Stephenson & Co. at Newcastle upon Tyne, with Robert Stephenson as manager, to build locomotives for the S & D and other railways. Pease was a prominent Quaker and was active towards the abolition of slavery.

Richard Trevithick (1771–1833) was the first to use high pressure steam in an engine instead of atmospheric pressure as in the condensing steam engines of Newcomen and Watt. He was born in Cornwall, but details of his early career and training are scanty; he taught himself about engines by observing them at the Cornish tin mines. About 1797 he built a steam engine for Herland mine and in 1800 a double-acting high-pressure engine for Cook's Kitchen mine. In 1796 he experimented with model steam locomotives and by the end of 1801 he had completed the first steam locomotive to pull a passenger carriage on a road. In 1803 a steam road carriage was tested in London, reaching a speed of 12 km/h (9 mph). At Coalbrookdale in Shropshire, also in 1803, he designed **the first locomotive to run on rails**, for the 914 mm (3 ft) gauge plateway system there. A model can be seen at the National Railway Museum at York, though it is not certain if the engine was built and if it ran.

His second locomotive was built while he was employed at the Penydarren Ironworks near Merthyr Tydfil in Wales to haul iron from Penydarren to the Glamorganshire Canal. It was set to work in February 1804, but weighing 5 tons it was too heavy for the cast-iron plateway rails. A third locomotive was built in 1805 by John Whinfield at Gateshead, County Durham, to a design by Trevithick. It was **the first locomotive to run on flanged wheels**. In 1808 he again attempted to popularize the steam locomotive by running one, named *Catch me who can*, on a circular track in London. The locomotive was a success, but the public was not sufficiently interested and after this he abandoned work on locomotives.

Richard Trevithick.

In 1809 he began a tunnel under the Thames, but the project failed. (See Brunel.) A steam threshing machine is recorded in 1811. In 1816 he went to Peru to supervise the erection of his engines at mines, but in the insurrection in the 1820s he lost all his money. He was found, penniless, by Robert Stephenson (qv) who assisted his repatriation. He took out his last patent, for the use of superheated steam, in 1832 and the following year he died in poverty in Dartford, Kent.

William James (1771–1837) was a railway surveyor and projector. He began as a land agent and surveyor but, dismayed by the oppressive conduct of canal companies towards mines in Staffordshire, he became interested in railways. He surveyed a line from Wolverhampton to Birmingham, and in 1803 made his first survey for a railway from Liverpool to Manchester. In 1809 he engineered the plateway from Gloucester to Cheltenham. His most important line was the Stratford on Avon & Moreton in Marsh Railway surveyed in 1821, built by Rastrick (qv), and opened in 1826. In 1822 he formed a Liverpool & Manchester Railway Company to build 'an engine railroad' and surveys were completed that year. The railway was built by George Stephenson and when it was opened in 1830 James's pioneering work was forgotten. He surveyed other lines all over England but he never gave sufficient attention to any one project and it was his more single-minded successors like the Stephensons who brought his schemes into effect and won all the fame.

William Hedley (1779–1843), pioneer of the steam locomotive. In 1805 he was appointed colliery viewer at Wylam in Northumberland, under Christopher Blackett. During the Napoleonic wars the prices of horses and fodder rose so high that Blackett was forced to consider steam locomotives. In 1812 Hedley carried out an experiment with a manually propelled carriage to prove that a locomotive with smooth wheels, as used earlier by Trevithick, would have adequate adhesion as opposed to the rack locomotives of Blenkinsop and Murray (qqv). His first locomotive was built in 1813, with the help of the enginewright Jonathan Forster and the blacksmith's foreman Timothy Hackworth (qv). A more successful locomotive was produced about 1814. Two Hedley locomotives of 1814–15, much reconstructed, are preserved: *Wylam Dilly* at Edinburgh Museum, and *Puffing Billy* at the Science Museum, London. George Stephenson (qv) at Killingworth Colliery nearby was almost certainly influenced by Hedley's work, but he never acknowledged it and the two engineers never became friends.

John Urpeth Rastrick (1780–1856) was born in Northumberland. After training with his father he joined John Hazeldine at Bridgnorth, Shropshire, where, in 1808, they built Trevithick's fourth locomotive *Catch me who can*. He also assisted Trevithick in the unsuccessful Thames tunnel. In 1814 he took out a patent for a steam engine and was soon experimenting with steam traction on railways. His first major work was the cast-iron road bridge over the Wye at Chepstow (1815–16). In 1817 he became managing partner in the firm of Foster, Rastrick & Co. of Stourbridge, Worcestershire, which built several early locomotives. In 1822–6 he constructed the tramway from Stratford on Avon to Moreton in Marsh, surveyed by William James (qv) which was the first line to use Birkinshaw's wrought-iron rails. In 1829 he completed the Shutt End railway in Staffordshire and for it he designed and built a locomotive, *Agenoria*, now preserved in the National Railway Museum at York. The *Stourbridge Lion* built for Horatio Allen (qv) was similar. Rastrick was one of the judges at the Rainhill Trials on the Liverpool & Manchester in 1829. His greatest work was the London & Brighton Railway, 1837–40 including the Merstham, Balcombe and Clayton tunnels and the magnificent Ouse viaduct.

George Stephenson (1781–1848) is perhaps the most famous name in the history of railways. He was the second son of Robert Stephenson, fireman at Wylam Colliery near Newcastle upon Tyne. With no formal education he gained his engineering experience working at various collieries, first as fireman and later as engineman, at the same time learning to read and write at a night school. In 1802 he married and the following year his only son Robert (qv) was born. His wife died of tuberculosis in 1806, and there followed a period of difficulty and hardship during which his father became incapable of further work and had to be supported as well as his mother. However, following his success in repairing a Newcomen pumping engine he was appointed enginewright at Killingworth Colliery in 1812 at a salary of £100 a year. His inventive

George Stephenson.

genius was first applied to the production of a safety lamp for miners. This was first tried on 21 October 1815. Unknown to each other, Sir Humphrey Davy had been working on the same problem and he produced a lamp on the same principle at about the same time.

Following the experiments with steam locomotives by Hedley (qv) at Wylam Colliery, Stephenson turned his attention to this problem and built his first locomotive in 1813–14. It could pull 30 tons up a gradient of 1 in 450 at 6.5 km/h (4 mph). In February 1815 he patented a locomotive in which the blast of the exhaust steam was used to create a draught for the fire. He provided further locomotives for the 13 km (8 mile) long Hetton Colliery Railway in County Durham, which he laid out and which was opened in 1822. Shortly after this he was appointed by Edward Pease (qv) to construct the Stockton & Darlington Railway for which he built the first locomotive, *Locomotion*, in 1825. This engine is preserved at North Road Station Museum, Darlington.

He was next appointed engineer to the Liverpool & Manchester Railway. Despite its progress of nearly a quarter of a century there were still doubts about steam locomotion. It was only after the Rainhill Trials on the L & M in October 1829 in which the prize of £500 was won by *Rocket*, specially constructed mainly by his son Robert, that the proprietors became convinced of the advantage of steam locomotives.

Stephenson was also chief engineer to the Manchester & Leeds, North Midland (Derby–Leeds), York & North Midland (Normanton–York) besides many shorter lines such as the Whitby & Pickering and the Leicester & Swannington. During construction of the North Midland Railway, Stephenson opened up limeworks at Ambergate, and collieries at Clay Cross near Chesterfield. It was near there, at Tapton House, that he spent his last years, taking up his hobby of horticulture. He died there on 12 August 1848 and was buried at Trinity Church, Chesterfield.

John Blenkinsop (1783–1831) was born on Tyneside. On 10 April 1811 he was granted a patent for a rack-rail system. The first engine to his order was built by Matthew Murray for the Middleton Colliery Railway, Leeds, in 1812. Its chief feature was a toothed wheel drive on to cogs on the side of one rail. At a test at Hunslet, Leeds, on 24 June 1812 it covered 2.4 km (1½ miles) in 23 minutes. Other Blenkinsop engines were used at Orrell Colliery near Wigan and at Willington, Kenton and Coxlodge collieries near Newcastle upon Tyne. A set of Blenkinsop wheels with rack rails from the Kenton & Coxlodge Railway is preserved in the National Railway Museum, York.

William Cubitt (1785–1861) was trained as a millwright in Norfolk. In 1807 he took out a patent for self-regulating windmill sails, and in 1817 he invented the treadmill for using the labour of convicts in prison for grinding corn. From 1826 to 1858 he practised as a civil engineer in London and was engaged in works on the Oxford and the Birmingham & Liverpool Junction canals. His principal work in railway engineering was the South Eastern Railway, which branched off from Rastrick's London & Brighton Railway at Redhill through the Weald of Kent to Folkestone. From here to Dover the line was carried in a succession of tunnels beneath the cliffs. The work involved the blasting of Round Down Cliff with one 8165 kg (18 000 lb) charge of gunpowder, exploded electrically on 26 January 1843.

In 1850–1 he superintended the erection of the Crystal Palace for the Great Exhibition in London, and in 1851 he was knighted at Windsor Castle. Other works included the floating landing stages on the Mersey at Liverpool and the iron bridge over the Medway at Rochester.

Timothy Hackworth (1786–1850), one of the most important figures in the early development of the locomotive. He was the eldest son of John Hackworth, foreman smith at Wylam Colliery, Northumberland, and was trained in the same craft, first under his father, who died in 1802, then under the supervision of Christopher Blackett, proprietor of the colliery. In 1807 he became foreman smith and was concerned with the design and construction of early locomotives built at Wylam with Jonathan Forster and William Hedley (qv). In 1813 he married Jane Golightly. Both were keen Methodists and Hackworth became a lay preacher.

From 1816 to 1824 he was foreman smith at Walbottle Colliery near Newcastle upon Tyne. After a short period

Timothy Hackworth.

Hackworth was the first engineer to establish the steam locomotive as a throughly reliable·machine. He introduced the eight-wheeled engine with bogie in 1813; side coupling rods instead of chains (S & D *Locomotion* 1825); spring loaded safety valve instead of weighted; self-lubricating bearings with oil reservoir; steam dome on boiler to obtain dry steam; inside cylinders and crank axle; valve gear reversed by single lever; and lap in slide valves to permit expansive working.

Marc Séguin (1786–1875) was a pioneer of the multi-tubular boiler and builder of the first steam locomotive in France. He was trained under Joseph Montgolfier, one of the brothers who invented the hot-air balloon. In 1820 he built an iron suspension bridge, his first major work. A steamship with a fire-tube boiler for service on the Rhône followed in 1825 and the next year he and the firm of E. Biot et Cie jointly obtained a concession for a railway between Lyon and Saint-Etienne which he surveyed. In 1827 he patented a multi-tubular boiler which he used on a steam locomotive, the first to be built in France, which he tested on the Saint-Etienne–Lyon Railway on 7 November 1829, less than a month after the Rainhill Trials on the Liverpool & Manchester Railway. He visited England in 1827–8 and met George Stephenson. Séguin published the first French study of railway engineering.

supervising the Forth Street Works of Robert Stephenson & Co., while George Stephenson was away on the Liverpool & Manchester Railway and Robert was in South America, he transferred to the Stockton & Darlington Railway and set up locomotive works at New Shildon. Here he built *Royal George* in 1827, the first six-coupled locomotive and the first in which the cylinders drove directly on to the wheels. His *Sans Pareil* of 1829 was entered in the Rainhill Trials and narrowly missed success. In the same year he designed coal staithes on the Tees at the new town of Middlesbrough. His next locomotive design was the 'Wilberforce' class of 0–6–0 with vertical cylinders at the rear driving a separate shaft connected to the wheels by coupling rods, so allowing all axles to be sprung. It had a greatly improved boiler with a heating surface of about 46 m² (500 ft²).

In 1833 he entered into a new contract with the S & D becoming responsible for locomotives and workshops but remaining free to operate his own business as a builder of locomotives and stationary engines. In 1838 he introduced his successful 0–6–0 type with inclined cylinders at the rear driving the front coupled wheels. One, named *Derwent*, is preserved at North Road Station Museum, Darlington. Three 0–6–0s built in 1838 for Nova Scotia, however, reverted to the old vertical cylinder arrangement. One, *Samson*, is preserved at New Glasgow, Nova Scotia.

In 1840 he gave up the S & D contract to develop his own works at Shildon, building locomotives, stationary engines and boilers. His last locomotive, 2–2–2 *Sans Pareil No. 2* of 1849 was purchased by the York, Newcastle & Berwick Railway and gave excellent service until 1881.

Robert Livingston Stevens (1787–1856), son of John Stevens (qv), American mechanical engineer and naval architect and pioneer of railroads and steam navigation. In 1830, on the establishment of the Camden & Amboy Railroad, he was elected president and chief engineer and he visited England to study locomotives and railways. On the voyage he designed the flat-bottomed rail (also attributed to Vignoles qv), now standard throughout the world, and had a quantity rolled in England. At the same time he designed a fish plate for joining rail ends, and the claw spike for holding rails to ties, or sleepers. In England he bought the Stephenson 'Planet' type 0–4–0, first named *Stevens* and later *John Bull*, which was erected by Isaac Dripps (qv) in 1831. At the Hoboken shops, New Jersey, he designed a cut-off valve gear for locomotives, improved boilers, and pioneered the burning of anthracite on locomotives.

William Fairbairn (1789–1874) was born in Scotland, trained on Tyneside and in 1817 started an engineering works in Manchester where he remained for the rest of his working life. Later he was joined by his two sons. Fairbairn & Sons built about 400 locomotives from 1839 to 1862. These included many bar-framed engines of Edward Bury's design. The most famous engines built by the firm were the 'Large Bloomers', 2–2–2s of McConnell's design for the Southern Division of the London & North Western Railway in 1852–4.

In 1845–9 Fairbairn devised the system of wrought-iron tubular girders used by Robert Stephenson on the Conway and Menai Strait bridges in North Wales and at Montreal. Fairbairn built many other bridges using this

William Fairbairn.

type of girder but of smaller section. In 1860 his firm rebuilt the timber viaducts at Mottram and Dinting on the Sheffield–Manchester Railway without interrupting the passage of about 70 trains daily. The firm wound up at about the time of his death.

Peter Rothwell (1792–1849) achieved distinction as a manufacturer of locomotives for many early railways. At an early age he joined his father at the Union Foundry, Bolton, of which he became manager, for a time being joined by Benjamin Hick (1790–1842). The first locomotive was a 2-2-0, *Union*, built for the Bolton & Leigh Railway in 1831. It had a vertical boiler and horizontal cylinders fixed to the framing, not to the boiler—an innovation. The most famous engines he built were the 2134 mm (7 ft) gauge 4-2-4 tanks to Pearson's design for the Bristol & Exeter Railway in 1853–4, with driving wheels 2743 mm (9 ft) diameter. Many other broad-gauge engines were built for the Great Western Railway.

Rothwell built engines for the London & Birmingham, Midland Counties, Grand Junction, Liverpool & Manchester, London & Southampton, London & North Western, London & South Western and Eastern Counties railways. The last engines were built in 1860; a total of 200. The firm later became the Bolton Iron & Steel Co. and for a time was managed by F. W. Webb, later the famous locomotive superintendent of the London & North Western Railway.

Thomas Edmondson (1792–1851), a native of Lancashire, was the originator of the standard railway ticket. He began in the cabinet-making trade. In 1836 he became a clerk on the Newcastle & Carlisle Railway where he quickly grew dissatisfied with the system of making out individual tickets for passengers. In 1837 he invented a machine for printing railway tickets on cards of a standard size, numbered consecutively, and a press for stamping dates on the tickets. The N & C was not interested in his invention, so Edmondson applied to the Manchester & Leeds Railway on which he was appointed at Manchester. His system was soon adopted for general use throughout Britain and in other parts of the world. He patented his invention and charged railways 10 shillings (50 p) a mile per year for using it.

Thomas Rogers (1792–1856), American locomotive engineer and founder of the Rogers Locomotive Works in 1837. In 1849 he introduced the link motion (valve gear) in America and he was one of the first engineers to apply balance weights for rotating parts. In 1850 he introduced the 'wagon-top', or tapered, boiler to give greater steam space over the firebox. This became a standard feature of early American locomotives. His works continued until 1905, producing about 6300 engines, before being absorbed by the American Locomotive Company (Alco).

Charles Blacker Vignoles (1793–1875) was one of the best known of the early railway civil engineers. He was born in Ireland and lost both his parents in infancy. The first part of his career was spent in the army; he became a surveyor in 1816. His principal railway work was on the lines forming the North Union Railway (Parkside–Wigan–Preston), after which he laid out the Dublin & Kingstown Railway, the first in Ireland. In 1837 he introduced the flat-bottomed rail section which bore his name and is now standard throughout the world. (See also R. L. Stevens.) During the 'Railway Mania' of 1846–8 he was engaged on many railways in Britain and Ireland. In 1847 he made the first of many visits to Russia where he carried out many railway projects and in 1853–5 he was responsible for the first railway in western Switzerland. His last important line was from Warsaw to Terespol in 1865.

Edward Bury (1794–1858), early locomotive engineer and originator of the bar frame universally used in American steam locomotive practice, was born in Salford, Lancashire, and in the early 1820s he set up his works in Liverpool. Here his works manager was James Kennedy who later became a partner in the firm of Bury, Curtis & Kennedy. His first locomotive, apart from an early unsuccessful attempt, was the 0-4-0 *Liverpool* in 1830, the first engine with inside cylinders and bar frames. Its wheels were 1829 mm (6 ft) in diameter, the largest up to that time. The upright cylindrical firebox with domed top became a standard feature of Bury's engines.

From 1837 he was locomotive superintendent on the London & Birmingham Railway at Wolverton, until succeeded by McConnell on 1 January 1847 when he was appointed to the Great Northern Railway as locomotive engineer. His work so impressed the management that in 1849 he was appointed general superintendent, but he resigned in 1850. That year the Liverpool works closed down. Two Bury engines survive today: the Furness Railway 0–4–0 No. 3 at the National Railway Museum, York; and the 2–2–2 No. 36 of the Great Southern & Western Railway at Cork Kent station in Ireland.

Matthias W. Baldwin (1795–1866), founder of the Baldwin Locomotive Works, Philadelphia, USA, the largest in the world. He was born in Elizabethtown, New Jersey, and became first a watch maker, then a tool maker and then a machinist. This brought him into contact with stationary steam engines and then locomotives. His first locomotive *Old Ironside* was built in 1832 and remained in service for over 20 years. His second, the 4–2–0 *E. L. Miller*, was a great advance and many of its features became standard American practice. In 1838 he introduced standardization using templates and gauges, and by 1840 he was using metallic packing for glands. His first European engine was built for Austria in 1841. Horizontal cylinders in identical castings, including half the smokebox saddle, were introduced in 1858 and soon became standard in America. In England, nearly half a century later, they were pioneered by Churchward on the Great Western Railway.

When he died in 1866 Baldwin's annual output was 120 engines; also in that year the 2–8–0 was introduced, becoming the most numerous type in America. The last Baldwin steam locomotive was built for India in 1955, bringing the total to about 75 000.

Ross Winans (1796–1877) became interested in railways in 1828 while in Baltimore. He joined Whistler, Knight and McNeill (qqv) on a journey to England to study railway construction. On his return to the USA he became locomotive engineer on the Baltimore & Ohio at the Mount Clare shops where he spent 25 years. Winans designed the first eight-wheeled passenger car in the world and is credited with the introduction of the car mounted on two bogies. In 1837 he built the first locomotive to be exported from the USA. In 1841 he built the first 0–8–0 locomotive, for the B & O, and in 1842 the first of vertical-boiler 'Mud Digger' 0–8–0s. In 1848 he brought out his 0–8–0 'Camel' type with wide firebox designed to burn anthracite and built over 100 for the B & O. He retired in 1860.

George Hudson (1800–71) was known as the 'Railway King'. He achieved considerable success as a draper in York, and at the age of 27 received a bequest of £30 000 which he invested in North Midland Railway shares. He quickly rose to important positions in the town, becoming Lord Mayor of York in 1837. In that year he was appointed chairman of the York & North Midland Railway, opened in 1839, and he became closely acquainted with George Stephenson. He next became actively engaged in extending the railway from York to Newcastle upon Tyne. He

George Hudson.

was instrumental in the formation of the Midland Railway by amalgamation of the Midland Counties, North Midland and Birmingham & Derby railways in 1844 and became chairman of the company. During the rush of railway speculation in 1844 he was in control of 1635 km (1016 miles) of railway. This was the period of his greatest success and, despite his rough north country accent and uncultivated manners, his acquaintance was sought by the leading persons in the country, even the Prince Consort.

As Hudson's power increased, however, his financial dealings became questionable and after paying dividends to the extent of £294 000 out of Eastern Counties Railway capital his fall was rapid. To his credit it must be said that he was the first person in control of railways who attempted to guide their development according to an overall plan, though his rule to 'Mak' all t' railways cum t' York' did not always lead to the best routes being chosen. The railway which suffered his most powerful opposition, the Great Northern, was in the end the one which really put York on the railway map.

George Washington Whistler (1800–49) pioneered many of the earliest railways in the USA. He began his career in the army, where he became friendly with William Gibbs McNeill (see below) whose sister became his second wife. In 1828 he and McNeill were sent to England to study locomotives and railway construction. On their return to ther USA they built the Baltimore & Ohio and the Paterson & Hudson River Railroads. In 1834 a son, James McNeill Whistler, was born in Lowell, Massachusetts, destined to become the famous American painter. After building the Western Railroad across the Berkshire

Mountains from Worcester to Albany in 1841, Whistler was invited by Tsar Nicholas I to survey and build the railway from Moscow to St Petersburg (now Leningrad). He went to Russia in 1842 and construction of the 676 km (420 mile) railway, one of the straightest in the world, began in 1844. He chose a gauge of 1524 mm (5 ft), standard on many early railways south of the Ohio River in the USA, and thus established the standard Russian gauge which was not, as is commonly assumed, adopted for strategic reasons. Construction became protracted, and in 1848 he succumbed to a cholera epidemic and died in St Petersburg on 7 April 1849.

William Gibbs McNeill (1801–53) was one of the pioneer civil engineers on railroads in the USA. His great grandfather had emigrated to America from Scotland with Flora Macdonald in 1746. He began his career in the army where he met George Washington Whistler (qv) who later married his sister. In 1823 he was asked to report on the feasibility and cost of a railway or canal across the Allegheny Mountains between Chesapeake Bay and the Ohio River, and he later surveyed the James River and Kanawha canals and the Baltimore & Ohio Railroad. In 1828, with Whistler, Jonathan Knight and Ross Winans (qqv) he was sent to England to study railway construction. He met George Stephenson and became convinced of the practicability of railways. With Whistler he became joint engineer on several railway projects in the eastern USA and was engaged as engineer on the Baltimore & Ohio (opened in 1829), Baltimore & Susquehanna, Paterson & Hudson River and several other lines. In 1837 he resigned from the army and became engineer for the state of Georgia, surveying railways from Cincinnati to Charleston. In 1851 he visited Europe, hoping to recover his health which had been severely damaged by overwork. In London he became the first American to be elected a member of the Institution of Civil Engineers. Soon after his return to the USA he died suddenly.

George Bradshaw (1801–53) was born in Salford, Lancashire. On leaving school he was apprenticed to an engraver and in 1821 he established an engraving business in Manchester where he specialized in the engraving of maps. In 1830 he produced the first of his maps of canals and inland navigations. In 1838 he produced the first of his railway maps. His first railway timetable appeared in 1839. In 1840 this became *Bradshaw's Railway Companion* with maps, and in December 1841 *Bradshaw's Monthly Railway Guide*. Among other publications were *Bradshaw's Continental Railway Guide* from 1847 and *Bradshaw's General Railway Directory and Shareholders' Guide* from 1848. While still a young man Bradshaw joined the Society of Friends (Quakers) and was prominent in philanthropic work.

The last Bradshaw timetable was No. 1521 published in June 1961. An almost complete collection was handed over to Manchester Public Library when Blacklock's Printing Works, successor to Bradshaw & Blacklock, closed in 1971.

Horatio Allen (1802–90), American locomotive pioneer and civil engineer. After graduating with high honours in mathematics at Columbia College in 1823 he started a career in law but soon changed to engineering. He began with the Delaware & Hudson Canal Co.; in 1824 he was appointed resident engineer of the Delaware & Susquehanna Canal and in 1825 resident engineer of the Delaware & Hudson Canal. Early in 1826 he was sent to England by the D & H to purchase rails for 25 km (16 miles) of railway and also four locomotives. At Liverpool he met George Stephenson, then engineer of the Liverpool & Manchester Railway. One engine was ordered from Robert Stephenson & Co. of Newcastle and three from Foster, Rastrick & Co. of Stourbridge. It was one of these, *Stourbridge Lion*, which was the first locomotive to run in North America. The locomotives were received in New York in the winter of 1828–9, but it was not until August 1829 that they were taken to the railway at Honesdale, Pennsylvania.

In 1829 Allen was appointed chief engineer of the South Carolina Railroad for which, in 1832, he designed the world's first articulated locomotive, a 2-2-0+0-2-2, which was built by the West Point Foundry in New York. Later he became consulting engineer for the New York & Erie RR and for the Brooklyn Bridge. In 1844 he became a member of the firm of Stillman, Allen & Co., building marine engines. He retired in 1870 and devoted himself to a life of study and invention. He was credited with the invention of the bogie coach (see Ross Winans) and an improved expansion valve gear.

Carl Ghega (1802–60) was one of the most outstanding European railway engineers. He was born in Venice and after graduating in mathematics at Padua University in 1819 he spent 17 years as an engineer on water supply works at Venice. In 1836 he was appointed engineer on the Kaiser Ferdinand's Nordbahn, the first steam railway in Austria. Later he laid out the Rabensburg–Brünen and Lundenburg–Olmüt railways. Ghega is best remembered as engineer of the Semmering Railway in Austria, the first 'mountain railway' in Europe, begun in 1848 and opened in 1854. It still ranks as one of the greatest pieces of railway engineering in Europe. At Semmering station is a large memorial to Ghega.

Robert Stephenson (1803–59), son of George (qv), ranks with Brunel and Locke as one of the greatest of early railway engineers. When aged only 20 he was placed in charge of the locomotive works in Newcastle upon Tyne which his father had founded under the name of Robert Stephenson & Company. In 1824 he visited South America for three years and there met Richard Trevithick, penniless, whom he helped to repatriate.

Under Robert Stephenson's direction the famous *Rocket* was built and entered successfully in the Rainhill Trials. He assisted his father on the Liverpool & Manchester, Leicester & Swannington and other railways and in 1833 was appointed engineer of the London & Birmingham Railway, completed in 1838.

Robert Stephenson.

It is for his great bridges that he is best remembered. Best known are the High Level Bridge at Newcastle (1846–9), Royal Border Bridge over the Tweed at Berwick (1850), and his great bridges built on the tubular system in conjunction with William Fairbairn (qv) at Conway (1846–8), Menai Strait (1846–50) and the Victoria Bridge over the St Lawrence at Montreal (1854–9).

Joseph Hamilton Beattie (1804–71) is famous for being the first to devise a means of burning coal on a locomotive without producing smoke, and for his feed-water heating apparatus. Details of his early career are obscure, but by 1839 he was assistant engineer on the London & Southampton Railway under Locke (qv). In 1850 he succeeded J. V. Gooch as locomotive superintendent on the London & South Western Railway (formerly London & Southampton) at Nine Elms, London. The first locomotive to be fitted with his coal-burning firebox and feed-water heater was a 1981 mm (6 ft 6 in) single-wheeler named *The Duke* in 1853. The firebox was in two parts, one of which burnt coal and the other coke. The coke fire burnt the smoke from the coal. This complicated arrangement was made obsolete by the firebox with brick arch and baffle plate in 1860. The trouble with the feed-water heater was that injectors (see Giffard) would not work with hot water, so that crosshead-driven boiler feed pumps had to be used. His 2-4-0 with outside cylinders achieved renown, two even being built for the East Lancashire Railway in 1857. Three of the tank-engine versions built in 1874–5, and much rebuilt since, continued in use at Wadebridge,

Cornwall, until 1962. Two are preserved, one in the National Collection.

Joseph Locke (1805–60), one of the principal early British railway engineers, was born near Sheffield and was educated at Barnsley Grammar School. In 1823 he was articled to George Stephenson and worked with him on the Liverpool & Manchester Railway. It was during the construction of the tunnel down to Liverpool Lime Street that Locke proved errors in Stephenson's survey which led to an estrangement. Locke's principal works were the Grand Junction (Birmingham–Warrington, begun by G. Stephenson), 1835–7; London–Southampton, 1836–40; Sheffield–Manchester, 1838–40; Lancaster–Preston, 1837–40; the Greenock, 1837–41; Paris–Rouen, 1841–3; Rouen–Le Havre, 1843; Barcelona–Mattaro, 1847–8; and the Dutch Rhenish Railway, 1856.

In 1840 Locke entered a partnership with John Edward Errington (1806–62) and together they constructed the Lancaster & Carlisle, 1843–6; East Lancashire, and Scottish Central, 1845; Caledonian (Carlisle–Glasgow and Edinburgh), 1848, and other Scottish lines.

Locke was noted for his avoidance of tunnels. There is no tunnel between Birmingham and Glasgow despite the obstacles of Shap and Beattock. He was also noted for the low cost of his lines, partly achieved by exploitation of human labour, and by long, heavy gradients.

Thomas Brassey (1805–70), one of the most famous railway contractors, was born and educated in Cheshire and articled to a land surveyor at the age of 16. In 1834 he became acquainted with George Stephenson and through him obtained a contract for Penkridge Viaduct on the Grand Junction Railway. This was followed by other GJR contracts under Locke. Following his marriage in 1831, his wife persuaded him to take up a career as a railway contractor and by 1850 he had works in progress throughout Britain and Europe. Other works were the Grand Trunk Railway in Canada, 1852–9; the Crimean Railway, with Peto and Betts (qqv), 1854; Australian railways 1859–63; Argentine railways, 1864; several Indian railways, 1858–65; and Moldavian railways, 1862–8.

Brassey was remarkable for his punctuality and thoroughness in his contracts, his power of mental calculation, skill in organisation, ability to delegate responsibility to his subordinates, and for humane treatment of navvies working under him. He was a man of unfailing courtesy and kindness, and scrupulous honesty.

Isambard Kingdom Brunel (1806–59) was the son of Marc Isambard Brunel (1769–1849), engineer of the Thames Tunnel, begun in 1825, completed 1843, and later adapted by John Hawkshaw (qv) as part of the East London Railway. I. K. Brunel worked with his father in the tunnel. His first major undertaking was the Clifton Suspension Bridge, Bristol, although this was not completed until after his death. In March 1833, when only 27, he was appointed engineer to the Great Western Railway between London and Bristol, laying out the line with bold

Isambard Kingdom Brunel.

Railway. In May 1837 he and Wheatstone took out a joint patent and persuaded the London & Birmingham Railway to experiment with a telegraph between London (Euston) and Camden Town. Its success led to its installation in 1839 on the Great Western Railway between London (Paddington) and West Drayton, which was extended to Slough in 1843. In 1845 it was instrumental in the arrest at Paddington of a murderer named Tawell who had boarded a train at Slough. From that moment the telegraph was established. In 1846, together with five partners, Cooke formed the Central Telegraph Co. which, by 1869, had achieved daily receipts of over £1000. Wheatstone was knighted in 1868 and Cooke in 1869.

Thomas Cook (1808–92) founded the great English firm of Thomas Cook & Son. He was born in Melbourne, Derbyshire, and after a succession of occupations he became interested in the Temperance Movement, and on 5 July 1841 he ran a temperance excursion on the Midland Counties Railway. Its success led to others and to the establishment of a business in Leicester which, in 1865, was transferred to London. In 1866 he arranged his first tours to the USA and from there followed many to other parts of the world, all at reduced rates. From 1948 control of Thomas Cook & Son was vested in the British Transport Commission. On 26 May 1972 it was sold for £22 500 000 to a consortium led by the Midland Bank.

William Fothergill Cooke.

engineering works and to the unprecedented gauge of 2134 mm (7 ft). He continued as engineer of the Bristol & Exeter, the South Devon (where he experimented unsuccessfully with atmospheric propulsion) and the Cornwall Railway; also the line from Swindon to Gloucester and South Wales. For this he devised a combination of tubular, suspension and truss bridge to cross the Wye at Chepstow, and he developed this design in his famous bridge over the Tamar at Saltash near Plymouth. This was completed just before his death in 1859. Besides railways Brunel designed and built steamships, the most famous being the *Great Western* of 1838, and the *Great Britain* of 1845. His greatest ship, the *Great Eastern*, was built for the Eastern Navigation Co. in 1858. Anxieties connected with this broke his health and he died the following year.

William Fothergill Cooke (1806–79), with Professor Charles Wheatstone (1802–75), pioneered the electric telegraph and thereby made one of the greatest contributions to the safety of railway operation. Cooke first became interested in the idea in 1836 and he experimented with it in a tunnel on the Liverpool & Manchester

Samuel Morton Peto (1809–89) stands second only to Brassey as one of the greatest of railway contractors. He served under an uncle and his cousin, Thomas Grissell, as a builder and in 1830 became a partner in the business for 16 years, during which period they carried out part of the Great Western Railway, and built the new Houses of Parliament, 1840–52, and Nelson's Column, 1843. In 1846 he became a partner with his brother in law, E. L. Betts (qv), and in 1847–8 they built the loop line of the Great Northern Railway, Peterborough–Boston–Lincoln. In 1850–4 they built the Oxford, Worcester & Wolverhampton Railway and in 1850–2 the Oxford–Birmingham line of the GWR. With Thomas Brassey (qv) he carried out railway contracts in Australia and Canada, and with Crampton (qv) built the London, Chatham & Dover Railway. During the Crimean War he built the first military railway, from Balaclava to Sebastopol, without profit or remuneration, thereby earning his baronetcy. From 1851 until its amalgamation with the London & North Western he was chairman of the Chester & Holyhead Railway. From 1847–78 he served in Parliament as Liberal representative first for Norwich, then Finsbury and finally Bristol.

Nathaniel Worsdell (1809–96) was the eldest son of Thomas Clarke Worsdell, builder of the tender for the Stephenson *Rocket*. In 1828 he began work on the Liverpool & Manchester Railway and with his father designed and built the earliest passenger coaches. In 1836 he succeeded his father as superintendent of the carriage department of the L & M. In 1837 he invented an apparatus for picking up and depositing mail bags on railways which was patented in 1838, but he never received any remuneration for this because the Post Office used a different system. He also invented a screw coupling, but using a single right-hand thread only.

The year his son Thomas William was born, 1838, he built the *Experience* coach for the L & M, consisting of three horse-carriage bodies on a railway-carriage frame, so establishing the design upon which future compartment coaches in Great Britain and Europe were based.

When the locomotive and carriage departments were transferred from Liverpool to Crewe in 1843 Worsdell moved there and played an important part in the development of the new town. He retired in 1880. He was a Quaker like his father and was renowned for his integrity. It was said of him that he would speak the truth if he had to die for it. His two brothers Thomas and George became noted railway engineers, and of his five sons Thomas William and Wilson became locomotive engineers on the North Eastern Railway, Henry worked on railways in India, and Robert also on the North Eastern Railway.

John Gray (1810–54) was the first engineer to use the balanced slide valve on locomotives, on the Liverpool & Manchester Railway in 1838. In 1839 he fitted a valve gear to the L & M *Cyclops* designed to utilise the expansion of steam. He was the first engineer to use a long-travel valve motion, about 152 mm (6 in) on the Hull & Selby Railway in 1840. Gray was among the first to discard the idea of a low centre of gravity as necessary for the safe running of locomotives. He was many years ahead of other locomotive engineers; indeed long-travel valve gear was not universally adopted in Britain until the 1920s.

Isaac L. Dripps (1810–92) was one of the first locomotive engineers in the USA. He began his training on steamboat engines in Philadelphia with a company which, in 1830–1, built the Camden & Amboy Railroad. Dripps was given the job of erecting the first locomotive when it arrived from Robert Stephenson & Co. in 1831, although he had not till then seen a locomotive, and he drove it on its trial run. In 1832 Dripps added a leading pony truck, and pilot, or 'cowcatcher'. In 1834–8 he introduced the first eight-wheeled freight engine. He remained on the C & A until 1853 when he became a partner in the Trenton Locomotive & Machine Works, New Jersey. In 1859 he became responsible for motive power on the Pittsburgh, Fort Wayne & Chicago RR until, in 1870, he took charge of the Altoona shops of the Pennsylvania RR, the biggest in the USA. He retired in 1878.

John Hawkshaw (1811–91) was responsible for the greatest number of major engineering works of the foremost 19th-century engineers. He was born near Leeds and was trained on roads with Charles Fowler and on harbours and canals with Alexander Nimmo. He was responsible for the construction of a large portion of the Lancashire & Yorkshire Railway between 1845 and 1853, including some tremendous viaducts in Yorkshire, and he was the first engineer to demonstrate conclusively that steam locomotives were capable of surmounting gradients steeper than 1 in 50 (2 per cent).

Other works included the Charing Cross and Cannon Street railway bridges and stations, London; the East London Railway utilizing Marc Brunel's Thames Tunnel; and the Severn Tunnel. With James Brunlees (1816–92) he was engineer to the original Channel Tunnel project 1872–86. Abroad he reported on the Suez and Panama canal projects and from 1862 to 1876 was engineer to the Amsterdam Ship Canal. His contributions to engineering literature were enormous and his various reports, articles and addresses make fascinating reading. He was knighted in 1873.

John Haswell (1812–97) was a Scottish engineer who settled in Vienna, having gone there originally to erect locomotives for one of Austria's first railways. In 1837 he planned and equipped a locomotive works, of which he became manager, in Vienna. Here he built some of the first locomotives on the European continent. He remained head of the works until 1882. In 1851 Haswell produced the first eight-coupled engine in Europe, *Vindebona*, for the Semmering Trials, and with his *Wein-Raab*, a large-boilered 0-8-0 with all parts accessible, in 1885, he established the pattern for European heavy freight engines for many years. He introduced the Stephenson Link Motion (see Howe, below) into Europe. His own inventions included a corrugated firebox without stays, and a rudimentary form of the Belpaire firebox, thermic syphons, and counter-pressure braking. In 1861 he built one of the first four-cylinder locomotives in Europe. His works also produced the first railway carriages and post office carriages in Austria. For his services he received two orders of knighthood from the emperor of Austria.

William Henry Barlow (1812–1902), civil engineer, trained at Woolwich dockyard and London docks. After six years on engineering works in Turkey he returned to England in 1838 and became assistant engineer on the Manchester & Birmingham Railway; in 1842 he became resident engineer on the Midland Counties Railway and in 1844 on the North Midland Railway. On the formation of the Midland Railway in 1844 he became chief civil engineer. In 1849 Barlow patented the saddle-back section rail which bore his name (it was much used on the Great Western Railway) and between 1844 and 1866 he took out many patents relating to permanent way. In 1862–9 he laid out the extension of the Midland Railway from Bedford to London and designed the great roof of St Pancras Station. With Sir John Hawkshaw in 1860 he completed the Clifton Suspension Bridge, begun by I. K. Brunel. He was responsible for the design of the second Tay Bridge, 1882–7.

William Howe (1814–79) was the inventor of the steam engine valve gear known as 'Stephenson's Link Motion'. He was born in County Durham and trained under Hackworth (qv) at New Shildon, later at the Vulcan Foundry, Lancashire, and at Liverpool. In 1840 he moved to Gateshead and joined Robert Stephenson & Co. It was here, as a foreman in 1842, that he devised the reversing gear using two eccentrics and a curved link. The idea was suggested to him in a sketch by an apprentice named Williams at the works. A similar link motion with two eccentrics had been designed in 1832 by William T. James of New York. It was fitted to a locomotive built for the Baltimore & Ohio RR, but the boiler exploded and it was abandoned. Howe's original model of his gear can be seen in the Science Museum, London.

It was immediately adopted by Stephenson who gave Howe full credit for the invention, and it was soon in universal use. It seems probable that the gear was used at first for reversing only, and that its use in expansive working, cutting off the steam to the cylinder before the end of the piston stroke, was discovered later.

John Ramsbottom (1814–92) is best remembered as the inventor of the water trough and the safety valve named after him. About 1839 he entered the locomotive works of Sharp, Roberts & Co., Manchester, and in 1842 became locomotive superintendent of the Manchester & Birmingham Railway with works at Longsight, Manchester. In 1846 the M & B became part of the newly formed London & North Western Railway but Ramsbottom remained at Longsight until 1857 when he succeeded Francis Trevithick as locomotive superintendent of the entire

Northern Division of the LNWR at Crewe. He invented the water trough in 1859 to enable locomotives to pick up water while in motion. It was patented in 1860 and was first installed at Mochdre on the Chester–Holyhead section in that year. The troughs were transferred to Aber on the same line in 1871. In 1862, with the ending of locomotive work under McConnell at Wolverton, Crewe became the locomotive headquarters for the entire railway. Ramsbottom retired from the LNWR in 1871, but in 1883 he became connected with the Lancashire & Yorkshire Railway and was partly responsible for the establishment of the LYR works at Horwich near Bolton.

Edward Ladd Betts (1815–72) was one of the most famous of the early railway contractors. He began his training under his father on the Bell Rock Lighthouse near Beaumaris in North Wales, and at the age of 18 was put in charge of the construction of the Dutton Viaduct on the Grand Junction Railway under Joseph Locke (qv). His principal works were the Chester & Holyhead Railway and other lines in North Wales. He then entered into partnership with S. M. Peto (qv) with whom he built much of the Great Northern Railway in 1848–9. With Peto he also built the Oxford–Birmingham line of the GWR and the Oxford, Worcester & Wolverhampton Railway. They also built railways in Russia and Argentina. With Peto and Thomas Brassey (qv) he built the Grand Trunk Railway in Canada including Robert Stephenson's tubular bridge over the St Lawrence at Montreal; and railways in Austria, France and Denmark. With Peto and Crampton (qv) he built the London, Chatham & Dover Railway. In 1843 he married Peto's youngest daughter.

William Barber Buddicom (1816–87) was born in Liverpool and in 1831–6 was apprenticed there with Mather, Dixon & Co. In 1836–8 he worked on the Liverpool & Manchester Railway, and later became resident engineer on the Glasgow, Paisley & Greenock Railway. In 1840 he was appointed locomotive superintendent of the Grand Junction Railway, which had amalgamated with the L & M, with his headquarters at Edge Hill, Liverpool. It was Buddicom who prepared the plans and estimates for the new works at Crewe, carried out under his successor Francis Trevithick. Frequent crank axle failures in the Bury locomotives then in use led Buddicom to design what became known as the 'Crewe type' engine about 1842. The cylinders were mounted in an outside framing with the smokebox sheeting continued in a curve over the cylinders. The type was much used on the LNWR, Highland, and Caledonian railways.

In 1841 he went to France to superintend the construction of rolling stock for the Paris & Rouen Railway then being built by Thomas Brassey and MacKenzie and of which Joseph Locke was engineer. A company was formed under the name of Allcard, Buddicom & Co. until 1851 when it became Buddicom & Co. When the Sotteville Works at Rouen were ready in 1842, Buddicom's firm entered into a contract for running the railway.

Crampton 4–2–0 *Le Continent* of 1852, and carriages of the same period.

Thomas Russel Crampton (1816–88) must rank as one of the most original of early locomotive engineers. He was born at Broadstairs, Kent, and from 1839 to 1844 he worked under Marc Brunel, and then for a short time with Daniel Gooch on the GWR at Swindon. It was here that he conceived his famous design for a locomotive with a large low boiler and a pair of large driving wheels behind the firebox.

In 1845 the first two of this type were built and others followed for the LNWR and other lines. The biggest was *Liverpool*, a 6–2–0 built by Bury, Curtis & Kennedy in 1848. It weighed 35 tons and had the largest boiler on any locomotive of that date. Its 2438 mm (8 ft) driving wheels and general majestic appearance earned it a gold medal at the Great Exhibition of 1851. Most Crampton engines were in France, the first 12 being built for the Northern Railway of France in 1848–9 by Derosne, Cail et Cie. Hundreds more were built in France and Germany. One of the French Cramptons, *Le Continent* built in 1852 for the Paris–Strasbourg Railway has been preserved for use on special trains. In 1889 Crampton 4–2–0 No. 604 achieved a world speed record of 144 km/h (89.5 mph) between Montereau and Sens on the Northern Railway in France.

As a civil engineer Crampton was partly responsible for the London, Chatham & Dover Railway and wholly for the Swanley Junction–Sevenoaks; Faversham–Herne Bay; and Strood–Dover lines; and railways in eastern Europe and Asia Minor. Besides an interest in the Channel Tunnel project he was responsible for laying the world's first submarine cable, across the Strait of Dover.

Daniel Gooch (1816–89) was the most distinguished member of a great family of engineers. He was born in Bedlington, Northumberland, son of John Gooch, manager of Bedlington Ironworks, and Anna, daughter of Thomas Longridge of Newcastle upon Tyne. He was apprenticed at Robert Stephenson & Co., Newcastle, and after experience at the subsidiary works of Tayleur at the Vulcan Foundry in Lancashire, and in Scotland, he applied to I. K. Brunel (qv) for the post of locomotive superintendent of the GWR and was appointed, at the age of only 21, in 1837.

After preliminary brushes with Brunel, whose misguided specifications for locomotives had resulted in some wretched machines being obtained, Gooch ordered engines of his own design from Newcastle which at once

Sir Daniel Gooch.

achieved a reputation for speed and reliability. His 2438 mm (8 ft) single-wheeler design of 1847, at that time one of the largest and most powerful in Britain, remained in production until 1878, and examples survived until the end of the broad gauge in 1892.

Gooch took a leading part in the establishment of the new locomotive works at Swindon from 1843 and made an active contribution to the development of the new town. In 1864 he resigned the post so as to lay the first Atlantic cable from Brunel's steamship *Great Eastern*. The first telegraph messages were sent across the Atlantic in 1866, and Gooch was made a baronet. The same year he returned to the GWR as chairman, remaining in this position until the last year of his life. During his chairmanship he guided GWR through difficult times, and in his last years threw all his energies into the Severn Tunnel project which was completed in 1887.

His brothers Thomas Longridge (1802–82) and John Viret (1812–1900) were both distinguished engineers, the first on the Manchester & Leeds Railway and the second as locomotive superintendent on the London & South Western and Eastern Counties railways.

James Brunlees (1816–92) was a civil engineer responsible for outstanding railway works. He learned surveying under Alexander Adie (1808–79) on the Bolton & Preston Railway and later with Locke and Errington on the Caledonian Railway. On completion of the latter in 1844 he became acting engineer under Hawkshaw (qv) on lines forming the Lancashire & Yorkshire Railway, until 1850.

He then became responsible for a succession of major railway projects: the Ulverston & Lancaster Railway, 1851, including viaducts across the Kent and Leven estuaries; the São Paulo Railway, Brazil, with its amazing rope-worked inclines, 1856; the Fell railway over Mont Cenis Pass between France and Italy, 1865; Solway Junction Railway including the viaduct over the Solway Firth, 1865–9; the Cleveland Extension, Yorkshire, with the 54.9 m (180 ft) high Skelton Beck Viaduct. With Douglas Fox (1840–1921) he built the Mersey railway tunnel. On completion of this in 1886 Brunlees and Fox were knighted. From 1872 to 1886 Brunlees was engineer with Hawkshaw to the original Channel Tunnel Company.

Ernst Werner von Siemens (1816–92) was born at Lenthe, Hanover. In 1834 he entered the Prussian Artillery and in 1844 took charge of the Artillery Workshops, Berlin. He is best remembered in railway circles for having built the first practical electric railway, for the Berlin Trades Exhibition, operated from 31 May to 30 September 1879 on a track about 550 m (600 yd) long. His brother **Sir William Siemens (1823–83)** was responsible for the Portrush–Giant's Causeway Tramway in Ireland, the first railway in the world to be run on hydro-electric power, opened on 28 September 1883.

John Fowler (1817–98) was born in Sheffield and trained under J. U. Rastrick on the London & Brighton Railway as a civil engineer. Later he became resident engineer on the Stockton & Hartlepool Railway on the completion of which, in 1842, he was appointed engineer, general manager and locomotive superintendent. From 1844 he worked on the lines from Sheffield to the east coast which became the Manchester, Sheffield & Lincolnshire Railway and, from 1898, the Great Central Railway. He designed the Pimlico railway bridge, the first across the Thames in London, finished in 1860. He was then engaged on the

Sir John Fowler, engineer of the Forth Bridge.

Metropolitan Railway, London, the first section of which was opened in 1863. For this he designed the first fireless locomotive, which was not a success.

In 1870 Fowler was appointed to a commission to advise on narrow-gauge railways in India, and he also visited Norway in this capacity. From 1875 he entered into partnership with Benjamin Baker (qv) and from 1883 to 1890 supervised the construction of the Forth Bridge in Scotland. In 1890 he received a baronetcy.

Charles Easton Spooner (1818–89)—the most famous name in the history of narrow-gauge railways. He was born at Maentwrog, Wales, where his father, James Spooner, had engineered the narrow-gauge tramway over the embankment, or the Cob, to Portmadoc. When the Act of Parliament for the Festiniog Railway (spelt with one f in the Act) was obtained in 1832 C. E. Spooner was only 14, but he assisted in the construction of this 600 mm (1 ft 11⅝ in) gauge railway from slate quarries at Blaenau Ffestiniog down to the coast at Portmadoc. When his father died in 1856 Spooner became engineer and manager. In 1863 powers were obtained to work the line with locomotives instead of horses (ascending) and gravity (descending), and at the same time the line was improved. In 1865 it opened for passengers, becoming the world's first passenger-carrying narrow-gauge line. It was visited by engineers from all over the world. The first 0-4-0 engines were built by George England, but in 1869 the first Fairlie double engines appeared. Some of the original engines are still at work, though much rebuilt.

Alfred Belpaire (1820–93) was the inventor of the firebox which bore his name. He was born in Ostend, Belgium, and in 1840 gained his engineering diploma in Paris. In that year the Belgian State Railways entrusted him with charge of the locomotive shops at Malines where his contemporary Egide Walschaerts (qv) began work. In 1850 he was appointed director of the rolling stock department at Brussels.

To obtain greater efficiency from the low-grade fuel burned on Belgian locomotives he produced his flat-topped firebox in 1860, in a round-top boiler which was tested on the 2-4-0 No. 1. In 1864 he abandoned this type and adopted the familiar form which facilitated the use of vertical and horizontal stays. It was used on all the Belgian State Railway engines from 1864 to 1884. At the end of 1884 he introduced new details, increasing both length and width of the grate, the area of which reached 6.8 m² (73.8 ft²) on some express engines on the Luxembourg line.

He also invented a combined screw and lever reverse for locomotives as well as a steam rail carriage (1878), the precursor of the rail motor. He designed large numbers of locomotives. The Belpaire firebox was first used in Britain on the 0-6-2 tanks designed by Thomas Parker and built in 1891 for the Manchester, Sheffield & Lincolnshire Railway. The first to be constructed in Britain were on 2-4-0s for the Malines Terneuzen Railway in Belgium built in 1872 by Beyer, Peacock & Co., Manchester. It was through the chief draughtsman of the MS&L who had been with Beyer, Peacock, that it was used on that railway. It was adopted as standard by G. J. Churchward (qv) on the GWR, and his designs influenced others right down to the series of standard engines built by British Railways from 1951 to 1959.

Egide Walschaerts (1820–1901) was the inventor of one of the most efficient and widely used valve gears on steam locomotives. He was born in Belgium and started work as a mechanic on the Belgian State Railways at Malines. In 1844 he invented his valve gear which was used successfully on an inside-cylinder 2-2-2 at Brussels in 1848. It was used on the Crampton engines Nos. 165–70, of the Northern Railway of France, built in 1859. In Belgium it was applied to all outside-cylinder engines, but the Stephenson Link Motion was preferred for inside cylinders. It was first used in the USA in 1874 and in Britain in 1876.

John Saxby (1821–1913) was the inventor of the interlocking of signals and points, thereby adding greatly to the safety of railway operation. He began his railway work on the London, Brighton & South Coast Railway as a carpenter. Following several accidents on the railway, one at London as a result of irregular operation, he designed and patented, in 1856, his system of interlocking. The first interlocking frame was installed on the LBSCR near Haywards Heath, Sussex. During his 22 years on the LBSCR he introduced important improvements on the 1856 patent. In 1861 he went into business on his own at Haywards Heath for manufacture of signalling apparatus and in 1862 he joined J. S. Farmer (1827–92) to form the firm of Saxby & Farmer at Kilburn on the LNWR near London, becoming sole signalling contractors to the LNWR and LBSCR. In 1871 they introduced the 'rocker and grid' interlocking frame. Another works was established near Paris in 1878, managed by Saxby's son James. Following the end of the partnership in 1888, Farmer remained at Kilburn until his death. The French works became part of John Saxby Ltd in 1889, and in 1893, with the Kilburn works, part of Saxby & Farmer Ltd. In 1903 the works was transferred to Chippenham in Wiltshire.

Henri Giffard (1825–82)—inventor of the injector for feeding water into boilers against pressure. He began his railway career in 1841 on the Paris–Saint Germain Railway. He devoted a great part of his life to the development of ballooning, on which he published two important treatises in 1851 and 1854. For his invention of the injector in 1859 he received the prize for mechanics from the Académie des Sciences in Paris. The injector eliminated the need for feed pumps and enabled locomotives to replenish their boilers while stationary. In 1863 Giffard was created a Knight of the Legion of Honour.

David Joy (1825–1903) is best remembered for his radial valve gear for steam engines, but he had many other inventions to his credit. He was born in Leeds and served an apprenticeship with Fenton, Murray & Jackson, the world's first locomotive-building firm. When this closed in 1843 he transferred to Shepherd & Todd, also in Leeds, and in 1846 to the Railway Foundry, Leeds. Here he worked on the design for the *Jenny Lind* 2-2-2 engine, forerunner of a famous type.

In 1850 Joy left to take charge of the Nottingham & Grantham Railway, then just opened, later becoming locomotive superintendent of the Oxford, Worcester & Wolverhampton Railway, 1852-6. He then returned to the Railway Foundry. In 1857 he patented a compound marine engine, also a steam reversing gear, the first in the world. At the same time he took out the first of his three patents for hydraulic organ blowers. In 1860 he invented a pneumatic hammer.

From 1862 to 1876 he ran a business of his own at Middlesbrough. He then became secretary to the Barrow Ship Building Company and it was here, in 1879, that he invented his radial valve gear. Its first use on a locomotive was in 1880 when F. W. Webb had it fitted to a 0-6-0 built at Crewe. The gear became standard on the LNWR and from 1886 on the Lancashire & Yorkshire Railway. The Joy gear has been criticized as mechanically unsound because it involved boring the connecting rod, but on all but the largest locomotives it gave satisfactory results.

Theodore Dehone Judah (1826–63) pioneered the first transcontinental railway in the USA. After training and working as a civil engineer on railroads in the Eastern States, in 1854 he moved to California as chief engineer of the Sacramento Valley RR, opened in 1856. While there he conceived the idea of a railway from California through the Sierras to connect with the lines in the Mississippi States. After strenuous efforts to achieve support in Washington and the Eastern States, in 1860 he announced that he had discovered a practical route through the mountains. With **Colis P. Huntington (1821–1900)** he formed the Central Pacific RR Co. and carried out a survey. In 1862 he secured an Act in Washington for the transcontinental railway. On his return to California friction developed between Judah and the Huntington group which led to the others buying him out. On his journey back to the east he contracted typhoid while crossing the Isthmus of Panama and he died in New York six years before the completion of his great project.

Sandford Fleming (1827–1915), pioneer of Canadian transcontinental railways, was born in Kirkcaldy, Scotland, and went to Canada in 1845. After gaining experience as a railway engineer under Casimir Gzowski on the Northern Railway, in 1864 he was appointed chief railway engineer of Nova Scotia where, in 1864-7, he built the railway from Truro to Pictou. Also in 1864 he was asked to survey a railway from Montreal to Halifax. In 1867 he was appointed chief engineer of the transcontinental railway which was a condition of the entry of British Columbia into the Confederation in 1871. On 16 July 1872 he began his great expedition across Canada, locating the route through the Yellowhead Pass and down the Thompson and Fraser river valleys to Vancouver. In 1880 the govern-

ment handed over construction to the Canadian Pacific Railway Co. and the railway was taken through the mountains by a more southerly route. He assisted in the survey through the Kicking Horse Pass, and Fleming and his party were the first white men to cross the Rockies by this route. The Yellowhead Pass was later used by the Grand Trunk Pacific and Canadian Northern Railways which became part of Canadian National.

In 1879 he urged the Canadian, Australian and British governments to lay a Pacific cable. Its completion between Vancouver and Australia in 1902 was his crowning success. From 1876 he took a leading role in forcing the adoption of the first standard time zones in North America which came into operation in 1883. Fleming designed the first Canadian postage stamp and founded the Royal Canadian Institute.

Eli Hamilton Janney (1831–1912) invented the automatic coupling universally used throughout Canada, the USA, Mexico and the USSR. Although he had no mechanical training, he became interested in the problem of coupling railroad cars automatically to end the frequent accidents with the link and pin couplings then in use, and in 1868 he patented an automatic coupler. A second patent in 1873 formed the basis of the present coupler. After exhaustive tests in 1874–6 it was adopted by the Pennsylvania RR, but it was not until 1888, after three more patents, that the coupling became universally adopted, and this was only when Janney had waived patent rights on the shape of the coupler.

Alexandre Gustav Eiffel (1832–1923) is best known for his famous tower in Paris, built in 1887-9; but he designed some of the greatest iron railway bridges in Europe including the Sioule and Neuvial viaducts on the Orléans Railway in France, 1868-9; the Tagus Bridge on the Caceres Railway in Spain in 1880 and the Tardes Viaduct in central France, 1883. With the great Douro Bridge at Porto, Portugal, in 1875 he established the form of his iron arched bridges of which the greatest is the Garabit Viaduct on the Southern Railway of France, 1882. By 1887 his bridges had consumed 38 000 tons of iron and steelwork.

William Arrol (1839–1913) was born near Paisley, Scotland. At 14 he began work with a local blacksmith and in 1863, after some years as a journeyman smith, he obtained employment with Blackmore & Gordon of Port Glasgow. By 1868 he had saved £85, half of which he spent on a boiler and engine with which he started a small works of his own near Glasgow. This formed the nucleus of the great Dalmarnock Works. Bridge building was added to his work and his first contract was for bridges on the Glasgow, Bothwell, Hamilton & Coatbridge Railway, 1874, including a long multi-span bridge over the Clyde at Bothwell. The Caledonian Railway then entrusted him with the bridge over the Clyde into Glasgow Central Station in 1875.

William Arrol.

In 1873 he had undertaken construction of a railway suspension bridge over the Firth of Forth to a design by Thomas Bouch and work actually began, but following the collapse of Bouch's Tay Bridge in 1879 it was stopped. His next important contract was the bridge carrying the North British Railway over the South Esk on the Montrose line. On this he gained experience which served him well when he undertook the second Tay Bridge, to the design of W. H. Barlow (qv), begun in 1882 and completed in 1887. It was the longest railway bridge in Europe.

Arrol's greatest contract was the Forth Bridge of 1882–90, after which he was knighted by Queen Victoria. Other great works included the steelwork for the Tower Bridge, London; the first Redheugh Bridge, Newcastle upon Tyne; three bridges over the Nile at Cairo; Queen Alexandra Bridge, Sunderland; the Scherzer lifting bridge at Barrow, and the second portion of the Clyde Bridge into Glasgow Central Station.

William Robert Sykes (1840–1917) was the inventor of the 'lock and block' signalling system. He began his railway career on the London, Chatham & Dover Railway in 1863 and very soon he had designed and installed the first electric signal repeater, showing the position of a signal out of sight of the signalman; an automatic recorder for showing what block signals a signalman had sent and received; and in 1864 he had installed at Brixton near London the pioneer length of track circuiting.

In 1872 he introduced automatic signals on the Metropolitan District Railway in London, operated electrically by the trains themselves. He patented his lock and block system in 1875 and, following favourable Board of Trade reports, it was installed on the LC & DR, Hull & Barnsley, Metropolitan District, Mersey, and Wirral Railways, and later on other systems. It was introduced in the USA in 1882, and then in Russia and Japan. Sykes also devised an electro-mechanical system for operation of points and signals. In 1899, when the LC & DR joined the South Eastern to form the South Eastern & Chatham Railway Sykes left the railway and formed the W. R. Sykes Interlocking Signal Company, but continued with the SE & CR Joint Managing Committee in a consultative capacity.

Benjamin Baker (1840–1907), civil engineer, was born in Somerset. From 1856 he served an apprenticeship at Neath Abbey Ironworks in South Wales. In 1860 he worked as assistant to W. Wilson on Grosvenor railway bridge and Victoria Station, London. In 1861 he joined the staff of John Fowler (qv) and was his partner from 1875 until Fowler's death in 1898. From 1861 he was engaged on the construction of the Metropolitan and District (Inner Circle) railways, London, and the extension to St John's Wood. Later he was one of the engineers responsible for the first London 'tubes', the City & South London opened in 1890 and the Central London line opened in 1900. In these Baker adopted a method suggested to him in 1875, by making the line drop out of one station and

Benjamin Baker.

rise into the next, to assist the starting and stopping. In 1896 he acted as joint engineer with W. R. Galbraith for the Baker Street & Waterloo Railway (Bakerloo Line).

From the early days of his career Baker had made a deep study of long-span bridges, and in 1872 he evolved the cantilever system which he adopted in his designs for the Forth Bridge near Edinburgh, begun in 1883 and opened in 1890. In addition Baker was responsible for many other works in Britain, Egypt and North America.

William Cornelius Van Horne (1843–1915) was the driving force behind the construction of the Canadian Pacific Railway. He was born in Illinois, USA, and at 14 he began as a telegraph operator on the Illinois Central RR. By 1864 he had become a train despatcher on the Chicago & Alton RR and in 1870 superintendent of transportation. Further promotion led to his appointment as general manager and later president of the Southern Minnesota RR which he restored to solvency. In 1881 there came his greatest opportunity when he was placed in charge of construction of the Canadian Pacific Railway. With tremendous energy he drove the vast project through to completion in 1886. He was president from 1888 until illness forced resignation in 1899. With health recovered, he directed construction of the Cuba Railway, 563 km (350 miles) long, opened in 1902. He next completed the railway from Puerto Barrios to Guatemala, 1903–8. He died in Montreal on 11 September 1915.

James Henry Greathead (1844–96) was the inventor of the tunnelling shield named after him. In 1869, when still only 24, he tendered for the construction of the Tower Subway (qv) under the Thames in London. To expedite the work he made his tunnelling shield, a wrought-iron cylinder forced forward by strong screws as material was excavated in front of it. The subway was opened in 1870. After working on various surface railway contracts, in 1884 he was engaged as engineer on the City & South London Railway, the world's first electric underground railway, opened in 1890. He was joint engineer with Sir Douglas Fox (1840–1921) on the Liverpool Overhead Railway, opened in 1893. With W. R. Galbraith he engineered the Waterloo & City Railway and with Sir John Fowler and Sir Benjamin Baker (qqv) he began the Central London Railway.

George Westinghouse (1846–1914), American engineer, invented the compressed-air brake widely used on railways. He began working this out in 1866, first producing the non-automatic 'straight-air' brake. The automatic brake, which applied itself if the train broke apart, was developed in 1872–3. Further improvements were made in 1886–7 to facilitate a more rapid brake application. From the beginning Westinghouse insisted on a rigorous standardization of details so that Westinghouse-fitted stock from any railways could be coupled. The Westinghouse Electric Company was formed in 1886; later other works were established in England and Europe. The principal British railways using the Westinghouse brake were the Great Eastern; London, Brighton & South Coast; North Eastern; North British and Caledonian. Other companies used the vacuum brake.

Alfred George de Glehn (1848–1936), locomotive engineer, was the son of Robert von Glehn who settled in London from the Baltic Provinces. When Alfred was still young they moved to France and changed the name to de Glehn. After training as an engineer Alfred de Glehn became technical head of the Société Alsacienne at Belfort where he was responsible for the construction of the first four-cylinder compound engine, Norther Railway No. 701, in 1886. This had low-pressure cylinders between the frames driving the first crank axle, and two high-pressure cylinders outside driving the second wheels by outside cranks. The driving wheels were not coupled. In its fully developed form as a 4–4–2 the de Glehn compound became used throughout France. The GWR in England bought three of these compound 4–4–2s. The de Glehn system was subsequently applied to a wide range of locomotive types. Some large de Glehn compound 4–4–2s and 4–6–2s were built for the Bengal–Nagpur Railway in India.

Magnus Volk (1851–1937) was born in Brighton, the son of a German clock maker, and was the builder of the first electric railway in Britain. In 1881 he gained a gold medal for a street fire alarm system and the following year he equipped his house with the first telephone and the first electric light in Brighton. In 1883 he completed the installation of electric light in the Brighton Pavilion and at the same time built a 610 mm (2 ft) gauge railway along the beach making use of a Siemens dynamo and a 2 hp Crossley gas engine. The first section of the railway opened on 4 August 1883, eight weeks before the Portrush & Giant's Causeway Tramway in Ireland (see Siemens). In 1884 the line was extended and the gauge changed to 838 mm (2 ft 9 in) and the rebuilt line was opened on 4 August 1884.

His most extraordinary venture was the Brighton & Rottingdean Seashore Electric Tramroad with a car like a ship on long legs which, at high water, actually ran through the sea. The line was about 4.5 km (2¾ miles) long. It was opened on 28 November 1896 and ran until January 1901.

August von Borries (1852–1906), pioneeer of locomotive compounding, studied in Berlin and from 1875 to 1902 was chief mechanical engineer of the Prussian State Railways. His first two-cylinder compound was built in 1880 and his first four-cylinder one in 1899. Among his numerous innovations in German locomotives was the use of nickel steel for boilers in 1891. From 1902 until his death he was professor of transport and machinery at the Berlin Technical School. He wrote extensively on locomotive matters.

George Jackson Churchward (1857–1933) was possibly the greatest of British locomotive engineers. At the age of

16 he was articled to John Wright, locomotive superintendent of the South Devon Railway at Newton Abbot. In 1876, when this became part of the Great Western Railway, Churchward transferred to Swindon under Joseph Armstrong. The following year Armstrong died and was succeeded by William Dean. In 1895 Churchward became assistant locomotive works manager and, in 1896, manager, and soon afterwards chief assistant to Dean. In this position he was given freedom to experiment with new boiler designs incorporating a high Belpaire firebox which appeared on most of the later Dean engines, including the famous *City of Truro*. In 1902 Dean retired and Churchward became superintendent. He had already produced his first 4–6–0, named *William Dean*. It was the forerunner of the 'Saint' class and later the 'Halls' and 'Granges'. He adopted a system of standard components such as boilers, cylinders, etc, combinations of which could be worked into a wide range of different locomotive designs. He was so impressed by the work of the de Glehn compound 4–4–2s in France that in 1903 he persuaded the GWR to buy one of these for trials. Two more were bought in 1905. For comparison he designed a four-cylinder simple 4–4–2, later rebuilt into a 4–6–0, the forerunner of the 'Stars', 'Castles' and 'Kings' and of his greatest engine *The Great Bear*, the first British 'Pacific', of 1908. From the French engines he adopted the high pressure of 15.8 kg/cm² (225 psi) and the generous bearing surfaces and from American practice the front end arrangement with long-travel valves, tapered boiler and cylindrical smokebox. Another innovation was his superheater at a time when the merits of superheating were still doubted on other railways. He retired at the end of 1921 but continued his close association with Swindon works until, on a misty morning on 19 December 1933, he was walking on the main line when he was struck and instantly killed by the 10.30 Fishguard express.

Dr Hugo Lentz (1859–1944), a locomotive engineer in Austria and Germany, was the inventor of the poppet valve gear for steam engines. He was trained in Hamburg and later served in the German navy. In 1887 he opened a works in Vienna where he built small steam engines to his designs and patents, later moving to Brno (now in Czechoslovakia) where he invented his poppet valve gear. In 1900 an engine with this gear was awarded a Grand Prix in Paris. In the same year he opened a works in Berlin. The first locomotive to be fitted with the Lentz gear was built by Hanomag of Hanover in 1902. Several other designs of valve gear followed, with oscillating and rotary cam drive. The rotary cam type was used by Gresley on several types of locomotive on the London & North Eastern Railway. By 1944 there were about 2000 locomotives with his valve gears in various countries. It was also extensively used in marine engines. (See also Caprotti.)

Karl Gölsdorf (1861–1916), Austrain locomotive engineer. His father Adolf (1837–1911) was locomotive engineer of the Austrian Southern Railways from 1885 to 1908. As locomotive engineer of the Austrian State Railways from 1891 until his death he produced over 60 designs of great elegance and ingenuity. In 1893 he introduced the two-cylinder compound and in 1901 his first four-cylinder compound. His first ten-coupled engine appeared in 1900. He designed the first 2–6–2 (1904), 2–6–4 (1908) and 2–12–0 (1911) in Europe, the last two being entirely new, and a 0–12–0 tank for the Abt rack system in 1912. He introduced a new valve gear which dispensed with the expansion link, and he is remembered particularly for his conveniently arranged footplate controls and his system of locomotive numbering which was widely used.

Hans Behn-Eschenburg (1864–1938) was a Swiss electrical engineer and a pioneer of high-voltage ac railway electrification, now adopted throughout the world. In 1892 he entered the firm of Maschinenfabrik Oerlikon (MFO) near Zürich and was engaged in the development of transformers and traction equipment. In 1897 he became chief electrical engineer. He introduced a three-phase induction motor in 1902, and in 1904 a practical single-phase traction motor used on the pioneer locomotive on the Seebach–Wettingen line and later on the Rhaetian, Lötschberg and other Swiss main lines. He became managing director of MFO in 1913.

Wilhelm Schmidt (1864–1924), the pioneer of high-degree fire-tube superheaters for boilers which revolutionized steam locomotive performance. He was born in Saxony and educated in Dresden. For 20 years he worked as an assistant to a locksmith in Brunswick where, in 1883, he established a works and built an engine to run on hot air and steam. This led to ideas for using superheated steam. In 1891 he moved to Kassel and there built an engine to work on superheated steam at 350°C (662°F). In 1898 the first locomotive superheater was used on the Prussian State Railways. It consisted of a large central flue with horizontal elements. A smokebox apparatus was employed on the Prussian State Railways in 1899 and in 1901 he introduced his final fire-tube type, first used that year on the Belgian Railways. Within ten years it was fitted to most large locomotives throughout the world, first in Britain in 1906 on a GWR 4–6–0 and on the Lancashire & Yorkshire Railway in a series of 0–6–0s introduced at Horwich by George Hughes.

Herbert Nigel Gresley (1876–1941) is famous as the engineer responsible for the world's fastest steam locomotive. From 1893 to 1897 he served an apprenticeship under F. W. Webb on the LNWR at Crewe and completed his training on the Lancashire & Yorkshire Railway under J. A. F. Aspinall. In 1905 he was appointed carriage and wagon superintendent on the Great Northern Railway at Doncaster. He was the first to introduce articulated carriages in Britain, in 1907, using one bogie to support the ends of two coaches. His bow-ended teak carriages were among the smoothest riding ever built.

In 1911 he succeeded H. A. Ivatt as locomotive superintendent. He remained in charge at Doncaster until his death, becoming chief mechanical engineer of the London & North Eastern Railway at the grouping of the railways in 1923. Most of the locomotives designed under him did good work, though some were terrible rough riders. His most famous achievements were the *Silver Jubilee* and *Coronation* streamlined trains in the mid-1930s. On 3 July 1938 his A4 class 4–6–2 No. 4468 *Mallard* achieved a world record speed, for a steam locomotive, of 201 km/h (125 mph) which has never been exceeded. *Mallard* is now in the National Railway Museum, York.

Arturo Caprotti (1881–1938), Italian engineer who designed a locomotive valve gear employing vertical poppet valves operated from a rotating camshaft as in internal combustion engine practice. It was first used on a 2–6–0 goods engine on the Italian State Railways in 1921. Its first application in Britain was on the LNWR 'Claughton' class 4–6–0 No. 5908 in 1926, resulting in a coal economy of 20.76 per cent. It was also applied with some success by the LNER to some four-cylinder 4–6–0s of Great Central design. In 1947 it was used on 20 Class 5 4–6–0s on the London, Midland & Scottish Railway, and in 1954 on the last British express locomotive, 4–6–2 No. 71000 *Duke of Gloucester*. Its last use on BR was on 30 standard class 5 4–6–0s in 1957. *Duke of Gloucester* has been reconstructed on the Great Central Railway at Loughborough.

André Chapelon (1892–1978) was one of the most outstanding engineers in the history of the steam locomotive, developing the French compound engine to a high degree of efficiency. After World War I he joined the Paris–Lyon–Méditerranée Railway; in 1925 the Paris–Orléans Railway, and in 1936 he became chief experimental engineer. In co-operation with M. M. Kylala in 1926 he perfected a double blast pipe which gave greater freedom to the locomotive exhaust. It was named the Kylchap blast pipe. His first rebuild of a 4–6–2 in 1929 and of a 4–8–0 in 1932 incorporated improvements which doubled the power output.

On the formation of the Société Nationale des Chemins de fer Français (SNCF) in 1938 he was appointed to the Department of Steam Locomotive studies of which he became chief. He achieved his greatest success with the 4–8–4 No. 242A1, rebuilt in 1942–6, largely during the German occupation of France. This engine, described on p. 122, could be claimed as the greatest steam locomotive ever built. Chapelon retired in 1953, but characteristically continued to produce calculations which, could they still be applied, would result in even greater steam locomotive efficiency.

The largest French express passenger locomotive, three-cylinder compound 4-8-4 No. 242A1, rebuilt by Chapelon in 1942-6 from a 4-8-2. The engine incorporated so many advanced design features as to justify its description as the greatest steam locomotive ever built. Progress with electrification and dieselization prevented construction of further examples of this type, and this magnificent machine was tragically broken up in 1960.

3

PERMANENT WAY

The term 'permanent way', meaning railway track, originated in the early days of British railway construction as a distinction between the contractors' temporary lines and the finished, or permanent, track. It is still in common use, as in 'P. W. Department, -Inspector, -gang, -machinery' etc. The Permanent Way Institution was founded in London in 1884 and incorporated in 1908.

RAILWAY GAUGES

Measurement between the inner edges of the rails

Standard gauge, 1435 mm or 4 ft 8½ in, is used in Great Britain, Canada, the USA, Mexico, Europe (except Ireland, Spain, Portugal, Finland and the USSR), North Africa, the Near Eastern countries, the Australian National Railways and New South Wales, China and South Korea; also Shinkansen in Japan, Western Australia and Victoria. In South America it is found in Paraguay, Uruguay, the Urquiza Region in Argentina, the Central and Southern Railways of Peru, Venezuela and short lines in Brazil.

France originally adopted standard gauge, but measured the gauge between the vertical axes of the rails which came to a round 1500 mm. This system of measurement was absurd because the actual gauge varied with the width of the rail heads and became 1445 mm (4 ft 8⅞ in). The French gauge was standardized at 1435 mm by the beginning of the 20th century, but in Algeria and Tunisia, on railways built by the French, the gauge of 1445 mm remained until fairly recently.

In Great Britain since 1966, and in several other countries, the standard gauge has been narrowed by 3 mm to 1432 mm (4 ft 8⅜ in) to reduce clearances and to obtain steadier running with modern motive power and rolling stock at high speeds.

Other Principal Gauges

Wide gauges

Gauge	Country
1676 mm (5 ft 6 in)	India, Pakistan, Bangladesh, Sri Lanka, Spain, Portugal, Argentina, Chile.
1600 mm (5 ft 3 in)	Ireland, South Australia, Victoria, Brazil.
1520 mm (4 ft 11⅞ in)	USSR, Finland, Mongolia. The gauge was officially narrowed from 1524 mm (5 ft 0 in) on 1 January 1972. Much of the old 5 ft gauge still exists.

Sub-standard Gauges

Gauge	Country
1067 mm (3 ft 6 in)	Queensland, South and West Australia, Tasmania, New Zealand, South Africa, Zimbabwe, Malawi, Ghana, Nigeria, Sudan, Japan, Indonesia, Newfoundland; some lines in Norway, Sweden, Ecuador and Chile.
1065 mm	South African Railways.
1050 mm (3 ft 5¼ in)	Algeria, Syria, the Lebanon and Jordan.
1 metre (3 ft 3⅜ in)	Principal lines in Burma, Thailand (Siam), Vietnam, Malaysia, East Africa and Cambodia, Brazil, Argentina, Chile, Bolivia; secondary lines in Switzerland, Portugal, Greece, India, Pakistan, Iraq.

Narrow Gauges (Less than 1 metre)

Gauge	Country
914 mm (3 ft)	Formerly extensively used in Colorado, USA, Ireland, and the Isle of Man. Still in use in Central America, Colombia, Peru, Mexico, Newfoundland.
891 mm (2 ft 11 in)	Some lines in Sweden.
800 mm (2 ft 7½ in)	Mountain and rack railways.
762 mm (2 ft 6 in)	Austria, Yugoslavia, Czechoslovakia, India, Sri Lanka (Ceylon), Wales (Welshpool & Llanfair Railway), and on the former Leek & Manifold Valley Railway in England.
750 mm (2 ft 5½ in)	Argentina, Brazil.
610 mm (2 ft) and 600 mm (1 ft 11⅝ in)	Sierra Leone and secondary lines in Wales, South Africa, India, Pakistan, southern Chile, north-west Argentina. Also the Lynton & Barnstaple and Ashover Light railways in England, both abandoned.
381 mm (1 ft 3 in)	Ravenglass & Eskdale and Romney, Hythe & Dymchurch Railways, England.
260 mm (10¼ in)	Wells Harbour and Wells–Walsingham Railways, Norfolk.

The first metre-gauge railway was probably that built by George Stephenson to connect his limestone quarry at Crich in Derbyshire with the limeworks beside the North Midland Railway at Ambergate. The first section was opened in March 1841 and the line was completed to Cliff Quarry in 1846. The railway worked until 24 May 1957 and the limeworks closed on 2 October 1965. Today the Cliff Quarry is the site of the Crich Tramway Museum.

Metre-gauge mineral railways were built in Algeria in 1865–6 and in Greece in 1869.

The earliest known passenger train service on a metre-gauge railway was operated by the Bombay, Baroda & Central India Railway between Delhi and Rewari, 84 km (52½ miles), opened to passengers on 14 February 1873.

The establishment of the metre gauge for secondary lines in India was somewhat devious. The choice of gauge was left to Lord Mayo (b. 1822 and Viceroy of India from 1869 until his assassination in 1872). He decided that the minimum width of a carriage to seat four aside should be 6 ft 6 in (2 m) and that the gauge should be not less than half that width. So the British Government agreed to a gauge of 3 ft 3 in (990 mm), but as a commission was then considering the introduction of the metric system in India the gauge was fixed at 1 metre, although another 90 years were to pass before the metric system was adopted. There are now 27 546 km (17 116 miles) of metre gauge route in India, Bangladesh and Pakistan.

The metre gauge holds second place in the world's route mileage. Out of about 1 126 500 km or 700 000 route miles about 112 600 km or 70 000 miles are metre gauge.

Third place is held by the 1067 mm (3 ft 6 in) gauge with a route length of 75 600 km (47 000 miles).

The largest metre-gauge system in Europe is the Greek Piraeus–Athens–Peloponnesus Railway (SPAP) with a route length of 800 km (497 miles). In September 1962 it was amalgamated with the Hellenic State Railways which now operates 960 km (597 miles) of metre-gauge lines and 1560 km (969 miles) of standard gauge.

The total route length of interconnected 1067 mm (3 ft 6 in) gauge operated by nine railway systems in southern Africa is 38 995 km (24 229 miles) made up as follows:

	km	miles
Benguela	1 415	879
Malawi	790	491
Mozambique	3 438	2 136
South Africa	22 891	14 223
Swaziland	316	196
Tan-Zam	1 860	1 156
Zaire	3 518	2 186
Zambia	1 297	806
Zimbabwe	3 470	2 156

A gauge of 5 ft (1524 mm) was used at first on the Eastern Counties, Northern & Eastern and London & Blackwall Railways, England.

For the Great Western Railway, England, I. K. Brunel adopted a gauge of 7 ft (2134 mm). After a while a ¼ in (6 mm) was added to give greater clearance. This was the

Lightning, one of Daniel Gooch's 2.4 m (8 ft) single-wheelers built for the GWR 2.1 m (7 ft) gauge.

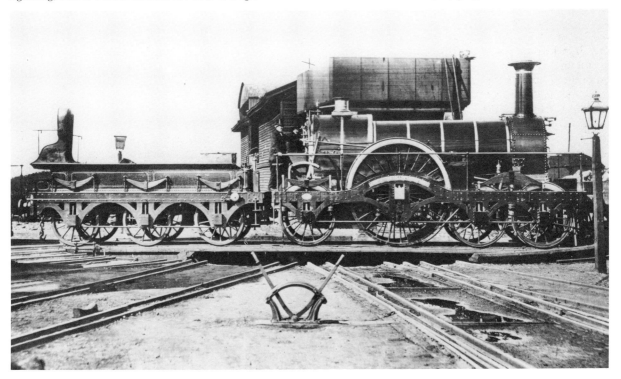

reverse of current practice which is to narrow the gauge by 3 or 4 mm to give steadier running at high speed.

A Royal Commission on railway gauges was appointed by the British Government on 25 June 1845. Its report, published in 1846, recommended that future railways should be built to standard gauge, except on the Great Western (where the standard gauge was always referred to as the 'narrow gauge'). The Gauge Act of 18 August 1846 left loopholes and so failed in its intention to standardize the gauge of British railways.

The last railway to be built to the 7 ft gauge was the 6.8 km (4¼ mile) branch of the West Cornwall Railway from St Erth to St Ives opened on 1 June 1877.

The last broad-gauge trains of the Great Western Railway ran on 20 May 1892. Gauge conversion was completed by 23 May.

In Ireland the first railway, the Dublin & Kingstown Railway, was built to the standard gauge. The Ulster Railway Co., incorporated by an Act of 1836 to build a line from Belfast to Armagh, adopted a gauge of 1880 mm (6 ft 2 in). The line was opened from Belfast to Portadown, 40 km (25 miles), in 1842. Further south, the Dublin & Drogheda Railway Co., also incorporated in 1836 to build a line of 51 km (32 miles), adopted a gauge of 1575 mm (5 ft 2 in). It was opened on 26 May 1844. The directors of the Ulster Railway complained about the gauge difference, but the Irish Board of Works decided that, as there was little prospect of the two lines being joined, it did not matter. In 1844, however, powers were sought to build the Dublin & Belfast Railway, to form a connection between Drogheda and Portadown, so the gauge question was referred to General Pasley, chief inspecting officer of railways, who consulted the leading authorities and decided upon the gauge of 1600 mm (5 ft 3 in) as the national gauge for Ireland, this being the mean of the various gauges in use. In seeking new powers to extend to Armagh, the Ulster Railway Co. was compelled to adopt the 1600 mm gauge before obtaining the Act of 1845, the year in which the Dublin & Belfast Company was incorporated. The Ulster Railway was converted to 1600 mm gauge in 1847 and the extension to Armagh was opened on 1 March 1848.

In 1871 there were 19 different gauges in use in the USA, ranging from 914 mm (3 ft) to 1829 mm (6 ft). Subsequently many 610 mm (2 ft) gauge lines were built.

Between 1867 and 1871 it was possible to travel from New York to St Louis on 1829 mm gauge tracks via the present Erie route to Dayton, Ohio, and the present Baltimore & Ohio through Cincinnati to St Louis. In 1868 the Missouri Pacific Railroad was converted from 1676 mm (5 ft 6 in) to standard, and in 1871 the Ohio & Mississippi (now the Baltimore & Ohio) Railroad from 1829 mm to standard. These influenced other conversions, and by 1887 nearly every important railroad in the USA was operating on standard gauge. The most outstanding exception was the Denver & Rio Grande Western Railroad which in 1888 operated a maximum of 2692 km (1673 miles) of 914 mm (3 ft) gauge.

The world's biggest gauge conversion was carried out on the Louisville & Nashville Railroad which was built to a gauge of 1524 mm (5 ft). On 30 May 1886 about 8000 men converted over 3220 km (2000 miles) of track to a gauge of 1447 mm (4 ft 9 in). Standard gauge was adopted gradually ten years later. One section foreman and his gang converted 17.7 km (11 miles) in 4½ h. One shop changed 19 locomotives, 18 passenger cars, 11 cabooses, 1710 revenue freight cars and several other works vehicles between dawn and dusk on 30 May. The total cost of the conversion was $195 095.69, minus $29 605 raised by the sale of redundant third rails.

Altogether 21 000 km (13 000 miles) of route in the southern states were converted at about the same time.

TRACK

The first steel rails were made by Robert Forester Mushet and were laid experimentally at Derby Station on the Midland Railway, early in 1857, on a heavily used line. They remained in use until June 1873.

The first steel rails on the London & North Western Railway were laid at Chalk Farm, London, in 1862.

The first steel rails in the USA were laid by the Pennsylvania Railroad in 1863 at Altoona and Pittsburgh under the supervision of John Edgar Thomson (1808–74), the third president of the PRR and himself an engineer.

Bessemer steel rails were first rolled in the USA at North Chicago Rolling Mills on 25 May 1865. By the end of the century they had almost completely replaced iron rails.

The first steel rails in Canada were used about 1871. In 1876 it was reported that there were 3659 km (2273¾ miles) of steel rails in Canada, about 45 per cent of the main routes.

The standard British flat-bottomed rails measure 159 mm (6¼ in) high, 140 mm (5½ in) wide across the foot, 70 mm (2¾ in) across the head and have a nominal weight of 55.8 kg/m (113 lb/yd). They are rolled in 18.3 m (60 ft) lengths. In Germany 30 m (98 ft 5 in) is common. They are then welded into continuous lengths first at the depot into 182.9 m, 219.5 m, 274.3 m or 402.3 m (600 ft, 720 ft, 900 ft or 1320 ft), and into greater lengths at the site.

London Transport use a 47.6 kg/m (95 lb/yd) 'bullhead' rail in chairs, mounted on sleepers of jarrah on underground lines.

The longest continuously welded rails in Australia are on the new standard-gauge line to Alice Springs opened in 1980 to replace the old 1067 mm gauge line. The rails are over 40 km (25 miles) long, on concrete sleepers. To avoid buckling in temperature up to 45°C (113°F) the rails are stretched under a tension of 120 tons. It is intended to complete the line to Darwin, to provide Australia with a north–south trans-continental line. (See chapter 5.)

USA railroads use rails of a standard length of 11.9 m (39 ft). Some, however, use lengths of 13.7 m and 18.3 m (45 ft and 60 ft). Rail weights on Class 1 railroads vary from 22.3 to 86.3 kg/m (45 to 174 lb/yd). On trunk lines the weights range upwards from 42 kg/m (85 lb/yd). Rail joints are generally staggered.

The railway spike with a hooked head, for holding flat-bottomed rails to sleepers, or ties, was designed in 1830 by Robert L. Stevens (qv), first president of the Camden & Amboy Railroad (now part of Conrail) in New Jersey. The first patent for a machine for making spikes was issued to Henry Burden of Troy, New York, in 1840. Stevens also designed the T-section iron rail and a 'fish-plate' for joining rail ends in 1830. Flat-bottomed iron rails, rolled in England, became standard on the Camden & Amboy Railroad in 1832. They were 76.2 mm (3 in) wide across the base, 50.8 mm (2 in) across the top, 88.9 mm (3½ in) high, with a 12.7 mm (½ in) thick web.

The record for laying the greatest length of track in one day was achieved during the construction of the Central Pacific Railroad in Utah on 28 April 1869 when 16.1 km (10 miles 56 ft) of a single track were laid. Charles Crocker (1822–88), in charge of construction, prepared the materials and briefed his men for several days beforehand. On the day over 4000 men, many of them Chinese, with hundreds of horses and wagons, were employed. The track advanced at 1.6 km (almost a mile) an hour, 800 men laying rails at the rate of about 73.1 m (140 ft) in 1 min 15 s, about as fast as a leisurely walk. Ahead of them were men preparing ties and spikes and behind them were the ballasters. The section included many curves on the western slope of Promontory Mountain where rails had to be bent. When work ended at 19.00 great quantities of material had been used, including 25 800 ties, 3520 rails 9.1 m (30 ft) long, 24 948 kg (55 000 lb) of spikes and 14 080 bolts. Each rail-handler had lifted 125 tons of iron during the day, in addition to his heavy tongs. To crown the achievement, one Jim Campbell drove a locomotive back over the new line at 64 km/h (40 mph).

The whole of this section was abandoned in 1942 and the rails were removed. The original rails, of course, had been replaced long ago. (See 'The world's longest water crossing', see p. 84.)

During construction of the Canadian Pacific Railway in autumn 1883, 183 m (600 ft) of track were laid in 4 min 45 s, certainly a record in Canada.

The term 'ballast' in connection with railway track originated on Tyneside. The ships which carried coal from Newcastle returned 'in ballast', laden with gravel and other material to maintain stability. This ballast was

Laying part of the record 16 km (10 mile) stretch on the Central Pacific Railroad, the greatest length of track laid in one day, on 28 April 1869.

dumped by the quays and was used to provide a solid bed for the tramways which carried the coal. The name 'ballast' was continued on the tramways and became a standard railway term.

SLEEPERS

The word 'sleeper' derives from the Old Norwegian *Sleip* and is related to the word 'slab'. *The Oxford English Dictionary* records its first use in England as early as 1607 as meaning 'a strong horizontal beam or baulk'. As 'a support for the rails of a tramway or railway' it is first recorded in Newcastle upon Tyne in 1789.

North Americans adopted the word 'tie'; the French *la traverse*. In German it is *die Schwelle*, meaning 'joist'.

British Rail replaces about 2 500 000 softwood sleepers annually. Each timber sleeper measures 2.6 m (8 ft 6 in) × 254 mm (10 in) × 127 mm (5 in) in softwood or 120 mm (4¾ in) in hardwood, usually jarrah. Concrete sleepers, cheaper than wood, are now used wherever possible.

The number of sleepers per kilometre in Britain varies from 1320 to 1540 (2124 to 2479 per mile) according to loadings, foundations, curves, etc. In exceptional situations as many as 1650 (2655 per mile) may be used.

The maximum British axle load is 25 tons, but in the USA, where loads can be up to 34 tons per axle, 1875 to 2188 ties per km (3000 to 3500 per mile) are used.

In Britain there are about 10 000 000 pre-stressed concrete sleepers in use. They measure 2.5 m (8 ft 3 in) long and weigh 267 kg (588 lb) with fastenings, compared with 107.5 kg (237 lb) for a chaired and creosoted wooden sleeper. They have an estimated life of 44 to 50 years, more than double that of a wooden sleeper. They became popular during the wartime timber shortage and are now standard for plain line. Mechanical handling has largely overcome the weight problem. Experiments are being made with concrete beams for points and crossings.

Until the general use of prefabricated track sections and sophisticated electronically controlled permanent way machines, track work was highly labour-intensive. This type of operation, at Surbiton, Surrey, in 1936, would cost about £1500 a week in wages today, that is, of course, if men of suitable intelligence and strength could be found prepared to undertake this kind of work.

Steel sleepers are extensively used on the continent of Europe and in other parts of the world. They can last from 40 to 50 or even 80 years and then still have scrap value. In Switzerland 70 per cent of the Federal system and the whole of the Rhaetian and other metre-gauge systems are laid with steel sleepers. Greece, Congo Republics, systems in west, east and South Africa use steel sleepers for 90–100 per cent of the track.

In India steel sleepers are used on 12 381 km (7694

miles) of 1676 mm (5 ft 6 in) gauge track and on 2306 km (1433 miles) of metre-gauge track.

In Britain steel sleepers are little used, largely because of the difficulty of packing ballast beneath. Corrosion can be minimized by resilient tar coatings or by the addition of a small percentage of copper to the steel.

Paved concrete track (PACT) consists of a continuous concrete slab on which the rails are fixed. This eliminates sleepers and ballast, significantly reduces maintenance, and provides a better line for high-speed trains, giving a smoother ride. The new track is highly suitable for use in tunnels, particularly the Channel Tunnel, and for rapid transit lines. It is already used on part of the new electric main line in Glasgow.

On French Railways PACT has been used in the new Sainte-Devote Tunnel under Monte Carlo and experimentally in a cutting near Limoges.

It has been used on 270 km (167 miles) out of 400 km (248 miles) of the 1975 extension of the Shinkansen from Okayama to Hokata in Japan.

In New Zealand it is used inside the new Kaimai Tunnel in the North Island (qv).

Before it is employed extensively on main passenger lines, train toilet facilities will have to be altered so that they no longer deposit waste on to the track. At present the ballast acts as an efficient filter-bed.

Track being laid in France for the TGVs (Trains à grande vitesse), known as LGV (Ligne à grande vitesse), uses rail of 60 kg/m (143 lb/yd). It is mounted on pre-stressed twin-block concrete sleepers weighing 245 kg (540 lb) each and 2.4 m (7 ft 10½ in) long, at 600 mm (23½ in) spacing, in ballast 320 mm (12½ in) deep.

The simplest, most ingenious and most effective rail fastening is probably the 'Pandrol'. The principal component is a spring-steel clip quickly driven into place with a hammer, and as easily removed. Its resilience makes it unaffected by vibration, it will not work loose, and it prevents 'rail creep' (the tendency for rails to move in the direction of the traffic when a train is braking). It is suitable for wood, concrete or steel sleepers, and on the last can be insulated for track-circuiting. Rail changing is simplified and the clips can be reused. It is eminently suitable for use with the new PACT construction. One of its greatest advantages is its low cost.

The clip was invented in 1957 by the Norwegian engineer Per Pande-Rolfsen who contracted his own name to form 'Pandrol'.

'Pandrol' rail fastenings were first used on British Railways in 1959, just south of Peterborough on the former Great Northern main line. Since then it has become standard on British Rail and the 50 millionth clip was delivered during 1972. Today more than 350 million Pandrol clips are in use. They are manufactured in 14 countries and used in 60.

Pandrol 'e' series clips generate higher clamping forces than the standard clips, of the same bar size.

Insertion and extraction have now been mechanized to reduce line-occupation periods. The 'Pandriver' travels

Pandrol rail clips on paved concrete track (PACT).

along the track at about 0.75 km/h (0.5 mph), enabling a man to place clips in position ahead of the machine ready for driving. The 'Pandrex' knocks out clips at a track speed of 3 km/h (2 mph).

'Fish-plates' for joining rail ends were introduced in 1847 by William Bridges Adams and Robert Richardson, and their use became general in Britain during the late 1840s and early 1850s. Previously the ends of rails rested in wide 'joint chairs' in which the rails could become loose. Standard fish-plates are 507 mm (1 ft 8 in) long with four holes at 127 mm (5 in) centres. Even with secure fish-plates the fracture of rail ends has always been a problem. During the 1930s the London, Midland & Scottish Railway experimented with short two-hole fish-plates which allowed the sleepers and chairs to be brought close to the rail ends to give better support. Modern track with heavy-section long-welded rails has practically eliminated this danger.

The first use of a 'steam navvy' or excavator on railway construction in England was on the West Lancashire Railway from Southport to Preston. One was purchased from Ruston, Proctor & Company of Lincoln for £1150 on 12 June 1877. Another was used in a chalk cutting at Upton on the Didcot, Newbury & Southampton Railway in 1879–81. The first extensive use of these machines was on the construction of the Hull & Barnsley Railway in 1881–3 and on the Great Central main line to London in 1894–7.

Earlier, a steam tunnelling machine, which had been intended for the siege operations before Sebastopol in 1855, was tried in the Colwall tunnel on the West Midland Railway between Worcester and Hereford. (The tunnel, 1433 m (1567 yd) long, was opened on 15 September 1861. In 1926 it was replaced by a new bore 1453 m (1589 yd) long.)

The latest weed-killing train on British Rail went into operation in the summer of 1975. It is able to operate at 72 km/h (45 mph) in both directions. It is the sixth type produced with Fisons Ltd in the past 20 years.

LONGEST STRAIGHTS

The world's longest straight stretch, 478 km (297 miles), is on the standard-gauge Transcontinental Railway of the Commonwealth Railways of Australia. It crosses the Nullarbor Plain from km 798 (mile 496) between Nurina and Loongana, Western Australia, to km 1276 (mile 793) between Ooldea and Watson, South Australia. It was completed in 1917. In one year 712 km (442 miles 44 chains) of track was laid, with a maximum for one day of 4 km (2 miles 40 chains), unballasted at the time. This is a record in Australia. (For the world record see p. 35.)

The Buenos Aires & Pacific Railway, Argentina (Central Region), is dead straight and almost level for 330 km (205 mile) between Junin and MacKenna, on the 1676 mm (5 ft 6 in) gauge line from Buenos Aires to Mendoza where it connects with the metre-gauge South Transandine line.

In the USA the longest straight is the 126.9 km (78.9 miles) on the former Seaboard Air Line Railway between Wilmington and Hamlet, North Carolina. ('Air Line' is an American term meaning 'direct'.) It is now part of the Seaboard Coast line which also has a 92.4 km (57.4 miles) straight between Okeechobee and West Palm Beach, Florida. Other long straights in the USA are:

Rock Island Railroad between Guymon, Oklahoma, and Dalhart, Texas, 114.2 km (71.9 miles)

Conrail (formerly New York Central, later Penn Central) between Air Line Junction (West of Toledo) and Butler, Indiana, 110.2 km (68.5 miles)

Monon Railroad between Brookston and Westville, Indiana, 103.8 km (64.5 miles)

Illinois Central Gulf between Edgewood and Akin Junction, Illinois, 101.3 km (62.9 miles)

Atlantic Coast line between Waycross and Kinderlou, Georgia, 96.7 km (60.1 miles)

There are, or were, five more lengths over 80 km (50 miles).

In Zimbabwe there is a 113 km (70 mile) straight between Sawmills and Dett on the Bulawayo–Waukie main line.

In Russia the Moscow & St Petersburg (Leningrad) Railway is almost straight and level for 644 km (400 miles). It was begun in 1843 and opened on 13 November 1951. It adopted the 1524 mm (5 ft) gauge, then standard in the Southern States of the USA, and so established the Russian standard gauge of 5 ft. (See G. W. Whistler.)

The longest straight in England is 29 km (18 miles) between Barlby and Brough on the 'down' line on the former North Eastern Railway Selby–Hull line (opened by the Hull & Selby Railway on 1 July 1840).

Next is the 21.9 km (13.6 miles) on the former Great Northern Railway Boston–Grimsby line between Boston and the site of Firsby South Junction, Lincolnshire, opened throughout on 1 October 1848. Originally it extended to Burgh-le-Marsh, another 3.9 km (2.4 miles).

The former South Eastern Railway between Tonbridge and Ashford, opened throughout on 1 December 1842, is nearly straight for 39 km (24 miles), but has a slight deviation between Staplehurst and Headcorn.

RAILWAY CURVES

In Great Britain curves are described by their radius in chains (1 chain=66 ft=20.12 m). European continental railways measure the radius in metres. In the USA railway curves are described by the number of degrees in the angle subtended at the centre of a circle of equal curvature by a chord 100 ft (30.5 m) long, so that the flatter the curve, the smaller is the angle. By the sine formula it can be easily worked out that a curve of 1° has a radius of 5734 ft or 86.9 chains or 1747.8 m. The radius of a curve is calculated by dividing 1747.8 or 86.9 by the number of degrees. Thus a curve of 10° has a radius of 174.78 m or 8.69 chains, suitable only for sidings or slow traffic. The number of degrees is obtained by dividing 5734 by the radius in feet, or 86.9 by the radius in chains, or 1747.8 by the radius in metres.

The radius of a curve, in feet, is obtained by measuring the versine, or offset, of the rail from the centre of a chord, usually of either 100 ft or 1 chain, and using the formula $R=3L^2/2V$ where L=length of chord in feet, and V is the versine in inches. In metric units the formula becomes $R=125L^2/V$ where R=radius in metres; L=length of chord in metres; V=versine in millimetres. On single lines the versine is measured on the outer, or 'high' rail and on double lines on the outer rail of the inner track.

Super elevation, or cant, obtained by tilting the track so that the outer rail is higher than the inner, is applied on curves to move the centre of gravity of vehicles towards the inside of the curve. Its extent depends on the radius of the curve and the speed of the traffic. The maximum cant is 152 mm (6 in).

Transition curves, with gradually increasing cant and reducing radius, are needed to ease a train smoothly from a straight track into a curve and in the reverse direction out again into a straight or a reverse curve.

Check rails are fitted to the inside of lower, or inner, rails on curves of less than 200 m (10 chains) radius in Britain. These guide the flanges of the inner wheels and reduce wear on the outer rail. Their use is known to date from 1729 or earlier when they were recorded on a wagonway at Ravensworth in County Durham. High check rails are also used on bridges and viaducts to guard against derailments.

The longest continuous curve in the USA is probably the Pontchartrain curve between Ruddock and Tunity in Louisiana on the Illinois Central Railroad, skirting the western shore of Lake Pontchartrain. It is 15.2 km (9.5 miles) long with only slight changes of radius.

The Southern Railway, shortly before entering New

Orleans, skirts the same lake on a curve nearly 14.5 km (9 miles) long.

The longest uniform curve is on the Texas & Pacific Railroad between Alexandria and Cheneyville, also in Louisiana. It has a radius of 10.5 km (6.5 miles) throughout its 9.2 km (5.7 miles).

DIRECTION OF RUNNING ON DOUBLE LINES

The first railway to be planned and built as a double line was the Liverpool & Manchester Railway, opened on 15 September 1830. Left-hand running was adopted from the start.

Sections of the Stockton & Darlington Railway had been doubled previously, but in the form of extended passing loops. Doubling between Brusselton Incline and Darlington was not undertaken until 1831–2.

The following British railways adopted right-hand running from the beginning:

The Clarence Railway in County Durham of which the first portion opened in 1833. It became part of the Stockton & Hartlepool Railway on 1 January 1851 and of the West Hartlepool Harbour & Railway Company on 17 May 1853. The right-hand running continued until its absorption by the North Eastern Railway on 1 July 1865.

The London & Greenwich Railway, the first railway in London, opened in 1836–8. Right-hand running was adopted very early in the line's history and it continued until changed to left-hand running on 26 May 1901.

The Manchester & Bolton Railway, opened on 29 May 1838, changed from right- to left-hand running when it was joined at Clifton by the East Lancashire Railway which opened on 28 September 1846.

The Newcastle & Carlisle Railway, opened on 18 June 1838, changed from right- to left-hand running on 7 March 1864, after its absorption by the North Eastern Railway in 1862.

Right-hand running operates on the following railways:

Europe: Austria (some sections), Bulgaria, Czechoslovakia, Denmark, Finland, Germany, Hungary, the Netherlands, Norway, Poland, Spain (the former Madrid, Zaragoza & Alicante Railway only), Turkey, the USSR and Yugoslavia. In France, trains in Alsace and parts of Lorraine run on the right, because these provinces were under German administration from 1870 to 1918.
Asia: China (some sections) and the USSR.
North America: Canada and the USA (except the Chicago & North Western Railroad).
Other countries use left-hand running or have no double-line sections.

Using modern signalling methods, several railways in parts of Europe and the USA are now equipped for either-direction running on both lines, with complete safety, so allowing one train to overtake another and thus increasing line capacity.

LOADING GAUGES

Britain pays a penalty for being first to build railways by suffering a restricted loading gauge with universal dimensions of only 3860 mm (12 ft 8 in) high by 2692 mm (8 ft 10 in) wide.

For most lines it is 3962 × 2743 mm (13 ft × 9 ft). Some sections exceeded this, e.g.: Great Western 4114 × 2946 mm (13 ft 6 in × 9 ft 8 in); Hull & Barnsley 4191 × 2819 mm (13 ft 9 in × 9 ft 3 in); Great Central 4089 × 2819 (13 ft 5 in × 9 ft 3 in); Midland 4191 × 2743 mm (13 ft 9 in × 9 ft); London & South Western 4064 × 2819 mm (13 ft 4 in × 9 ft 3 in); LNWR, London, Brighton & South Coast, and Lancashire & Yorkshire 4115 × 2743 mm (13 ft 6 in × 9 ft). The widest stock in Britain was on the Liverpool–Southport electric line, 3048 mm (10 ft).

The world's largest loading gauge for standard-gauge lines is in the USA: 4724 mm × 3277 mm (15 ft 6 in × 10 ft 9 in).

The Indian loading gauge for 1676 mm (5 ft 6 in) gauge lines is 4470 × 3200 mm (14 ft 8 in × 10 ft 6 in). In 1961 it was decided to increase it to 4724 × 4110 mm (15 ft 6 in × 13 ft 6 in).

The standard for European lines, as recommended by the Berne Conference, is 4279 mm × 3150 mm (14 ft 0½ in × 10 ft 4 in). **Australian standard-gauge** lines are about the same 4267 mm × 3200 mm (14 ft × 10 ft 6 in).

The world's biggest loading gauge is the Russian standard for the 1520 mm (4 ft 11⅞ in) gauge: 5302 mm × 3413 mm (17 ft 4¾ in × 11 ft 2 in).

The South African loading gauge for its 1065 mm (3 ft 6 in) gauge lines is larger than the British standard: 3962 mm × 3048 mm (13 ft × 10 ft).

The biggest loading gauge on metre-gauge lines is on the East African Railways 4115 mm × 3200 mm (13 ft 6 in × 10 ft 6 in), considerably larger than the British standard.

The Channel Tunnel will provide the world's largest loading gauge: 5400 mm (17 ft 8½ in) high and 4000 mm (13 ft 1½ in) wide.

4

RAILWAY ORGANIZATION

The first public goods railway in Great Britain to be sanctioned by Parliament was the Surrey Iron Railway, on 21 May 1801. The gauge was 1219 mm (4 ft) and it opened from Wandsworth to Croydon on 26 July 1803. It was extended by the Croydon, Merstham & Godstone Railway, incorporated by Act of Parliament on 17 May 1803, and opened from Croydon to Merstham on 24 July 1805. The engineer was William Jessop (qv) assisted by his son Josias (1781–1826).

The first railway amalgamation to be authorized by Act of Parliament was the formation of the North Union Railway on 22 May 1834, uniting the Wigan Branch Railway with the Wigan & Preston Railway.

The first conference of railway managers was held in Birmingham, on 19 January 1841, to draw up a code of rules, signalling, etc.

The Railway Clearing House, whose function was to settle rates for through traffic over different British railway companies' systems, began operating on 2 January 1842. The Irish Railway Clearing House was established on 1 July 1848.

The year when the greatest number of railway Acts was passed was 1846, during the 'Railway Mania', when 272 Bills received the Royal Assent in Britain.

The largest British railway scheme ever approved by Parliament in one Act was in the Great Northern Railway Act of 26 June 1846, authorizing a railway from London to York via Peterborough, Grantham, Newark, Doncaster and Selby and a branch from north of Peterborough to Boston, Lincoln and Gainsborough to form a loop rejoining the main line near Bawtry, a total of 376 km (233½ miles) with a capital of £5 600 000.

Eleven Acts of Parliament were obtained for the Uxbridge & Rickmansworth Railway. It was incorporated by Act of 1861, then abandoned after four more Acts, reincorporated in 1881 and abandoned again, after three more Acts, in 1888. In 1895 a third company was incorporated and in 1899 a further Act was obtained. Construction was never even started.

The last main line into London, the Great Central Railway (formerly the Manchester, Sheffield & Lincolnshire Railway) was opened to passengers on 15 March 1899. Coal traffic had begun on 25 July 1898 and general freight began on 11 April 1899. The railway was pioneered by Edward Watkin when he was chairman of the MS & L, the Metropolitan and the South Eastern railways and of the Channel Tunnel Company. He saw the London Extension as part of a main line linking Manchester, London and Paris. The Act of 28 March 1893 for the 'London Extension' of the MS & L authorized **the greatest amount of capital in any British railway Act**, £6 200 000, equivalent in 1985 to £220 100 000. The name 'Great Central' was adopted on 1 August 1897.

The GCR became part of the London & North Eastern Railway on 1 January 1923.

Under the Railways Act of 19 August 1921, a total of 123 separate British railway companies were amalgamated into four groups; the London, Midland & Scottish, the London & North Eastern, the Great Western and the Southern. Certain inter-group joint companies continued to operate separately. The Grouping came into effect on 1 January 1923.

All Irish railways wholly in the 'Free State' (Eire), both 1600 mm (5 ft 3 in) and 914 mm (3 ft) gauge, were grouped into the Great Southern Railways on 1 January 1925.

The London Transport Executive was formed under the Transport (London) Act of 1969 which transferred the operation of the Underground Railways and the red buses from the former London Transport Board to the Executive, and financial and policy control to Greater London Council from 1 January 1970. The Executive owned 383 km (238 miles) of railways of which 378 km (235 miles) is electrified with third rail at 600 V dc, and operates over 248 km (154 miles) of route. The red buses run over 2799 km (1739 miles) of roads.

The background history goes back to the Act of 13 April 1933 when the London Passenger Transport Board was established to take over the Metropolitan Railway, the Metropolitan District Railway, the London Electric Railway, the Central London Railway, the City and South London Railway, all the streets tramways (now abandoned) and nearly all bus and coach undertakings in its area. It became part of the British Transport Commission on 1 January 1948 and was renamed the London Transport Executive. On 1 January 1963 it was again renamed, becoming the London Transport Board when the British Transport Commission was dissolved under the 1962 Transport Act.

Under the Transport (London) Act 1969, control of LT finance and policy was transferred to Greater London Council from 1 January 1970 and operation of the red buses and underground railways passed to the new London Transport Executive. The green buses and coaches passed to London Country Bus Services Limited.

On 29 June 1984, under the London Regional Transport Act of 26 June, it was renationalized and renamed London Regional Transport. In April 1985 its various services were divided up and the railways became London Underground Limited.

The Irish Transport Company (Coras Iompair Eireann), formed under the Eire Transport Act of 19 November 1944, began operation on 1 January 1945. Under this Act the Great Southern Railways and the Dublin United Transport Company Limited were merged.

From 1 October 1958 the portion of the Great Northern Railway in the Irish Republic was merged with CIE. From 2 February 1987 the railways in the Irish Republic became a separate division uinder the title Iarnród Éireann (Irish Rail) and now operates as a subsidiary company of CIE.

BRITISH RAIL

The proposal to nationalize British Railways was first announced by the Government on 19 November 1945. Canals and long-distance road haulage were included.

The Transport Act received the Royal Assent on 6 August 1947, nationalizing British railways and canals from 1 January 1948.

At nationalization, British Railways operated about 32 190 km (20 000 miles) of route with 20 024 steam, 55 diesel and diesel-electric and 16 electric locomotives. There were 6701 stations of which 4815 handled freight. The system was divided into regions: Scottish, North Eastern, London Midland, Eastern, Western and Southern. On 1 January 1967 the Eastern and North Eastern Regions were combined.

Under the guidance of Dr. Richard Beeching, BR reduced its network from 30 209 km (18 771 miles) in 1960 to 21 342 km (13 261 miles) in 1969.

Although the statutory regional structure was abolished by the Transport Act of 1968, it has been continued from 1 January 1969 by the BRB as part of its management structure.

The Transport Act (Northern Ireland) 1948, incorporated the Ulster Transport Authority. The Northern Ireland Road Transport Board, the Belfast & County Down and the Northern Counties railways and other transport services were acquired by 1 April 1949. The portion of the Great Northern Railway in Northern Ireland was taken over from 1 October 1958.

On 1 April 1968 its assets were handed over to Northern Ireland Railways Company Limited, incorporated under the Transport Act (Northern Ireland) 1967.

The original BR crest, a lion astride a wheel, was introduced in 1948. In 1956 it was replaced by a rampant lion holding a wheel. The abbreviated title 'British Rail' and its new emblem, two horizontal lines and two arrow heads, were adopted in the summer of 1964. The emblem began to appear on rolling stock in February 1965.

The first British Rail combined timetable operated from 6 May 1974 to 4 May 1975.

At 31 March 1987 British Rail operated 16 729 km (10 395 miles) of route of which 1703 km (1058 miles) were open for passenger traffic only, 12 600 km (7829 miles) for passenger and freight traffic, 2366 km (1470 miles) for freight only. There were 2405 passenger stations and 123 freight stations. Rolling stock consisted of 2338 diesel locomotives, 243 electric locomotives, 3 steam locomotives (597 mm gauge), 197 High Speed Train power units, 3276 locomotive-hauled passenger carriages, 2625 diesel multiple-unit trains, 7034 electric multiple-unit trains, 712 HST carriages, and 1659 non-passenger-carrying vehicles (parcels, mail etc). Freight stock consisted of 2027 covered, 24 866 open, 6297 flat and 459 bulk material wagons. BR total staff at 31 March 1987 numbered 173 760.

British Rail is endeavouring to increase its manpower efficiency by flexible rostering of train crews, single-manning of traction units, elimination of guards on many passenger and freight trains, and 'open' stations, but progress is impeded by trade unions because of fear of unemployment. The fear has some basis: in 1983 BR reduced its staff by 5979, amounting to 4 per cent. The result of a rigid 8 hour shift for footplate staff is that each man spends an average of 3 h 58 min driving. Men engaged on passenger trains drive an average of about 29 000 loaded train-km (18 000 train-miles) in a year, about twice the mileage of an average motorist. An average of only 6600 train-km (4100 train-miles) are worked by freight train crews per year, but some of this is at slow speeds, as on 'merry-go-round' trains when loading and unloading.

The newest piece of main-line construction in Britain is the Selby deviation, south of York, to enable the Selby coalfield to be worked under the old main line north of Selby. Work began in April 1980. In its 22.8 km (14 miles) there are 36 bridges and culverts. The new railway came into use on 1 October 1983 and the former North Eastern line from Selby to Chaloner Whin Junction, York, was closed and later dismantled. The new railway, designed for speeds of 200 km/h (124 mph), bypasses Selby where there was a severe speed restriction.

Other large British railway contracts in recent times were the new Woodhead Tunnel, 1949–54, which was abandoned on 18 July 1981; the Harecastle deviation north of Stoke on Trent in 1964–6; the deviation round the collapsed Penmanshiel Tunnel between Berwick and Edinburgh, opened on 20 August 1979; the Merseyrail Loop and Link (p. 171) and the London Underground extension to Heathrow (p. 170).

A long-awaited connection, the 'Windsor Link' just

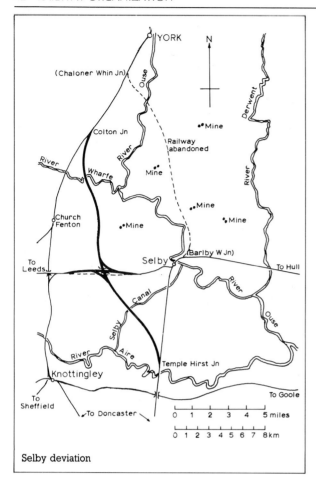

Selby deviation

Fares on London Regional Transport, after a period of reduction during which there was an enormous increase in passenger loadings, were almost doubled in 1982 when they became the highest fares in the world. In 1983, when a zonal fare structure was introduced, the number of commuters entering London by car fell from 197 000 to 180 000 per day, a drop of 9.4 per cent. In terms of accident costs and time saved by other road users, including buses, this was worth £25 m in a year. The travel-card scheme introduced in May 1983 resulted in a gain to London Transport of £23 m in one year.

Comparisons between road and rail transport are difficult to make because the costs of road transport are spread so widely. Expenditure on British roads in 1985–6 was £2930 m. In 1988, a 50-seat coach was charged £84 vehicle excise duty a year, compared with £100 for a private car. It operated from coach stations provided by local rate payers, and on roads paid for by tax payers and so, with lower costs, it was able to attract passengers from the railways by charging lower fares. By contrast, BR is expected to provide and maintain track, substructure, line equipment, signalling, station and other buildings and rolling stock out of its income.

In Britain, where roughly half the cost of petrol is tax, it clearly benefits the government if public transport becomes more expensive and inconvenient, thereby encouraging people to use private cars. Ironically, deregulation of buses, by throwing bus services into confusion, benefited the railways.

BRITISH RAIL WORKSHOPS

British Rail Engineering Limited, formed in January 1970 to enable BR workshops to compete with private engineering firms by tendering for outside work, is a wholly owned subsidiary of the British Rail Board. From 1987 the former BREL works at Doncaster, Eastleigh, Glasgow and Wolverton returned to direct control of the British Railways Board to form British Rail Maintenance Ltd. BREL now comprises the works at Crewe, Derby and York and the foundry at Horwich, Lancashire.

The 24-hour time system was introduced on Italian Railways in 1898. Between then and 1912 it was adopted by Belgium, France, Portugal and Spain. Thomas Cook & Son first used it in the Cook's Continental Timetable in December 1919. It was adopted by British Railways in its timetables in summer 1964.

Cook's Continental Timetable was first issued in March 1873. From January 1977 it became the **Thomas Cook International Timetable** with the addition of a 64-page section of services outside Europe.

over 1 km long joining the former Lancashire & Yorkshire and London & North Western lines in Manchester, was opened on 16 May 1988. It facilitates through north–south services via central Manchester for the first time since the railways arrived there in the 1830s and 1840s.

On the same day the Thames Link was opened to provide through services between the east Midlands and south-east England via the reopened Snow Hill Tunnel in London. Another Snow Hill tunnel, under Birmingham, was reopened on 5 October 1987 to serve a new central station on the site of the former GWR Snow Hill station.

Fares, Costs and Income

The fixing of a fare structure is a problem of great complexity, and of fine balance between fares which fail to cover costs and fares which drive passengers on to other forms of transport. BR is making positive efforts to attract passengers by lower fares at times when trains are lightly used, thus spreading the load throughout the day.

The Transport Act of 1968 enabled the Secretary of State for the Environment to make grants for the maintenance of unremunerative passenger services, in particular where these provided an important social service. In 1987 the grant amounted to nearly £900 m. In the same year, passengers on BR made 689.4 million journeys, travelling a total of 30 812 million km.

RAILROADS OF THE USA

The following States had railroads open before 1835:

State	Route	Date
Alabama	Tuscumbia–Decatur	1834
Connecticut	Northwich–Killingly	1832
Delaware[1]	Newcastle–Frenchtown	1831
Florida	Tallahassee–Port Leon	1834
Louisiana	New Orleans–Lake Pontchartrain	1831
Maryland	Baltimore–Ellicott's Mills	1830
Michigan	Detroit–St Joseph	1832
New Jersey[1]	Camden–South Amboy	1834
New York	Albany–Schenectady	1831
Pennsylvania[1]	Leiperville–Ridley Creek	1809
South Carolina	Charleston–Hamburg	1833
Virginia	Weldon, N.C.–Petersburg, Virginia	1833
West Virginia	Baltimore–Harpers Ferry	1834

[1] The three earliest States in the Federation admitted 1787.

The State with the highest railroad mileage is Texas, with 20 602 km (12 802 miles) in 1986. Its first railroad, from Harrisburg to Alleyton, was opened in 1860. Next is Illinois with 17 971 km (11 167 miles); the earliest line was Jacksonville to Meredosia opened in 1838.

The smallest mileage is in the District of Columbia, 76 km (47 miles).

Early railroads in the USA were given land grants, or loans, by the Federal Government under an Act passed by President Millard Fillmore on 20 September 1850. By 1871 the Government had granted 53 000 000 ha (131 000 000 acres) of land, then worth about $125 000 000, to cover 80 railroads, for the construction of about 30 600 km (19 000 miles) of route. This amounts to less than one-thirteenth of the total mileage built. Yet in exchange all American railroads were required to carry Government freight at half price and mail at a 20 per cent reduction. When Congress repealed this provision in 1945, from 1 October 1946, it was calculated that the railroads had saved the Government about $1 250 000 000, or ten times the value of the original land grants.

Some early railroads, however, were dishonest or ruthless. In the 1860s a group of railroad tycoons in North Carolina received $6 000 000 in bonds from the Federal Government for building 150 km (93 miles) of railroad worth under $1 000 000.

In 1867 Cornelius Vanderbilt, having gained control of two New York City lines, cut off rail access to Manhattan, thereby forcing the New York Central into his net, afterwards voting himself a personal bonus of $6 000 000 in stock. When his successor, his son William, was asked if he ran the NYC for the public benefit, he replied 'The public be damned!' By the 1870s the Americans regarded their railroads as 'Public enemy No. 1'. Some of the legislation against which the railroads are fighting today originated in this period. They brought much of it upon themselves.

The Interstate Commerce Commission (ICC) was created by Act of Congress signed by President Grover Cleveland on 4 February 1887. It regulates rates, services and abandonments of services among railroads, motor carriers, pipelines, inland water-carriers and freight forwarders engaged in interstate commerce. While it regulates 100 per cent of railroad traffic, it regulates only 39 per cent of inter-city road haulage, 14.6 per cent of river and canal traffic, 4.4 per cent of coastal sea traffic and 1.1 per cent of Great Lakes traffic.

In the early 1900s the Interstate Commerce Commission encouraged road and water traffic to compete with the railroads (understandably, in view of their over-exercised monopoly) by providing generous Federal assistance in the form of highways and waterways.

This pattern continues today. While the USA railroads pay 24 per cent of their profits in taxes, road operators pay 5 per cent, air lines 4 per cent, and water-carriers nothing. In addition, the competing carriers receive Federal assistance amounting to thousands of millions of dollars. In 1986 the railroads of the USA paid a total of $2 507 924 in taxes, while receiving meagre Federal assistance, totally out of proportion to the contribution they make to the national economy.

The railroads are divided into Classes I, II and III. Class I railroads are those with an annual operating revenue of about $88 600 000 (1986). The basic amount increases with inflation. In 1983 there were 31 Class I railroads which moved about 98 per cent of the freight, operated 94 per cent of rail mileage, and accounted for 94 per cent of all railroad employees. In addition there were 26 Class II line-haul railroads, about 142 switching and terminal companies (all Class III) and about 270 Class III line-haul railroads.

Standard Time was introduced in North America on 18 November 1883, when nearly 100 'local times' observed by the railroads were abolished. There are four time zones: Eastern, Central, Mountain, and Pacific, all one hour apart. Standard Time was sponsored and put into effect by the General Time Convention of Railway Managers, now part of the Association of American Railroads (see below), but it was not until 19 March 1918 that Congress passed the Standard Time Act, making this the official time.

The General Time Convention of Railway Managers, a predecessor of the Association of American Railroads, adopted the first standard code of train rules on 14 April 1887.

Since 1916 the USA has abandoned nearly 80 500 km (50 000 miles) of railroad. This is almost 2.5 times the maximum railway mileage in Great Britain, in 1930.

The largest railroad abandonment in the USA was the 871 km (541 miles) New York, Ontario & Western on 29 March 1957. Next were the Missouri & Arkansas, 539 km (335 miles) in 1948; and the Colorado Midland (see below), from Colorado Springs to Glenwood Springs, 356 km (221.3 miles) in 1919.

The Association of American Railroads, with headquarters in Washington, was formed on 12 October 1934 by amalgamation of the American Railway Association, The Association of Railway Executives, Railway Accounting Officers' Association, Railway Treasury Officers' Association, and the Bureau of Railway Economics. It acts as joint agency in research, operation, traffic, accounting and finance. Nearly all important railroads in the USA, Canada and Mexico are members.

The Department of Transportation, with headquarters in Washington, was established on 15 October 1966 by Public Law 89–670, and began operation on 1 April 1967. Eleven offices were transferred to it from other Federal agencies. It develops national transport at the lowest costs consistent with safety and efficiency, co-ordinates transport policies of the Federal Government, and administers the Uniform Time Act.

The Staggers Rail Act of 14 October 1980 at last relieved the railroads of a substantial amount of regulation, freeing them to make their own rates, the ICC retaining control only where the railroads have 'market dominance'. Greater freedom is given to abandon unprofitable routes and for the merging of railroad companies into larger organizations. While considerably easing the burden on the railroads, it still leaves them at a disadvantage in competition with other forms of transport which continue to receive substantial public assistance.

Railroads carry 70 per cent of the coal in the USA, 74 per cent of canned and frozen foods, 46 per cent of the meat and dairy products, 71 per cent of household appliances, 76 per cent of automobiles and parts, 86 per cent of pulp and paper, 78 per cent of timber, 63 per cent of chemicals and 68 per cent of primary metal products.

If the railroads in the USA were to shut down for one week the national income for the year would be reduced by nearly 6 per cent. An 8-week shut-down would reduce the gross national product for the year by 24 per cent and increase unemployment by 22 per cent.

The National Railroad Passenger Corporation, known as 'Amtrak', was formed under the Rail Passenger Service Act of 31 October 1970. It took over the passenger services of 22 leading railroads of the USA. Operations began on 1 May 1971. The principal companies remaining outside were the Southern, Denver & Rio Grande Western, and the Rock Island & Pacific. Amtrak now operates about 200 trains daily over about 37 970 route km (23 594 route miles) connecting 440 cities in the USA, and into Canada, with 396 locomotives and 1929 passenger cars including sleepers, diners, dome cars and chair cars. Its aim is 'To make the trains worth travelling again.'

In 1986 it carried 20 326 000 revenue passengers a total of 8 067 421 000 km. The average passenger journey was 400 km (249 miles).

In an attempt to achieve greater efficiency, many of the railroad companies of the USA are combining into large corporations. One of the first was the Penn Central, formed on 1 February 1968 by the merging of the Pennsylvania and New York Central railroads. On 31 December 1968 the New York, New Haven & Hartford Railroad became part of the PC, which then owned 31 935 km (19 853 miles) and operated nearly 35 400 km (22 000 miles) of railroad. Of these, 1170 km (727 miles) were electrified in 16 State, two Canadian Provinces and the District of Columbia. It carried nearly 3000 freight trains every 24 h with 4041 locomotives (174 electric and 3867 diesel-electric), 3109 passenger cars (including 766 multiple-unit electric cars) and 165 495 freight cars and other vehicles, and 2270 cabooses.

Penn Central is now part of Conrail (Consolidated Rail Corporation), formed on 1 April 1976. The new system is 27 353 km (16 996 miles) long and extends from the Mississippi River and Lake Michigan in the west, Canada on the north and the Ohio River on the south, to the Atlantic Coast. It serves major industrial areas such as St Louis, Chicago, Indianapolis, Columbus, Detroit, Toledo, Cleveland, Buffalo and Pittsburgh, connecting them with Boston, Providence, New York, Philadelphia, Baltimore and Washington in the North East and the Middle Atlantic States. It covers 16 States in the USA and two Canadian Provinces, and is divided into seven Regions and 28 Divisions. The Regions are: Atlantic, Central, Eastern, North East, Northern, Southern, Western. It includes the following systems: Central Railroad of New Jersey; Erie Lackawanna Railway Company; Lehigh & Hudson River; Lehigh Valley Railroad Company; Penn Central Transportation Company; Pittsburgh & Lake Erie Railroad Company; Reading Company; Pennsylvania–Reading Seashore Lines.

The Burlington Northern Railroad was formed on 2 March 1970 by the merging of the Chicago, Burlington & Quincy, the Great Northern, the Northern Pacific and the Spokane, Portland & Seattle railroads. In November 1980 it absorbed the St Louis–San Francisco; it operates 44 382 km (27 578 miles) of route, and extends from Chicago to Vancouver and Seattle. BN also operates the Colorado & Southern Railway and the Fort Worth & Denver Railway.

The Chessie System was incorporated in Virginia on 26 February 1973. It acquired control of the Chesapeake & Ohio Railway Company and the Baltimore & Ohio Railroad which had already amalgamated on 4 February 1963, and the Western Maryland Railway. In November 1980 it merged with the Seaboard Coast Lines to form the CSX Corporation, operating 39 937 km (24 816 miles) of route.

On 1 June 1982 the Norfolk Southern Corporation was formed by the merging of the Norfolk & Western Railway, 12 555 km (7802 miles), and the Southern Railway System, 16 185 km (10 057 miles). It now operates 28 198 km (17 522 miles).

In 1983 another large merger formed the Union Pacific Corporation from the Missouri Pacific Railroad,

16 878 km (10 488 miles); the Union Pacific Railroad, 14 638 km (9096 miles), and the Western Pacific Railroad, 2390 km (1486 miles). Total route length is 34 458 km (21 412 miles).

Other USA railroads operating more than 16 000 km (about 10 000 miles) are the Atchison, Topeka & Santa Fe, 19 108 km (11 873 miles) and the Southern Pacific Transportation Co., 15 633 km (9714 miles).

RAILWAYS OF CANADA

The story of railway development in Canada is almost synonymous with that of the development of the country. The earliest railways are mentioned in the first chapter. Because railways had been built to different gauges which threatened future railway unification, the Province of Canada appointed a Royal Commission in 1845 to study the gauge question. Until the financing of a 'main line' became a major issue, the Commission was slow in consulting various authorities. While this was going on, the St Lawrence & Atlantic Rail Road (which, together with the Atlantic & St Lawrence Rail Road in the USA, linked Montreal with Portland, Maine, to provide an ice-free port for Montreal in winter), was built to a gauge of 1676 mm (5 ft 6 in) and opened in 1847–52.

Despite a majority of professional opinion against the 1676 mm gauge, the Commission recommended it in deference to economic and political developments. On 31 July 1851 the Province of Canada legislated to make this 'Provincial Gauge' a pre-condition of financial assistance, so strengthening the Guarantee Act of 1849.

In 1852 the Grand Trunk Railway was incorporated by an Act which also amalgamated the Quebec & Richmond; St Lawrence & Atlantic; Old Grand Trunk; Grand Junction; Toronto, Guelph & Sarnia; and Main Trunk, with a total length of 2216 km (1377 miles).

The Great Western Railway of Canada was empowered by various Acts between 1834 and 1858 to build a line from Niagara Falls to Windsor, Ontario, opposite Detroit, via Hamilton and London, 369 km (229 miles). The main line was begun at London in 1847 and the company was forced to adopt the 1676 mm gauge before opening from Niagara Falls to London in 1853 and to Windsor in 1855. However, it installed a third rail on the main line in 1867 to provide standard gauge. The total length was 555 km (345 miles) including main line 369 km (229 miles); Hamilton–Toronto 51 km (38 miles); Galt branch 19 km (12 miles); and Sarnia branch 82 km (51 miles).

At the time of the Confederation of Nova Scotia, New Brunswick, Quebec and Ontario to form the nucleus of the Dominion of Canada on 1 July 1867, there were 15 railways totalling 4015 km (2495 miles), employing 9391 persons. There were 485 locomotives, 310 first class and 374 second class passenger cars which carried a total of 2 920 000 passengers in the year, and 4214 freight cars which carried 2 260 000 tons.

The Intercolonial Railway was incorporated on 12 April 1867. A condition of the Confederation was the building of a railway from Halifax, Nova Scotia, through New Brunswick to the Saint Lawrence at or near Quebec, to be started within six months. For economic and military reasons the railway followed a route via Campbelltown on the Bay of Chaleur and across to the Saint Lawrence which it followed up to Rivière du Loup. Throughout Nova Scotia and into New Brunswick it was built to the 1676 mm gauge. It was opened from Halifax to Truro in 1858 and to Amherst in 1872. The main line from near Newcastle, New Brunswick, to Trois Pistoles on the Saint Lawrence, about 476 km (290 miles), was standard gauge. Amherst to Rivière du Loup on the St Lawrence was opened on 1 July 1876. By then the 1676 mm-gauge line from Levis, opposite Quebec, to Rivière du Loup had been built by the Grand Trunk. It was acquired by the Intercolonial in 1879.

The Dominion Government repealed the Provincial Gauge in 1870 by which time most Canadian and USA railways had adopted standard gauge. Conversion of the Grand Trunk Railway took until 1874. The Intercolonial between Halifax and Truro (and St John) was converted to standard gauge by 1875 and the remainder of the route soon afterwards; by 1876 a standard-gauge line connected Halifax and Levis.

Prince Edward Island entered the Confederation in 1873 while its railway system was under construction. The 338 km (210 miles) of route were taken over by the Federal Government and opened for traffic in April 1875. Railways on Prince Edward Island grew to a total of 448 km (297 miles), all standard gauge.

In 1882 the Grand Trunk and Great Western Railways were amalgamated, making a total of 1455 km (904 miles) of route, together with another 761 km (473 miles) of line in western Ontario. The Grand Trunk Western Railroad was formed in 1893 by amalgamation of the Grand Trunk properties in the State of Michigan to provide a through route to Chicago.

In 1885 the Canadian Pacific Railway transcontinental line was completed (to be mentioned later). After a few years the section beween Fort William on Lake Superior and Winnipeg was becoming congested. To avoid this and also to obtain a share in the long-haul traffic to the Pacific, the Grand Trunk proposed a second transcontinental route, formed of the National Transcontinental Railway (Monkton–Winnipeg) and the Grand Trunk Pacific onwards to the Pacific. This, together with the third transcontinental route, the Canadian Northern, is described in chapter 5.

Soon after opening the transcontinental line, the Canadian Northern was in financial difficulties and, following careful consideration by the Government, *Canadian National Railways* was formed to acquire the Canadian Northern Railway. In 1919 the Grand Trunk Pacific was allowed to go into receivership. On 21 May 1920 the Government took formal possession of the Grand Trunk Railway and in September 1920 met the debenture obligations as *de facto* proprietor of the Grand Trunk Pacific. The Grand Trunk Acquisition Act was passed on 5 November 1920. In 1923, under an Order in Council, the control of all Government railways including the Grand Trunk and the Intercolonial Railways passed to the Canadian National Railways under a president and board of directors appointed by the Government. In 1949 the Newfoundland Railway was absorbed, adding 1135 (705 miles) of 1067 mm (3 ft 6 in) gauge route. Of this, 880 km (547 miles) were on the main 'Overland Route' from St John's to Port aux Basques.

In 1923 the Canadian National Railways had 33 109 km (20 573 miles) of route. CN offers one of the world's longest railway journeys: Halifax–Montreal, 1352 km (840 miles), and to Prince Rupert on the Pacific, another 4998 km (3105 miles), a total of 6350 km (3946 miles). It serves all ten provinces, and a branch reaches Churchill on Hudson Bay in Manitoba. North of Edmonton the Northern Alberta Railway, joint CPR and CN, operates 1485 km (923 miles) of route and from Roma Junction near Peace River on this system, CN operates the Great Slave Lake Railway, 607 km (377 miles), opened in 1964 to the Great Slave Lake in North West Territories.

Canadian National also operates a highway transport service, coastal steamers, a chain of large hotels, and a telecommunications service. Air Canada, an autonomous subsidiary of CN, operates Canadian and international air services.

In 1985 CN freight traffic totalled 126 917 million ton-km. Rolling stock consisted of 1870 diesel-electric locomotives, 14 electric locomotives (operating on 63 km of electrified route at 2700 V), and 82 396 freight cars. The now familiar CN monogram was adopted in 1960. The total route length of CN standard-gauge lines is 35 792 km (22 240 miles). In Newfoundland (Terra Transport) are 990 km (615 miles) of 1067 mm gauge.

The oldest charter of a constituent of the **Canadian Pacific Railway** was that incorporating the St Andrews & Quebec Railroad Company in March 1836 for a railway from St Andrews, New Brunswick, to Lower Canada. The oldest operating constituent of the CPR was La Compagnie du Chemin à Rails du Saint Laurent at du Village d'Industrie, 19 km (12 miles) long from Village d'Industrie (now Joliette, Quebec) to Lanoraie on the Saint Lawrence about 56 km (35 miles) north east of Montreal. Regular services began on 6 May 1850. It came into the possession of what is now CP Rail with the purchase of the Eastern Division of the Quebec, Montreal, Ottawa & Occidental Railway in September 1885, and part of it is still in use.

The completion of the CPR transcontinental route is described in chapter 5.

Canadian Pacific announced its new corporate identification programme on 17 June 1968, from which date its various interests became known as CP Rail, CP Air, CP Ships, CP Transport (road vehicles), CP Express, CP Hotels and CP Telecommunications. On 5 July 1971 supplementary Letters Patent were issued to the company changing its corporate name from 'Canadian Pacific Railway Company' to 'Canadian Pacific Limited' in English and to 'Canadien Pacifique Limitée' in French. CP Rail operates a total of 23 623 km (14 679 miles) of route, all standard gauge. Rolling stock consists of 1200 diesel-electric locomotives, 60 000 freight cars and 4500 miscellaneous work vehicles.

VIA Rail Canada was incorporated on 12 January for the purpose of revitalizing all passenger services, to manage and to market them on an efficient commercial basis, so reducing the financial burden on the Government. The first joint CP/CN timetable was issued, under the VIA symbol, in October 1976. VIA purchased all CN and CP Rail's passenger equipment in 1978. From 1 April 1979 VIA assumed full financial responsibility for the passenger services formerly operated by CN and CP Rail. In 1985 7.8 million passenger journeys were made, a total of 3010 passenger-km (1870 miles). VIA operates over 28 962 km (17 997 miles) of route with 126 diesel locomotives, 30 diesel locomotives for LRC (Light Rapid Comfortable) train sets, 76 diesel railcars and 674 coaches.

AUSTRALIAN RAILWAYS

Australian railway development was piecemeal, each colony forming its own policy without regard to future unification. Details of the earliest railways are given in chapter 1. By the time of the constitution of the Australian Commonwealth, on 9 July 1900, Australia had 20 126 km (12 506 miles) of railways of three gauges.

Today the standard gauge forms only 36.16 per cent of the total route length of Australian Railways. There have been several Government reports, since the first in 1857, recommending unification of the Australian railways on the standard gauge, but attempts to carry out the recommendations have failed because of the high cost. Progress is already being made on standardization of main routes between states and principal cities.

The Australian National Railways Commission came into existence on 1 July 1975 to control the former Commonwealth Railways and also the Tasmanian and non-metropolitan South Australian Railways which were transferred to it on 1 March 1978. As the Commonwealth Railways its function was to operate lines connecting different states. Its earliest line was opened in 1879. It now controls a total route of 7450 km (4629 miles) which includes 2001 km (1243 miles) of 1600 mm gauge; 3636 km (2259 miles) of standard gauge; and 1813 km (1127 miles) of 1067 mm gauge.

In New South Wales the Government railways were taken over by the Public Transport Commission of NSW in October 1972. Under the Transport Authorities Act of 1980 this was dissolved on 1 July 1980 and replaced by two separate organizations: the Urban Transport Authority (UTA) and the State Rail Authority (SRA), both under the control of the Minister for Transport. The SRA operates 9908 km (6157 miles) of standard-gauge route. The following table shows route-kilometres of Government-owned railways of three gauges in each State and Territory on 30 June 1979. Some state systems operate into neighbouring states.

State	1600 mm	1435 mm	1067 km	Total km
New South Wales	328[1]	9 820[2]	–	10 148
Victoria	5 448	332[3]	–	5 856
Queensland	–	113	10 114	9 789
South Australia	2 537[4]	1 871	1 536	5 944
Western Australia	–	1 212[6]	4 169[5]	6 501
Tasmania	–	–	864	864
Northern Territory	–	–	278	278
Australian Capital Territory	–	8	–	8
Australian total	8 396	14 243	16 749	39 388

[1] Part of Victorian Railways system.
[2] Includes 47 km of 1435 mm gauge line from Broken Hill to Cockburn operated by ANR.
[3] Includes 12 km of 1435 mm/1600 mm dual-gauge line which operates in the Melbourne metropolitan area.
[4] Includes 153 km of the Adelaide metropolitan railway system operated by South Australian State Transport Authority.
[5] Excludes 148 km of 1067 mm/1435 mm dual-gauge line which is included in the 1435 mm length.
[6] Excludes 1005 km of 1435 mm gauge ore railways.

LARGE RAILWAY SYSTEMS, WORLD WIDE

Argentina

The railways of Argentina were built largely with foreign capital. They were nationalized in 1948 and **Argentine State Railways** was established in 1956. As in Australia, there are three gauges: 1676 mm, about 21 500 km (13 360 miles); standard, or 1435 mm about 3000 km (1864 miles); and metre, about 10 000 km (6214 miles). There are six divisions: Roca, Mitre, San Martin, and Sarmiento, all 1676 mm gauge. Urquiza division is standard gauge and Belgrano is metre gauge. The total route length is 34 509 km (21 443 miles). Of this only 209 km (130 miles) is electrified, 0.6 per cent of the total route.

Brazil

Brazilian Federal Railways (Rede Ferroviaria Federal SA; RFFSA) was established on 30 September 1957. It is divided into four regions and operates 20 695 km (12 860 miles) of route, mostly metre, but including 13 km (8 miles) of 762 mm (2 ft 6 in) gauge and 1859 km (1155 miles) of 1600 mm (5 ft 3 in) gauge.

China

The railways of China were nationalized in 1908. The system developed piecemeal with unconnected lines all over the vast country. In 1949 the **Chinese People's Republic Railways** was established and since then the system has grown from around 20 000 km to 54 000 km (12 428–33 555 miles) in 1985. China is building about 1000 km (621 miles) of new railway route every year and hopes to achieve 80 000 km (49 711 miles) by 2000. About 2600 km (1616 miles) are electrified at 25 kV 50 Hz.

France

French National Railways (Société National des Chemins de fer Français; SNCF) was formed on 31 August 1937 and it took over the operating concessions of the major French railway companies on 1 January 1938. On 1 January 1983 the SNCF became a public corporation. At 31 December 1986 the total standard-gauge route length was 34 541 km (21 463 miles), of which 11 488 km (7139 miles) were electrified. The SNCF also operates a few km of metre-gauge route, notably the Savoy Railway (St Gervais–Martigny) and the Cerdagne Railway. In January 1983 the metre-gauge Corsican Railways became part of the SNCF, 232 km (144 miles).

Czechoslovakia

Czechoslovak State Railways was first established in 1919 and was re-established in May 1945. It operates 12 844 km (7981 miles) of standard gauge of which 3507 km (2179 miles) are electrified; 177 km (110 miles) of metre and 600 mm (1 ft 11½ in) gauge and 101 km (63 miles) of the Russian 1520 mm (4 ft 11⅞ in) gauge, total 13 130 km (8159 miles).

Germany

The German Federal Railway (Deutsche Bundesbahn; DB) was formed by the State Railways Act of 13 December 1951 to operate the lines in West Germany. On 31 December 1985 it consisted of 27 628 km (17 168 miles) of standard gauge, of which 11 396 km (7081 miles) were electrified at 15 kV 16⅔ Hz.

The German State Railway (Deutsche Reichsbahn) was established on 1 April 1920. On 11 October 1924 (by the Railway Act of 30 August, amended by the Act of 13 March 1930), the system was made independent of the Government. It was placed once more under State control on 30 January 1937. After the Second World War the name denoted only the system in East Germany. Today it operates 14 231 km (8843 miles) of standard gauge of which 2321 km (1442 miles) are electrified at 15 kV 16⅔ Hz; and 1012 km (629 miles) of narrow gauge.

India

The Indian Railway Board was constituted in its present form in 1951. The total route operated, 61 850 km (38 433 miles), includes the following gauges:

Gauge	Route length km (miles)	
1676 mm (5 ft 6 in)	33 553	(20 850)
Metre gauge	24 051	(14 945)
762 mm (2 ft 6 in) } 610 mm (2 ft 0 in) }	4 246	(2 638)

About 6440 km (4002 miles) of 1676 mm gauge route are electrified. The system is divided into nine zonal administrative units.

Italy

Italian State Railways (Ferrovie dello Stato; FS) was formed in 1905–7. It operates 16 066 km (9983 miles) of standard gauge of which 8843 km (5495 miles) are electrified at 3000 V dc. Also 71 km (44 miles) of 950 mm gauge in Sicily.

The mountainous nature of the country has necessitated numerous bridges and tunnels. There are 43 158 bridges and viaducts with over 10 m (33 ft) length of clearance. Of these, 39 091 are of masonry and 4067 of steel of which 77 masonry and 31 steel bridges and 36 viaducts have a clearance over 100 m (328 ft) long. There are 1849 tunnels totalling 911 km (566 miles), a distance further than from London to Inverness. The longest is the Apennine, 18 519 m (11 miles 892 yd), and 21 others are over 5 km (3 miles) long. New lines are under construction with more large bridges and long tunnels. (See list of tunnels.)

Japan

The railways of Japan were purchased by the Government on 31 March 1906, and on 5 December 1908 a Railway Board was set up. A Ministry of Railways (established on 15 May 1920), was finally absorbed, together with Telecommunications, into the Ministry of Transport on 18 May 1945. On 1 June 1949 the Government railways were reorganized into a public corporation under the title of **Japanese National Railways**. From April 1978 JNR was split up into seven separate railway companies:

Company	Route length km (miles)	
East Japan Railway	7454	(4632)
West Japan Railway	5091	(3164)
Hokkaido Railway	2542	(1580)
Kyushu Railway	2101	(1306)
Central Japan Railway	1984	(1233)
Shikoku Railway	837	(520)

Japan Freight Railway Co. operates nationwide freight services. Shinkansen Property Corporation leases the 1835 km (1140 miles) of standard-gauge passenger facilities to the passenger railway companies. The title 'Japan Rail' covers the whole organization. Of the 21 091 km (13 106 miles) of 1067 mm (3 ft 6 in) gauge lines 5493 km (3413 miles) are electrified at 1500 V dc; 2174 km (1351 miles) at 20 kV 50 Hz and 1371 km (852 miles) at 20 kV 60 Hz. The Shinkansen (meaning New Main Line) system is electrified at 25 kV at both 50 Hz and 60 Hz. In 1984 JNR carried 6884 million passengers and 75 million tonnes of freight.

Mexico

Ferrocarriles Nacionales de Mexico was formed in 1908. It operates 14 913 km (9267 miles) of standard-gauge route; 397 km (247 miles) of 914 mm (3 ft 0 in) gauge; and 18 km (11 miles) of mixed gauge; total 14 680 km (9122 miles).

Poland

Polish State Railways at present operate 23 707 km (14 731 miles) of standard-gauge route of which 8902 km (5532 miles) are electrified at 3000 V dc. There are also 654 km (406 miles) of the Russian 1520 mm (4 ft 11⅞ in) gauge and 651 km (405 miles) of various narrow gauges.

Romania

Romanian State Railways (Caile Ferate Romane; CFR) operates 10 515 km (6534 miles) of standard gauge of which 2367 km (1471 miles) is electrified at 25 kV 50 Hz; also 568 km (353 miles) of 610 mm (2 ft) and 762 mm (2 ft 6 in) gauge.

South Africa

South African Railways was formed in 1910 on the unification of the Cape, Orange River, Transvaal and Natal Colonies. It operates 23 821 km (14 803 miles) of 1065 mm (3 ft 6 in) gauge of which 5781 km (3592 miles) are electrified at 3 kV dc; 861 km (535 miles) at 50 kV ac and 1266 km (787 miles) at 25 kV ac, a total of 7908 km (4914 miles). There are also 559 km (347 miles) of 610 mm (2 ft) gauge.

Spain

Spanish National Railways (Red Nacional de los Ferrocarriles Españoles; RENFE) was formed under the Law of 27 February 1943. It operates 12 691 km (7886 miles) of 1676 mm (5 ft 6 in) gauge, of which 6181 km (3841 miles) are electrified at 1650 and 3000 V dc.

Sweden

Swedish State Railways (Statens Järnvägar; SJ) was formed in 1856. Of its total route length of 10 819 km (6723 miles) of standard gauge 6955 km (4322 miles), 64 per cent, is electrified at 15 kV 16⅔ Hz.

USSR

Sovetski Zhelezno-Dorozhni; SZD (Soviet Metal Roadway). By 1913 the Russian railway network comprised 25 state and 13 private lines. The entire system was nationalized after the Revolution of 1917.

In 1986 the total route length of 1520 mm (4 ft 11⅞ in) gauge was 142 968 km (88 839 miles) of which 23 280 km (14 466 miles) was electrified at 25 kV 50 Hz and 27 309 km (16 969 miles) at 3 kV dc, altogether 35.38 per cent of the system. The Russian gauge was 1524 mm (5 ft) until 1 January 1972 when the standard was narrowed by 4 mm to give steadier running at high speeds. In 1986 the SZD carried 4077.6 million tonnes of freight. Passenger journeys totalled 4345 million.

5
WORLD RAILWAYS

THE EXTREMITIES

Continent	Place	Country	Lat/Long	Gauge	Comments
EUROPE					
North	Litsnayamari	Murmansk Oblask, USSR	69°39'N	1520 mm	330 km (205 miles) north of Arctic Circle. (See Note 1)
South	Algeciras, nr Gibraltar	Spain	36°8'N	1676 mm	
East	Khalmer-Yu	USSR	64°48'E	1520 mm	
West	Tralee	Ireland	9°42'W	1600 mm	Opened 1859. (See Note 2)
ASIA					
North	Labytnangi	USSR	66°43'N	1520 mm	(See Note 3)
South	Bentjulak	Indonesia (Java)	8°0'S	1067 mm	Indonesian State Railways
East	Nemuro	Japan (Hokkaido)	145°34'E	1067 mm	
West	Just north of Izmir	Turkey	27°0'E	standard	Opened 1866
AFRICA					
North	Bizerte	Tunisia	37°16'N	standard	
South	Bredasdorp	S. Africa	34°36'S	1065 mm	
East	Djibouti	Djibouti	42°50'E	metre	Terminus of railway to Addis Ababa, Ethiopia
West	Dakar	Senegal	17°24'W	metre	
NORTH AMERICA					
North	Dome, near Fairbanks	Alaska, USA	64°55'N	standard	Alaska RR opened June 1923. (See Note 4)
South	Miami	Florida, USA	25°46'N	standard	(See Note 5)
East	St Johns	Newfoundland, Canada	52°54'W	1067 mm	Canadian National. Opened 29 June 1898
West	Anchorage	Alaska, USA	150°3'W	standard	Alaska RR. (See Note 6)
SOUTH AMERICA					
North	Santa Marta	Colombia	11°15'N	914 mm	
South	Puerto Gallegos	Argentina	51°5'S	750 mm	Ramal Ferro Industrias Rio Turbio, opened 1958. (See Note 7)
East	Cabedelo	Brazil	34°48'W	metre	
West	Paita	Peru	81°7'W	standard	
AUSTRALIA					
North	Darwin	Northern Territory	12°28'S	1067 mm	Out of use. Rebuilding to standard gauge.
South	Foster	Victoria	38°42'S	1600 mm	(See Note 8)
East	Ballina	NSW	153°36'E	standard	
West	Geraldton	W Australia	114°36'E	1067 mm	

The extremities of British Rail are:

North	Thurso	Caithness	58°36'N	Former Highland Railway, opened 28 July 1874
South	Penzance	Cornwall	50°7'N	GWR (West Cornwall Railway) opened 11 March 1852. (See Note 9)
East	Lowestoft	Suffolk	1°44'E	Former Great Eastern Railway opened 3 May 1847
West	Between Arisaig and Morar	Inverness-shire	5°53'W	Former West Highland Railway opened 1 April 1901

Notes

1 The most northerly railway in the world was a 2.4 km (1½ mile) long 889 mm (2 ft 11 in) gauge line at King's Bay, Spitsbergen, on latitude 79°N, only 1207 km (750 miles) from the North Pole. It connected coal mines with the harbour and was used in summer only. It was built in 1917 and had five German 0-4-0 tank engines. The line was closed in 1929 but was reopened from 1945 to 1949.

Litsnayamari, at present the most northerly point on any railway, is at the end of a 32 km (20 mile) extension for goods trains only from Pechenga, 69°33'N, which is the most northerly point on a 'main line' railway.

In the USSR work is in progress on a 400 km (250 mile) railway to the tip of the Yamal Peninsula, from Vorkuta to Kharasavei, 73°N, on the coast of the Karu Sea, which will make this the world's most northerly railway. It will serve towns and settlements in the Yamal Peninsula. Gas from rich deposits in the area will be piped parallel to the railway. The route will involve a ferry across the Baydaratskaya Gulf, 60 km (37 miles) wide for which special ice-breaking train ferries will be used. The main problem is permafrost, but Soviet railway engineers have considerable experience with this. Heavy bridging and tunnelling will be required through the Urals.

At Narvik in Norway, 68°40'N, the Lapland iron-ore railway, opened in July 1903, is about 209 km (130 miles) north of the Arctic Circle.

The Norwegian iron ore terminal at Narvik, 68°40'N, 209 km (130 miles) north of the Arctic Circle, on 1 May 1979.

Invercargill Station, New Zealand, 46°26'S, the world's most southerly station.

2 In 1887 a branch was opened from Tralee to Fenit, 9°51'W, but this became disused about 1972. Previously the honour was shared by Valentia Harbour, Co. Kerry, Ireland, terminus of the 1600 mm (5 ft 3 in) gauge branch of the Great Southern & Western Railway from Killorglin opened on 12 September 1893; and by Dingle, Co. Kerry, terminus of the 914 mm (3 ft) gauge Tralee & Dingle Railway, opened on 31 March 1891, both 10°15'W. These are now abandoned.

The furthest west on the European mainland is at Cascais, 9°25'W, terminus of a 1665 mm (5 ft 6 in) gauge branch about 29 km (18 miles) west of Lisbon in Portugal.

3 The line from Chūm to Labytnangi crosses the Urals at about 67°N.

4 Farthest north and west was reached about 1910 by the now closed Seward Peninsula Railroad at Nome, 165°24'W. Its northern end was at Lane's Landing, north of 65°N.

5 The border with Mexico is taken as the southern boundary of North America.

6 The farthest west is actually about 80 km (50 miles) along the railway north west of Anchorage.

7 The Ramal Ferro Industrias Rio Turbio is an isolated 750 mm (2 ft 5½ in) gauge Argentine Coal Board line from Puerto Gallegos to the Rio Turbio coal mines at the southern foot of the Andes in Argentina, close to the frontier with Chile. It runs due west from the South Atlantic coast for about 261 km (162 miles) and is used mainly to transport coal for shipment by sea from Puerto Gallegos. The coal is carried in block trains of up to 1700 tons hauled by Japanese-built 2–10–2 tender engines, the largest and most powerful locomotives ever built for this gauge. Winds in this region frequently reach 161 km/h (100 mph).

From 1910 to 1948 a 610 mm (2 ft) gauge railway operated at Ushuaia in southern Argentina at 54°40′S, 68°5′W. One of the locomotives has been preserved.

At the Atlantic port of Deseado in Argentina, latitude 47°45′S, is the terminus of the 1676 mm (5 ft 6 in) gauge railway from Colonia Las Heras.

8 If the 'continent' is taken as Australasia then the furthest south is Bluff, New Zealand (S Island), 46°33′S, and furthest east is Gisborne (N Island), 177°59′E, both 1067 mm (3 ft 6 in) gauge.

9 Until 5 October 1964 the most southerly point was Helston, Cornwall, 50°6′N.

GRADIENTS

Railway gradients in Britain are described as a ratio, e.g. 1 in 100. In North America a 'per cent' description is used for the units rise per 100 horizontal units. In some European continental countries a 'pro mille' (‰) or per 1000 description is used: e.g. 25‰=2.5 per cent=1 in 40.

The steepest railway in the world is the Swiss funicular (cable-worked) incline between Piotta and Piora (Lake Ritom) in Canton Ticino, with a gradient of 1 in 1.125 (88 per cent). It is closely approached by the Châtelard–Barberine funicular south of Martigny, Switzerland, with a gradient of 1 in 1.15 (87 per cent). Both lines were built for transport of materials for hydro-electric schemes and were later adapted for passengers.

The steepest railway in the USA is the 472 m (1550 ft) long cable-worked incline down to the famous 'hanging bridge' at the bottom of the Royal Gorge, Colorado. It has a gradient of 64.6 per cent, or 1 in 1.55. It was opened on 14 June 1931. The engineer was George F. Cole. The journey takes 5 minutes.

The steepest incline over which regular passenger trains are worked is the 1 in 11 (9 per cent) between Chedde and Servoz, on the metre gauge electric Chamonix line of the South-Eastern Region of the French National Railways, opened on 25 July 1901.

The steepest standard-gauge incline on the French National Railways (SNCF) is 1 in 23 (4.3 per cent) between Urdos and Les Forges on the French side of the Somport Tunnel in the Pyrenees.

Another steep gradient on the SNCF is 1 in 16.5 (6.06 per cent) on the metre-gauge Cerdagne Railway in Languedoc.

The steepest adhesion-worked incline in Great Britain was the 1 in 14 (7 per cent) Hopton Incline on the Cromford & High Peak Railway in Derbyshire, opened in 1831 and closed in 1967. It was originally chain worked.

The original C & HPR included five other cable-worked inclines with gradients ranging from 1 in 7 (14.3 per cent) to 1 in 16 (6.25 per cent), and a short one at Whaley Bridge, worked by a horse gin and endless chain, which continued in use until 9 April 1952.

The steepest main-line gradient in the USA is the Saluda Hill on the Southern Railway, 54.7 km (34 miles) south of Ashville, North Carolina. The grade is 1 in 21.4 (4.7 per cent).

The steepest standard-gauge incline in the USA was on the north side of the Ohio River at Madison, Indiana, on the Madison & Lafayette Railroad, opened on 1 April 1839. It was 2 km (7040 ft) long and rose 131 m (431 ft) on a gradient of about 1 in 17 (5.89 per cent).

From 1866 it formed part of the Jeffersonville, Madison & Indianapolis Railroad, whose master mechanic Reuben Wells designed a massive 0–10–0 tank engine, built in 1868, to work the incline. The engine can still be seen today, in the Children's Museum, Indianapolis.

The world's greatest 'main-line' inclines are on the 1600 mm (5 ft 3 in) gauge São Paulo Railway in Brazil. The railway has to rise about 800 m (1700 ft) from the port of Santos to São Paulo in a distance of 79 km (49 miles). The British engineer James Brunlees (qv) built the first line in 1851–7. It included a single-track incline 8.5 km (5.3 miles) long on a gradient of 1 in 10 (10 per cent). It was worked by a cable on the 'tail-end' principle.

In 1900 a new double-track line was opened, 11 km (6.8 miles) long worked in four inclined sections with continuous cables. The old incline remained in use for freight.

By 1958 traffic on the inclines was nearing their limit of 9 000 000 tons per annum, so in 1968 it was decided to rebuild the original incline for rack operation, electrified at 3000 V dc. The new incline was opened in 1974. It includes a concrete viaduct 260 m (853 ft) long at Grota Funda and a span of 63 m (206 ft) over the River Mogi. It is operated by rack and adhesion locomotives of 2820 kW (3800 hp) and has a capacity of 21 000 000 tons per annum at only a third of the operating cost of the cable incline. The 1900 cable inclines are being retained for emergency use, and as a tourist attraction.

The steepest gradient over which standard-gauge passenger trains were worked by adhesion in Great Britain was probably the Lowca Light Railway in Cumbria which was 1 in 17 (5.9 per cent) between Rose Hill and Copperas Hill. Between 2 June 1913 and 31 May 1926 passenger trains were worked over it by the Furness Railway and its successor, from 1 January 1923, the LMS.

The Chequerbent Incline section of the Kenyon–Leigh–Bolton branch of the London & North Western Railway in Lancashire, once 1 in 30 (3.33 per cent), was so affected by mining subsidence that a short stretch became 1 in 19.5 (5 per cent). The line was originally part of the Bolton & Leigh Railway, the first public railway in Lancashire, opened on 1 August 1928. Passenger services ran from 13 June 1831 to 3 March 1952.

On the 1219 mm (4 ft) gauge Glasgow Subway there are gradients of 1 in 18 (5.5 per cent) and 1 in 20 (5 per cent) on the sections under the Clyde.

Several railways with rope-worked inclines carried passengers at one time. The best known was the Beck Hole Incline near Goathland on the Whitby & Pickering Railway, 1 in 10 (10 per cent), which carried passengers from 1836 to 1865. A runaway disaster led to the construction of the present deviation line through Goathland.

The steepest gradient in Britain over which standard-gauge passenger trains work today is the 1 in 27 (3.7 per cent) on the Mersey Railway from the bottom of the Mersey Tunnel up to James Street Station, Liverpool. (See Merseyrail.)

From Middleton Junction to Oldham the branch of the Lancashire & Yorkshire Railway, opened in 1842, rose for 1.2 km (¾ mile) at 1 in 27. Passenger services ended in 1958 and the line was closed completely on 7 January 1963.

The Pwllyrhebog Incline on the Pwllyrhebog branch of the Taff Vale Railway in South Wales, opened in 1863, climbed at 1 in 13 for 0.8 km (½ mile), then at 1 in 29 and 1 in 30. Trains were assisted by a rope and winding engine. It was closed on 1 July 1951. For working the incline the

locomotive superintendent Tom Hurry Riches (1846–1911) designed the 'H' Class 0–6–0 tanks of which three were built by Kitson, Leeds, in 1884. They had a dome over a firebox, especially designed to avoid its becoming uncovered by water on the steep incline.

In Scotland the Causewayend Incline near Manuel, about 3 km (2 miles) west of Linlithgow, Stirlingshire, included 804 m (½ mile) at 1 in 23 (4.34 per cent). The Commonhead Incline near Airdrie included a short stretch of 1 in 23. Passenger trains ran until 1 May 1930 on both these lines.

On the former Brecon & Merthyr Railway in Wales, in the 11.7 km (7.3 miles) from Talybont-on-Usk to Torpantau the line climbed 281.9 m (926 ft) on gradients of 1 in 38–40 (2.63–2.5 per cent).

The Canterbury & Whitstable Railway in Kent, opened on 3 May 1830, included 543 m (594 yd) at 1 in 28 (3.5 per cent).

The slightest gradient to be indicated on British Railways is 1 in 14 400 between Pirbright Junction and Farnborough on the Surrey/Hampshire border. Similar gradients are indicated at Wimbledon and Surbiton on the same line.

The self-acting inclined plane on which descending loaded wagons pull empties up was patented by Michael Menzies, a Scottish advocate, in 1750.

The principle was first used on the Schulenberg Railway in the Harz Mountains in Germany in 1724.

The world's toughest and longest gradient is on the standard-gauge Central Railway of Peru. In 172 km (107 miles) the line rises 4775 m (15 665 ft). This gives an *aver-*

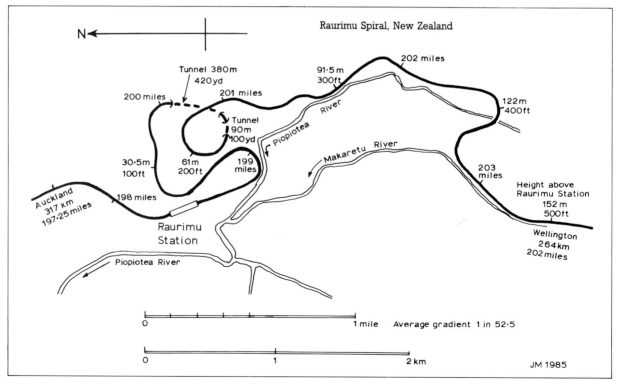

Raurimu Spiral, New Zealand

age gradient of 1 in 36 (2.8 per cent), but this includes stations and reversing switches. The normal gradient is 1 in 25 (4 per cent), with long stretches of 1 in 20 (5 per cent), or steeper. The line was begun by Henry Meiggs (1811–77) in 1870 and completed to Oroya in 1893, and it was opened to Huancayo, 332 km (206 miles), on 8 September 1908.

On the Burma State Railways the line between Mandalay and Lashio climbs for 19.3 km (12 miles) continuously at 1 in 25 (4 per cent). This section includes the Gokteik Viaduct (see Chapter 6).

The steepest main line in Australia is 1 in 33 (3 per cent) up the Blue Mountains between Sydney and Lithgow, New South Wales.

The steepest adhesion-worked railway in Australia was 1 in 19 (5.3 per cent) between Campbelltown and Camden, New South Wales. It was opened as a tramway in 1879 and became a branch of the railway system in 1901. It was closed on 31 December 1962, though an enthusiasts' special was run over it the following day. Normal trains consisted of a carriage and two wagons hauled by a '20' Class 2-6-4 tank engine. On Good Fridays up to three pilgrims' specials were run, eight or nine coaches with two '20' Class engines in front and one behind.

Australia's steepest railway was a section of the 1067 mm (3 ft 6 in) gauge Emu Bay Railway in Tasmania where the line rose at 1 in 16 (6.2 per cent) between Queenstown and Strahan. An Abt track was used. It was closed in 1963.

The most remarkable railway location in New Zealand is the Raurimu Spiral on the North Island Main Trunk Railway from Auckland to Wellington, south of Taumarunui. In 48 km (30 miles) it has to climb 636 m (2086 ft) to the edge of the Waimarino Plateau. In the last 11 km (7 miles) it climbs 213 m (700 ft). Several surveys in 1886–7 failed to produce a satisfactory route. This was at last achieved in 1898 by R. W. Holmes, a senior engineer of the Public Works Department. The spiral location increases the distance from Raurimu to the National Park from 5.6 km (3½ miles) to 11 km (7 miles).

ZIGZAG INCLINES, OR SWITCHBACKS[1]

The use of zigzag or switchback locations on railways for overcoming abrupt height differences dates back to the 1840s when they were used on a coal line at Honesdale in Pennsylvania, and on the Ithaca & Oswego Railroad, New York. Their first use on a main line was on the Great Indian Peninsula Railway at Bhore Ghat on the line from Bombay to Poona, begun in January 1856 and opened on 14 May 1863. With a ruling grade of 1 in 37 (2.7 per cent), 25.5 km (15.9 miles) long, it overcame a height difference of 558 m (1831 ft) from Karjat at the foot up to Khandala. There were 25 tunnels totalling 5.653 km (2 miles 475 yd). On the Bombay–Calcutta main line the incline up the

[1] The word 'switchback' can also mean alternating up and down gradients.

Thull Ghat was begun in 1857 and opened on 1 January 1865. It was originally 15 km (9.3 miles) long, rising 296 m (972 ft) with a ruling gradient of 1 in 37 (2.7 per cent) and 13 tunnels, totalling 2.315 km (1 mile 772 yd) and including **the highest viaduct in India**, the Ehegaon Viaduct (qv). Realignment of the Thull Incline, begun in October 1913 and brought into use in September 1918, abolished the zigzags. The line to Poona was similarly realigned and electrified, in 1929.

While these lines were under construction, the Great Western Railway of New South Wales was being laid out over the Blue Mountains west of Sydney, by John Whitton (1819–98). At Lapstone, *c.* 64 km (*c.* 40 miles) from Sydney, it climbed the mountain face by the 'Little Zig Zag', opened on 13 July 1867, and 80 km (50 miles) further descended again by the 'Great Zig Zag' at Lithgow, opened on 18 October 1869. The Lapstone zigzag was bypassed by the Lapstone deviation in 1892 and this in turn was avoided by the Glenbrook deviation in 1913.

The Lithgow zigzag was bypassed by the deviation line opened on 16 October 1910. Both zigzags are now accessible by road and on foot, and on 30 August 1975 trains began running on a 1067 mm (3 ft 6 in) gauge railway laid on the middle section of the Lithgow zigzag by the Lithgow Switchback Railway Co-operative Society, using preserved locomotives and rolling stock. The area is now administred by the Zig Zag Trust, Lithgow.

The next use of the principle for main-line work was on the Peru Central Railway (qv), 1870–93, and on the Darjeeling Himalayan Railway, opened in July 1881. They can also be found on the 1067 mm (3 ft 6 in) gauge Cuzco–Santa Ana Railway in Peru.

Besides their use for temporary lines, such as over the Cascade Mountains during the construction of the first Cascade Tunnel in 1892–1900 (qv), other examples of zigzag locations are too numerous to list fully.

In England the most notable zigzag railways were both freight-only lines, on the North Eastern Railway: down to the Loftus iron-mine near Skinningrove, Cleveland, opened on 21 April 1865, and from Tweedmouth down to the dock, opened on 16 October 1878. The Skinningrove branch was closed on 1 May 1958 and the Tweedmouth Dock branch in 1965.

MOUNTAIN AND RACK RAILWAYS

The first railway with a central rack was the Jefferson Incline on the north bank of the Ohio River near Madison, Indiana, built in 1847. The eight-coupled engines had a separate vertical-cylindered engine for driving the rack mechanism.

The first mountain rack railway was opened on 3 July 1869. It was built by Sylvester Marsh (1803–84) to carry passengers to the 1918 m (6293 ft) summit of Mount Washington in New Hampshire, USA. The railway is standard gauge, 4.8 km (3 miles) long, and has a maximum gradient of 1 in 3.1 (32.26 per cent). A wrought-iron ladder-type rack was used.

Nicholas Riggenbach (1817–99) designed a similar rack, patented in 1863, and first used on the 7.3 m (4½ mile) standard-gauge line from Vitznau to the summit of the Rigi, Switzerland, opened on 23 May 1871. The last 3.2 km (2 miles) were opened on 27 June 1873 to a summit level of 1750 m (5741 ft). It was electrified on 3 October 1937.

The Riggenbach rack is used also on the metre-gauge Brünig and Bernese Oberland railways in Switzerland.

Roman Abt (1850–1933) invented his rack system in 1882. It was first used in 1885 on a railway at Blankenburg in the Harz Mountains.

Three-quarters of the world's rack railways use the Abt system in which two or sometimes three flat steel bars having teeth in their upper edge are fixed side by side so that the gap in one comes opposite the tooth of the next or, in the triple rack, a third of the space of one tooth.

The steepest rack railway in the world is the Mount Pilatus Railway in Switzerland, with a gradient of 1 in 2 (50 per cent). A special rack was devised by Edward Locher (1840–1910). It has horizontal teeth on each side which prevent any possibility of slipping or derailment. The railway was opened on 4 June 1889 with steam and was electrified on 15 May 1937.

One of the original steam locomotives and cars descending the Pilatus Railway, Switzerland, showing the Locher rack which prevents over-riding or derailment.

For this railway a gauge of 800 mm (2 ft 7½ in) was chosen. Roman Abt adopted this as his standard and it was used for 11 mountain railways in Switzerland, and others elsewhere.

The Snowdon Mountain Railway in Wales, 800 mm (2 ft 7½ in) gauge, uses the Abt double rack and Swiss-built steam locomotives. It was opened on 6 April 1896. In its 7.3 km (4½ miles) it climbs from Llanberis to the summit at 1064 m (3493 ft) on gradients of 1 in 5.5 (18 per cent).

The Abt system is used on 'main lines' on the Furka–Oberalp and Brig–Visp–Zermatt railways in Switzerland.

The first rack railway in Australia and also the steepest was a 1067 mm gauge line built by the Mount Lyell Mining & Railway Co. on the west coast of Tasmania, from the mine at Lyell near Queenstown to King River at Teepookana. It was opened in 1894 and in 1899 extended to Regatta Point on Macquarie Harbour. The Abt rack extended for 7.3 km (4½ miles) at a maximum gradient of 1 in 16. The original locomotives were used until it closed in 1963.

The world's first electric mountain rack railway was the Gornergrat Railway at Zermatt, Switzerland, opened on 20 August 1898. It is metre gauge, 9.3 km (5.8 miles) long, with Abt rack and operates on three-phase ac at 725 V. With a summit at 3088 m (10 134 ft) it is the second highest railway in Europe and the highest in the open.

The highest railway in North America is the Manitou & Pike's Peak Railway in Colorado. This standard-gauge line is 14.3 km (8.9 miles) long with an average gradient of 1 in 6 (16.66 per cent). The lower terminus is at 2298 m (7538 ft) and the summit is 4300 m (14 109 ft). On Windy Point Hill it climbs for 3.2 km (2 miles) at 1 in 4 (25 per cent). It was opened on 1 June 1891 with steam-power, using Vauclain compound Abt system rack locomotives. These worked until 1958 when a petrol-driven railcar was introduced. In 1959 a diesel-electric locomotive was tried and was followed in 1961 by two diesel-electric single-unit railcars built by the Swiss Locomotive & Machine Works, Winterthur. Another two came in 1968. The newest cars are two diesel-hydraulic twin-unit sets built by SLM and delivered in 1976. One of the steam locomotives is preserved at Manitou and another at the Colorado Railroad Museum at Golden near Denver.

The highest railway in Europe is the metre-gauge Jungfrau Railway in Switzerland, opened on 1 August 1912. At Jungfraujoch it is 3454 m (11 332 ft). The upper section is entirely in a tunnel, 7.123 km (4 miles 750 yd) long. Strub rack is used.

Switzerland's only steam mountain railway is now the Brienzer Rothorn Railway, 800 mm (2 ft 7½ in) gauge with Abt rack. It was opened on 17 June 1892. The summit is at 2349 m (7707 ft).

John Barraclough Fell (1815–1902) invented the centre-rail friction-drive system named after him in 1863–9. It was devised for the railway over the Mont Cenis Pass, opened in 1868 and used until the Mont Cenis Tunnel was completed in 1871.

A similar system had previously been invented by C. E. Vignoles and John Ericsson and jointly patented on 7 September 1830.

The Fell centre-rail is used on the 1067 mm (3 ft 6 in) gauge Snaefell Mountain Railway in the Isle of Man, but for braking purposes only. The electric cars climb to the top, 620 m (2034 ft), by adhesion. It was opened on 21 August 1895. On 1 June 1957 the undertaking was transferred to the Manx Government.

The first and only railway to the top of a volcano was built on Vesuvius in Italy. The funicular railway, with gradients as steep as 1 in 1.9 (52.6 per cent), was opened in 1880 to the summit station at 1213 m (4012 ft) just below the crater.

The composer Luigi Denza (1846–1922) wrote a popular song 'Funiculi-Funicular' to celebrate the occasion. Richard Strauss thought this was a Neapolitan folk-song and incorporated it in the Finale of his symphonic fantasy *Aus Italien* (1886)

The railway was destroyed in the eruption on 20 March 1944. It has been replaced by a bus between Pugliano and Lower Station and a chair lift from there to the crater.

ALTITUDES

The Central Railway of Peru is not simply the world's highest railway; it is also the most wonderfully engineered. It climbs from just above sea-level at Callao to 4783 m (15 694 ft) in Galera Tunnel in a distance of 173.5 km (107.8 miles) and drops again to Oroya, 3726 m (12 224 ft), in a further 49 km (30 miles), by means of six double zigzags and one single zigzag on the main line and three double zigzags on the Morococha Branch. There are 67 tunnels and 59 bridges, some of which are major engineering works in themselves.

This standard-gauge line was laid out and constructed under the direction of Henry Meiggs, but he died in 1877 when construction had reached Cacray, and further work was delayed by the Peru-Chile War in 1879. In 1893 it was completed to Oroya along the route already laid out by Meiggs. The mountain above the summit is named Mount Meiggs, after the great engineer and contractor. Heights, distances and dates are shown on the adjoining map.

In April 1955 a spur was opened from the Morococha Branch at La Cima to the Volcán Mine overlooking Ticlio, reaching a world record altitude of 4830 m (15 848 ft), but it has recently been abandoned and dismantled.

The world's highest railway junction is at Ticlio, 4758 m (15 610 ft), on the Central Railway of Peru. There the line divides, the main line passing beneath Mount Meiggs in the Galera Tunnel (qv) and the Morococha Branch climbing to the world's highest railway summit at La Cima, to rejoin the main line at Cut-Off above Oroya.

SUMMITS IN COLORADO

The highest adhesion-worked summit in North America was on Mount McClellan, 4159 m (13 644 ft), reached by the Argentine Central (later Argentine & Gray's Peak) Railway, from Silver Plume, Colorado, a 914 mm (3 ft) gauge line built by Edward Wilcox in 1906. The 1 in 16.67, or 6 per cent, grades and switchbacks were worked by

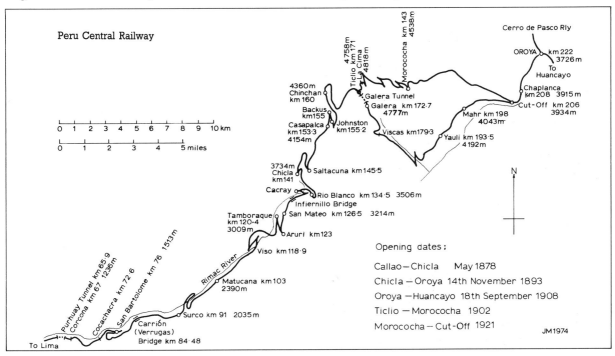

Peru Central Railway

Opening dates:

Callao—Chicla   May 1878
Chicla—Oroya 14th November 1893
Oroya—Huancayo 18th September 1908
Ticlio—Morococha 1902
Morococha—Cut-Off 1921

JM 1974

Shay geared engines (qv) which could pull two or three Colorado & Southern cars to the summit. Petrol cars were introduced in 1914. The 9.6 km (6 mile) long railway closed in 1917. (See also **'The highest railway in North America'**.)

The highest adhesion-worked standard-gauge line was the Denver & Salt Lake Railroad or 'Moffat Road' over Rollins or Corona Pass, at an altitude of 3560 m (11 680 ft). Opened in 1904 it was used until the Moffat Tunnel was completed in 1928. It is now a road.

The record was then held by the branch of the Denver & Rio Grande Western from Leadville up to Ibex, Colorado, at an altitude of 3509 m (11 512 ft). This was closed in 1944.

The Colorado Midland was a standard-gauge railway from Colorado Springs to Leadville and Grand Junction, completed in 1890. West of Leadville it climbed to a 659 m (720 yd) long tunnel under Hagerman Pass at a height of 3515 m (11 530 ft). In 1891 this was replaced by the Busk–Ivanhoe Tunnel, 2864 m (1 mile 1372 yd) long at a height of 3337 m (10 984 ft), considerably shortening the route and reducing the climb and curvature. The entire railway was abandoned in 1919.

The highest summit on a through line in North America is 312 m (10 239 ft) at Tennessee Pass Tunnel on the standard-gauge Denver & Rio Grande Western Railroad north of Leadville. Before the 785 m (859 yd) long tunnel was opened in 1890 the earlier 914 mm (3 ft) gauge line crossed the pass at 3177 m (10 424 ft). In November 1945 a new concrete-lined tunnel, 777 m (850 yd) long, was opened and the original timber-lined tunnel was abandoned.

The Denver, South Park & Pacific Railroad, a 914 mm (3 ft) gauge line completed from Denver to Gunnison in 1882, crossed the Continental Divide in Alpine Tunnel, 539.5 m (590 yd) long, at an elevation of 3512 m (11 523 ft). From Como a branch, completed in 1882, reached Breckenbridge over the Boreas Pass at 3503 m (11 493 ft) and in 1884 over Fremont Pass at 3450 m (11 318 ft) to Leadville. On 12 January 1899 the DSP & P became part of the Colorado & Southern Railroad.

The last train passed through Alpine Tunel on 10 November 1910; the remainder of the system closed in 1937. The section from Leadville to Fremont Pass was rebuilt to standard gauge and reopened in 1943. It is operated by the Burlington Northern, successor to the Colorado & Southern since 1970. At the Fremont Pass this branch reaches a height of 3450 m (11 318ft). A spur from here to a mill of the Climax Molybdenum Company on the pass reaches a record height of 3472 m (11 390 ft). **This is now the highest adhesion-worked railway summit in North America.**

The Silverton Northern (1906–41), 914 mm (3 ft) gauge, reached a height of 3408 m (11 180 ft) at Animas Forks.

The eastern approach to Hagerman Tunnel on the Colorado Midland Railway in 1890 during work on the Busk–Ivanhoe Tunnel in the lower centre.

Above: An early scene on the Ferdinands Nordbahn, the first railway in Austria, 1840.

Right: A Bury 2–2–0 on the London & Birmingham Railway, 1845.

Right: Euston Station on the London & Birmingham Railway, opened in 1838. A scene by T. T. Bury (1811–77).

Above: An early scene on the Ludwigsbahn, Nuremberg to Fürth, the first railway in Germany.

Left: A Canadian Pacific 2-6-0 of 1888 with an inspection car standing on a steel cantilever bridge, a new replacement of a wooden structure 1905. Probably Surprise Creek in the Beaver Valley, in the Selkirk Mountains, British Columbia.

Heraldic devices of various British railways.

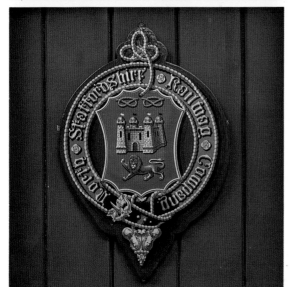

Top: Climbing the 1 in 25 to Cumbres Pass, 3053 m (10 015 ft) round Windy Point on the Cumbres & Toltec Scenic Railroad in Colorado. This is the highest narrow gauge summit, on the longest preserved railway. The leading engine is doing most of the work because it comes off at the summit, but the rear engine has to take the train on to Antonito.

Above: Double Fairlie locomotive *Merddin Emrys* at Porthmadog on the 600 mm (1 ft 11⅝ in) gauge Festiniog Railway, the world's first passenger-carrying narrow-gauge railway. The engine was originally built at the railway's Boston Lodge Works in 1879 and has been several times rebuilt since, last in 1988.

Above right: Trains at the summit station on the Gornergrat Railway, Switzerland 3088.7 m (10 133 ft), the world's first electric rack railway and the highest open-air station in Europe.

Right: Near La Cima on the Morococha branch of the Peru Central Railway, 4817 m (15 806 ft) above sea level, the world's highest railway summit.

Above: Forth Bridge from South Queensferry. Opened 100 years ago on 4 March 1890, this is still the world's greatest railway bridge.

Left: No. 40158 crossing the Forth Bridge on a south-bound express on 10 May 1980. The bridge, still the greatest of its kind in the world, was built 100 years ago.

Top: Mineral train hauled
by QJ Class 2–10–2 on the
Yangtse River Bridge
approach viaduct, Nanking.

Above: Ouse Viaduct on the London to Brighton railway,
designed by Daniel Mocatta and John Urpeth Rastrick, and
built in 1840. It has 37 spans of 9.14 m (30 ft) and a
maximum height of 28 m (92 ft).

Above: The world's longest-span concrete-arch railway bridge, Pfaffenberg–Zwenberg Bridge on the Tauern Railway in Austria.

Left: A mixed train crossing the Landwasser Viaduct on the metre-gauge Rhaetian Railway in Switzerland. The viaduct is 65 m (213 ft) high and is laid out on a curve of 120 m (394 ft) radius and on a gradient of 1 in 50.

Overleaf: Aerial picture of Sydney Harbour Bridge and Opera House, Australia.

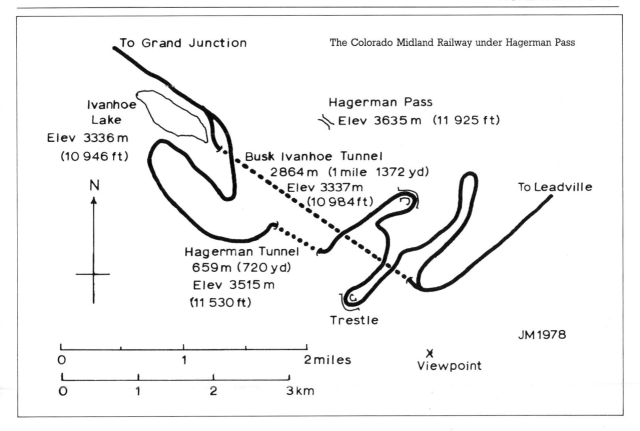

To Grand Junction

The Colorado Midland Railway under Hagerman Pass

Ivanhoe
Lake
Elev 3336 m
(10 946 ft)

N

Hagerman Pass
Elev 3635 m (11 925 ft)

Busk Ivanhoe Tunnel
2864 m (1 mile 1372 yd)
Elev 3337 m
(10 984 ft)

To Leadville

Hagerman Tunnel
659 m (720 yd)
Elev 3515 m
(11 530 ft)

Trestle

JM 1978

0   1   2 miles

0   1   2   3 km

x
Viewpoint

The remaining summits over 3050 m (10 000 ft) were on 914 mm (3 ft) gauge lines:

Marshall Pass, 3306 m (10 846 ft), on the Denver & Rio Grande main line to Gunnison, opened 1881, closed 1955.

Lizard Head, 3124 m (10 248 ft) on the Rio Grande Southern Railroad, opened in 1891 and closed in December 1951.

Colorado & Southern Leadville line, 3111 m (10 207 ft), opened in 1884.

Monarch, Denver & Rio Grande Western 3093 m (10 148 ft), opened in 1883. This is now standard gauge.

Cumbres Pass, 3053 m (10 015 ft), on the Denver & Rio Grande Western from Antonito to Durango, opened in 1880. Today it is operated as a tourist line by the Cumbres & Toltec Scenic Railroad.

OTHER SUMMITS

The highest railway summit in Canada is at the Great Divide on the Canadian Pacific Railway, 1435 m (5332 ft), where it crosses the Alberta–British Columbia boundary.

A railway into Tibet, from Sining to Lhasa, 2200 km (1367 miles), was begun in 1959 by the Chinese People's Republic Railways. It will cross the Tangla Pass between Tsinghai Province and Tibet at an altitude of about 5000 m (16 400 ft), making it the world's highest railway. Much of the southern section will be over 4000 m (13 000 ft) above

The south-east end of the abandoned Busk–Ivanhoe tunnel, 2864 m (1 mile 1372 yd) long, which took the Colorado Midland Railway under Hagerman Pass at a height of 3337 m (10 984 ft), 178 m (564 ft) lower than the earlier Hagerman tunnel. Photographed on 18 August 1977.

sea level and will involve numerous long tunnels, one about 5800 m (3.6 miles) long. The first 835 km (519 miles) was opened on 1 October 1979, including a 32 km

Amid the wild grandeur of northern Perthshire, No. 47635 heads an express from Inverness to Glasgow over Druimuachdar Summit, the highest on British Railways, 452 m (1484 ft) above sea level, on 28 May 1986.

Two snow ploughs used on the former North Eastern Railway between Darlington and Tebay, opened in 1861 and closed in 1962, which crossed the Pennines at a height of 417 m (1370 ft). This line experienced some of the worst snowdrifts in Britain.

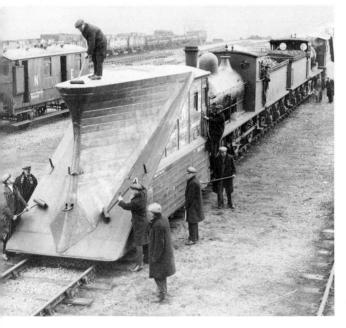

(20 mile) causeway across a salt lake. Passenger trains began running to Telinha, 523 km (325 miles), taking 17 h from Sining, on 20 October 1981.

The highest summit on British Rail is at Druimuachdar, 452 m (1484 ft), between Dalnaspidal and Dalwhinnie on the former Highland Railway main line from Perth to Inverness, opened in 1863.

In 1902 a 12.4 km (7¼ mile) branch was opened from the Caledonian Railway Glasgow–Carlisle main line, at Elvanfoot, to Wanlockhead, the highest village in Scotland. The station was at a height of 431 m (1413 ft), but the line climbed to 456 m (1498 ft). It closed on 2 January 1939.

At Waenavon in South Wales the London & North Western Railway reached a height of 427 m (1400 ft). It was closed to passengers on 5 May 1941 and closed entirely on 23 June 1954.

On the Great Western Railway, England, the terminus of the branch to Princetown on Dartmoor was at a height of 418 m (1373 ft). It was closed on 5 March 1956.

Stainmore Summit, on the former Stockton & Darlington Kirkby Stephen line, was 417 m (1370 ft) above sea-level. It was opened in 1861 and closed on 22 January 1962.

At Weatherhill, County Durham, on the former Stanhope & Tyne Railway, later the North Eastern Railway, the rails stood at 420 m (1378 ft). From here a private mineral branch, opened in 1846, ascended to about 509 m (1670 ft) at the top of the incline down to Rookhope. **This was the highest point reached by standard-gauge rails in Britain.** A private passenger service operated over it until about 1921. It is now abandoned, but is an interesting walk.

The lowest point on British Rail is the bottom of the Severn Tunnel, 43.9 m (144 ft) below Ordnance Datum.

The lowest point reached by any surface railway in the world was in Israel: Jisr el Majame near Samakh (Zemach), 246.5 m (808.4 ft) below sea-level. There the 1042 mm (3 ft 5¼ in) gauge line from Haifa to Derraa crossed the River Jordan, south of the Sea of Galilee, 76.3 km (47.4 miles) from Haifa. At Derraa it joined the Hedjaz Railway from Damascus to Medina. It was begun in 1901 and opened through to Medina, on 31 August 1908. The Haifa-Derraa section was closed in 1949 and all trace of the track in the Jordan Valley has now vanished.

The Nanjiang Railway in China, 476 km (296 miles) between Turpan and Korla in the Xinjiang Uygur Autonomous Region, opened on 7 August 1984, passes through the Turpan Basin, **the lowest in China**, at 154 m (505 ft) below sea level.

By the Salton Sea in California, the Southern Pacific main line is about 61 m (200 ft) below sea level.

The rails in the Seikan tunnel under the Tsugaru Straits between Honshu and Hokkaido in Japan are 240 m (787 ft) below sea level. (See chapter 7.)

Israel Railways have projected a line from Eilat on the Gulf of Aqaba to Sodom south of the Dead Sea, where it will be about 366 m (1200 ft) below sea level. When built, this will be the lowest possible surface railway.

Mine railways are working at far greater depths.

Principal Railway Summits over 1000 m (3250 ft) above sea-level[2]

Summit	Railway	Gauge	Altitude m	Altitude ft
La Cima	Peru Central, Morococha Branch[3]	standard	4 818	15 806
Condor	Bolivian National (former Antofagasta & Bolivia), Potosi Branch[4]	metre	4 787	15 705
Galera Tunnel	Peru Central[3]	standard	4 781	15 688
Caja Real	Yauricocha, Peru[3]	standard	4 602	15 100
Chaucha	Yauricocha, Peru[3]	standard	4 564	14 974
Km 41	Yauricocha, Peru[3]	standard	4 538	14 888
Chorrillos	Argentine Railways (North Transandine)	metre	4 475	14 682
Crucero Alto	Southern of Peru[3]	standard	4 470	14 666
Yuma	Bolivian National (former Antofagasta & Bolivia)[4]	metre	4 401	14 440
Alcacocha	Cerro de Pasco, Peru	standard	4 385	14 385
La Raya	Southern of Peru	standard	4 314	14 153
Pike's Peak	Manitou & Pike's Peak, Colorado, USA	standard[1]	4 302	14 109
Jeneral Lagos	Bolivian National (former Arica–La Paz)	metre	4 257	13 963
La Cima	Cerro de Pasco, Peru	standard	4 214	13 822
Cuesta Colorado	Bolivian National	metre	4 137	13 573
El Alto	Guaqui–La Paz	metre	4 106	13 471
Escoriani	Bolivian National	metre	4 057	13 310
Between Potosi and Sucre	Bolivian National	metre	4 033	13 231
Comanche	Bolivian National (former Arica–La Paz)	metre	4 031	13 225
Kenko	Bolivian National (former Antofagasta & Bolivia)	metre	4 004	13 134
Muñano	Argentine Railways (North Transandine)	metre	4 000	13 120
Ascotan	Bolivian National (former Antofagasta & Bolivia)	metre	3 959	12 982
Socompa	Antofagasta–Salta (Argentina)[5]	metre	3 908	12 822
Tres Cruces	Argentine Railways	metre	3 693	12 116
Urbina	Guyaquil–Quito (Ecuador)	1067 mm (3 ft 6 in)	3 609	11 841
Pumahuasi	Argentine Railways	metre	3 559	11 674
Climax spur	Burlington Northern (former Colorado & Southern), USA	standard	3 472	11 390
Jungfraujoch	Jungfrau, Switzerland	metre	3 454	11 332
Fremont Pass	Burlington Northern (former Colorado & Southern), USA	standard	3 450	11 318
Villazon	Villazon–Atocha (Bolivian National)	metre	3 447	11 308
Iturbe	Argentine Railways	metre	3 343	10 965
La Cumbre	Chilean Transandine	metre[1]	3 191	10 466
Tennessee Pass Tunnel	Denver & Rio Grande Western, Colorado, USA	standard	3 116	10 239
Monarch	Denver & Rio Grande Western, Colorado, USA	standard	3 093	10 148

Summit	Railway	Gauge	Altitude	
			m	ft
Gornergrat	Gornergrat, Switzerland	metre[1]	3 088	10 134
La Cima	National Railways of Mexico	standard	3 054	10 020
Cumbres Pass	Cumbres & Toltec Scenic Railroad (former Denver & Rio Grande Western), Colorado, USA	914 mm (3 ft)	3 053	10 015
El Oro	National Railways of Mexico	standard	3 041	9 977
Silverton	Denver & Rio Grande Western, Colorado, USA	914 mm (3 ft)	2 831	9 288
Veta Pass	Denver & Rio Grande Western, Colorado, USA	standard	2 817	9 242
Moffat Tunnel	Denver & Rio Grande Western, Colorado, USA	standard	2 817	9 242
Timboroa	East African	metre	2 783	9 131
Schneefernerhaus	Bavarian Zugspitz, Germany	metre[1]	2 650	8 692
Nanacamilpa	National Railways of Mexico	standard	2 561	8 400
Acocotla	National Railways of Mexico	standard	2 542	8 337
Near Addis Ababa	Franco Ethiopian	metre	2 470	8 104
Sherman	Union Pacific, Wyoming, USA	standard	2 443	8 013
Las Vigas	National Railways of Mexico	standard	2 415	7 923
Near Asmara	Northern Ethiopian	950 mm (3 ft 1½ in)	2 412	7 911
Kikuyu	East African	metre	2 395	7 857
Asmara	Eritrean	metre	2 394	7 854
Rothornkulm	Brienzer Rothorn, Switzerland	800 mm (2 ft 7½ in)[1]	2 349	7 707
Quezaltenango	Guatemalan State	standard	2 332	7 650
Raton Pass	Santa Fé, USA, Colorado/New Mexico	standard	2 312	7 586
Soldier Summit	Denver & Rio Grande Western, Utah	standard	2 268	7 440
Ghoom	North Eastern, India (former Darjeeling Himalayan)	610 mm (2 ft)	2 258	7 407
Bernina Hospice	Rhaetian, Switzerland	metre	2 257	7 403
Asit	Turkish State	standard	2 256	7 402
Kan Mehtarzai	Pakistan	762 mm (2 ft 6 in)	2 222	7 291
Nilgiri Hills	Nilgiri, India	metre[1]	2 217	7 275
Nurabad	Iran State (Trans Iranian, southern section)	standard	2 217	7 275
Furka Tunnel	Furka–Oberalp, Switzerland	metre	2 163	7 098
Sierra Nevada	Southern Pacific, USA	standard	2 147	7 043
Gaduk	Iran State (Trans Iranian, northern section)	standard	2 112	6 929
Tip Top, near Colorado Springs	Chicago, Rock Island & Pacific, USA	standard	2 097	6 880
Nederhorst	South African	1065 mm (3 ft 6 in)	2 095	6 871
Pilatus	Pilatus, Switzerland	800 mm (2 ft 7½ in)[1]	2 070	6 791
Kleine Scheidegg	Wengernalp, Switzerland	800 mm (2 ft 7½ in)[1]	2 061	6 762
Oberalp Pass	Furka–Oberalp, Switzerland	metre	2 045	6 711
Rochers de Naye	Glion–Rochers de Naye, Switzerland	800 mm (2 ft 7½ in)[1]	1 973	6 473
Belfast	South African	1065 mm (3 ft 6 in)	1 970	6 463
Schynige Platte	Schynige Platte, Switzerland	800 mm (2 ft 7½ in)[1]	1 967	6 453
Nuria	Mountain Railways Co., Spain (Ribas–Caralps–Nuria)	metre[1]	1 964	6 443
Shelabagh	Pakistan	1676 mm (5 ft 6 in)	1 950	6 398
Near Butte, Montana	Burlington Northern (former Northern Pacific), USA	standard	1 929	6 329
Near Butte, Montana	Chicago, Milwaukee & Pacific, USA	standard	1 925	6 317
Mount Washington	Mount Washington, New Hampshire, USA	standard[1]	1 918	6 293
Montenvers	Chamonix–Montenvers, France	metre[1]	1 913	6 276
Pattipola	Sri Lanka Government	1676 mm (5 ft 6 in)	1 898	6 226
Albula Tunnel	Rhaetian, Switzerland	metre	1 823	5 981
Shafter	Western Pacific, USA	standard	1 799	5 903
Hoch Schneeberg	Austrian Federal	metre[1]	1 798	5 898
Near Zebdãni	Syria	1050 mm (3 ft 5½ in)	1 794	5 885
Kolpore	Pakistan	1676 mm (5 ft 6 in)	1 791	5 874
Puerto de Navacerrada	Spanish National	1676 mm (5 ft 6 in)	1 761	5 777

Summit	Railway	Gauge	Altitude	
			m	*ft*
Rigi-Kulm	Arth–Goldau–Rigi; and Rigi, Switzerland	standard[1]	1 750	5 741
Johannesburg	South African	1065 mm (3 ft 6 in)	1 748	5 735
Arosa	Rhaetian, Switzerland	metre	1 742	5 715
Wendelstein	Wendelsteinbahn, Austria	metre[1]	1 723	5 653
Near Marandellas	Rhodesia Railways	1067 mm (3 ft 6 in)	1 688	5 538
Between Tananarive and Antsirabe	Madagascar Railways	metre	1 687	5 534
Zermatt	Brig–Visp–Zermatt, Switzerland	metre[1]	1 650	5 415
Wolfgang	Rhaetian, Switzerland	metre	1 633	5 358
Great Divide	Canadian Pacific	standard	1 625	5 332
Monte Generoso	Monte Generoso, Lugano, Switzerland	800 mm (2 ft 7½ in)[1]	1 620	5 315
Between Peking and Suiyuan	Peking–Suiyuan, China	standard	1 585	5 200
Col de la Perche, Cerdagne	French National	metre	1 585	5 200
Col de Puymorens tunnel, Toulouse–Barcelona	French National	standard	1 561	5 121
Near El Alto	Costa Rica Northern	1067 mm (3 ft 6 in)	1 547	5 075
Paisano, Texas	Southern Pacific, USA	standard	1 547	5 075
Taurus	Turkish State	standard	1 494	4 900
Between Beirut and Zahle	Lebanon State	1050 mm (3 ft 5½ in)	1 487	4 879
Leysin	Aigle–Leysin, Switzerland	metre[1]	1 453	4 767
La Molina	Spanish National	1676 mm (5 ft 6 in)	1 420	4 659
Kalaw	Union of Burma Railways	metre	1 405	4 610
La Cañada	Spanish National	1676 mm (5 ft 6 in)	1 380	4 526
Near Ben Lomond	State Rail Authority of New South Wales, Australia	standard	1 377	4 517
Brenner Pass	Austrian Federal	standard	1 370	4 495
Mekiri	Nigerian	1067 mm (3 ft 6 in)	1 370	4 495
Crows Nest Pass	Canadian Pacific	standard	1 359	4 459
Le Buet (Chamonix)	French National	metre	1 337	4 386
Near Batna	Algerian National	standard	1 313	4 308
Arlberg Tunnel	Austrian Federal	standard	1 313	4 308
Mont Cenis Tunnel	Italian State	standard	1 306	4 284
Taugevatn, near Finse	Norwegian State (Bergen–Oslo line)	standard	1 301	4 265
Saanenmöser	Montreux–Bernese Oberland, Switzerland	metre	1 275	4 183
Rivisondoli	Italian State	standard	1 267	4 156
Lötschberg Tunnel	Bern–Lötschberg–Simplon, Switzerland	standard	1 240	4 068
Near Horse Lake	British Columbia Railway, Canada	standard	1 208	3 963
Canfrane	French/Spanish National	standard	1 188	3 898
Tauern Tunnel	Austrian Federal	standard	1 183	3 381
Col de la Croix Haute	French National (Grenoble–Veynes)	standard	1 164	3 827
Connaught Tunnel	Canadian Pacific	standard	1 154	3 787
St Gotthard Tunnel	Swiss Federal	standard	1 151	3 780
Château de Lugarde	French National (Bort–Neussargues)	standard	1 136	3 727
Yellowhead Pass	Canadian National	standard	1 133	3 717
Maan	Hedjaz	1050 mm (3 ft 5¼ in)	1 128	3 700
Snowdon	Snowdon Mountain, Wales	800 mm (2 ft 7½ in)[1]	1 064	3 493
Arcomie	French National	standard	1 052	3 451
Mont Dore	French National	standard	1 049	3 442
Kolasin	Jugoslav State	standard	1 032	3 385
La Bastide	French National Cévennes	standard	1 025	3 363

[1] Whole or part rack.

[2] Abandoned railway summits in Colorado, USA, over 3050 m (10 000 ft) are listed earlier in this chapter.

[3] The Central and Southern Railways of Peru and the Yauricocha Railway became part of the Peruvian National Railways on 1 December 1972.

[4] In 1907 the Antofagasta & Bolivia Railway built a branch from Ollogue in Chile, close to the Bolivian border, to copper-mines at Collahuasi, reaching a height of 4826 m (15 835 ft) at Punto Alto. It is now disused beyond Yuma, 4401 m (14 440 ft). The Condor summit on the Potosi Branch is now **the highest over which passenger trains are worked**. The Bolivian lines of the A. & B. were nationalized on 1 November 1964.

[5] The Antofagasta–Salta Railway is divided between the Chilean National Railways and the Argentine Railways North Western Region.

TRANSALPINE RAILWAYS

The first transalpine railways were those over the Semmering, opened on 15 May 1854, and the Brenner Pass (Austria–Italy) opened on 24 August 1867. This is the only main line which crosses the Alps without a major tunnel, and its altitude of 1370 m (4496 ft) makes it one of the highest main lines in Europe.

The only metre-gauge transalpine route was opened on 1 July 1903 and forms part of the Rhaetian Railway in Switzerland. Between Chur and St Moritz the railway passes through the Albula Tunnel, 5865 m (3 miles 134 yd) long, at an altitude of 1823 m (5981 ft). It is the highest of the principal Alpine tunnels.

From St Moritz to Tirano in Italy the Bernina Railway, opened throughout on 5 July 1910, crosses the Alps in the open at an altitude of 2257 m (7403 ft). **It is the highest through railway in Europe.**

The first railway across the main range of the Alps was opened over the Mont Cenis Pass on 15 June 1868. It operated with the centre-rail friction-drive system invented in 1863–9 by John Barraclough Fell. It worked until 18 September 1871 when the Fréjus or Mont Cenis Tunnel was opened. This, **the first of the major Alpine tunnels**, was begun on 31 August 1857 and took 14 years to complete. It is 13 657 m (8 miles 555 yd) long and links the Italian and French railway systems, but is operated by the Italian State Railways.

When construction of the tunnel began it was wholly in the Kingdom of Piedmont. The eastern end of the line became French territory in 1861. The French Government then took over a half share of the construction cost from King Victor Emmanuel. When opened, the line was operated by the Paris, Lyon, Mediterranean Co.

The St Gotthard Railway and Tunnel were opened to goods traffic on 1 January 1882 and to passenger trains on 1 June 1882. The 14 998 m (9 miles 662 yd) long tunnel with double track, was begun on 13 September 1872. The engineer Louis Favre (b. 1826) died of a heart attack inside the tunnel on 18 July 1879. The two bores met on 28 February 1880.

In this tunnel, in 1879, diamonds were successfully used for the first time in rock drills.

The principal railway through the Alps from east to west is the Arlberg Railway in Austria. It was completed with the opening on 20 September 1884 of the Arlberg Tunnel for double track, 10 250 m (6 miles 650 yd) long. It traverses a greater distance through magnificent mountain scenery than any other railway in Europe.

The Simplon Railway between Switzerland and Italy was completed with the opening on 1 June 1906 of the first single-line Simplon Tunnel, 19 803 m (12 miles 537 yd) long. The second tunnel was opened on 16 October 1922 and is 19 823 m (12 miles 559 yd) long.

The second railway between Austria and Italy was opened by the Austrian Federal Railways on 7 July 1909 after the completion of the Tauern Tunnel, 8551 m (5 miles 551 yd) long, near Bad Gastein. (See also chapter 6.)

The value of the Simplon route was greatly increased by the opening of the single-track Berne–Lötschberg–Simplon Railway on 15 July 1913. It included the 14 612 m (9 miles 140 yd) double-track Lötschberg Tunnel under the Berner Oberland Mountains. The tunnel deviates from a straight line to avoid a section where, on 24 July 1908, an inrush of water and rock caused the loss of 25 lives. The railway has now been doubled throughout.

TRANSCONTINENTAL RAILWAYS

The longest railway in the world is the Trans-Siberian, from Moscow to Vladivostok—9297 km (5777 miles). It was opened in sections. The first goods train reached Irkutsk on 27 August 1898.

Through communication was established on 3 November 1901 by ferry across Lake Baikal, and via the Chinese Eastern Railway through Manchuria. In 1904, while Lake Baikal was frozen over, rails were laid across the ice, but the first locomotive plunged through a gap and was lost.

The Circum–Baikal line, round the south of the lake, was opened on 25 September 1904. The 1931 km (1200 mile) Amur line, opening up through travel entirely on Russian soil, was begun in 1908 and completed in 1916.

According to the Thomas Cook International Timetable the Trans-Siberian Express covers the journey in 7 days 2 hours.

The Baikal–Amur Northern Main Line, 3145 km (1954 miles) long, begun in 1938, will shorten the distance over the Trans-Siberian Railway by about 500 km (310 miles). The far eastern section, Komsomolsk–Urgal, 350 km (217 miles), was opened on 2 July 1979 and the Kunerma–Krasnoiarsk section in May 1982. Its construction involved 380 million m³ of earthwork, including 200 m³ of hard rock or permafrost ground. There are nine tunnels totalling 32 km (20 miles), 139 large bridges or viaducts and 3762 smaller bridges or culverts, on the whole route. The largest bridges at present completed are across the Lena, 500 m long; Amur, 1500 m; and Zeya, 1100 m. Of the longest tunnels, three are finished: Baikal, *c.* 6700 m (4.2 miles); Nagorny, *c.* 1300 m (0.8 mile); and Dusse-Alin, *c.* 1800 m (1.1 miles). The longest tunnel, Severomuisky, or North Mui, which was begun in 1978, is *c.* 15 400 m (9.6 miles) long, of which 4600 m (2.9 miles) are completed, and the Kodar tunnel, *c.* 2100 m (1.3 miles), is started. Work in North Mui tunnel is hampered by hot and cold springs. The engineers decided to go round it by a 30 km (18.6 mile) avoiding line on which the first track was completed on 14 July 1981. This line climbs 1000 m (3281 ft) and has numerous bridges but it is not wholly suitable for revenue traffic. Another deviation, 60 km (37 miles) long, is under construction for freight and passengers. It has three tunnels totalling 6 km (3.7 miles).

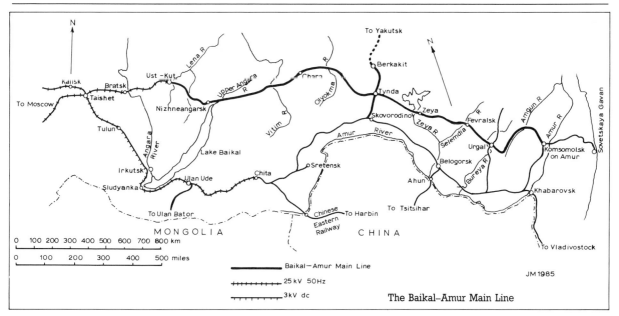

N

To Yakutsk

Berkakit

Kaiisk Ust -Kut Chara
Bratsk Tynda
Taishet Nizhneangarsk Skovorodino Zeya
To Moscow Fevralsk
Tulun Selemdia Urgal Komsomolsk on Amur
Lake Baikal Belogorsk
Irkutsk Amur River Ahun
Sludyanka Sretensk Khabarovsk

To Ulan Bator Chita
Chinese To Harbin To Tsitsihar
MONGOLIA Eastern Railway CHINA

0 100 200 300 400 500 600 700 800 km
0 100 200 300 400 500 miles

To Vladivostock

——————— Baikal–Amur Main Line
+++++++++ 25 kV 50Hz
————————— 3kV dc

JM 1985

The Baikal–Amur Main Line

The western portion between Ust Kut and Tynda was brought into use early in 1984 and a passenger service was introduced between Tynda and Moscow, 7560 km (4698 miles). The section from Tynda to Urgal was opened on 7 November 1984, but although through trains are running, the line is still not ready to be handed over to USSR Railways for full operation. Work is now to go ahead on the 830 km (516 miles) from Berkakit to Yakutsk. (See map.)

The construction of more than 1200 km (746 miles) presented numerous unique problems. For 9 months of each year snow falls often to depths of 2 m (6.5 ft). Much of the ground is permanently frozen to depths of 5 to 300 m (16–984 ft) at temperatures of −1° to −5°C (30° to 23°F). Air temperatures range from −58° to 36°C (−74° to 97°F); even at the latter temperature, the permafrost ground thaws down to only 1 to 1.5 m (3 to 5 ft). Care has to be taken to preserve the natural conditions maintained by the permafrost area. There is high earthquake activity, sometimes up to 6, 8 and 9 on the Richter scale; from 1979 to 1982 there were 4000 earthquakes in the area. For 750 km (466 miles) from the western end the railway crosses high mountain ranges: the Baikal, North Mui, Udokan, and Stanovoy. Other construction difficulties were caused by thermal karsts (eroded limestone liable to sudden collapse), heaving ground, talus (scree slopes), areas threatened by avalanches and rock slides, and areas of saturated bog. Many bridges and buildings are supported on piles, some driven to depths as great as 28 m (92 ft). Information such as this makes it understandable that construction has taken so long.

Practically all excavation and track laying is by mechanical means. Track lies on a bed of sand 200 mm (8 in) thick and rock ballast 250 mm (10 in) deep. Rails of 65 kg/m (131 lb/yd) are in 25 m (82 ft) lengths, laid on timber sleepers 46 per length, 1840 per km. The railway will open up vast mineral resources and is expected to generate employment for 40 000 staff, bringing yet more prob-

lems, such as water supply and sewage disposal. All buildings must be highly insulated and triple-glazed to make human life possible in this inhospitable region.

In the mountain section electric traction at 25 kV 50 Hz will be used, with thyristor-controlled locomotives of class VL80R of 6520 kW, fitted with regenerative braking. Tests have been carried out with eight-axle VL84 class locomotives of 7600 kW.

Electrification of the Trans-Siberian Railway, partly on 3000 V dc and more recently on 25 kV 50 Hz, had reached Karimskaya, 6284 km (3905 miles) from Moscow, by 1980. By 1990 USSR Railways hopes to have electrified the entire Trans-Siberian Railway.

The first railway from the Atlantic to the Pacific was the 1524 mm (5 ft) gauge Panama Railroad, 77 km (48 miles) long, across the Isthmus of Panama, between Aspinwall and Panama. It was opened on 28 January 1855. Surveys were made as early as 1828. Its Atlantic end is further west than its Pacific end.

The first big step towards an American transcontinental railroad was taken on 21 April 1856 when trains first crossed the Mississippi between Rock Island, Illinois, and Davenport, Iowa.

The first American transcontinental railroad was completed on 10 May 1869 when the last spike was driven at Promontory, north of the Great Salt Lake, Utah, uniting the Central Pacific and Union Pacific railroads. Because the point of joining had not been previously established, and because the companies were receiving up to $48 000 a mile in Federal loans for track-laying, rival grading gangs passed one another and the UP gangs went on constructing 362 km (225 miles) of parallel grading until they were officially stopped. The section from Promontory to Ogden was taken over by the Central Pacific.

The railway ran from Omaha, Nebraska, to Sacramento,

California, 2776 km (1725 miles). The old Western Pacific Railroad (no relation to the present Western Pacific) was opened from Sacramento to Oakland opposite San Francisco, a further 148 km (92 miles), on 8 November 1869. It was consolidated with the Central Pacific on 23 June 1870. Passengers crossed by ferry to San Francisco.

Through communication between the Atlantic and Pacific coasts was finally established in 1877 when the first bridge was opened across the Missouri near Omaha. The present bridge, 533.4 m (1750 ft) long, was built in 1886.

The Central Pacific became a part of the Southern Pacific Railroad when that company was formed in 1884. It was fully absorbed in 1958.

The Lucin Cut-off across the Great Salt Lake, totalling 166 km (103 miles), was opened on 8 March 1904 and shortened the journey between Ogden and Lucin by 67.6 km (42 miles), making the original Promontory route redundant. (See 'The world's longest railway water crossing', p. 84.) The old line, however, with its curves equivalent to 11 complete circles, was not abandoned until 1942.

A short section at Promontory was relaid in 1969 for the enactment of the Centenary celebrations. For the benefit of crowds of visitors the 'last spike' suffered numerous drivings and extractions.

The first railway across Canada, the Canadian Pacific, was completed at a place named Craigellachie in Eagle Pass, British Columbia, when the eastern and western sections were joined on 7 November 1885. Its completion within ten years was a condition of British Columbia entering the Confederation, on 20 July 1871. The first sod was cut on 1 June 1875 at Fort William, on the left bank of the Kaministiquia River. The main contract was signed on 21 October 1880, by which year 1126 km (700 miles) were under construction. The Canadian Pacific Railway Company was incorporated on 15 February 1881; construction began on 2 May 1881, and throughout 1882 4 km (2.5 miles) of track were laid every day. The Prairie section was finished as far as Calgary on 18 August 1883 and the Great Lakes section on 16 May 1885, thanks to the devotion and energy of William Cornelius Van Horne. The section through the rock and muskeg north of Lake Superior was almost as difficult as the construction through the British Columbia mountains.

Transcontinental services began with the departure of the first train from Montreal on 28 June 1886. It arrived at Port Moody on 4 July. The 19.3 km (12 mile) extension to Vancouver was opened on 23 May 1887.

From Montreal to Vancouver, the 4633 km (2879 mile) journey takes 3 days on 'The Canadian' transcontinental train.

An alternative route through the Rockies at Crow's Nest Pass, through a rich coal region close to the USA border, was begun in 1897 and completed in 1930. It crosses the great Lethbridge Viaduct over the Oldman (formerly Belly) River, and another viaduct 45.8 m (147 ft) high over the same river at Fort Macleod. (See also Tunnels, chapter 7.)

Top: Two days before the driving of the Golden Spike at Promontory on 10 May 1869, one of the last westbound covered wagon trains met the first train from California on the north shore of the Great Salt Lake, Utah. This was Govenor Leland Stanford's special train pulled by the 4-4-0 *Jupiter* on its way to the last spike ceremony a few miles east. Photographed by Alfred A. Hart of Sacramento on 8 May 1869.

Above: Donald A. Smith (later Lord Strathcona and Mount Royal) driving the last spike on the Canadian Pacific Railway at Craigellachie at 09.22 Pacific Time on 7 November 1885.

Canada's second transcontinental railway began in eastern Canada as the Grand Trunk Railway. By 1900 the GTR owned and operated a network of lines covering Ontario and Quebec. This included the former Great Western Railway with which it amalgamated in 1882, and also the Grand Trunk Western to Chicago, and a line from Montreal to the Atlantic at Portland, Maine. After

unsuccessful proposals to extend westwards through the USA, the GTR finally agreed that the Government should build the Eastern Division of the National Transcontinental Railway between Moncton and Winnipeg. The newly created Grand Trunk Pacific Railway, as a subsidiary of the GTR, should build from Winnipeg to the Pacific Coast at Prince Rupert, 885 km (550 miles) north of Vancouver. With Government aid the GTP was built to the same high standards as the Grand Trunk had been.

Both the National Transcontinental Eastern Division and the Grand Trunk Pacific were begun in 1905. The

Three Canadian Pacific ST11 4–6–0s pounding up the 'Big Hill' in the Kicking Horse Pass with eight coaches of the transcontinental train on the 6.6 km (4.1 miles) of 1 in 22¼ before the spiral tunnels were built in 1909.

National Transcontinental was opened in stages from June to November 1915. It included the great Quebec Bridge (qv) over the St Lawrence, not opened until 1917. The GTP was completed at a point 671 km (417 miles) east of Prince Rupert on 7 April 1914 and complete services began in September.

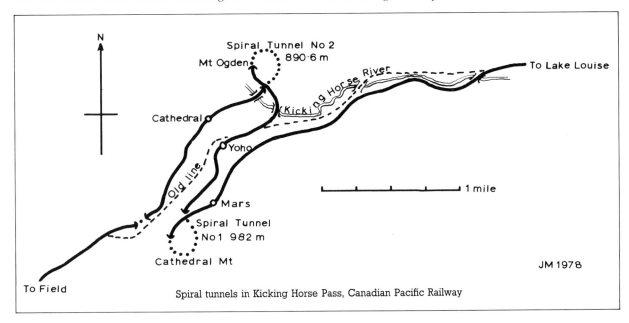

Spiral tunnels in Kicking Horse Pass, Canadian Pacific Railway

From Winnipeg, the GTP passed through Edmonton and through the Yellowhead Pass. There it made the lowest crossing of the Rockies, with the easiest grades, of any North American transcontinental railway.

The Canadian Northern Railway, Canada's third transcontinental line, was inspired by two men, William Mackenzie (1849–1923) and Donald Mann (1853–1934). It was made up of a number of separately incorporated railways and by 1903 had grown to 554 km (344 miles) in the east, and to 2192 km (1362 miles) in the west. By 1905 the western lines had reached Edmonton and Prince Albert, and in the east Hawkesbury was linked to Ottawa. Surveys through the Yellowhead Pass began in 1908 and on 4 October 1915 the Canadian Northern was opened to Vancouver, through the Fraser River Canyon which it shared with the Canadian Pacific. The Canadian Northern had now grown to 15 067 km (9362 miles) and extended from Quebec to Vancouver, with additional lines in Nova Scotia and in the USA (the Duluth, Winnipeg & Pacific).

In 1917, to aid the war effort, over 161 km (100 miles) each of the Grand Trunk Pacific and the Canadian Northern tracks were removed between Lobstick Junction, Alberta, through the Yellowhead Pass, to Red Pass Junction, where the Prince Rupert and Vancouver lines diverged, to make a joint line of the two competing sections.

One of the last and largest works on the Canadian Northern was Mount Royal Tunnel, 5073 m (3 miles 268 yd), which carried the line directly into Montreal. It

Eastbound 'Super Continental' of the Canadian National Railways crossing Yellowhead Pass, 1133 m (3717 ft), the lowest crossing of the Canadian Rockies.

was opened on 21 October 1918. Shortly afterwards it became part of Canadian National Railways, the formation of which was described in chapter 4.

In the USA no single railroad company operates from the Atlantic to the Pacific, with the possible exception of the Southern Pacific (see below). Following the Union Pacific–Central Pacific, the other major transcontinental routes were completed as follows:

☐ **The Atchison, Topeka & Santa Fe** from Kansas City joined the Southern Pacific from California at Deming, New Mexico, on 8 March 1881. The Santa Fe completed its own through route from Chicago to California on 1 May 1888.

☐ **The Southern Pacific** from California to New Orleans on the Gulf of Mexico was formally opened on 12 January 1883. It was completed near the old bridge across the Pecos River at its confluence with the Rio Grande, at the border with Mexico.

☐ **The Northern Pacific, the first to the Pacific North-west**, was completed at Gold Creek, Montana, on 8 September 1883.

☐ **The Oregon Short Line and the Oregon Railway & Navigation Company**, forming the Union Pacific route to the Pacific North-west, were connected at Huntingdon, Oregon, on 25 November 1884.

□ **The Great Northern Railway** between the Great Lakes and Puget Sound at Everett, Washington, was completed on 6 January 1893.

On the Pacific Coast Extension of the **Chicago, Milwaukee & St Paul** (now the Chicago, Milwaukee St Paul & Pacific, or The Milwaukee Road) the last spike was driven at Garrison, Montana, on 19 May 1909.

□ **The Western Pacific**, the western extension of the Denver & Rio Grande main line from Denver to Salt Lake City, was opened throughout to San Francisco on 22 August 1910, making its famous passage through the Feather River Canyon and forming, with the D & RGW, one of the finest scenic routes through the mountains.

The first train from the Atlantic to the Pacific was the 'Transcontinental Excursion' consisting of Pullman 'Hotel Cars', sponsored by the Boston Board of Trade in May 1870. It took 8 days from Boston to San Francisco. A daily newspaper was published on the journey.

The first regular through sleeping-car service between the Atlantic and Pacific coasts of the USA did not begin until as late as 31 March 1946. Before that a change had to be made at Chicago or St Louis.

The first South African transcontinental railway linked Cape Town and Durban at Heidelberg in the Transvaal on 10 October 1895.

Another African transcontinental route was completed in 1928. It runs from Benguela, Angola, via the Congo and Rhodesia to Beira in Portuguese East Africa.

The standard gauge Trans-Australian Railway from Port Augusta to Kalgoorlie, 1693 km (1052 miles), was opened on 22 October 1917. Across the Nullarbor Plain it traverses the world's longest straight stretch, 478 km (297 miles) long. At Kalgoorlie it connected with the Western Australian 1067 mm (3 ft 6 in) gauge line from Perth. With the conversion of the Kalgoorlie–Perth section (Western Australia) and of the section from Port Pirie to Broken Hill (South Australia) from 1067 mm to standard gauge, completed on 29 November 1969, a through route entirely on standard gauge was opened up from Perth to Sydney, 3960 km (2461 miles). The section from Perth to Northern is dual-gauged. The 'Indian Pacific Express' was inaugurated on 1 March 1970 by the opening of the new standard-gauge route from Sydney to Perth.

In 1889 an isolated 1067 mm gauge line was opened from Darwin, Northern Territory, southwards to Pine Creek—a distance of 233 km (145 miles). It was extended in stages, reaching Larrimah just north of Birdum in 1929, a total of 503 km (312 miles), leaving a gap of 1000 km (622 miles) to Alice Springs, terminus of the 1067 mm gauge Central Australian Railway from Marree.

This was closed on 1 January 1981 following the opening, by HRH Princess Alexandra on 9 October 1980, of a new line from Tarcoola, on the Trans-Australian Railway in South Australia, to Alice Springs, 832 km (517 miles). This is the first section of the standard-gauge North–South Continental Railway. Construction began in April

1975 and completion in 5½ years is probably a record for a line over 500 miles long. The new railway follows a different route from the former 1067 mm (3 ft 6 in) gauge line completed on 2 August 1929. Work has already begun on the 1504 km (934 mile) extension to Darwin, due for completion in 1988–9.

The Transandine Railway between Los Andes, Chile, and Mendoza, Argentina, was opened on 5 April 1910. It is metre gauge with Abt triple-rack sections, and climbs to an altitude of 3191 m (10 466 ft) at the 3167 m (3463 yd) long La Cumbre Tunnel.

At Mendoza it connects with the 1676 mm (5 ft 6 in) gauge line from Buenos Aires. The total distance is 1448 km (900 miles).

Passenger services between Los Andes and Mendoza were suspended indefinitely in 1979 because of a substantial drop in demand. Freight traffic has increased.

The Northern Transandine Railway from Antofagasta, Chile, to Salta, a distance of 904 km (562 miles), is metre gauge and was completed in 1948. It reaches a height of 4475 m (14 682 ft) at Chorrillos; 4000 m (13 120 ft) at Muñano and over 3050 m (10 000 ft) at four other summits. At Salta it connects with the metre-gauge main line from Buenos Aires.

One of the most formidable railway construction projects of recent times is being undertaken by Soviet Railways (SZD). This is a railway across the Caucasus, 182 km (113

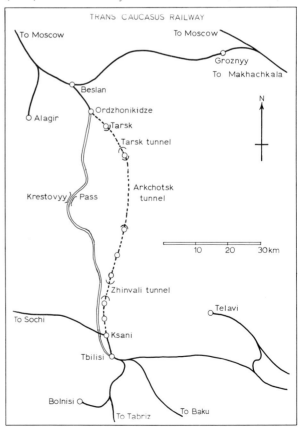

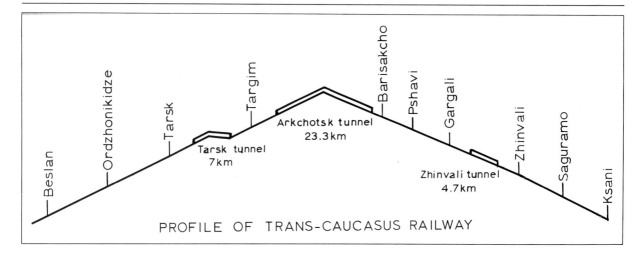

PROFILE OF TRANS-CAUCASUS RAILWAY

miles) long from Ordzhonikidze to Ksani north of Tbilisi (Tiflis). The railway climbs to a summit of 1400 m (4593 ft) inside the 23.3 km (14.5 mile) long Arkchotsk Tunnel, with gradients of 1.23 per cent (1 in 81) on the north side and 0.95 per cent (1 in 105) on the south. Altogether there will be 26 tunnels totalling 42 km (26 miles) including Tarsk Tunnel 7 km (4.3 miles) long and Zhinvah tunnel 4.7 km (2.9 miles) long; 40 viaducts totalling 6 km (3.7 miles) and 11 km (6.8 miles) of retaining walls. Earthworks amount to 22 million m³ (777 million ft³). Some measure of the difficulties to be faced can be gained from the fact that the line was first projected in the 1860s and, despite its strategic importance, it is only by modern engineering techniques and experience gained on the Baikal–Amur Main Line that construction can be tackled. The railway will be double track with rails 65 kg/m (131 lb/yd) and will be electrified at 25 kV 50 Hz. Trains up to 4000 tonnes will be hauled by single VL85 eight-axle electric locomotives rated at 10 000 kW (13 410 hp). Journey times between Moscow and Tiflis will be shortened by 24 h for freight and 7 to 8 h for passenger trains. Work is expected to take about ten years.

NARROW-GAUGE RAILWAYS (less than 1 m gauge)

The current fascination with narrow-gauge railways is generally speaking because they stopped progressing about 1900–10 and so represent steam railways of that period or earlier.

Many such lines were built to open up backward areas and their ultimate closure in the face of road competition can be seen more as a measure of their success than of their failure.

The world's first public narrow-gauge railway was the 600 mm (1 ft 11⅝ in) gauge Festiniog Railway in Wales, engineered by James Spooner (1789–1856) and opened for slate traffic on 20 April 1836. Trains ran by gravity from Blaenau Ffestiniog to Portmadoc and empties were pulled back by horses which rode down on the trains. Steam locomotives were introduced, for the first time on a

narrow-gauge railway, in 1863 by Charles Easton Spooner (qv), son of James. Passenger traffic officially began on 6 January 1865, but passengers had been carried unofficially for years before that. Traffic declined during the Second World War and the railway was closed in 1946. In 1954 the Festiniog Railway Society Limited was formed, and passenger services were resumed on 23 July 1955.

James Spooner was also engineer to the 686 mm (2 ft 3 in) gauge Tal-y-llyn and Corris railways in Wales.

The first narrow-gauge railroad in the USA was the 914 mm (3 ft) gauge Denver & Rio Grande Railway from Denver to Colorado Springs, opened on 26 October 1871. The locomotive *Montezuma* was the first narrow-gauge passenger engine built or operated in the USA.

After attaining a maximum of about 4800 km (3000 miles) the 914 mm (3 ft) gauge in Colorado was finally abandoned in the late 1960s. The 72 km (45 mile) long Durango–Silverton Branch and the Alamosa–Durango line between Antonito and Chama, 105 km (65 miles), over the Cumbres Pass, 3053 m (10 015 ft), were preserved as tourist attractions. At present the Cumbres & Toltec Scenic Railroad (CATS) is the **longest preserved railway in the world**, and the highest, and to many the most scenic.

Typical of the Colorado 3 ft lines was the Uintah Railroad which, in 21 km (13 miles), had 233 curves from 434 m (1425 ft) to 22 m (72 ft) radius, including 27 sharper than 34.7 m (114 ft) radius. It had 8 km (5 miles) at a record 7.5 per cent or 1 in 13.3 and crossed into Utah at 2572 m (8437 ft) at Baxter Pass. It was abandoned in 1938.

In contrast, the Denver & Rio Grande Western between Villa Grove and Alamosa, Colorado, in the heart of the Rockies, was dead straight for 85 km (52.82 miles), falling from 2408 m (7900 ft) to 2301 m (7550 ft) at Alamosa.

The 3 ft gauge was used on the White Pass & Yukon Railway, 178.5 km (111 miles) long, of which 32 km (20 miles) were in Alaska and the rest in Canada. It was **the first railway in Alaska**, opened in stages from 21 July 1898 and completely from Skagway to Whitehorse on 8 June 1900. This railway is now closed.

The first 610 mm (2 ft) gauge line in the USA was the Bedford & Billerica Railroad which opened on 28 November 1877. There were 14 systems operating 2 ft gauge in the USA, ten of which were in Maine. The last to close was the Monson Railroad in December 1944.

The total mileage of narrow-gauge railroad in the USA in 1890 was about 10 000 (16 000 km), operated by about 500 independent companies.

Ireland's first 914 mm (3 ft) gauge line opened in 1875. Over 800 km (500 miles) were built. The last line, the West Clare, closed on 1 February 1961.

The first narrow-gauge railway to carry standard-gauge wagons on transporter trucks was the 762 mm (2 ft 6 in) gauge, 16.8 km (8¼ mile) long Leek & Manifold Valley Light Railway in Staffordshire. It opened on 27 June 1904 and closed on 10 March 1934. The transporters were designed by the engineer, Everard Richard Calthrop (1857–1927), for the Barsi Light Railway, India, of which he was also engineer, but they were first used on the Manifold Valley line. They are now widely used in several countries, on different gauges.

British Rail's only steam railway is the 597 mm (1 ft 11½ in) gauge Vale of Rheidol Railway, Wales. It opened on 22 December 1902 from Aberystwyth to Devil's Bridge and is 19 km (12 miles) long.

One of the world's most spectacular narrow-gauge railways is the 610 mm (2 ft) gauge Darjeeling Himalayan Railway in India. It was opened from Siliguri, then the northern terminus of the Eastern Bengal Railway from Calcutta, to Darjeeling in July 1881. From Sukna, 162 m (533 ft) above sea-level, and about 563 km (350 miles) from the sea, 11 km (7 miles) beyond Siliguri, the railway climbs for 64 km (40 miles) mostly at 1 in 25 (4 per cent) to a height of 2557 m (7407 ft) at Ghoom. From there it drops to 2076 m (6812 ft) at Darjeeling. The total length is 82 km (51 miles). The line includes five spiral loops and three reversing zigzags to gain height. One loop includes the sharpest curve on the line, 18 m (59½ ft) radius.

A branch of 45 km (28 miles) along the magnificent Teesta River Valley to a station below Kalimpong was opened in 1915. This is now closed.

Throughout most of its existence, the railway has been worked by 0-4-0 saddle tanks of a type built in 1888 by Sharp Stewart in Glasgow. For a time a 0-4-0+0-4-0 Garratt was used, built by Beyer Peacock, Manchester, in 1910. It was their second design and the first normal simple-expansion Garratt with the cylinders at the outer ends.

The greatest narrow-gauge engineering in India is on the 762 mm (2 ft 6 in) gauge Kalka–Simla Railway, in the north-west Himalayan foothills. It was built in 1899–1903 to give access to Simla where the Indian Government made its summer headquarters. From a height of 653 m

(2143 ft) at Kalka where it connects with the 1676 mm (5 ft 6 in) gauge line from Delhi, it climbs by gradients of 1 in 33 to a height of 2075 m (6808 ft) at Simla in 95 km (59 miles). There are 103 tunnels, the longest being Barogh, 1144 m (1251 yd). The track is of 'main-line' standard with 29.76 kg/m (60 lb/yd) rails.

The principal steam locomotives were the 'K' Class 2-6-2 tanks, first built in 1908 by the North British Locomotive Company, Glasgow.

The title of the smallest public railway, if taken to mean operating a public service, could be claimed by the Wells Harbour Railway at Wells-next-the-Sea in Norfolk. The 260 mm (10¼ in) gauge line, 1.1 km (¾ mile) long, was opened on 1 July 1976. It operates a frequent passenger service in summer between Wells and the beach.

The same operator has constructed the Wells & Walsingham Light Railway to the same gauge along the track bed of the former Great Eastern line from Fakenham to Wells. With a length of 6.5 km (4 miles) this is **the longest 260 mm gauge railway in Britain** and probably in the world. Trains began running along this line on 7 April 1982.

Another claimant for the title could be the 260 mm gauge Mull & West Highland Narrow Gauge Railway in Scotland which runs for 1.7 km (about 1 mile) along the east coast of Mull from near the ferry terminal at Craignure to Torosay Castle. The title is still claimed also by the 381 mm (15 in) gauge Romney, Hythe & Dymchurch Railway in Kent. The reader is left to make his, or her, own choice.

2-6-4T *Lady of the Isles* at Torosay on the 10¼ in gauge Mull Railway, the only railway in the Scottish Islands, on 19 September 1987. The railway was opened on 22 June 1984.

6

BRIDGES AND VIADUCTS

RAILWAY BRIDGES

One of the world's oldest bridges still carrying a railway is that built in 1810 as an aqueduct to carry the Paisley & Johnstone Canal over the River Cart near Paisley, Scotland. It was converted to a railway in 1885, becoming part of the Glasgow & South Western system.

The first iron railway bridge in the world carried the Stockton & Darlington Railway over the River Gaunless at West Auckland. It was built in 1825 and was replaced in 1901. It has been re-erected at the National Railway Museum, York.

The first skew-arch masonry railway bridge in Britain, also on the Stockton & Darlington Railway, carried the Haggerleases Branch over the River Gaunless at an angle of 27°. It was built, at a cost of £420, in 1829. Though closed on 30 September 1963, it still stands.

To carry the Middlesbrough extension of the Stockton & Darlington Railway across the River Tees, Timothy Hackworth designed a plate-girder bridge but, as it was an untried design, the directors made the unwise choice of a suspension bridge designed by Capt. Samuel Brown RN. It was built in 1830 at a cost of £2200 and was 125.6 m (412 ft) long with a main span of 85.7 m (281 ft 4 in). The 4.9 m (16 ft) wide deck was supported by 110 rods from 12 chains. Its lack of rigidity resulted in its replacement by a cast-iron girder bridge, opened on 27 May 1844, with three spans of 27 m (89 ft) and two of 9.5 m (31 ft). This in turn was replaced by plate-girder spans in 1906.

The flexibility of the suspension bridge under a concentrated load made it unsatisfactory for railway use. With the development of modern designs it is now coming back into use, for example in Japan. One was used in France in 1910, the Gisclard suspension bridge (qv); others have been used for several rapid transit railways. In Zaire a suspension bridge with a main span of 520 m (1706 ft), carrying a single-line railway and a road over the Matadi River about 150 km (118 miles) above its mouth, was completed in 1984.

The only transporter bridge to carry railway vehicles was built in 1916 to connect the soap and chemical works of Joseph Crosfield & Son Ltd on both sides of the River Mersey at Warrington, Lancashire. It has a span of 57 m (187 ft) at a height of 23 m (75 ft). Although it has been out of regular use since 1964, it is maintained in working order.

RAILWAY BRIDGES OVER 61 METRES (200 FT) HIGH

The world's highest railway bridge spans the Mala Rijeka Gorge near Kolasin at a height of 198 m (650 ft) on the Belgrade–Bar line in Yugoslavia. It consists of five steel spans on concrete piers. The railway was opened on 1 June 1976 after nearly 25 years of work. It includes 254 tunnels, totalling 114 km (71 miles). The summit at Kolasin is at 1032 m (3386 ft).

The Pfaffenberg–Zwenberg Bridge on an improved alignment on the south ramp of the Tauern Railway in Austria (opened on 25 July 1909) is a great concrete arch with a span of 200 m (660 ft). It is **the world's longest**, and has a height of 120 m (394 ft). The bridge was opened on 30 July 1971, and it eliminated two tunnels and a smaller bridge and considerable sharp curvature.

Further improvements on the south ramp of the same railway include the Falkenstein Bridge, 396 m (1299 ft) long and 75 m (246 ft) high with one span of 120 m (394 ft) and one of 150 m (492 ft). This was begun on the day the Pfaffenberg–Zwenberg Bridge was opened, and came into use on 13 July 1974, shortening the route by 167 m (549 ft).

On the same day, 13 July 1974, work began on yet another great bridge, the Lindischgraben Bridge, with a span of 154.4 m (505 ft), 100 m (328 ft) high, opened on 3 November 1977. These new works reduce curvature from a miminum of 250 m (820 ft) radius to 450 m (1476 ft) radius and enable speeds to be raised from 60 km/h to 90 km/h (37 to 56 mph). Work has now begun on improvements to the north ramp.

The Gokteik Viaduct, Burma, carries the metre-gauge Lahsio line 251 m (825 ft) above the River Nam Pan Hse. The tallest of the 18 steel towers stands on the natural tunnel over the river and is 97.5 m (320 ft) high. The viaduct was built in 1900 by the Pennsylvania Steel Company of the USA. It is 688.6 m (2260 ft) long, consisting of sixteen spans of 12.2 m (40 ft), seven spans of 18.3 m (60 ft) and ten spans of 36.6 m (120 ft).

The highest viaduct in India is the Ehegaon Viaduct on the line up the Thull Ghat, built in 1865. It is 58 m (190 ft) high and consists of three main girder spans of 42.7 m (140 ft), and two masonry arches of 12 m (39 ft 9 in) at each end. The total length is 229 m (750 ft). The girders were renewed in 1897.

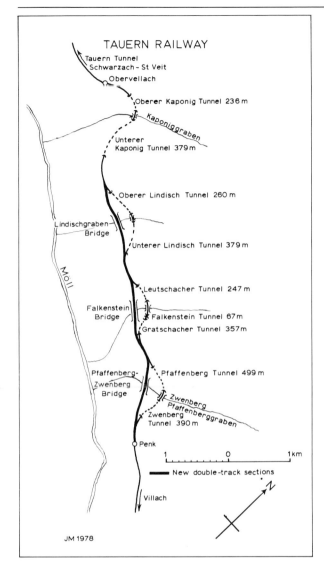

TAUERN RAILWAY

Tauern Tunnel
Schwarzach - St Veit
Obervellach
Oberer Kaponig Tunnel 236 m
Kaponiggraben
Unterer Kaponig Tunnel 379 m
Oberer Lindisch Tunnel 260 m
Lindischgraben Bridge
Unterer Lindisch Tunnel 379 m
Möll
Leutschacher Tunnel 247 m
Falkenstein Bridge
Falkenstein Tunnel 67 m
Gratschacher Tunnel 357 m
Pfaffenberg-Zwenberg Bridge
Pfaffenberg Tunnel 499 m
Zwenberg
Pfaffenberggraben
Zwenberg Tunnel 390 m
Penk
Villach

New double-track sections

JM 1978

It was built by Thomas Bouch in 1859 and was 317 m (1040 ft) long and 60 m (196 ft) high. It was closed in 1962 and dismantled in 1963.

The world's longest span concrete arch railway bridge is the Pfaffenberg–Zwenberg Bridge in Austria (see above). The second longest is the Esla Viaduct in Spain on the single-line 1676 mm (5 ft 6 in) gauge Sierra de la Culebra Railway, between Zamora and Pueblo de Sanabria near Andavias. It is 481 m (1578 ft) long, with a main arch over the Rio Esla of 197 m (645 ft) span, and about 84 m (275 ft) high. It was opened in 1940. The height varies with the level of the water in the reservoir.

Next in order are: Plougastel Bridge at Brest, France, opened in 1929, with a span of 186.5 m (612 ft); Stockholm, Sweden, opened in 1935, with a span of 181 m (593 ft). These carry both rail and road. The bridge over the Aare at Berne, Switzerland, with a span of 151 m (495 ft) was built in 1937–41 to replace the former lattice-girder steel spans, and carries four tracks into Berne Station.

Previously the record was held by the Langwies Bridge on the metre-gauge Chur–Arosa section of the Rhaetian Railway in Switzerland, built in 1912–13. This has a span of 96 m (315 ft) and a height of 62 m (203 ft).

The longest-span masonry arch railway bridge is the Salcano Bridge carrying the railway from Trieste to Jesenice across the Isonzo Gorge at Salcano, about 16 km (10 miles) north of Gorizia (Görz), with a span of 85 m (279 ft) and a total length of 226 m (741 ft). It was built by the Austrian State Railway and opened on 19 July 1906. It was demolished during the First World War and was temporarily replaced by a Wagner military bridge. The territory was ceded to Italy in 1919 and in 1927–8 the bridge was rebuilt to the original design by Italian State Railways. In 1947 it was again transferred and it now belongs to Yugoslav Railways.

The highest masonry railway bridge in Europe is near Corte in Corsica carrying the metre-gauge Corsica Railway over a gorge at a height of 100 m (328 ft).

On the metre-gauge Rhaetian Railway in Switzerland, the Solis Bridge over the Albula River is 89 m (292 ft) high with an arch of 42 m (138 ft). It was built in 1902. The Wiesen Bridge, built in 1908–9, crosses the Landwasser River at a height of 88 m (289 ft) with a span of 55 m (180 ft).

The highest railway bridge in Great Britain was the iron Crumlin Viaduct in Wales, built by T. W. Kennard for the Newport, Abergavenny & Hereford Railway and opened in June 1857. It was 60 m (197 ft) high with a total length of 505 m (1658 ft). It was demolished in 1965. The highest is now the Ballochmyle Viaduct (see below).

The highest railway bridge in England was the Belah Viaduct in Westmorland on the South Durham & Lancashire Union line of the former Stockton & Darlington Railway.

Ballochmyle Viaduct, carrying the former Glasgow & Southern Western Railway over the Ayr gorge, from the south west. It is now the highest railway bridge in Britain and also the largest masonry arch.

The largest masonry arch railway bridge in Britain is the central span of the Ballochmyle Viaduct over the River Ayr on the Glasgow & South Western main line from Glasgow to Carlisle in Scotland. It was begun in March 1846 and finished in March 1848. The arch has a semi-circular span of 55 m (181 ft), c. 30 cm (1 ft) longer than the Wiesen Bridge in Switzerland. It carries the line 51.5 m (169 ft) above the river-bed. **It is now the highest railway bridge in Great Britain.**

Railway Bridges over 61 m (200 ft) high

Bridge	Railway	Position	Height m	Height ft	Date Opened	Details
Mala Rijeka Viaduct	Yugoslav Railways (JZ)	Kolasin on Belgrade–Bar line	198	650	1 June 1976	Steel spans on concrete piers
Vresk	Iranian State	220 km (137 miles) from Bandar Shah on Caspian Sea, Trans Iranian line	152	500	1938	Masonry arch 55 m (181 ft) span
Fades Viaduct	French National	Clermont-Ferrand–Montluçon line (via Volvic)	132.5	435	1909	Steel spans on masonry piers 465 m (1526 ft) long
Khotur	Iranian State	Khotur River near Khoi	131	430	1973	Steel arch spans 223 m (732 ft)—9 spans. Total length 443 m (1455 ft)
Victoria Falls	Zimbabwe Railways	Livingstone	128	420	1904	Steel arch span 152 m (500 ft). Total length 198 m (650 ft)
Pfaffenberg–Zwenberg	Austrian Federal	Mallnitz–Spittal	120	394	30 July 1971	World's longest span concrete arch railway bridge, 200 m (660 ft) span. Double track. Replaced steel bridge on old line 68 m (223 ft) high; main span 56 m (184 ft)
Viaur	French National	Tanus, Rodez–Albi	116	381	1902	Steel cantilever span 220 m (722 ft)
Garabit Viaduct	French National	Neussargues–Mallnitz	112	367	1884	Steel arch 165 m (541 ft) span. Formerly 122 m (400 ft) high
Müngstner	German Federal	Müngsten, over River Wupper	107	350	1897	Double track. Main steel arch span 160 m (525 ft)
Rio Grande	Costa Rica	Near San José	105	346		
Vance Creek	Simpson Timber Co.	Shelton, west of Tacoma, Washington, USA	105	346	1928	Steel arch span 128.8 m (422 ft 6 in)
Tramo Sobre	Former Buenos Aires Great Southern, Argentina	Rio Negro	104	344		
Viaduct No. 2	Turkish State	Between Konakler and Günaykoy on Izmir–Afyonkarahisar line, 199.3 km from Izmir	103	338	1900	Lattice girders below rail-level—6 spans of 30 m (98 ft). Total length 195 m (640 ft)
Faux-Mau-Ti	Chinese People's Republic	Kunming–Hekou (and Hanoi)	102	335	1910	Main span 55 m (180 ft 6 in) over Nam Ti River
Rio Chinipas	Chihuahua–Pacific Mexico	On the Ojinago–Topolobampo line	101	330		Steel trusses on concrete piers. Total length 310 m (1019 ft)
Corte	Corsica	Corte	100	328	1894	Masonry arch
Lindischgraben	Austrian Federal	Tauern Railway Obervellach–Penk	100	328	3 Nov 1977	Concrete arch span 154 m (505 ft). Total length 283 m (928 ft)
Ten Tze	Chinese People's Republic	Yunnan section	c. 100	c. 328	1910	

Müngstener Bridge, the highest in Germany, built in 1897,
carrying a double-track railway 107 m (350 ft) above the
River Wupper near Solingen, with a span of 160 m (525 ft).

Bridge	Railway	Position	Height		Date Opened	Details
			m	ft		
Sitter	Bodensee–Toggenburg, Switzerland	Near St Gallen	99	324	3 Oct 1910	Steel span 120 m (394 ft) on stone piers
Malleco	Chilean State	Collipulli, on Santiago–Puerto Montt line	97.5	320	26 Oct 1890	7 steel spans on steel towers. Total length 347 m (1138 ft). Over Rio Malleco River
Gokteik	Union of Burma Railways	Mandalay–Lashio	97.5	320	1900	Steel trestle over River Nam Pan Hse which flows through a natural tunnel 251 m (825 ft) below the track
Pecos	Southern Pacific, USA	352 km (219 miles) west of San Antonio, Texas	97.5	320	21 Dec 1944	Continuous steel cantilever 424 m (1390 ft) long. Central span 114.15 m (374 ft 6 in) long, over Pecos River. Replaced an earlier steel structure built in 1892

Bridge	Railway	Position	Height m	ft	Date Opened	Details
Crooked River Canyon	Oregon Trunk Railroad, USA	Madras–Bend, Oregon	97.5	320	1911	Steel arch span 103.63 m (340 ft)
Mahoka Viaduct	New Zealand	34 km (21 miles) south of Waiora on Napier–Gisborne line, North Island	97	318	June 1937	Steel trestle 277 m (908 ft) long
Lethbridge Viaduct	Canadian Pacific	Oldman (formerly Belly) River, Alberta	95.7	314	1909	34 spans on steel towers 1624 m (5327 ft) long
Deep Creek	British Columbia Railway, Canada	Lillooet–Quesnel	95	312	Aug 1921	Lattice steel spans on steel towers
Stoney Creek	Canadian Pacific	East of Connaught Tunnel	93.6	307	1894	Replaced wooden trestle built 1886
Kinzua Viaduct	Erie Lackawanna Railway, USA	Bradford, Pennsylvania	92	301	Sept 1900	Steel trestle 626 m (2053 ft) long with 41 spans of 18.28 m (60 ft). Replaces iron trestle built 1882
Hurricane Gulch	Alaska Railroad	269 km (167 miles) north of Anchorage	90	296	18 Aug 1921	Two-hinged steel arch. Total length 280 m (918 ft)
Solis	Rhaetian Railway, Switzerland	Thusis–Filisur	89	292	21 Oct 1902	Masonry arch 42 m (138 ft) span over Albula River
Wiesen	Rhaetian Railway, Switzerland	Davos–Filisur	88	289	1 July 1909	Masonry arch 55 m (180 ft) span over Landwasser River
Trisanna	Austrian Federal Arlberg line	St Anton–Landeck	87.4	287	20 Sept 1884	Main steel span 120 m (393 ft 8 in) on masonry piers
Drau	Austrian Federal	Bleiburg–Wolfsberg	87	285	1963	5 steel spans on concrete piers. Total length 428 m (1404 ft)
Ulla Viaduct	Spanish National	Sierra de la Culebra line	86	282	1959	Masonry; 219 m (718 ft) long
Here Dere	Turkish State	Near Radjoun	85.3	280		Steel truss bridge
Lawyers Creek Trestle	Burlington Northern, USA (former Northern Pacific)	Craigmont, Idaho	84	276		Steel trestle 407 m (1335 ft) long
Esla	Spanish National Sierra de la Culebra line	Zamora–Pueblo de Sanabria, near Andavias	84	276	1940	Total length 481 m (1578 ft). Main concrete arch span 197 m (645 ft)
Paderno d'Adda	Italian State	Over Adda River at Paderno d'Adda	80.7	265	1 July 1889	Iron arch by Gustav Eiffel. Span 150 m (492 ft). Total length 226 m (873 ft)
Nirihuao River	Argentine	20 km (12 miles) east of San Carlos de Bariloche, Rio Negro	80.4	264	1934	Steel arch span 70 m (229 ft 8 in). Carries 1676 mm (5 ft 6 in) gauge San Antonio–Bariloche line
Vecchio	French National (Corsica)	4 km (2½ miles) north of Vivario	80	262	1894	Steel truss on stone piers 140 m (459 ft) long
Gisclard suspension bridge	French National	Mont Louis–La Cabanasse	80	262	18 July 1910	Carries metre-gauge Cerdagne line over River Tet. Length 234 m (768 ft); main span 151.5 m (497 ft)

Bridge	Railway	Position	Height m	ft	Date Opened	Details
Niagara Canyon	Canadian Pacific	22.5 km (14 miles) north of Victoria, Vancouver Island on Nanaimo line	79	260	*c.* 1912	Steel cantilever 161 m (529 ft) long. Replaced wooden trestle. Used from 1884 to 1910 to carry main CPR line across Fraser River south of Lytton, BC.
North Rangitikei	New Zealand	Mangaweka Deviation, North Island	79	260	18 Nov 1981	
Meienreuss (middle bridge)	Swiss Federal	St Gotthard line, above Wassen	79	260		Concrete arch faced in stone. Replaced steel bridge of 1882
Makatote	New Zealand	11 km (7 miles) south of National Park, North Island	78.6	258	10 July 1908	Steel trestle 262 m (860 ft) long
Bietschtal	Lötschberg, Switzerland	Brig–Goppenstein	78	255	15 July 1913	Steel span 95 m (312 ft)
Waikare	New Zealand	Just north of Putorino, North Island	78	255	Aug 1937	Steel trestle 1868 m (613 ft) long
South Rangitikei	New Zealand	Mangaweka Deviation, North Island	78	255	18 Nov 1981	315 m (1033 ft) long
Carrion	Peru Central	84.48 km (52 miles) from Callao	77	253	1937	Steel truss on steel towers. Length 219 m (720 ft). Replaced the 1891 bridge which replaced the Verrugas Bridge of 1870
Isorno	Centovalli, Ticino, Switzerland	Intragna	77	253	27 Nov 1923	Steel arch 90 m (295 ft) span over Isorno River
Van Staaden's Gorge	South African	Port Elizabeth–Avontour line	76	250	1905	Steel trestle 195.7 m (642 ft) long. Carries 610 mm (2 ft) gauge line
Ingiustria	Centovalli, Ticino, Switzerland	Corcapolo–Verdasio	76	249	27 Nov 1923	Masonry viaduct; 3 arches 25 m (82 ft) span
Falkenstein	Austrian Federal Tauern line	Mallnitz–Spittal	75	246	13 July 1974	Two concrete arches of 120 m (394 ft) and 150 m (492 ft) span
Grandfrey Viaduct	Swiss Federal	Fribourg	74.7	245	2 July 1860	Over Saane River
Puente de las Vacas	International Railways of Central America 914 mm (3 ft) gauge	Near Guatemala	74.7	245		Steel trestle
Tunkhannock Creek Viaduct	Erie Lackawanna, USA	Nicholson, Pennsylvania	73.15	240	7 Nov 1915	Double-track, reinforced concrete viaduct 724 m (2375 ft) long with 12 arches of 63.4 m (208 ft) and an approach arch of 30.5 m (100 ft) at each end
Göltzchtal Viaduct	German state (DR)	Reichenbach–Plauen, Vogtland, East Germany	73.15	240	1851	Arched viaduct in 4 tiers with brick piers and granite arches, 570 m (1870 ft) long

Bridge	Railway	Position	Height		Date Opened	Details
			m	ft		
Brallos	Hellenic Railways Organization Ltd	Over Kifissos River on Athens–Thessaloniki line 8 km south of Brallos Tunnel	73.2	240	6 Sept 1908	Steel trestle
Tardes Viaduct	French National	Montluçon–Eygurande	73	240	1883	Built by Gustav Eiffel
Altier	French National	Altier River nr Ville Fort	73	240	1870	Two-tier masonry viaduct 246 m (807 ft) long
Niagara Gorge	Conrail, USA (formerly Michigan Central)	Niagara Falls, New York/ Ontario	73	240	16 Feb 1925	Braced spandrel steel arch, span 195 m (640 ft). Replaced 1883 cantilever bridge
Kawhatau	New Zealand	Mangaweka Deviation North Island	73	240	18 Nov 1981	
Trout Creek	Canadian Pacific	11.7 km (7.3 miles) west of Penticton, British Columbia	72.5	238	1915	188 m (618 ft) long. 2 plate girder spans of 13.7 m (45 ft) and 1 of 79.2 m (260 ft) and 176.2 m (250 ft) lattice deck truss and 2 timber spans
Makohine Viaduct	New Zealand	11 km (7 miles) south of Mangaweka, North Island	72.5	238	1902	Steel trestle 228.6 m (750 ft) long
Staircase Viaduct	New Zealand	West of Springfield, South Island	71.6	235	1914	Steel trestle 146.3 m (480 ft) long
Waikoau Viaduct	New Zealand	45 km (28 miles) north of Napier, North Island	71.6	235	Aug 1937	Steel trestle 160 m (525 ft) long
Gennessee River Bridge	Erie Lackawanna, USA		71.3	234		Steel trestle
Cottonwood River Viaduct	British Columbia Railway, Canada	Quesnel–Prince George	71.3	234	1952	Steel trestle
Altier Viaduct	French National	Alès–La Bastide	70	230	16 Mar 1870	Masonry viaduct 246 m (870 ft) long
Maliko Gulch Trestle	Kahului Railway, Hawaii	Maui Island	70	230		
Felizon Gorge	Dolomites Railway	North of Cortina d'Ampezzo	70	230	15 June 1921	Lattice girder bridge 27.2 m (90 ft) long
Castellaneta	Italian State	Bari–Taranto	70	230	1928	Masonry viaduct; arches 25.5 m (83 ft 7 in) span. Replaced iron viaduct opened 15 September 1868
Gidur Viaduct	Turkish State	Between Hacikiri and Bucak on Ulukisla–Yenice section, 69.7 km (43 miles) from Ulukisla	69	226	1918	Steel spans on masonry piers. Total length 215 m (705 ft)
Cize–Bolozon	French National	Ain Gorge near Nantua	69	226		Two-tier masonry viaduct
Niagara Gorge	Canadian National Railways	Niagara Falls, New York/ Ontario	68.9	226	1897	Steel arch bridge 237.7 m (780 ft) long, span 167.6 m (550 ft). Replaced suspension bridge of 1855. Carries road beneath railway
Jocketa Viaduct	German State (DR)	Near Plauen, Vogtland	68.3	224	1851	Granite arches 279 m (915 ft) long
Cisco	Canadian National	11 km (7 miles) south of Lytton	68	222	4 Oct 1915	Steel arch 129.5 m (425 ft) span over Fraser River

Bridge	Railway	Position	Height m	ft	Date Opened	Details
Devils Canyon	Atchison, Topeka & Santa Fe, USA	41.8 km (26 miles) west of Winslow, Arizona	68	222	1944	Replaced 1900 trestle
Arbutus Canyon	Canadian Pacific	24 km (15 miles) north of Victoria, Vancouver Island	67	220		141 m (462 ft) long. 6 deck plate girder spans on steel towers. Replaced timber trestle.
Dead Horse Gulch	White Pass & Yukon	Between Glacier and White Pass, Alaska	66	215	Feb 1899	Cantilever span. 914 mm (3 ft) gauge line. Closed.
Maungaturanga Viaduct	New Zealand	24 km (15 miles) south of Waiora, North Island	65.5	215	June 1937	Steel trestle 243.8 m (800 ft) long
Matahoura Viaduct	New Zealand	5.6 km (3½ miles) south of Putorina, North Island	65.5	215	Aug 1937	Steel trestle 141 m (463 ft) long
Landwasser Viaduct	Rhaetian. Albula line, Switzerland	Filisur	65	213	2 Oct 1902	Masonry viaduct 6 arches of 20 m (65 ft 7 in) span
Angerschlucht	Austrian Federal Tauern line	Hofgastein	65	213	7 July 1909	Steel arch 110 m (361 ft) span
Torres Querido	Spanish National	Cuenca–Utiel	65	213		Masonry viaduct, 23 arches over Narboneta River
North and South Bisanseto	Japan Rail	Honshu–Shikoku	65	213	10 Apr 1988	Two suspension bridges back to back, with central spans of 990 m (3248 ft) and 1100 m (3609 ft)
Fontpédrouse (Séjourné) Viaduct	French National Cerdagne line metre gauge	Mont Louis–Villefranche–Conflent	65	213	18 July 1910	Masonry viaduct 236.7 m (777 ft) long. Centre arch in 2 tiers. Named after the engineer, Paul Séjourné (1851–1939)
Ruinacci	Centovalli, Switzerland	Camedo	65	213	27 Nov 1923	Steel arch 65.92 m (216 ft) span
Pembina River Viaduct	Canadian National	103 km west of Edmonton, Alberta	65	213	1909	Steel trestle 274 km (900 ft) long
Poughkeepsie	Conrail (former New York, New Haven & Hartford)	120 km (75 miles) north of New York City	64.5	212	1889	Cantilever bridge over Hudson River, 2063 m (6768 ft) long including 2 cantilever spans of 167 m (548 ft), 2 spans of 160 m (525 ft) and 2 anchor spans of 61 m (201 ft)
Chamborigaud	French National	Luëch Valley near Alés	64	210		Masonry viaduct 387 m (1269 ft) long
Weissenbach Viaduct	Bodensee–Toggenburg, Switzerland	St Gallen–Herisau	64	210	3 Oct 1910	Masonry viaduct 282 m (925 ft) long
Polvorilla	Argentine, North-Western Region, North Transandine	8 km (5 miles) west of Antonio de Los Cobres, Salta	64	210	1941	Steel trestle 225 m (738 ft) long on 6 piers on curve of 200 m (10 chains) radius. Carries metre-gauge line at altitude of 4267 m (14 000 ft)
Grueize Viaduct	French National 'Ligne des Causses'	Near Marvejols	63.4	208	3 May 1884	Masonry viaduct 218.8 m (717 ft) long
Enfer	French National	Crucize River near Marvejols	63	207	1884	Masonry viaduct 219 m (718 ft) long
Black Lick Viaduct	Virginian, USA	Over Black Lick Creek near Princeton, W Virginia	63	207		227 m (910 ft) long

Bridge	Railway	Position	Height		Date Opened	Details
			m	ft		
Bralo Viaduct	Hellenic State	On Livadia–Lianokladi section	63	207	6 Sept 1908	Steel trestle 320 m (1050 ft) long. 4 spans: 3 × 106 m (347 ft) and 120 m (394 ft)
Busseau	French National	Montluçon–St Sulpice	62	203	1864	Steel spans on masonry piers 264 m (866 ft) long
Margologio Viaduct	Centovalli, Italy	Verigo–Marone	62	203	27 Nov 1923	Masonry viaduct 3 × 29 m (95 ft)
Langwies	Rhaetian Railway Chur–Arosa section, Switzerland	Langwies	62	203	12 Dec 1914	Concrete arch 96 m (315 ft) span
Morlaix Viaduct	French National	Place des Octages, Morlaix	61.2	201	1861	Masonry viaduct in 2 tiers 285 m (935 ft) long
Eglisau	Swiss Federal	Eglisau	61	200	1897	Steel lattice span of 90 m (295 ft) over Rhine. Masonry arch approaches. Total length 457 m (1500 ft)
Douro (Pont de Pia Maria)	Portuguese	Porto	61	200	1877	Steel arch, similar to Garabit Viaduct, France, also by Gustav Eiffel. Total length 354.5 m (1163 ft). Main span 160 m (525 ft)
Cowlitz River	Cowlitz, Chehalis & Cascade Railway, Washington, USA	Cowlitz River	61	200		Timber trestle
Gouritz River	South African	Worcester–Mosel line near Albertinia	61	200	1931	Steel cantilever

This list is intended to be comprehensive, but I am conscious of several bridges whose height could not be established. The height of a bridge above ground or water is the dimension which concerns the design or maintenance engineer the least, and consequently it is not always mentioned in details of the bridge. Also, heights are variable. Sometimes they are measured from a stream-bed, or from water-level which, under the Garabit Viaduct in France, for example, can be raised by a dam, so reducing the height of the bridge above water. Variations occur again at the upper end where measurements are sometimes given to the underside of the bridge, or to rail-level, or to the top of a parapet. In this list I have tried to establish the height of the rails above ground or water.

THE WORLD'S LONGEST RAILWAY BRIDGES

The earliest of the long railway bridges was the Victoria Bridge across the St Lawrence River at Montreal. The original bridge, begun in 1854 and opened on 17 December 1859, was a single-line tubular structure designed by Robert Stephenson. It was 3.1 km (1 mile 1668 yd) long and carried the Grand Trunk Railway, later part of the Canadian National Railways. It had a central span of 107 m (350 ft) and 24 other spans of 73.8 to 75.3 m (242 to 247 ft).

The smoke nuisance and increasing traffic led to its reconstruction under engineer Joseph Hobson as an open girder bridge carrying double track and two roadways on the original piers. When reopened on 13 December 1898 it was named the 'Victoria Jubilee Bridge'.

Tay Bridge in Scotland, 3.6 km (2 miles 364 yd) long carries the Edinburgh–Aberdeen line across the Tay Estuary at Dundee. The original single-line bridge designed

by Thomas Bouch (1822–80) was opened on 1 June 1878. Cast-iron columns were badly designed and made, and construction was poorly supervised. On 28 December 1879 the centre spans were blown down in a gale while a train was crossing. Of the 78 passengers and crew there were no survivors.

The present double-track bridge, designed by W. H. Barlow and built by William Arrol (qqv), was opened on 20 June 1887. The deck trusses of the original bridge were reused as the centre girders of the present deck spans.

The Storstrøm Bridge, Denmark, opened on 26 September 1937, connects the islands of Zealand and Falster. It carries a single-line railway, a road and a footpath, and has a total length over water of 3200 m (10 500 ft). It consists of steel spans on concrete piers: from Zealand 21 plate-girder deck spans, alternately 57.8 m (189 ft 6 in) and 62.2 m (204 ft) span, 3 bow-string truss spans of 103.9 m (340 ft), 137.8 m (450 ft) and 103.9 m giving a clearance of 25.5 m (83 ft 8 in) above mean sea-level, and 26 more plate-girder spans. The bridge took 4 years to build.

The Hardinge Bridge over the Ganges in Bangladesh north of Calcutta was opened on 4 March 1915. It has 15 steel spans of 106.7 m (350 ft) and a length of 1.8 km (1 mile 207 yd) between abutments. The main piers are carried down to a depth of 48.8 m (160 ft) below the lowest water-level and were the deepest foundations of their kind in the world. It consumed more than 1 100 353 m³ (38 860 000 ft³) of masonry and 1 700 000 rivets. The engineer was R. R. Gales.

It carried the main line northwards from Calcutta to Siliguri at the foot of the Himalayas. The bridge was damaged in the 1971 conflict and was temporarily repaired in 1972–4.

Britain's longest railway bridge, or viaduct, is the original London & Greenwich Railway, the first railway in London. It is about 6 km (3.7 miles) long and consists of 878 brick arches. It was designed by Lt. Col. G. T. Landmann (later engineer of the Preston & Wyre Railway) and was opened to an intermediate station at Deptford on 14 December 1836 and to Greenwich on 24 December.

One of the highest masonry viaducts in Britain is the Dee Viaduct at Cefn, Wales, on the Shrewsbury–Chester line. It is 45 m (148 ft) high and is 466 m (1530 ft) long, with 19 arches of 18.3 m (60 ft) span. It was designed by Henry Robertson (1816–88), engineer of the Shrewsbury & Chester Railway, and was built in 1848 by Thomas Brassey.

It is closely rivalled by the Templand Viaduct of 14 arches, carrying the former Glasgow & South Western Railway 44 m (145 ft) above the Lugar Water north of Old Cumnock.

The greatest number of viaducts per mile on a British railway is in Cornwall. In the 120 km (75 miles) between

The second Tay Bridge, opened on 20 June 1887, seen from Wormit opposite Dundee on 29 July 1961. Wormit station in the foreground was closed on 5 May 1969. The bases of Bouch's ill-fated bridge can be seen beside the later piers.

Saltash and Penzance there are 34 viaducts.

The Settle & Carlisle line of the former Midland Railway has 19 viaducts and 14 tunnels in 116 km (72½ miles).

The earliest and largest 'elastic arch' railway bridge in Britain is at West Wylam on the former North Wylam Branch of the North Eastern Railway, Northumberland. It was designed by William George Laws on the principle of Leather's bridge over the Aire at Leeds, and has a span of 74.7 m (245 ft). It was built by the Scotswood, Newburn & Wylam Railway and was opened in October 1876, becoming part of the North Eastern system in 1883. It was the 'father' of the arch bridges at Newcastle upon Tyne, Sydney, the Hell Gate in New York, and others. The railway was closed on 11 March 1968, but the bridge remains, and is used as a footbridge.

The first cable-stayed railway bridge in Europe, Lyne Bridge, carrying the Virginia Water–Chertsey line of the Southern Region of British Rail over the new dual four-lane M25 motorway, was completed at the end of 1978. It consists of two skew spans of 55 m (180 ft) formed of continuous concrete beams, at an angle of 28° to the motorway. The towers stand 26 m (85 ft) above the tracks. The cable stays are primarily intended as external prestressing cables. It was formally opened by Sir Peter Parker, then chairman of British Railways, on 7 February 1979. The first trains crossed on 12 February.

The greatest of all railway bridges, and the oldest railway cantilever bridge is the Forth Bridge in Scotland, opened on 4 March 1890. It was designed by John Fowler (1817–98) and Benjamin Baker (1840–1907) and built by William Arrol. The three cantilever towers are 110 m (361 ft) high and the double-track railway is carried 47.5 m (156 ft) above high water. The two main spans are 521 m (1710 ft) and the total length of the bridge is 2528 m (8298 ft).

Work began in November 1882. The main columns, 3.7 m (12 ft) diameter, stand on piers 18.3 m (60 ft) diameter and rise to a height of 104 m (343 ft), leaning inwards from 36.5 m (120 ft) apart at the base to 10 m (33 ft) at the top, 110 m (361 ft) above high water. The piers of the shore towers are spaced 47 m (155 ft) apart and the Inchgarvie piers 82.3 m (270 ft).

The bridge consumed over 54 000 tons of steel, the Inchgarvie piers supporting 18 700 tons and the other piers 16 130 tons each. All this was held together by 6 500 000 rivets, themselves representing over 4000 tons. The piers consumed 21 000 m³ (740 000 ft³) of granite masonry, 35 400 m³ (46 300 yd³) of rubble masonry, 49 000 m³ (64 300 yd³) of concrete and 21 000 tons of cement. Of the 4500 workers employed on the bridge 57

Forth Bridge from the top of the north tower in 1961. This, the greatest of all railway bridges, celebrates its centenary on 4 March 1990. It was built by William Arrol to designs by Benjamin Baker and John Fowler. The pier of Thomas Bouch's abandoned suspension bridge project can be seen beside the base of the Inchgarvie tower, surmounted by a lighthouse. The precision of the work, on a gigantic scale, can be gauged from the position of the south tower, dead in line with the central tower.

The Inchgarvie pier of the Forth Bridge, the pier of Bouch's abandoned bridge, and the new road bridge, from Inchgarvie, on the occasion of a visit by members of the Stephenson Locomotive Society in August 1967.

were killed in accidents. Work was completed, at a cost of £3 000 000, at the end of 1889 and the first train crossed on 22 January 1890. Since then it has needed constant painting by up to 29 men taking about 3 years to apply c. 45 000 litres or 56 tons of paint to the 59 ha or 145 acres of steelwork. On completion of this it was time to start again. Since 1976 four painters have used two small diesel-powered paint-sprayers which can spray paint at up to 8.3 litres a minute and pump up to a height of 61 m (200 ft), each powering two spray-guns. The paint used is a British Rail formulation with red oxide.

The largest steel arch span in the world is the Sydney Harbour Bridge in New South Wales, with a main span of 503 m (1650 ft). It was opened on 19 March 1932 and carries two railway tracks, eight road lanes, footway and cycle track each of 3 m (10 ft), at a height of 51.8 m (170 ft). Its total length is 1149 m (3770 ft). Originally it had four rail tracks, two of which were used by trams until 1958 when they were converted to road lanes.

The chain of bridges carrying 1067 mm (3 ft 6 in) gauge tracks between Kojima on Honshu Island and Sakaide on Shikoku Island in Japan, begun in 1978, was opened to passenger trains on 10 April 1988. The first test trains crossed on 11 January. The length of elevated structures totals 12.3 km (7.6 miles) across five small islands including 9.4 km (5.8 miles) over the Seto inland sea. There are three suspension bridges: the North Bisanseto Bridge with a central span of 990 m; South Bisanseto Bridge with a span of 1.1 km (0.7 miles); and Shimotsuiseto Bridge with a span of 940 m (3084 ft); two cable-stayed bridges

with central spans of 420 m (1378 ft) and one cantilever truss bridge. With side spans and viaducts the structures are continuous. The Bisanseto bridges extend back to back for 3.4 km (2.1 miles) giving 65 m (213 ft) headroom over a channel 85 m (279 ft) deep. The spans consist of a massive girder 30 m (98 ft) wide and 13 m (43 ft) deep with four road lanes on top and, at present, two 1067 mm (3 ft 6 in) gauge tracks inside the girder, electrified at 1500 V dc, with room for standard-gauge Shinkansen tracks to be added later. These are by far the world's largest suspension bridges carrying road and rail traffic. Together with the Seikan Tunnel (see chapter 7) these bridges complete the uniting by rail of the four main islands of Japan. Kyushu and Honshu were connected in 1942 by the (old) Kanmon Tunnel, 3.6 km (2.2 miles) long.

Work on another rail link between Kobe on Honshu and Naruto on Shikoku was begun in 1976. This will include two large suspension bridges: Oh-Naruto Bridge with a centre span of 876 m (2874 ft) and the Akashi Kaikvo Bridge with a centre span of 1.8 km (1 mile 186 yd), the longest in the world. It will carry a six-lane express road and a double track 1067 mm gauge railway.

The Tohoku Shinkansen crosses the Kitakami River on a bridge 3.9 km (2 miles 350 yd) long, opened on 23 June 1982.

Yangtse River Bridge, looking towards Nanking. With approaches this is the second longest railway bridge in China.

The world's longest railway bridge, opened in September 1985, carries the line from Heze in Shandong Province, China, to Xinxiang in Henan Province over the Huang He (Yellow) River. It is 10.3 km (6 miles 684 yd) long. Details have not yet been found. This is the 14th bridge over the Yellow River to be built in the past 35 years. Before 1949 there were only two. Another, opened in July 1981 near Jinan in Shandong, is 5.7 km (3 miles 952 yd) long including approaches.

The Yangtse River Bridge at Nanjing in Kiangsu province, with approach spans, measures 6.8 km (4 miles 452 yd). The river section consists of ten through truss spans of 157 m (515 ft), totalling 1574 m (5174 ft) between abutments, with a road on top. The piers go down 70 m (230 ft) below the water surface. The bridge consumed a million tons of concrete and 100 000 tons of steelwork, took 7000 workers ten years to build, and was competled in 1968. It was designed and built entirely by the Chinese.

SOME NORTH AMERICAN BRIDGES

The oldest railroad bridge in the USA still in use is at Mount Clare, Baltimore, across Gwynn's Falls. It is a stone arch of 24.4 m (80 ft) span with a clearance of 13.4 m (44 ft) above the water. It carries the double-track Baltimore & Ohio Railroad and was opened in December 1829.

The oldest stone viaduct in the USA is the Thomas Viaduct of eight arches carrying the Washington Branch of the Baltimore & Ohio Railroad across the Patapsco River in Maryland, completed on 4 July 1835. It was built in local granite by McCartney, contractor, who erected a monument at one end bearing his own name. The viaduct has eight elliptical arches about 17.7 m (58 ft) span and is 188 m (617 ft) long and 18.3 m (60 ft) high. The engineer was Benjamin Henry Latrobe (1806–78).

The first iron tubular bridge in the USA was built in 1847 at Bolton, Maryland, on the Baltimore & Ohio Railroad.

The first iron truss bridge, also built in 1847, was near Pittsfield, Massachusetts, on the Boston & Albany Railroad.

The first all-steel bridge was opened in 1879 at Glasgow, Missouri, on the Chicago & Alton Railroad. It was 823 m (2700 ft) long.

The world's first successful railway suspension bridge was built across the Whirlpool Rapids below Niagara Falls by John A. Roebling (1806–69) who developed the modern wire-cable suspension bridge. It measured 250 m (821 ft 4 in) between the towers and carried a single-line railway on the upper deck 68.9 m (226 ft) above the water, and a road beneath. It was opened on 18 March 1855, and it connected the Great Western Railway of Canada with

the railways of the USA. It was replaced by a steel arch bridge, constructed round the suspended span, in 1897.

The highest railroad bridge in North America is the Vance Creek Bridge at Shelton, west of Tacoma in Washington State, USA. It is owned and maintained by the Simpson Timber Company, and it was built in 1928 by the American Bridge Company. It is of steel construction with a main arch span of 128.8 m (422 ft 6 in) carrying the rails 105.8 m (347 ft) above the floor of Vance Creek. The total length of the bridge is 252 m (827 ft 4 in).

The highest railroad bridge on a main line in North America is the Pecos Bridge, carrying the Southern Pacific Railroad over the Pecos River a few miles above its confluence with the Rio Grande, 352 km (219 miles) west of San Antonio, Texas. The original high bridge, which took 103 days to build, was completed in March 1892. It replaced the earlier line, opened on 5 January 1883, which ran down into the Rio Grande Gorge and across the Pecos by a low-level bridge in 1882.

The present bridge, opened on 21 December 1944, is a continuous cantilever steel structure, 413.8 m (1390 ft) long with seven spans, the longest being 114.1 m (374 ft 6 in). It carries a single line, 97.5 m (320 ft) above the river.

The Oregon Trunk Railroad crosses the Crooked River Canyon at a height of 97.5 m (320 ft) by a single steel arch span of 103.6 m (340 ft). It was designed by Ralph Modjeski (1861–1940), engineer of the Huey P. Long, San Francisco Bay, and other bridges, and was erected in 1911.

The Pit River Bridge on the Southern Pacific in Shasta County, California, about 22.5 km (14 miles) north of Redding was, when opened on 24 May 1942, one of the highest railway bridges in the world. It was built by the US Federal Government as part of the California Central Valley Water Project. Bids for construction of the bridge were received on 5 October 1939.

It is a riveted steel through Warren truss bridge carrying a double-track railroad, and a road above the top chords. The total length of the road deck is 1093 m (3588 ft) and of the rail deck 839.4 m (2754 ft). The longest of the 13 spans is 187.5 m (615 ft). The greatest height was just east of pier 3, under span 5, where the rails were 132 m (433 ft) above the bed of the old Pit River. Pier 3 is 108.8 m (357 ft) high and contains about 26 750 m^3 or 70 000 tons of concrete.

On completion of the Shasta Dam, the water in the reservoir rose to 9.2 m (31 ft) below the bridge. The bridge is owned by the US Government Bureau of Reclamation.

The Kinzua Viaduct, south of Bradford, Pennsylvania, is 626 m (2053 ft) long and carried the Erie Railroad across a valley at a height of 92 m (301 ft), making it the third highest railroad bridge in the USA. The original iron trestle viaduct was begun on 10 May 1882 and was completed in four months at a cost of $167 000. In 1900, from May to September, the viaduct was rebuilt in steel. It has 41 spans

of 18.3 m (60 ft). It is now out of use, but under a preservation order and with no funds for maintenance it is rusting away.

The largest reinforced-concrete viaduct in the USA carries the double-track line of the Delaware, Lackawanna & Western Railroad across Tunkhannock Creek at Nicholson, Pennsylvania. It is 724 m (2375 ft) long with 12 arches of 63.4 m (208 ft) span and an approach arch of 30 m (100 ft) at each end, and is 73.1 m (240 ft) high.

The highest railway bridge in Canada is the Lethbridge Viaduct, carrying the Canadian Pacific Railway over the Oldman (formerly Belly) River in Alberta at a height of 95.7 m (314 ft). It was completed in 1909 and is 1623.6 m (5327 ft) long with 34 spans on steel towers. It consumed 12 000 tons of steel and is dead straight.

The world's largest cantilever span is the Quebec Bridge over the St Lawrence River, Canada, opened on 3 December 1917 by the Canadian National Railways. It had cost $ Can 22 500 000 (then £4 623 000). The total length of 987 m (3238 ft) includes a main span of 548.6 m (1800 ft) and shore spans of 171.4 m (562 ft 6 in). The central suspended span of 205.7 m (675 ft) is the second one to be built. The first collapsed, causing the loss of ten lives

Top: A train of logs of the Simpson Lumber Company crossing the Vance Creek Bridge in Washington, USA, the highest railway bridge in North America, 105.8 m (347 ft) above the floor of Vance Creek.

Above: Quebec Bridge, the world's longest cantilever span, carrying the Canadian National Railways' line across the St Lawrence River.

while being hoisted into position on 11 September 1916 and now lies at the bottom of the river.

The first attempt by the Phoenix Bridge Company of Pennsylvania to erect a bridge here ended in disaster on 29 August 1907 when the south cantilever collapsed, killing 75 of the 86 men working on it.

The Stoney Creek Bridge on the Canadian Pacific Railway 6.5 km (4 miles) east of the Connaught Tunnel was originally built in 1886 as a timber Howe-truss deck-type bridge of two spans of 61 m (200 ft) and one of 30 m (100 ft) supported on timber towers. At the time it was the highest wooden bridge in the world.

In 1893–94 it was replaced by a steel arch span of 102.4 m (336 ft) designed by H. E. Vautelet and erected by the Hamilton Bridge Company of Ontario without interruption to traffic. It was unique in being probably the only parallel double-chorded arch with its main hinge-pins in its lower chord, unlike the Garabit Viaduct in France in which the chords converge at the springings.

In 1929 the bridge was reinforced by an additional arch on each side, additional supports for the railway, and new deck girders. From track-level on the centre-line of the bridge to the bottom of the gorge the height is 93.6 m (307 ft). (See map p. 94.)

On Vancouver Island, British Columbia, the Malahat Logging Company's railway was carried across Bear Creek by a wooden trestle at a height of 77.5 m (254 ft), 274 m (900 ft) long. It was demolished in the 1950s. It claimed to be one of the largest wooden bridges in the world.

America's longest drawbridge span of 160 m (525 ft) forms part of the Atchison, Topeka & Santa Fe Railroad bridge over the Mississippi at Fort Madison Iowa, Illinois, opened in 1927.

The longest swing spans on American railroads are the Willamette River Bridge at Portland, Oregon, of 159 m (521 ft), completed in 1908; and the East Omaha Bridge over the Missouri of 158 m (519 ft) completed in 1903.

The longest railroad vertical-lift bridge span carries the Baltimore & Ohio Railroad connection to the Staten Island Rapid Transit across Arthur Kill, New York. It was opened on 25 August 1959 and replaces the earlier swing bridge. The centre span of 170 m (558 ft) is suspended from two 65.5 m (215 ft) steel towers. It can be raised to its maximum height of 41.1 m (135 ft) or lowered to its closed position 9.5 m (31 ft) above the water in 2 minutes.

The second longest carries the New Haven & Hartford Railroad across the Cape Cod Canal, Massachusetts. It was built in 1933–5. The 165.8 m (544 ft) span can be raised from 2.1 m to 41.1 m (7 ft to 135 ft) in 2½ minutes.

The world's longest stone arch railway bridge over a river carries the former Pennsylvania Railroad over the Susquehanna at Rockville, Pennsylvania. It was built in 1902 to replace the iron truss bridge of 1877 and is 1122 m (3680 ft) long.

The longest simple-truss span on USA railroads is the 219.5 m (720 ft) of the Chicago, Burlington & Quincy (now Burlington Northern) Railroad's Metropolis Bridge over the Ohio River, opened in 1917. The truss is 33.5 m (110 ft) deep. It was designed by Ralph Modjeski (see 'Crooked River Bridge', and 'Benjamin Franklin Bridge').

The longest continuous-truss railroad-bridge span in the USA is the 236.2 m (775 ft) of the Sciotville Bridge, also over the Ohio River, opened in 1918.

The world's longest railway water crossing is on the Southern Pacific Railroad, USA, across the Great Salt Lake, just west of Ogden, Utah. The original Central Pacific line climbed over Promontory at a maximum height of 1496 m (4907 ft). It was on this section that the record track-laying length was laid and the last spike was driven.

The Lucin Cut-off was opened on 8 March 1904. It crossed the lake on a 32 km (20 mile) long trestle which required 38 256 piles and other timber from 10.36 km² (4 miles²) of forests in Louisiana, Texas, Oregon and California. Gradually the trestle was filled in to form an embankment until latterly 19.1 km (11 miles 1509 yd) remained. As most of it was single-track, and it was several times attacked by fire, it was the most vulnerable part of the Southern Pacific system. In May 1960 198 m (650 ft) were burnt out.

In 1955 work began on a broad embankment 20.4 km (12.68 mile) long to replace the trestle. A total of 34 673 000 m³ (45 480 000 yd³) of rock, sand and gravel were consumed, mostly from quarries on Promontory Point. A maximum of 1 835 000 m³ (2 400 000 yd³) was placed in one month. For the base of the fill 11 738 139 m³ (15 352 000 yd³) was dredged from the lake to a maximum depth of 26 m (85 ft) below the water surface to a width of 183 m (600 ft). The top of the fill, 4 m (13 ft) above water, is 16 m (53 ft) wide.

The new line was opened on 27 July 1959. Together with the crossing of the Bear River by the Bagley Fill, the total length of embankment in the water is 44.4 km (27.6 miles).

A railway which went out to sea was the 206 km (128 mile) long Key West Extension, Florida. It was built by Henry Morrison Flagler (1830–1913), was begun in 1905, partly wrecked in a 201 km/h (125 mph) hurricane in 1909, and was opened to Key West on 22 January 1912. Between the mainland and Key West there were 27.8 km (17¼ miles) of bridges and 32 km (20 miles) of embankment through shallow water. The remainder was on the 'keys'. The longest bridge was the 11 km (7 mile) long steel girder Little Duck Viaduct. The railway was closed after being damaged by a hurricane on 2 September 1935 and has been replaced by a road. The rail journey took 3¾ hours.

The World's Longest Railway Bridges

Bridge	Length m	ft	Date opened	Details
Huey P. Long, New Orleans, USA	7 082	23 235	16 Dec 1935	Owned by the New Orleans Public Belt RR and used by the Southern Pacific, Missouri Pacific and Texas & Pacific RRs. Crosses Mississippi by 8 river cantilever spans totalling 1074 m (3524 ft). Main channel span 241 m (790 ft).
Yangtze River, Nanjing, China	6 772	22 218	1 Oct 1968	River section of 10 spans of 157 m (515 ft), total 1577 m (5774 ft), carries road above and double-track railway below. Piers go down 70 m (230 ft) below water surface.
London–Greenwich	c. 6 000	c. 19 000	14 Dec 1836	Viaduct of 878 brick arches. World's longest brick viaduct.
Hell Gate, New York	5 862	19 233	1917	Steel arch span of 298 m (977 ft 6 in) and long approaches including a 4-span bridge nearly 366 m (1200 ft) long across Little Hell Gate, and two 53.5 m (175 ft) spans over Bronx Kill. Carries 4 tracks of former Pennsylvania RR, now Conrail, 43 m (140 ft) above water.
Paglia Viaduct	5 400	17 716	29 Apr 1980	Reinforced concrete throughout. On Rome–Florence Direttissima.
Savannah River, S. Carolina, USA	3 692	13 000	1909	Plate girder and truss spans on concrete piers, and 1 swing span. Carries single line of Seaboard Coast Line RR at Hardeeville. Clearance above water 3.6 m (12 ft).
Lower Zambezi, Mozambique	3 678	12 064	1934	33 main spans of 793 m (262 ft 5 in), 7 of 50.3 m (165 ft), 6 approach spans 22.2 m (66 ft 5 in) at east end and a steel trestle viaduct at west end. Carries 1067 mm (3 ft 6 in) gauge railway from Marromeu to Tete.
Venice Viaduct, Italy	3 600	11 811	1846	222 arches across Lake of Venice. Road alongside.
Tay, Scotland	3 552	11 653	20 June 1887	Main steel spans total 3130 m (10 269 ft). Carries double-track Edinburgh–Dundee line. Replaces former single-line bridge opened 1 June 1878 and which was blown down on 28 December 1879.
Storstrøm, Denmark	3 212	10 537	26 Sept 1937	Carries a railway, 5.5 m (18 ft) road, and cycle path.
Victoria, Montreal	3 135	10 284	17 Dec 1859	Built by Robert Stephenson as a single-line tubular bridge with central span of 100.5 m (330 ft) and 24 spans of 73.7–75.2 m (242–247 ft). Rebuilt as a double-track steel-truss bridge and reopened as Victoria Jubilee Bridge on 13 Dec 1898. Carries Canadian National railway over St Lawrence River.
Upper Sone, India	3 064	10 052	27 Feb 1900	Carries Calcutta–Delhi main line over River Sone near Sasaram.
Ohio River, USA	3 011	9 877	1929	177 spans; height 28 m (92 ft). Carries Conrail (formerly New York Central) between Louisville, Kentucky, and Jeffersonville, Iowa. Replaced 1895 bridge.
Yellow River, Chengehow, China (old)	3 009	9 873	Nov 1905	102 spans. Carries Peking–Hankow Railway across Hwang Ho (Yellow) River.
Yellow River, Chengehow, China (new)	2 899	9 511	1950s	Double track, 71 steel-plate girder spans of 40 m (131 ft) on concrete columns 3.6 m (11.8 ft) diameter.
Godavari, India	2 772	9 096	6 Aug 1900	Carries Calcutta–Madras line over Godavari River.
Forth, Scotland	2 529	8 298	4 Mar 1890	Steel cantilever structure. Two main spans 521 m (1710 ft). Carries double-track Edinburgh–Dundee line 47.5 m (150 ft) above high water.
Benjamin Franklin, Philadelphia, USA	2 527	8 291	4 July 1926	Suspension bridge. Central span 533.4 m (1750 ft), 42.7 m (140 ft) above the Delaware River. Carries rapid transit trains between Philadelphia and Camden.

Bridge	Length		Date opened	Details
	m	ft		
Rendsburger	2 454	8 051		Over Nord-Ostsee (Kiel) Canal.
St Charles, Missouri, USA	2 400	7 876	1936	Steel cantilever structure on concrete and masonry piers, carrying the single-line Wabash RR 16.7 m (55 ft) above the Missouri River. Main bridge 500.4 m (1645 ft); max span 183 m (600 ft).
Cairo, Illinois, USA	2 396	7 864	1899	Carries Illinois Central Gulf RR over Ohio River. Height 31.1 m (102 ft). Steel truss spans on masonry piers.
Amur, Khabarovsk, USSR	2 300	7 546	1916	On Trans-Siberian Railway. 22 spans. Longest in Russia.
Newark Bay, New Jersey, USA	2 259	7 411	1926	Steel deck-plate-girder spans on concrete piers, and two vertical lift spans of 65.8 m (216 ft) and 40.8 m (134 ft), rising to give a clearance of 41.4 m (135 ft). Carries Jersey Central RR between Bayonne and Elizabeth.
Pont de Cubzac, France	2 198	7 211	1886	Crosses River Dordogne at St Andre de Cubzac near Bordeaux. Iron girder spans; max height 20.5 m (67 ft).
Mahanadi, India	2 106	6 909	11 Mar 1900	Carries South Eastern Railway over Mahanadi River at Cuttack
Salado, Santa Fé, Argentina	2 044	6 705	1892	Carries 1676 mm (5 ft 6 in) gauge single track of Argentine Central Region over River Salado. Longest in Argentina.
Izat, Allahabad, India	1 945	6 381	1 Jan 1905	40 spans of 45.7 m (150 ft). Carries the North Eastern Railway across the Ganges.
Havre de Grace, Maryland, USA	1 877	6 108	Jan 1910	Replaced 1886 bridge. Carries Baltimore & Ohio RR across the Susequehanna River. 40 steel spans.
Hardinge, Bangladesh	1 798	5 900	4 Mar 1915	15 spans of 106.7 m (350 ft) and 6 land spans of 22.9 m (75 ft). Clearance at high water 12.2 m (40 ft). Carries former Bengal & Assam Railway over the Ganges near Sara.
Santiago del Estero, Argentina	1 788	5 868	1891	Carries 1676 mm (5 ft 6 in) gauge single-track branch of Argentine Central Region over River Dulce.
Rakaia, South Island, New Zealand	1 744	5 720	1939	Replaces trestle bridge built in 1870s. 143 steel-plate spans of 12.2 m (40 ft) on concrete piers. Clearance above water 2.7 m (9 ft).
Martinez–Benicia, California, USA	1 708	5 603	1930	Steel spans on concrete piers. Central lift span 100 m (328 ft) giving max clearance of 41.1 m (135 ft). Carries Southern Pacific across arm of San Francisco Bay.
Yangtze River, Wuhan, China	1 670	5 479	Oct 1957	Double-track railway; road above. Continuous steel truss. Main spans 1156 m (3793 ft); approaches 514 m (1686 ft).
Lethbridge Viaduct	1 623	5 327	1909	Carries Canadian Pacific Railway over Oldman River, Alberta, at a height of 95.7 m (314 ft). Highest and longest in Canada.
Ohio River, Louisville, Kentucky, USA	1 604	5 263	1918	Carries double track of Conrail (former Pennsylvania RR). Steel truss spans, max 192 m (630 ft).
A. H. Smith Memorial Bridge, Castleton, New York, USA	1 602	5 255	1924	52 steel girder spans on steel towers and 2 steel through-truss spans of 183 m (600 ft) and 124 m (408 ft) on concrete piers. Clearance 44.1 m (145 ft). Carries Conrail (former New York Central) across Hudson River.
Lake Pend d'Oreille, near Sanspoint, Idaho, USA	1 453	4 767	1902	78 deck-plate-girder spans of 15.2 m (50 ft) and 4 through-plate-girder spans of 23 m (75 ft) and 2 of 30.5 m (100 ft) and 1 pin-connected draw span of 60.9 m (200 ft). Clearance 9.8 m (32 ft). Carries Burlington Northern (former Northern Pacific) RR.
Batraki, USSR	1 438	4 719	1880	Carries Syzran–Kuibishev line over Volga River by 13 through steel truss spans of 107 m (350 ft).
Moerdyk, Netherlands	1 400	4 592	1880	14 spans of 100 m (328 ft). Carries Antwerp–Rotterdam Railway across the Hollandsch Diep.

Bridge	Length m	ft	Date opened	Details
Ohio River, Pittsburgh, Pennsylvania, USA	1 388	4 555	1933	Carries 2 tracks of Conrail (former Pennsylvania RR). Steel truss spans, max 157 m (515 ft).
Fuji River, Japan	1 373	4 505	1 Oct 1964	On Shinkansen system. Steel through-truss spans.
Sacramento River Viaduct, California, USA	1 325	4 346		71 steel spans on steel towers and 3 deck-truss spans. Carries Southern Pacific RR.
Memphis, Tennessee, USA	1 235	4 509	1917	Steel cantilever structure on concrete and masonry piers. Max span 241 m (791 ft). Carries double-track Chicago, Rock Island & Pacific RR and 2 carriageways across Mississippi. Clearance 35.6 m (117 ft).
Yellow River Bridge, Tsinan, China	1 225	4 020	1911	Single track. 9 steel truss and 3 cantilever spans on piers. Clearance 19.1 m (62 ft 8 in).
Ava, Burma	1 203	3 948	1934	9 spans of 109.7 m (360 ft); 1 of 79.2 m (260 ft) and 6 of 18.3 m (60 ft). Carries metre-gauge line of Burma Railways across the Irrawaddy River from Ava (east bank) to Sagaing.
Yellow River, Fengling Ferry, Shansi, China	1 194	3 918		Double-track deck truss on 23 cylindrical concrete piers.
Rotterdam Viaduct, Netherlands	1 180	3 870		Carries Rotterdam–Dordrecht line through Rotterdam by 59 steel spans of 14–16 m (46–52 ft) and 6 approach spans, on masonry and steel piers. Tracks are 7 m (23 ft) above ground-level.
Sheyenne River Viaduct, Valley City, N Dakota, USA	1 177.4	3 863	1908	3 deck-plate-girder spans of 30.8 m (101 ft), 27 of 23 m (75 ft), 1 of 18.3 m (60 ft), 30 of 13.7 m (45 ft), all on steel towers, and timber trestle 45.7 m (150 ft). Max height above ground 49.4 m (162 ft). Carries single line of Burlington Northern (former NP) RR.
Weldon, N Carolina, USA	1 165	3 822	1910	Steel truss and plate-girder spans on concrete piers. Longest span 46 m (152 ft). Clearance above water 26 m (85 ft). Carries single line of Seaboard Coast Line RR.
Susquehanna River Bridge, Rockville, Pennsylvania	1 161	3 808	1902	48 masonry arch spans of 21.3 m (70 ft). Carries 4 tracks of Conrail (former Pennsylvania RR).
Sydney Harbour, New South Wales, Australia	1 149	3 770	19 Mar 1932	Main steel arch span 503 m (1650 ft); headway 51.8 m (170 ft); south approach 1 span 72.5 m (238 ft), 4 of 53.2 m (174 ft 6 in); north approach 5 spans of 50.9 m (167 ft). Carries double-track railway, road, tramway and footways.
Tsien-Tang-Kiang, Hangchow, China	1 073	3 420	1937	Steel truss spans on piers. Carries single-track Chekiang–Kiangsi Railway and road.
Upington, South Africa	1 071	3 514		Crosses Orange River with steel spans of 9.1 m (30 ft), 24.4 m (80 ft) and 30.5 m (100 ft).
Harrisburg Viaduct, Pennsylvania, USA	1 069	3 507		46 arches. Carries Reading Co Line across Susquehanna River. Max low-water clearance 22.7 m (74 ft 6 in).
Ford Madison, Iowa, USA	1 020	3 347	1927	Steel deck-girders and through-truss spans on concrete and masonry piers, and draw-span of 160 m (525 ft). Carries double track of Santa Fé RR and road across Mississippi. Replaced single-track bridge of 1887.
St Louis Bay, USA	1 015	3 330	1908	2 draw spans of 146 m (479 ft) and 129.5 m (425 ft); 1 pin-truss span 48.7 m (160 ft). Remainder pile and timber trestle. Carries Burlington Northern (former NP) RR between Superior, Wisconsin, and Duluth, Minnesota.
Kiso River, Japan	1 001	3 284	1 Oct 1964	On Shinkansen system.
Quebec, Canada	987	3 238	3 Dec 1917	Steel cantilever bridge. Main span 548.6 m (1800 ft) including suspended span of 205.7 m (675 ft); shore spans 168.2 m (562 ft 6 in). Carries track of Canadian National Railways over the St Lawrence.

7

TUNNELS

The world's first railway tunnel was an underground line at Newcastle upon Tyne, built in 1770.

Chapel Milton Tunnel on the Peak Forest Tramway in Derbyshire, was opened on 1 May 1800. This was a plateway with L-section rails. At Ashby de la Zouch in Leicestershire, a tunnel 282 m (308 yd) long was built for the Ticknall Tramway (which also used L-section rails) in 1800–5. It was enlarged by the Midland Railway for the Ashby–Melbourne Branch, opened on 1 January 1874. Passenger trains ran until 22 September 1930. Hay Hill (or Haie Hill) Tunnel on the Forest of Dean Tramroad in Gloucestershire was opened in September 1809 and was 973 m (1064 yd) long. In 1854 it was enlarged by Brunel to accommodate the 2134 mm (7 ft) gauge Forest of Dean Branch from the South Wales Railway to Cinderford. It was converted to standard gauge in 1872 and was closed on 1 August 1967. Talyllyn Tunnel on the Hay Railway in Breconshire, Wales, was opened on 7 May 1816 and was 616 m (674 yd) long. In 1860 it became part of the Brecon & Merthyr Railway and was enlarged in 1862. It was closed on 2 May 1964.

The first railway tunnel to be used for passenger traffic was Tyler Hill Tunnel on the Canterbury & Whitstable Railway, opened on 4 May 1830. It was 766 m (838 yd) long. Passenger traffic ended on 1 January 1931 and the line closed completely on 1 December 1952.

The second was the single-line tunnel, 265 m (290 yd) long and only 3.7 m (12 ft) high, leading to the Crown Street terminus of the Liverpool & Manchester Railway at Liverpool, opened on 15 September 1830. Passenger traffic continued until 15 August 1836 when Lime Street Station was opened. Next was Glenfield tunnel on the Leicester & Swannington Railway, opened on 17 July 1832. It was 1642 m (1796 yd) long. Passenger trains ran until 24 September 1928 and the tunnel was closed completely on 4 April 1966.

The first underwater public railway tunnel was the Thames Tunnel on the East London Railway. The two parallel bores were built by Marc Brunel (1769–1849), begun in 1825 and opened on 25 March 1843 for pedestrian traffic. They were incorporated in the East London Railway under the supervision of the engineer Sir John Hawkshaw and opened on 7 December 1869. The railway now forms part of the London Regional Transport system.

Britain's longest railway tunnel is the Severn Tunnel built by the Great Western Railway to shorten the route

East or English end of the Severn Tunnel at the time of its completion in 1886. The longest tunnel on British Railways.

between London and South Wales. It was opened on 1 September 1886 after 14 years' work. It is 7 km (4 miles 628 yd) long, but of this length only about 2 km (1¼ miles) are actually under water even at high tide. The engineer was Sir John Hawkshaw (1811–91).

Turkey intends to build a tunnel between Istanbul and Haydarpasa to connect the European and Asian systems of Turkish State Railways. This was announced on 20 September 1977, but work has not yet started.

The longest underwater tunnel in the USA is the Bay Area Rapid Transit (BART) Trans Bay Tube carrying rapid transit trains beneath the bay between San Francisco and Oakland. It is 5.8 km (3.6 miles) long. It was opened on 14 September 1974.

The 1837 m (2009 yd) long single-track St Clair Tunnel, linking Canada and the USA under the St Clair River between Sarnia and Port Huron, was opened on 27 October 1891 for freight and on 7 December for passengers. It cost $2 700 000. In 1908 it was electrified with single-phase ac 3300 V, 25 Hz. It was operated by the St Clair Tunnel Company, a subsidiary of the Grand Trunk Railroad of Canada which gained access to Chicago by a series of links which became the Grand Trunk Western. The GT and its subsidiaries including 2598 km (1614 miles) in the USA came into the possession of the Canadian Government on 21 May 1920. It became part of the Canadian National system in 1959. When the use of diesel locomotives became universal the electrification through the tunnel was dismantled.

The Grand Trunk's main competitor, the then Michigan Central, also built a tunnel under the St Clair River, between Detroit and Windsor in 1906–10. This consists of two single-track tubes 2553 m (2792 yd) long, of which 813 m (889 yd) are beneath the water. This section was built by dredging a trench and sinking the pairs of steel tubes into it. It was originally electrically operated, but as in the St Clair Tunnel the electrification was abandoned with the advent of diesel-traction.

The Channel Tunnel first came into prominence in 1874 when the South Eastern Railway obtained Parliamentary powers to sink experimental shafts and in 1881 to acquire lands between Dover and Folkestone. The Submarine Continental Railway Company Limited, incorporated on 12 December 1881, took over the SER works and drove a pilot tunnel about 1920 m (2100 yd) out under the sea. The chief engineer was Sir John Hawkshaw. Work was suspended in 1883, largely for military reasons. In 1875 a Channel Tunnel Company and a French Submarine Railway Company obtained powers to carry out works and the latter drove a 2.4 km (1½ mile) gallery under the sea from Sangatte. In 1886 the English company was absorbed by the Submarine Continental Company and in 1887 the name became the 'Channel Tunnel Company'. The original SER interests are now held by the British Railways Board.

In July 1957 the Channel Tunnel Study Group was formed to carry out extensive economic, traffic and revenue, and engineering studies. In March 1960 it submitted its report, recommending a twin railway tunnel, and on 6 February 1964 the British and French governments decided to go ahead with the project. Survey work was completed in October 1965. In 1966 it was proposed that private capital should be raised for the tunnel, being repaid through a royalty arrangement on all goods and traffic using the tunnel. It was emphasized that the tunnel would not be built at the taxpayer's expense.

Work began in 1974 and considerable progress had been made both on the British side, at the Shakespeare

Cliff site, and on the French side when the British government under Harold Wilson forced the abandonment of the project in January 1975.

The political decision to divide responsibility between the British and French governments, financing companies, project managers and railways prevented co-ordinated planning and was a major influence in the British government's decision. The Cairncross Report (*The Channel Tunnel and alternative cross-Channel Services*, HMSO, 1975) stated: 'We have been conscious as our work proceeded that everything seemed to be happening in the wrong order. In the face of all adverse circumstances the tunnel remains the cheapest and most efficient method of handling cross-Channel traffic.' After its abandonment there was an enormous increase in cross-Channel juggernaut traffic obstructing British roads.

Faith in the project was now too firmly rooted for it to die and, after much discussion of various schemes, including ridiculously ill-conceived ideas for a bridge, a half-bridge-half-tunnel, and a 'drive through' tunnel for motor vehicles, a positive scheme for a twin-bore railway tunnel was finalized and a decision to proceed with it was made by the British and French governments on 20 January 1986. Following this, a Concession was granted to the Channel Tunnel Group/France Manche under which the partners, known as Eurotunnel, have the right to build and to operate the tunnel over a period of 55 years from the coming into force of the Concession in 1987. The contract, at a price of £2750 million, was signed in August 1986, and work on the tunnel was resumed on both sides of the Channel. By the time of the public share offer in November 1987 much further progress had been made.

The two rail tunnels will be 7.6 m (25 ft) diameter and 49.4 km (30.7 miles) long of which 38 km (23.6 miles) will be under the sea. A central service tunnel 4.8 m (15 ft 9 in) diameter will be connected to the running tunnels by transverse passages 3.3 m (11 ft) diameter at intervals of 375 m (410 yd).

The tunnel will pass through a mixture of chalk and clay known as chalk marl, which is ideal for tunnelling and is impervious to water, about 100 m (328 ft) below sea level, giving a normal thickness of rock above the tunnels of

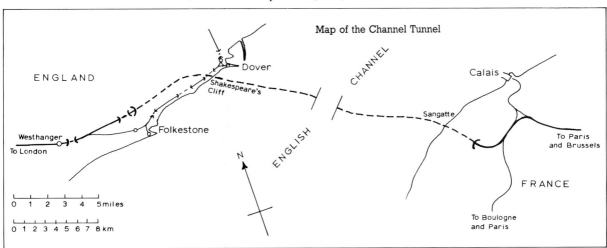

about 40 m (150 ft). The security of the rock is well shown by the pilot bore driven under the sea from the British side in 1882 and untouched since, which is still structurally sound. Break-through of the service tunnel is expected in 1990 and it is planned to open the tunnel to traffic in 1993.

Two types of train will use the tunnel: purpose-built shuttle trains owned and operated by Eurotunnel to carry freight and passenger road vehicles with their drivers and passengers; and passenger and freight trains operated by European railways linking the railway networks of Britain, France and continental Europe. As an example it is expected that trains will run from London to Paris in 3 hours. The capacity of the tunnel will be about 20 trains an hour in each direction. No advance booking or prepayment will be necessary. Elaborate precautions have been worked out to avoid the spread of dangerous diseases through the tunnel. It is expected that the tunnel will give a great boost to traffic on British and European railways and there should be a welcome reduction in heavy lorry traffic on our roads.

A view inside the Seikan Tunnel during construction. With a length of 53.8 km (33.4 miles) it is by far the longest railway tunnel in the world and at a depth of 240 m (787 ft) below sea level it is the world's lowest railway. The branch tunnel on the left is an access tunnel for construction purposes.

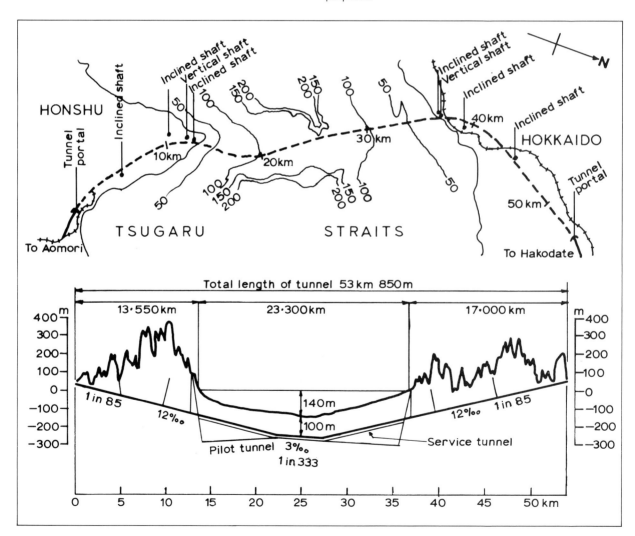

The Seikan undersea railway tunnel between Honshu and Hokkaido in Japan, 53.8 km (33.4 miles) long with 23.3 km (14.4 miles) undersea, has a maximum depth below sea-level of 240 m (786 ft). Work began in 1964 on shafts and pilot tunnels and was completed in 1987. The tunnel passes 100 m (328 ft) below the sea-bed in badly faulted granite containing water-filled seams of broken rock, compared with the clay-chalk of 'cheese-like consistency' with no faults expected in the Channel Tunnel.

Approach gradients are 1 in 83.3 (1.2 per cent). Work delayed by serious flooding: one flood in January 1974 halted work for a year.

The pilot tunnel was holed through on 27 January 1983, after 19 years of work. This will be the drainage tunnel and is about 100 m (328 ft) below the sea bed, which is 140 m (459 ft) deep. At this time the main tunnel was 94 per cent complete with less than 3000 m (3280 yd) to finish. It was holed through on 8 March 1985. The tunnel is

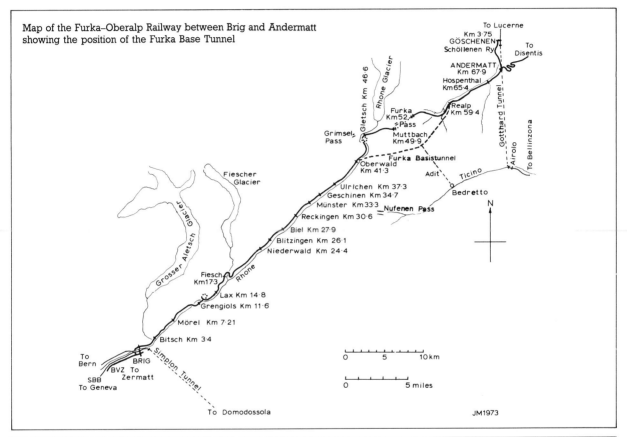

Map of the Furka–Oberalp Railway between Brig and Andermatt showing the position of the Furka Base Tunnel

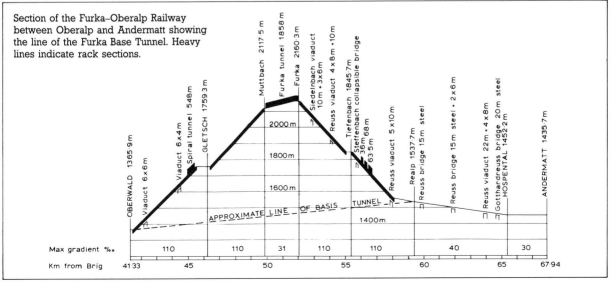

Section of the Furka–Oberalp Railway between Oberalp and Andermatt showing the line of the Furka Base Tunnel. Heavy lines indicate rack sections.

11 m (36 ft) wide to accommodate two standard-gauge tracks, but for the present two 1067 mm (3 ft 6 in) gauge tracks have been laid through, on concrete slabs. Provision is made for third rails for standard-gauge to be added later.

The first test train ran through on 21 October 1987 and the tunnel was opened for passenger trains on 13 March 1988. The total cost was 650 billion Yen, or 4.5 billion US dollars. It is unlikely that the tunnel will ever pay for itself in financial terms, but in human terms its value is incalculable. For example, in a typhoon in September 1954 five ferries were sunk and 1430 people were drowned. On average the ferry service is suspended over 80 times a year because of storms in the Tsugaru Straits. When it runs, the ferry from Amori to Hakodate takes 4 hours for the 113 km (70 miles).

Tunnels on Japanese railways total over 2000 km (1243 miles). Partly because of scarcity of land, much of the Shinkansen railway system is carried underground in long tunnels. Japan now has more of the world's longest tunnels than any other country.

The planned extension of the Shinkansen from Morioka to Amori, to connect with the Seikan Tunnel, includes a 26.5 km (16.5 mile) tunnel at Hokkoda and another of 25.8 km (16 miles) at Iwate.

The new Furka Base Tunnel on the metre-gauge Furka–Oberalp Railway in Switzerland, is 15 381 m (9 miles 968 yd) long and is the longest tunnel entirely in Switzerland. It cuts out the section between Oberwald and Realp over the Furka Pass which had to be closed every winter, so enabling the railway to operate all the year round, providing a vital link between the Cantons of Wallis and Graubünden. Regrettably, it also cuts out the spectacular view of the Rhône Glacier above Gletsch. Construction was facilitated by an adit 5221 m (3 miles 422 yd) long from Bedretto in the Ticino Valley. The tunnel was holed through on 30 April 1981. The first train passed through on 25 June 1982 from Oberwald to Realp. The tunnel includes two passing loops.

In Graubünden, Switzerland, a new tunnel on the metre-gauge Rhaetian Railway between Klosters and Susch in the Lower Engadin has been started. It will be 20 km (12.9 miles) long. It is expected to cost 455 million Swiss Francs and to be open in 1995. There will be two portals at Klosters, one for Rh B trains and the other further south at Stützbach for car ferry trains. The two tunnels will join 2.2 km (1.4 miles) from Klosters station.

The longest tunnel in Scotland is Greenock, on the former Caledonian Railway from Glasgow to Gourock, 1920 m (1 mile 340 yd), opened on 1 June 1889.

The longest tunnel in Wales is the Ffestiniog, 3407 m (2 miles 206 yd), on the Llandudno Junction to Blaenau Ffestiniog Branch of the former London & North Western Railway, opened on 22 July 1879.

The highest tunnel in Britain was at Torpantau on the Brecon & Merthyr Railway in Wales, 609 m (666 yd) long. The west portal was 400 m (1313 ft) above sea-level. It was opened on 1 May 1863 and closed on 2 May 1964.

Today the highest is Shot Lock Hill Tunnel on the Settle & Carlisle section of the former Midland Railway, at an altitude of about 349 m (1153 ft). It was built in 1872–3 and is 97 m (106 yd) long. Freight traffic began on 2 August 1875 and passenger traffic on 1 May 1876.

The deepest tunnel in England is Cowburn between Chinley and Edale in Derbyshire, 267 m (875 ft) below the surface at its deepest point. It is 3384 m (2 miles 182 yd) long. The tunnel was built by the Midland Railway and opened on 6 November 1893.

The total number of tunnels in Great Britain was 1049 in 1938. By then several lines had been abandoned and the total could have been about 1060. This includes 'long bridges' classed as tunnels.

Europe's longest tunnel north of the Alps is Lieråsen between Asker and Brakerøya on the Oslo–Drammen line in Norway, begun in 1963 and opened on 3 June 1973. It is 10.7 km (6 miles 1142 yd) long, shortens the rail journey between Asker and Drammen by 12.5 km (7.8 miles) and permits speeds up to 120 km/h (74½ mph).

The longest tunnel on French Railways is the Somport Tunnel, actually between France and Spain. It is 7874 m (4 miles 1572 yd) long, and was opened on 18 July 1928. It carries a single line, and is operated by the French National Railways (SNCF).

One of Europe's shortest railway tunnels is the Moutier III tunnel between Moutier and Roches on the single-track main line from Basel to Bienne in Switzerland. It is 6.8 m (22 ft) long. (See photo.) Moutier IV tunnel is 8.2 m. Another is Di Molino tunnel on the St Gotthard Railway, 6.5 m long (21 ft).

The longest railway tunnel in China is the 14.3 km (8.9 mile) double-track Dayaoshan tunnel on the nearly-completed section of the Beijing–Guangzhou railway south of Hengyang. The entire railway is 2310 km (1435 miles) long and is largely an upgrading of earlier routes with many new sections. Double-tracking of the Beijing–Hengyang section was completed about 1980.

China's second longest tunnel, the 8.5 km (5.3 miles) Jundushan tunnel on the Datong–Quinhuangdao line was completed on 26 December 1987. Information about the exact length of these tunnels is not yet available.

The longest tunnel in Canada for over 70 years was the 8083 m (5 mile 39 yd) Connaught Tunnel in the Selkirks on the Canadian Pacific Railway. The headings met, below the 2890 m (9483 ft) peak of Mount Macdonald, on 19 December 1915. The double-track bore, opened on 6 December 1916, replaced the difficult route over the

Rogers Pass which reached an altitude of 1323 m (4340 ft) and was threatened every winter with snow blockage despite 6.5 km (4 miles) of snow-sheds. It shortened the route by 7.2 km (4½ miles), lowered the summit by 165 m (540 ft) and eliminated curves amounting to seven complete circles.

Track was singled in 1959 to give greater clearances for 'piggyback' trains. At its deepest point the crown of the tunnel lies beneath a mile of rock.

In July 1984 work began on a 33.4 km (21 mile) long deviation from just south of Stoney Creek Bridge, along a 1225 m (4020 ft) long bridge section, built on a 41 degree slope above the Beaver River, through a tunnel 1858 m (1 mile 271 yd) long, across a bridge over Connaught Creek, leading to the main tunnel 14 723 m (9 miles 260 yd) long. This passes 91.4 m (300 ft) below the north-east end of Connaught Tunnel and 256 m (840 ft) below Rogers Pass. The tunnel is 5 m (17 ft) wide, 6 m (20 ft) on curves, and

One of Europe's shortest tunnels, Moutier III Tunnel, 6.8 m (7.4 yd) long, at km 74.6 between Moutier and Roches BE on the single-track main line between Basel and Bienne and Geneva, Switzerland. Photographed on 8 August 1984.

Western portal of Connaught Tunnel during construction in 1916. The original line over Rogers Pass can be seen above the trees. With a length of 8 km (5 miles 39 yd) it was Canada's longest tunnel until the opening of the new deep-level tunnel 14.7 km (9 miles 260 yd) long.

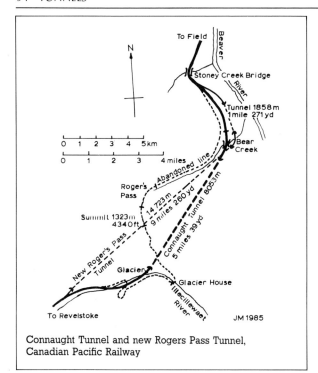

Connaught Tunnel and new Rogers Pass Tunnel,
Canadian Pacific Railway

West end of Kojak Tunnel, 3.9 km (2 miles 770 yd) long, on
the Quetta–Chaman line in Pakistan. Begun in 1884 and
completed in 1891, it is still the longest tunnel on the
Indian sub-continent.

7.9 m (25 ft 10 in) high above rail level. At near mid-point
a vertical shaft 348.9 m (1145 ft) deep provides ventilation
controlled by a door under the shaft. The tunnel was broken through in October 1986. The work involved construction of eight bridges totalling 1724 m (5658 ft) and
excavation of 1.14 million metres^3 of overburden and
349 600 metres^3 of rock. The new line, intended for westbound trains, rejoins the old route about 6 km (3.8 miles)
beyond the south-west end of Connaught Tunnel and
reduces the grades from 1 in 45 (2.2 per cent) to 1 in 100
(1 per cent). The engineering team was headed by John
Fox, Vice President, engineering special products. It is the
largest project undertaken by CP Rail since the completion of the transcontinental line in 1885. It came as a
result of the recent Western Grain Transportation Act
which, for the first time in decades, made grain transport
by rail profitable.

The longest tunnel in the Southern Hemisphere is on a
30 km (18.6 mile) long industrial mining line between
Toquepala and Cuajone in Peru, officially opened on
6 December 1975. It is 14.7 km (9.1 miles) long. Tunnels
on the line total 27 km (16.8 miles), leaving only 3 km
(1.9 miles) in the open.

The longest tunnel in New Zealand measures 8.8 km (5½
miles) and pierces the Kaimai Range, forming part of a
new 24 km (15 mile) cut-off line between Apata and
Waharoa in the North Island. It was opened on 12 September 1978. The tunnel is straight, on a gradient of 1 in
333 (0.3 per cent) rising from west to east. Paved concrete
track (PACT, qv) is used throughout for the single line.

Also in the North Island is the single-track Rimutaka
Tunnel on the railway from Wellington to Masterton. It

was opened on 3 November 1955 and is 8798 m (5 miles
821 yd) long. It replaced the line over the Rimutaka
Ranges, involving the famous Fell incline of 5 km (3
miles) at 1 in 14–16 opened on 12 October 1878.

The Otira Tunnel in the South Island, New Zealand,
between Christchurch and Greymouth, is 8563 m (5 miles
564 yd) long and was opened on 4 August 1923. It has a
gradient of 1 in 33 (3 per cent), rising from Otira to Arthur
Pass, and at the time of building it was the longest tunnel
in the British Empire and fifth longest in the world. It is
electrically worked, at 1500 V dc.

New Zealand Railways have over 180 tunnels, totalling
about 85 km (53 miles).

The longest tunnel in Argentina carries a 1676 mm (5 ft
6 in) gauge freight-only single line of the D. F. Sarmiento
National Railway (formerly Buenos Aires Western Railway) under the city of Buenos Aires. It is 4.8 km (about 3
miles) long and was opened on 14 February 1916. The
line leaves the surface tracks 1.2 km (¾ mile) west of Once
de Septiembre Station and from the tunnel entrance
descends at 1 in 67 to reach an average depth of 15 m
(49 ft) below street-level, and emerges in the Port Zone. It
is electrified with the standard 800 V dc third rail through
the tunnel and with overhead conductors in the Port
Zone.

The longest tunnel in Chile is Las Raices on the 1676 mm
gauge branch from Pua to Lonquimay, about 625 km (388
miles) south of Santiago. It is 4545 m (2 miles 1450 yd)
long.

The longest railway tunnel in South Africa is the twin-
bore Hilton Road Tunnel between Boughton and Cedara

on the Natal main line, 4948 m (3 miles 131 yd) long. Next are the Hidcote Tunnels, 3295 m (2 miles 84 yd). Both are on the South African Railways system. No others are over 1609 m (1 mile) long.

A new tunnel under the Hex River Pass near Worcester, under construction, 13.4 km (8 miles 574 yd) long, will be the longest in South Africa.

TUNNELS IN THE USA

On its 408 762 km (254 000 miles) of railroad in 1916 the USA had 1539 tunnels with a total length of 515 km (320 miles). This total number was only 50 per cent more than the total on 32 902 km (20 445 miles) in Great Britain in 1930.

The longest railway tunnel in North America is the Henderson Tunnel in Colorado. It is really a long mine adit, built by the Climax Molybdenum Company (a section of Amax Inc) to tap an immense body of molybdenum ore buried deep inside Red Mountain on the Continental Divide. The ore was discovered in 1975 just after the death of Robert Henderson who pioneered the exploration and after whom the mine is named. Shafts were sunk in the Clear Creek Valley near Empire 96 km (60 miles) west of Denver for access to the ore body. The main shaft, 8.5 m (28 ft) in diameter and 945 m (3100 ft) deep, is the largest shaft in North America.

For extraction of the ore a tunnel was bored about 15.4 km (9.6 miles) long on a rising gradient of 1 in 33 (3 per cent), emerging in the Williams Fork Valley on the west side of the Continental Divide. The exact length of the tunnel is difficult to establish because it has only one open end; the other end is inside the mine. A 7.7 km (4.8 mile) open stretch leads to the only suitable site which could be found within a radius of 40.2 km (25 miles) of the mine, where there was enough flat area for the extensive processing and storage facilities without spoiling the environment.

Driving of the tunnel began at the west portal on 10 January 1971, and it was holed through on 15 July 1975 with a vertical error of 127 mm (5 in) and a horizontal of only 25 mm (1 in). Surveying calculations had to allow for the curvature of the earth. The finished tunnel is 4.6 m (15 ft 2 in) high and 5 m (16 ft 6 in) wide, and contains a double-track 1067 mm (3 ft 6 in) gauge railway. In the centre is a ventilation shaft 3.4 m (11 ft) in diameter and 483 m (1585 ft) deep to exhaust hot air from the tunnel. Its site was so remote that helicopters had to be used to transport men and materials. The altitude of the east end of the tunnel, 945 m (3100 ft) underground, is 2286 m (7500 ft), and the west portal is 2766 m (9075 ft) above sea-level.

The remarkable series of zigzags which carried the Great Northern Railway from Spokane to Seattle over the mountains during the construction of the first Cascade Tunnel, 1892–1900. This also was abandoned in 1929 when the new base tunnel was opened, the longest 'through' railway tunnel in the USA.

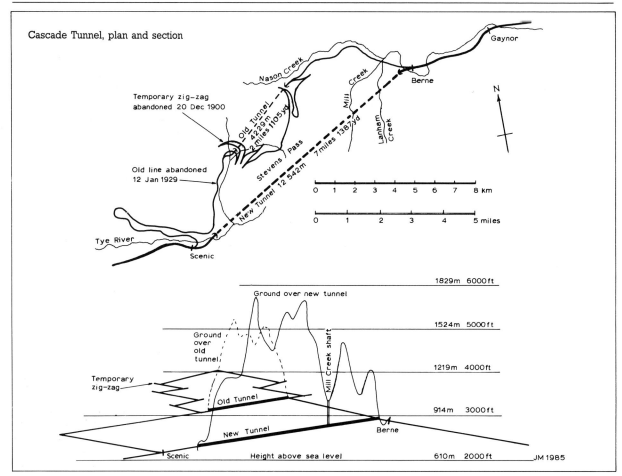

Cascade Tunnel, plan and section

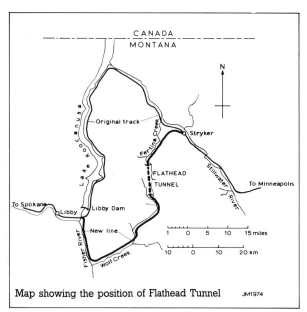

Map showing the position of Flathead Tunnel   JM 1974

Operation of the railway, which came into use in August 1976, is completely automatic. Six unmanned trains operate at a constant speed of 40 km/h (25 mph) between the mine and the processing mill. Each train, with four locomotives, one at each end and two in the middle, carries 660 tons of ore in 30 cars and makes 45 trips in 24 h. The locomotives were built by ASEA (Allmanna Svenska Elektriska Aktiebolaget) of Stockholm, and were designed to withstand a temperature range of −45.6°C (−50°F) to 29.4°C (85°F). Within the mine loading area the locomotives use a 600 V dc overhead system. From there to the processing mill a 1400 V dc overhead system is employed, fed by six transformer rectifiers from a 13.8 kW supply.

At a rate of extraction of 30 000 tons of ore per day it is expected that the known ore body will take 30 years to mine.

The longest through tunnel in the USA is the Cascade Tunnel on the Great Northern (now Burlington Northern) main line from Spokane to Seattle in Chelan and King Counties in Washington State. It is 12 542 m (7 miles 1387 yd) long. It was opened on 12 January 1929 and replaced an earlier line which climbed to a summit tunnel 4229 m (2 miles 1109 yd) long. While this was being built, trains crossed the summit by a spectacular series of zigzags in a line 19.7 km (12¼ miles) long. This opened in 1892 and was used until completion of the tunnel in 1900 (see map).

The second longest tunnel in the USA and seventh longest in the world, is the Flathead Tunnel in north-west

Montana, also on the Great Northern. It was made necessary by the Federal Government's Libby Dam project which flooded much of the former main line beneath Lake Koocanusa. It is on a new 96 km (59½ mile) diversion and passes under the Elk Mountain from Wolf Creek to Fortina Creek.

Guided by laser beam, the workers holed through on 21 June 1968 after 630 days, drilling from both ends. The tunnel is 12 479 m (36 970 ft) or 10 ft under 7 miles, including a 'cut and cover' section 509 m (1670 ft) long at the western end, and is 5.5 m (18 ft) wide and 7.2 m (23 ft 6 in) high above rail-level.

The tunnel was officially opened on 7 November 1970, the special train running from Libby to Stryker via the new line and returning via the old route.

The north portal is closed by a door after the passage of a train and two 2000 hp fans, 2616 mm (103 in) in diameter with a capacity of 8963 m³ (307 000 ft³) per min, clear the fumes from the tunnel in 17 min and provide cooling air for the engines as they pull up the grade towards the east.

The third longest tunnel is the Moffatt Tunnel, 9997 m (6 miles 373 yd), under James Peak, Colorado, on the Denver & Salt Lake Railroad, the 'Moffat Road'.

In 1921 the people of Denver and nearby counties voted and passed a bond issue of $15 470 000 to construct the Moffat Tunnel, thus creating the 'Moffat Tunnel District'. Work began in 1921 and the tunnel was holed through on 12 February 1927. It was opened on 27 February 1928, at an altitude of 2822 m (9257 ft), replacing the original line over the Rollins, or Corona, Pass at an altitude of 3554 m (11 660 ft). With the Dotsero Cut-off it shortened the route from Denver to Salt Lake City by 278 km (173 miles). The original pioneer bore carries water from the western slope of the Rockies to Denver where it is part of the main supply.

On 11 April 1947 the D & SLRR merged with the Denver & Rio Grande Western Railroad which rents the tunnel from the Moffat Tunnel District. The bonds matured in 1982.

The most difficult tunnel in America was the Hoosac Tunnel on the Boston & Maine Railroad in Massachusetts, on the main line from Boston to Albany. It was begun in 1851 and took 14 years to complete, at a cost of $20 000 000. The engineer was Herman Haupt (1817–1905). It was opened on 9 February 1875 and is 7562 m (4 miles 1230 yd) long. In 1911 it was electrified at a cost of $541 000. The electrification was abandoned on 24 August 1946 when the entire operation went over to diesels.

The shortest tunnel in the USA is Bee Rock Tunnel near Appalachia, Virginia, on the Louisville & Nashville line from Corbin, Kentucky, to Norton, Virginia, opened in 1891. It is 9 m (10 yd) long.

A natural tunnel was used on the Bristol–Appalachia section of the Southern Railway system at Glenita about 72 km (45 miles) west of Bristol, Tennessee. In the course of surveying the line along the Stock Creek Valley in 1880, the party reached a natural amphitheatre with a rock wall 61 m (200 ft) high and an arched tunnel entrance 27 m (90 ft) high and 36.5 m (120 ft) wide into which the stream flowed. It was eroded by waters east of Purchase Ridge forcing through the mountain wall into Clinch Basin. The tunnel was found to be 240 m (788 ft) long and averaged 30 m (100 ft) high and 40 m (130 ft) wide. After blasting through about 5 m (16 ft) of rock the engineers were able to construct the railway formation beside the stream.

AUSTRALIAN RAILWAY TUNNELS

The first railway tunnel in Australia was the double-track Elphinstone Tunnel on the 1600 mm (5 ft 3 in) gauge Victorian Government Railways Bendigo line north-west of Melbourne, opened in 1862. It is 382 m (418 yd) long and lies on a gradient of 1 in 60 (1.66 per cent) and a curve of 120.7 m (60 chains) radius, and is still in use.

The longest railway tunnel in Australia is Cox's Gap Tunnel, 1931 m (1 mile 352 yd). The 241 km (150 mile) single line from Sandy Hollow to Margvale, New South Wales, was sanctioned in 1927 but, because of economic depression, construction was not begun until 1937 and was further delayed by the war. This tunnel and four others were completed in 1949 but rails were not laid and the tunnels were used for road traffic. In 1982 the railway was completed from Sandy Hollow to Ulans coal mines and was opened in September.

The double-track Woy Woy tunnel, on the State Railway Authority of NSW north coast line between Sydney and Newcastle, was opened in July 1886. It is 1789 m (1 mile 197 yd) long.

There are two spiral tunnels in Australia, one on the Brisbane to Sydney main line at Cougal just south of the Queensland–New South Wales border, opened in 1932; and one at Bethungra on the Sydney–Melbourne main line, in southern New South Wales, opened in 1946.

The worst tunnel in Australia was the single line Otford Tunnel on the NSW Railway's Illawarra line south of Sydney, opened in 1886. It was 1550 m (1695 yd) long on a gradient of 1 in 40 (2.5 per cent) against loaded trains. Engine crews suffered so much from smoke inhalation and scalding that, after a forced ventilation system was installed with little success, a deviation was built and opened on 10 October 1920 and the tunnel was abandoned.

In Tasmania the longest tunnel is at Rhyndaston on the 1067 mm (3 ft 6 in) gauge single-track main line from Hobart to Launceston, opened on 13 March 1876. It is 1207 m (1320 yd) long.

RAILWAYS WITH MANY TUNNELS

The railway with the greatest number and length of tunnels is the Chengtu–Kunming railway in China, in the mountainous provinces of Szechwan and Yunnan. In its 1085 km (674 miles) it has 427 tunnels and 653 bridges. There is an average of one large or medium sized bridge for every 1.7 km and a tunnel for every 2.5 km. The combined length of tunnels and bridges exceeds 400 km (about 250 miles). The difficulties of access and construction were enormous. In the Shamulata tunnel an underground river broke in and poured 12 000 tons of water into the workings every 24 h. In a tunnel in the Chinsha River valley the men had to work in a temperature of 40°C (104°F).

The railway was begun in 1958 and was opened on 1 July 1970. It is one of the greatest feats of railway engineering in the world, and Chinese engineers are justifiably proud of it.

Another Chinese railway which approaches this record is the new line from Zhicheng in Hubei province to Liuzhou in Guanxi Zhuang, opened on 1 January 1983. In its 885 km (550 miles) it has 396 tunnels of a total length of 172.3 km (107 miles) and 476 bridges totalling 52.2 km (32 miles).

Since 1949 the Chinese People's Republic Railways have built about 4000 tunnels with a total length of about 1000 km (1120 miles).

In 1978 track laying was completed on the 475 km (295 mile) line from Tulufan to Kuerhle in the north-west province of Sinkiang, begun in July 1971. The major work was Koeihsien tunnel, about 6 km (3¾ miles) long under the Tienshan mountain range.

The railway with the greatest number of tunnels in Europe is the Sierra de la Culebra Railway, Spain. Between Puebla de Sanabria and Carballino, 173 km (107½ miles), there are 182 tunnels amounting to 78 km (48½ miles). The longest is the 5949 m (3 miles 1226 yd) Padornelo Tunnel, opened in 1957–9.

The Bergen–Oslo line in Norway has 178 tunnels in 491 km (305¾ miles), amounting to 36.2 km (22½ miles). It was opened on 1 December 1909.

In Japan, the San-yo Shinkansen standard-gauge line from Okayama to Hakata, 398 km (247 miles), opened on 10 March 1975. There are 111 tunnels totalling 222 km (140 miles) and representing 56 per cent of the whole route. They include the Aki Tunnel, 13 030 m (8 miles 169 yd); Shin Kanmon, 18 713 m (11 miles 1105 yd); Kita-Kyushu 11 747 m (7 miles 528 yd) and Bingo, 8900 m (5 miles 933 yd).

A new iron-ore railway in Brazil, 397 km (247 miles) long, from Belo Horizonte to steelworks at Volta Redonda, was begun in May 1975. Much remarkable engineering was involved including 99 tunnels totalling 72.4 km (45 miles) and viaducts 39 km (24 miles). The longest tunnel, 8.7 km (5.4 miles), is at the 1124 m (3688 ft) summit at Bom Jardim beneath the Serra da Mantiqueira. Eight viaducts are over 60 m (197 ft) high; the highest is over the valley of Córrego Bela Vista, the tallest pier of which measures 81.8 m (268 ft 4 in).

Mounting costs resulted in the suspension of track laying in December 1983. Works have been completed from mines at Jeceaba to Saudade near Redonda, 309 km (192 miles), at a cost of US $600 million.

The highest tunnel in the world is the Galera Tunnel on the Central Railway of Peru, opened on 14 November 1893. It is 1176 m (1287 yd) long at an altitude of 4781 m (15 688 ft). (See map of Peru Central, p. 55.)

Compressed-air rock drills were first used in tunnel construction in the Hoosac Tunnel, USA, in 1855. (see p. 97.) In Great Britain they were first employed in the Clifton Tunnel on the Clifton Extension Railway, Bristol, in 1874.

An illustration of the type of engineering throughout the Chengtu–Kunming Railway, China, opened in July 1970. The railway has the most, and greatest length, of tunnels of any comparable length of line in the world.

The World's Longest Railway Tunnels

Tunnel	m	miles	yd	Date	Railway	Position
Siekan*	53 850	33	809	13 Mar 1988	Japan Rail	Honshu–Hokkaido
Daishimizu	22 228	13	1426	Mar 1980	Japan Rail	Jōmō-Kogen–Echigo
Simplon No 2	19 823	12	559	16 Oct 1922	Swiss Federal	Brig–Iselle
Simplon No 1	19 803	12	537	1 June 1906	Swiss Federal	Brig–Iselle
Shin Kanmon	18 713	11	1105	10 Mar 1975	Japan Rail	Honshu–Kyushu
Apennine	18 519	11	892	12 Apr 1934	Italian State	Florence–Bologna
Rokko	16 250	10	171	15 Mar 1972	Japan Rail	Osaka–Shinkobe
Furka Base	15 381	9	968	28 June 1982	Furka–Oberalp Switzerland	Oberwald–Realp
Haruna	15 350	9	933	15 Nov 1982	Japan Rail	Jōmō-Kogen–Echigo
Gotthard	14 998	9	562	1 Jan 1882 (a)	Swiss Federal	Göschenen–Airolo
Nakayama	14 650	9	180	15 Nov 1982	Japan Rail	Takasaki–Jōmō-Kogen
Lötschberg	14 612	9	140	15 July 1913	Bern–Lötschberg–Simplon	Goppenstein–Kandersteg
Haruna*	14 350	8	1612		Japan Rail	Takasaki–Jōmō-Kogen
Hokuriku	13 870	8	1089	10 June 1962	Japan Rail	Maibara–Fukui
Mont Cenis (Fréjus)	13 657	8	855	17 Sept 1871	Italian State	Turin–Modane
Shin Shimizu	13 500	8	684	15 Nov 1982	Japan Rail	Takasaki–Niigata
Aki	13 030	8	170	10 Mar 1975	Japan Rail	Mihara–Hiroshima
Cascade	12 542	7	1397	12 Jan 1929	Burlington Northern USA	Spokane–Seattle Washington
Flathead	12 479	7	1327	7 Nov 1970	Burlington Northern USA	Libby–Whitefish, Montana
Kitakyushu	11 747	7	528	10 Mar 1975	Japan Rail	Kokura–Hakata
Kubiki	11 353	7	96	May 1969	Japan Rail	Nou–Nadachi
Zao*	11 210	6	1698		Japan Rail	Fukushima–Shin-Shiroishi
San Donato	10 954	6	1419	1986	Italian State	Rome–Florence diretissima
Lieråsen	10 700	6	1142	3 June 1973	Norwegian State	Oslo–Drammen
Santa Lucia	10 262	6	662	22 May 1977	Italian State	Naples–Salerno
Arlberg	10 250	6	650	20 Sept 1884	Austrian Federal	Bludenz–St Anton
Moffat	9 997	6	373	27 Feb 1928	Denver & Rio Grande Western USA	Denver–Glenwood Springs
Ichinoseki	9 730	6	79	23 June 1982	Japan Rail	Ichinoseki–Kitakami
Shimizu	9 702	6	50	1 Sept 1931	Japan Rail	Doai–Tsuchitaru
Orte	9 371	5	1443	29 Apr 1980	Italian State	Rome–Città della Pieve
Kvineshei	9 064	5	1112	17 Dec 1943 (b)	Norwegian State	Kristiansand–Stavanger
Bingo	8 900	5	933	10 Mar 1975	Japan Rail	Fukuyama–Mihara
Kaimai	8 850	5	878	12 Sept 1978	New Zealand Govt	Waharoa–Apata, North Island
Rimutaka	8 798	5	821	3 Nov 1955	New Zealand Govt	Upper Hutt–Featherston, North Island
Uonuma	8 650	5	658	15 Nov 1982	Japan Rail	Urasa–Nagoaka
Ricken	8 603	5	608	1 Oct 1910	Swiss Federal	Wattwil–Uznach
Grenchenberg	8 578	5	581	1 Oct 1915	Swiss Federal (c)	Moutier–Grenchen
Otira	8 563	5	564	4 Aug 1923	New Zealand Govt	Christchurch–Brunner, South Island
Tauern	8 551	5	551	7 July 1909	Austrian Federal	Bad Gastein–Spittal
Fukuoka	8 488	5	482	10 Mar 1975	Japan Rail	Kokura–Hakata
Haegebostad	8 474	5	467	17 Dec 1943 (b)	Norwegian State	Kristiansand–Stavanger
Ronco	8 291	5	277	4 Apr 1889	Italian State	Genoa–Milan
Hauenstein (new)	8 134	5	95	8 Jan 1916	Swiss Federal	Tecknau–Olten

The World's Longest Railway Tunnels

Tunnel	m	miles	yd	Date	Railway	Position
Tenda	8 099	5	60	30 Oct 1914	Italian State	Turin–Nice
Fukushima	8 090	5	46	23 June 1982	Japan Rail	Koriyama–Fukushima
Connaught	8 083	5	39	6 Dec 1916	Canadian Pacific	Field–Revelstoke
Karawanken	7 976	4	1683	1 Oct 1906	Austrian Federal	Rosenbach (Austria)– Jesenice (Yugoslavia)
Borgallo	7 972	4	1679	1 Aug 1894	Italian State	Parma–La Spezia
New Tanna	7 958	4	1663	1 Oct 1964	Japan Rail	Tokyo–Shizuoka
Somport	7 874	4	1572	18 July 1928	French National	Oloran (France)–Jaca (Spain)
Tanna	7 804	4	1493	1 Dec 1934	Japan Rail	Tokyo–Shizuoka
Ulriken	7 662	4	1338	1 Aug 1964	Norwegian State	Bergen–Oslo
Hoosac	7 562	4	1230	9 Feb 1875	Boston & Maine USA	North Adams, Mass (Boston–Albany)
Monte Orso	7 562	4	1230	28 Oct 1927	Italian State	Rome–Naples
Lupacino	7 514	4	1178	24 Sept 1958	Italian State	Aulla–Lucca
Castiglione	7 390	4	1040	24 Feb 1977	Italian State	Rome–Florence
Vivola	7 355	4	1004	28 Oct 1927	Italian State	Rome–Naples
Monte Adone	7 132	4	760	22 Apr 1934	Italian State	Florence–Bologna
Jungfrau	7 123	4	750	1 Aug 1912	Jungfrau, Switzerland	Above Lauterbrunnen
Toyohara	7 030	4	647	23 June 1982	Japan Rail	Nasu-Shine-Shirakawa
Severn	7 011	4	628	1 Sept 1886	British Rail	Swindon–Newport
Shin-Kinmeiji	6 822	4	419	10 Mar 1975	Japan Rail	Shin-Iwakuni– Tokuyama
Itsukaichi	6 640	4	220	10 Mar 1975	Japan Rail	Hiroshima-Shin-Iwakuni
Ohirayama	6 585	4	160	10 Mar 1975	Japan Rail	Tokuyama–Ogori
San Giacomo	6 514	4	83	12 May 1977	Italian State	Savona
Marianopoli	6 475	4	42	1 Aug 1885	Italian State	Valledolmo–Enna, Sicily
Tsukiyono	6 460	4	25	15 Nov 1982	Japan Rail	Jōmō-Kogen– Echigo-Yuzawa
Turchino	6 446	4	10	18 June 1894	Italian State	Genoa–Asti
Wochein (Podbrdo)	6 339	3	1652	9 July 1906	Yugoslav State	Jesenice–Nova Gorica
Zlatibor	6 202	3	1503	1 June 1976	Yugoslav State	Belgrade–Bar
Sozina	6 170	3	1466	1 June 1976	Yugoslav State	Belgrade–Bar
Mont d'Or	6 097	3	1388	16 May 1915	French National	Vallorbe (Switzerland)
Urasa	6 020	3	1302	15 Nov 1982	Japan Rail	Urasa–Nagaoka
Col de Braus	5 949	3	1226	30 Oct 1928	French National	Turin–Nice
Padornelo	5 949	3	1226	1959	Spanish National	Puebla de Sanabria– Carballino
Albula	5 865	3	1134	1 July 1903	Rhaetian, Switzerland	Filisur–Samaden
Gyland	5 717	3	972	17 Dec 1943 (b)	Norwegian State	Kristiansand– Stavanger
Sant'Oreste	5 710	3	962	6 Dec 1976	Italian State	Rome–Florence
Totley	5 697	3	950	6 Nov 1893 (d)	British Rail	Sheffield–Chinley
Metropolitana	5 666	3	910	28 Sept 1925	Italian State	Naples
Shin Karikachi	5 647	3	896	Oct 1966	Japan Rail	Ochiai–Shin Karikachi
Cravere	5 573	3	813	June 1980	Italian State	Busselino–Salbettrand
Peloritana	5 446	3	676	20 June 1889	Italian State	Palermo–Messina, Sicily
Tanze	5 433	3	660	May 1984	Italian State	Busselino–Salbettrand
Puymorens	5 414	3	641	21 July 1929	French National	Foix (France)– Puigcerda (Spain)
Monte Massico	5 378	3	601	28 Oct 1927	Italian State	Rome–Naples
Senzan	5 361	3	583	10 Nov 1937	Japan Rail	Shikoku
Gravehalsen	5 312	3	529	10 June 1908	Norwegian State	Bergen–Oslo

The World's Longest Railway Tunnels

Tunnel	m	miles	yd	Date	Railway	Position
Fukasaka	5 173	3	379	1 Oct 1957	Japan Rail	Omi-Shintsu–Shinhikida
Biassa II	5 146	3	348	14 Nov 1933	Italian State	Genoa–La Spezia
S Elia-Ianculla	5 142	3	343	5 Dec 1960	Italian State	Reggio Calabria–Brindisi
S Cataldo	5 141	3	342	30 July 1894	Italian State	Agropoli–Supri (Naples–Reggio Calabria)
Mount Royal	5 073	3	268	21 Oct 1918	Canadian National	Montreal
Ohara	5 063	3	256	11 Nov 1955	Japan Rail	Ohara–Katsuura
Otowayama	5 045	3	247	1 Oct 1964	Japan Rail	Tokyo–Osaka
Amanus	4 905	3	83	1918	Turkish State	Adana–Aleppo
Woodhead New (e)	4 888	3	66	14 June 1954 (f)	British Rail	Sheffield–Manchester
Standedge (g)	4 888	3	66	5 Aug 1894	British Rail	Stalybridge–Huddersfield

(a) For goods traffic; passengers from 1 June 1882. .
(b) Wartime opening under German Occupation. Full traffic began 1 March 1944.
(c) Grenchenberg Tunnel owned by the Bern–Lötschberg–Simplon Railway but worked by Swiss Federal Railways.
(d) For goods traffic; passengers from 1 June 1894.
(e) Superseded two single-line tunnels 4848 m (3 miles 22 yd) long, opened 23 December 1845 and 2 February 1852.
(f) Formally opened 3 June 1954. Railway closed 18 July 1981.
(g) Two adjacent single-line bores opened 1 August 1849 and 12 February 1871 were abandoned in October 1966.
* Under construction.
On the Paola–Cosenza line a base tunnel 14 944 m (9 miles 502 yd) was started about 1969 and is still unfinished.

One of the world's most extraordinary railway tunnels: Corry Brothers' Tunnel on the Canadian Pacific Railway in the Lower Kicking Horse Canyon near what is now Palliser. The first tunnel, completed in 1884, was abandoned in 1887 after severe contraction and the line was taken round the hill on sharp curves. This second tunnel, 213 m (233 yd) long and timber lined like the first, was opened in 1906 and was later lined in concrete. After further trouble the hill was removed completely in the 1950s and the tunnel lining was left as a snow shelter.

8

MOTIVE POWER – STEAM

LOCOMOTIVE TYPES

Steam locomotives are generally referred by the system of wheel arrangements invented in 1900 by Frederic M. Whyte (1865–1941), an official of the New York Central Railroad. It can easily be worked out from the examples below. All locomotives are imagined facing to the left.

2-2-2	oOo
2-4-0	oOO
4-4-2 ('Atlantic')	ooOOo
0-4-0	OO
0-6-0	OOO
4-6-2 ('Pacific')	ooOOOo
2-8-0	oOOOO
2-10-4	oOOOOOoo

The European continental countries use an axle system, thus a 4–6–2 is a 2C1, or in France and Spain a 231. Germany and Switzerland denote the number of driving-axles as a fraction of the total number of axles: for example, a 4–6–2 is a 3/6, a 2–8–0 a 4/5.

Electric and diesel locomotives are referred to by a letter indicating the number of driving axles: A is one, B two, C three and D four.

A locomotive on two four-wheeled bogies with a motor to each axle is a Bo-Bo. The small 'o' indicates that the axles are not coupled. If the wheels were coupled it would be a BB. A locomotive on two six-wheeled bogies with all axles driven but not coupled is a Co-Co; if the axles are coupled it is a CC; if the centre axle is not driven it is an A1A-A1A. If the trucks are articulated by a connection taking buffing and drag stresses a plus sign is used; for example the locomotives of the Furka–Oberalp and Brig–Visp–Zermatt railways in Switzerland are Bo+Bo.

Richard Trevithick's locomotive of 1803. It is reported to have pulled a load of 10 tons and 70 passengers for a distance of 14 km (9 miles) at Penydarren in Glamorgan, South Wales on 21 February 1804.

STEAM LOCOMOTIVE DEVELOPMENT

The steam locomotive owes its origin to the high cost of obtaining and maintaining horses in Great Britain during the Napoleonic wars when the prices of horses and fodder rose considerably. At the same time coal was cheap. Richard Trevithick (qv), the inventor of the high-pressure steam engine which superseded the low-pressure condensing, or atmospheric, steam engines of Newcomen and Watt, had experimented with model steam locomotives since 1796. In 1800, on the expiry of James Watt's patent, Trevithick built a double-acting high-pressure steam engine. As the name implies in this the steam acted on both sides of the piston.

Trevithick's first railway locomotive was designed in 1803 at Coalbrookdale ironworks in Shropshire for the 914 mm (3 ft) gauge plateway there. A model of it can be seen in the National Railway Museum at York and a full-size reproduction is displayed at Telford station in Shropshire. It had a single horizontal cylinder mounted inside the boiler and it had flat-tyred wheels with no flanges. There is no evidence that this locomotive actually ran, or even that it was built; it might have been too heavy for the rails on which it was intended to run.

Trevithick's second locomotive was built while he was employed as engineer at the Penydarren Ironworks near Merthyr Tydfil in South Wales. On 22 February 1804 it pulled 10 tons of iron, 70 men and five extra wagons for 15 km (9½ miles) at nearly 8 km/h (5 mph). This had a return-flue boiler, steam blast in the chimney, and all four wheels driving, by gearing. Drawings of it can be seen at the Science Museum, London. A full-size working replica of this locomotive was built in 1981 as a project of the

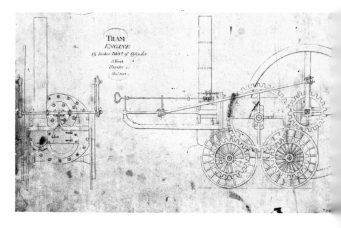

Welsh Industrial and Maritime Museum, part of the National Museum of Wales, Cardiff.

The locomotive was introduced to Northumberland by Christopher Blackett, proprietor of Wylam Colliery. He ordered an engine on Trevithick's principle through his engineer John Steel and it was built at Gateshead, County Durham, by John Whinfield. However, when it was tried in 1805 it was too heavy at over 5 tons and was rejected. **It was the first locomotive to have flanged wheels.**

In 1808 Trevithick's fourth locomotive, named *Catch me who can*, was built by J. U. Rastrick (1780–1856) at Hazeldine's Foundry at Bridgnorth, Shropshire, for demonstration on a circular track in London. Nothing seems to be known of the actual form of this locomotive.

The short 'D'-pattern slide-valve was introduced by Matthew Murray at Leeds, in 1806.

The first commercially successful locomotive was most probably that built by Matthew Murray in 1812 to an order by John Blenkinsop for the 1245 mm (4 ft 1 in) gauge Middleton Colliery Railway, Leeds. It ran on four

flanged wheels which were free, and was propelled by a toothed wheel which engaged a rack on the side of one rail. The two vertical cylinders, 229 × 559 mm (9 × 22 in) drove cranks set at right angles and geared to the rack wheel. It weighed about 5 tons. The engine went into service on 12 August 1812.

The spring-loaded safety valve was introduced in 1812 by James Fenton (1815–63) at Leeds.

The first locomotive built entirely at Wylam, Northumberland, was by William Hedley (qv), assisted by Timothy Hackworth and Jonathan Forster, in 1813. It ran on four flanged wheels and had a 1219 mm (4 ft) diameter boiler

Agenoria, shown at work on the Pensnett Railway in 1860. It was built by Foster and Rastrick at Stourbridge, Worcestershire, in 1828, similar to *Stourbridge Lion* built for the Delaware & Hudson RR in the USA. These were the last of the 'Grasshopper' type, so called because of the system of links above the boiler to retain the piston rods in the axis of the cylinders before the use of a crosshead. *Agenoria* is preserved in the National Railway Museum at York.

Blenkinsop locomotive of the Middleton Railway, Leeds, the first commercially successful steam locomotive, built by Matthew Murray in 1812.

3 m (10 ft) long. The two vertical cylinders at the rear drove the wheels through levers and connecting-rods to a centre jack-shaft geared to the two axles. It was known as the *Grasshopper*.

The next two engines built at Wylam in 1814–15 were of the same type but ran on eight wheels to spread the load on the light track until the cast-iron rails were replaced by wrought iron in 1830. Two more 'Grasshopper'-type engines on four wheels were built by Foster and Rastrick at Stourbridge, Worcestershire, as late as 1828. One, named *Agenoria*, was put to work on the Shutt End Railway from Lord Dudley's Colliery at Kingswinford to the Staffordshire & Worcestershire Canal. It is now in the National Railway Museum, York.

The other, named *Stourbridge Lion*, was sent to the USA, where it was tried on the Carbondale–Honesdale Railroad on 8 October 1829, the day before the opening. (See 'Early Railroads in the USA'.)

The locomotive bogie was patented by William Chapman in 1813.

A locomotive propelled by two legs working at the rear and pushing it along was patented on 22 May 1813 by William Brunton (1777–1851). An example was built at Butterley, Derbyshire, for Newbottle Colliery near Newcastle. In 1815 it was fitted with a new boiler which exploded on 31 July 1815 killing five, fatally injuring nine and maiming 43 others.

George Stephenson's first locomotive, named *Blücher*, was completed at Killingworth near Newcastle upon Tyne on 25 July 1814. It had a boiler 863 mm (2 ft 10 in) in diameter and 2.5 m (8 ft) long, in which the two 203 × 610 mm (8 × 24 in) cylinders were mounted vertically along the centre. They drove the wheels through counter-shafts geared to the two driving-axles.

In February 1815 Stephenson with Ralph Dodds, viewer at Killingworth Colliery, patented an engine in which the wheels were driven directly and coupled by either rods or chains.

The first engine under this patent was built in 1815. Its wheels were coupled by rods working on cranked axles. **This was the first use of cranked axles in a locomotive**, but they were abandoned as not strong enough and for a time wheels were connected by endless chains.

The loose-eccentric valve gear was introduced by George Stephenson in 1816 with the assistance of Nicholas Wood, and was used on the 'Rocket'- and 'Planet'-type engines until 1835.

Carmichael's valve gear with a single fixed eccentric was introduced in 1818. The end of the eccentric rod was fixed to two V-shaped 'gabs' in the form of an X which could be raised to engage the forward valve-pin or lowered to engage the backward pin. These pins were at opposite ends of a centrally pivoted lever.

The first locomotive to have its wheels coupled by rods was *Locomotion* No. 1 of the Stockton & Darlington Railway, built by George Stephenson in 1825. The two vertical cylinders 241 × 610 mm (9½ × 24 in) were in line along the centre of the single-flue boiler and each drove one of the axles through rods and crank-pins on the wheels. Because these cranks were set at right angles, one end of each coupling-rod had to be attached to a return crank.

The first four-cylinder locomotive was built by Robert Wilson of Newcastle upon Tyne, and was sold to the Stockton & Darlington Railway at the end of 1825. The vertical cylinders were in pairs on each side of the engine and drove the rear wheels.

The multi-jet blast-pipe was introduced in 1826 by Sir Goldsworthy Gurney (1793–1875). The fusible plug (a soft metal plug in the firebox crown which melts if uncovered by water and allows steam to damp down the fire) and expansion valve gear (allowing steam to be used expansively) were also introduced by him in the same year. He is best known for his steam road carriages.

The first six-coupled locomotive was Hackworth's *Royal George* built at Shildon, County Durham, in 1827. It was also the first engine in which the cylinders drove directly on to the wheels without intermediate gearing or levers. The piston-rods, however, were guided by Watt-type parallel motion, not a crosshead. Cylinders were 279 × 508 mm (11 × 20 in) and exhausted into a single blast-pipe. It weighed 8.4 tons.

The multi-tubular boiler was patented in 1827 by Marc Séguin (qv) and it was used on the first French steam locomotive, built by him and first tested on 7 November 1829 on the Saint-Etienne–Lyon Railway, opened in 1830. A forced draught was provided by two rotary fans on the tender, driven by the wheels. The engine weighed nearly 6 tons in working order and could haul 30 tons on a gradient of 1 in 167 at 7.2 km/h (4½ mph). A model of this engine can be seen in the Science Museum, London.

The first locomotive in which the wheels were driven directly from the piston-rod working in a crosshead was Stephenson's 0-4-0 for the Bolton & Leigh Railway where it was named *Lancashire Witch* in 1828. The 229 × 610 mm (9 × 24 in) cylinders mounted on the rear of the boiler drove the front coupled wheels which were 1292 mm (4 ft) diameter. This engine also incorporated expansion valve gear in a primitive form. It was the first locomotive to be entirely suspended on leaf springs.

Throughout the 1820s the steam locomotive remained an experimental machine. Its first opportunity to establish itself as a reliable form of motive power came in October 1829 at the Rainhill Trials on the Liverpool & Manchester Railway. A prize of £500 was offered by the company to the builder of a locomotive which, with a steam pressure not above 50 lb/in², could travel to and fro with a load of

20 tons over a course of 2.8 km (1¾ miles). Four locomotives were entered: *Rocket* by George Stephenson and his son Robert, then 26 years old, who did most of the design work; *Novelty*, built by John Braithwaite (1797–1870) to a design by John Ericsson (1803–89); *Sans Pareil* by Timothy Hackworth; and *Perseverence* by Timothy Birstall. The last was withdrawn before the competition. A curious entry was *Cycloped* powered by a horse walking on a moving platform, designed by Thomas Shaw Brandreth (1788–1873). It achieved a speed of 24 km/h (15 mph).

The prize was won by *Rocket.* This incorporated the same arrangement of sloping cylinders as on the *Lancashire Witch*, but only 203 × 419 mm (8 × 16½ in). It was the first engine to combine a multi-tubular boiler and a blast pipe. The latter was a device which, by directing the exhaust steam up the chimney, created a draught through the fire. Driving wheels were 1435 mm (4 ft 8½ in) diameter, equal to the track gauge, and the weight of the engine was 4½ tons.

Novelty was the first inside-cylinder (or inside-connected) locomotive, driving on to a crankshaft. The 152 × 305 mm (6 × 12 in) vertical cylinders drove the front axle through bell cranks. It was also the first well-tank engine.

In the USA a locomotive similar to *Cycloped* was designed by D. C. Detmold for the South Carolina Canal & Railroad in 1830. It was named *Flying Dutchman* and won a $300 prize. On an experimental trip it pulled 12 passengers at 19 km/h (12 mph).

The bar-frame and haycock firebox first appeared in the 0–4–0 *Liverpool*, built by Edward Bury (qv) largely to the design of James Kennedy (1797–1886). It was tried on the Liverpool & Manchester Railway in June 1830, two months before the line opened. It had 304 × 457 mm (12 × 18 in) cylinders driving on to a cranked axle. It was a highly advanced engine at the time. The inside cylinders became standard British practice and the bar-frame standard American practice. The multi-tubular boiler and smokebox were replacements soon after construction.

It was sold to the Petersburg Railroad, USA, in 1833. (See 'North American Locomotives', below.)

The first engine to be built with a smokebox was the Stephensons' *Phoenix*, built in 1830 for the Liverpool & Manchester Railway. The *Rocket* was soon afterwards rebuilt with this feature which became universal.

Stephenson's 2–2–0 engine *Planet* built in 1830 for the Liverpool & Manchester Railway had inside cylinders enclosed within the smokebox. **It was the first engine to be built with outside sandwich frames and outside bearings**, a feature of British practice which survived in Stephenson's designs for many years. (The 'sandwich' frame consisted of a slab of oak or ash between two iron plates.)

Hackworth's first inside-cylinder 0–4–0 was built at Shildon in 1830 for the Stockton & Darlington Railway and was named *Globe.* The 229 × 406 mm (9 × 16 in) cylinders were mounted beneath the driving-platform at the rear.

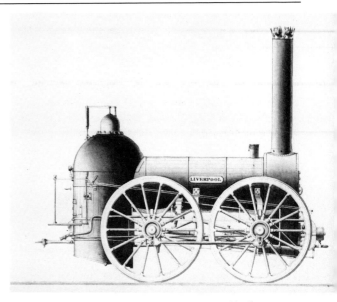

Edward Bury's inside-cylinder 0–4–0 *Liverpool* built at Liverpool in 1830 for the Liverpool & Manchester Railway. It established the bar frame construction for which Bury was famous.

The first locomotive in which the outside cylinders were attached to the frame instead of to the boiler was the *Union* built by Rothwell, Hick & Rothwell of Bolton, Lancashire, in 1831 for the Bolton & Leigh Railway. It was a 2–2–0 with a vertical boiler, 229 × 457 mm (9 × 18 in) cylinders and 1524 mm (5 ft) driving-wheels.

The first locomotive of Stephenson's 'Planet'-type inside-cylinder 0–4–0 to be delivered to America was originally named *Stevens* in honour of John Stevens (see 'Early Railroads in the USA'), but was renamed *John Bull.* It went into service on the Camden & Amboy Railroad on 12 November 1831. Because of a tendency to leave the rails, a two-wheeled truck and pilot was fitted in front by Isaac Dripps (1810–92), master mechanic on the C & A. This was **the first locomotive pilot, or 'cowcatcher'**. It ran until 1865 and is now preserved in the Smithsonian Institution, Washington, DC. In 1893 it travelled to the Chicago World's Fair under its own steam.

The classic British 'single-wheeler' was established by Robert Stephenson in a patent on 7 September 1833. It was a development of the 'Planet' type with a pair of wheels behind the firebox, becoming a 2–2–2, the success of the design resulting from the outside framing which allowed space for an adequate firebox.

The first engine, named *Patentee*, was built at Newcastle upon Tyne in 1833 for the Liverpool & Manchester Railway. It soon became widely adopted in Britain and abroad and was the design upon which the famous Gooch 'Singles' of the Great Western Railway were based. It was developed also into the 0–4–2 and 0–6–0 goods engines.

First experiments with piston-valves were made by Robert Stephenson in 1832. A design was prepared for a locomotive for the Liverpool & Manchester Railway, but there is no evidence of their behaviour, or that they were in fact used.

The 'petticoat' blast-pipe was also introduced by Robert Stephenson in 1832, by flaring the base of the chimney and extending it down into the smokebox to achieve a better smokebox vacuum.

A steam-trumpet was introduced on the Leicester & Swannington Railway following an accident at a road crossing on 4 May 1833.

The steam whistle was invented by Adrian Stephens (1795–1876) at Dowlais Works, Wales, in 1832–3 and was used on locomotives from 1835. It was reported in use on the Newcastle & Carlisle Railway on 28 June 1836 on the opening of the Hexham–Haydon Bridge section. It spread to North America in 1836 and France in 1837.

The steam-brake was introduced by Robert Stephenson in 1833, and was incorporated in his 'Patentee'-type 2-2-2.

The first inside-cylinder 0-6-0, a development of the Stephenson 'patent' type, was built by Robert Stephenson in 1833.

The bogie was first used on a British locomotive in 1833 on J. & C. Carmichael's 0-2-4 engine for the 1372 mm (4 ft 6in) gauge Dundee & Newtyle Railway.

The 'gab motion' (valve gear) operated by four fixed eccentrics was first used by Forrester & Company, Liverpool, in 1834-6, and R. & W. Hawthorn of Newcastle upon Tyne in 1835. Robert Stephenson & Company used the gear first on the 'patent'-type 0-4-2 *Harvey Combe* built in 1835.

The cylindrical smokebox was introduced in the USA in 1834 and was common there by the mid-1850s. It became established in Great Britain about 1900, but the old 'D' type was still being made by the London, Midland & Scottish and the Southern railways in the 1930s.

The balanced slide-valve was first patented by Hiram Strait of East Nassau, New York, on 25 June 1834. Its purpose was to eliminate the direct pressure of the steam on the top of the valve. It was first used on a railway engine by John Gray on the Liverpool & Manchester Railway in 1838. George W. Richardson patented an improved balanced slide-valve in the USA on 31 January 1872.

The first 'tank' locomotives were *Victoria* and *Comet* built by Forrester & Co. of Liverpool for the Dublin & Kingstown Railway in 1835. In so far as it carried its fuel and water on its own frame, *Novelty* could be described as

a tank locomotive. In German-speaking countries tank locomotives are known as 'Tenderlokomotiven'. A tender locomotive is referred to as 'Lokomotive mit Schlepptender'.

John Gray's expansion valve gear was first used in 1839 on the North Midland Railway. It was a complicated gear known as the 'Horse Leg' motion. Its purpose was to cut off the steam at different positions of the piston stroke to allow the remaining work to be done by the expansion of the steam.

The variable blast-pipe was introduced by Peter Rothwell (qv) of Bolton, Lancashire in 1839. It was in the form of a hollow cone which could be raised or lowered inside the blast-pipe orifice from a lever on the footplate. It was used on Sharp's heavy goods engines of 1848-9.

The locomotive superheater was introduced by R. & W. Hawthorn of Newcastle upon Tyne in 1839.

Long-travel valves, giving greater cylinder efficiency, were first used on the Hull & Selby Railway by John Gray (qv) in 1840. They had about 152 mm (6 in) travel.

They first became established in the USA. It was about 1900 before they were regularly used in England, on the Great Western Railway by G. J. Churchward (qv) and in 1909 by George Hughes (1865–1945) on the Lancashire & Yorkshire Railway, but it was nearly 30 more years before they were universally adopted in Britain.

Hall's brick arch in the firebox for smokeless combustion of coal was first tried in 1841. Previously, engines had burned coke or, as in North America, wood. It did not come into general use for several years but is stated to have been used on the Scottish North Eastern Railway by Thomas Yarrow from about 1857.

The Stephenson 'Long-boiler' locomotive was introduced in 1841, with the *North Star* for the 1524 mm (5 ft) gauge Northern & Eastern Railway. To obtain a large heating surface with a longer boiler, without increasing the wheelbase, the firebox was placed behind the rear axle. Mainly 4-2-0s, 2-4-0s and 0-6-0s were built to this design, but they were unsteady at speed.

The first British application of sanding gear, to sprinkle sand on the rails to help the driving-wheels to grip, was applied by Robert Stephenson in 1841.

The Stephenson (or Howe) Link Motion—valve gear with two fixed eccentrics—was first used on locomotives for the North Midland Railway by Robert Stephenson in 1843.

The 'stationary-link' motion was first used by Daniel Gooch (qv) on the Great Western Railway and by his brother John Viret Gooch (1812–1900) on the London & South Western Railway in 1843.

Walschaerts valve gear was invented by Egide Walschaerts (qv) in 1844. It was first used on a Belgian inside-cylinder 2–2–2 in 1848. In France it was applied on six Crampton engines built in Paris for the Chemins de fer du Nord in 1859. Its first use in Great Britain was on a Fairlie 0–6–6–0 built by the Yorkshire Engine Company, Sheffield, in 1876, and used on the East & West Junction Railway until converted by the makers to a 2–6–6–2 in 1881 for sale to the Nitrate Railways, Peru. In 1878 it was used on a 0–4–4 tank built by the Fairlie Engine Company, London, for the Swindon, Marlborough & Andover Railway. For its first use in the USA in 1874 see 'North American Locomotives' below.

The dial pressure gauge, replacing the mercurial gauge, was first proposed in Germany by Schinz in 1845. S. S. Smith of Nottingham patented and manufactured one in 1847 which interested George Stephenson. He used it on his colliery boilers at Clay Cross. It was perfected in 1849 by Eugene Bourdon (1808–84) of Paris.

The balancing of locomotive driving-wheels was first applied on the London & Birmingham Railway in 1845 as a result of experiments with models carried out in Birmingham by George Heaton of Shadwell Street Mills. His models are preserved in the Museum of Science and Industry, Birmingham.

The first three-cylinder locomotive was built by Robert Stephenson in 1846 as a private venture. It was tested on the London & Birmingham Railway and, following modification, was sold to the Newcastle & Berwick Railway.

The compounding of locomotive cylinders, using the steam twice, first at boiler pressure and then in partly expanded form at a lower pressure, was invented by John Nicholson in the locomotive department of the Eastern Counties Railway, England. It was patented and first applied by the engineer of the railway, James Samuel (1824–74), in 1850. It was known as 'continuous expansion' and, in fact, the expanded steam was used in both high and low pressure cylinders.

The double-beat regulator valve was introduced by John Ramsbottom (qv) on the London & North Western Railway in 1850. His famous **duplex safety-valve** was introduced in 1856 together with the **screw reverser**, instead of the hand lever, and the **displacement lubricator**. The screw reverse had already been used on the 1219 mm (4 ft) gauge Padarn Railway locomotives in North Wales in 1848 built in accordance with a patent by T. R. Crampton (qv). One of these is preserved at Penrhyn Castle near Bangor.

The first all-steel tyres for locomotive wheels were produced by Alfred Krupp (1812–87) of Essen, Germany, in 1851 and examples were displayed at the Great Exhibition in London in that year. The first manufacturer in the USA was James Millholland (1812–75) of the Philadelphia & Reading Railroad in the early 1850s. In Great Britain they were introduced by Naylor and Vickers on the London & North Western Railway in 1859.

Steel tyres lasted for 322 000 to 483 000 km (200 000 to 300 000 miles), compared with 96 500 km (60 000 miles) for iron tyres.

The drop-grate, to facilitate fire-cleaning, was introduced by Edward Bury in 1852.

A smokebox superheater for steam locomotives was used in 1852 by J. E. McConnell (1815–83) at Wolverton on the London & North Western Railway.

Feedwater-heaters were first tried in 1854 by Joseph Hamilton Beattie on the London & South Western Railway and were first applied in 1855. His double firebox and combustion-chamber, enabling engines to burn coal without producing smoke, were introduced in 1859.

The straight-link motion, invented by Alexander Allan (1809–91), was first used on locomotives of the Scottish Central Railway in 1854.

The firehole deflector plate to assist combustion was first applied by G. K. Douglas on the Birkenhead, Lancashire & Cheshire Junction Railway early in 1858.

The combination of brick arch and firehole deflector plate was devised by Charles Markham (1823–88) while assistant locomotive superintendent on the Midland Railway under Matthew Kirtley (1813–74) at Derby. It was first used in 1859 on a Midland engine. It enabled coal to be burnt without the complication of the Beattie firebox.

The steam injector (for forcing water into a locomotive boiler against pressure) was invented by Henri Giffard (qv), the French balloonist, and was first used on locomotives by Sharp Stewart & Company, Manchester, in 1859. By 1860 nearly 30 injectors were in use on British locomotives. It was introduced in the USA by William Sellers (1824–1905) in 1860. In the first year he supplied no fewer than 2800.

A steel locomotive firebox was first tried by Alexander Allan on the Scottish Central Railway in 1860. Steel fireboxes became general in American practice, but European engineers tended to continue with the copper firebox.

Steel boilers in place of wrought iron were first used by George Tosh on the Maryport & Carlisle Railway in 1862.

Steam tenders were introduced on the Great Northern Railway, England, in 1863 by Archibald Sturrock (1816–1909), the locomotive superintendent. Fifty were built, to increase the power of his 0–6–0 goods engines. Various troubles, including heavy maintenance costs, and complaints from men who were 'driving two engines and only getting paid for one' led to their withdrawal.

Some were rebuilt into small locomotives in 1870–3 by Isaac Watt Boulton (1823–99) at his famous 'siding' at Ashton-under-Lyne near Manchester.

While Sturrock was the first to use steam tenders extensively, they were first applied by the Verpilleux brothers, of Rive-de-Gier, France, who patented the invention on 26 September 1842.

The radial axlebox was invented by William Bridges Adams (1797–1872) and was first used on a 2–4–2 tank for the St Helens Railway in Lancashire, built by Cross & Company of St Helens in 1863.

The first successful locomotive piston valves were used in 1868 by Josiah Evans (1820–73) at Haydock Colliery, Lancashire. Six 0–6–0 outside-cylinder well tanks with split-ring piston valves and outside Stephenson link motion were built from 1868 to 1887. The third, *Bellerophon*, built in 1874, has been restored on the Keighley & Worth Valley Railway in Yorkshire. It is the oldest locomotive with piston valves.

The counter-pressure brake, in which the engine is reversed so that the cylinders act as compressors thereby absorbing power and avoiding wear on tyres and brake-blocks, especially on long inclines, was first used with water-injection by F. Holt on the South Staffordshire Railway in 1856. The Le Châtelier system, using hot water, was introduced on the London & North Western Railway in 1868.

The water-tube firebox was introduced by Johann Brotan (1843–1923) in Austria about 1870. His semi-water-tube boiler was first used in 1902 and over 1000 were built in the following 25 years.

The first successful compound locomotives were built by Anatole Mallet (1837–1919) in 1876. They were 0–4–2 tank engines for the Bayonne–Biarritz Railway in France.

Gresham's automatic vacuum brake was invented by James Gresham (1836–1914) and was first used in 1878. By this system the brakes are automatically applied on both portions of the train if it breaks in two. Gresham began his work on brakes while with Sharp Stewart & Company, Manchester. There, in 1864, he began improving the Giffard injector by providing means for adjusting the combining cone in relation to the steam cone.

Joy valve gear, which takes its drive from the connecting rod, was first used on a LNWR 0–6–0 in 1880. (See David Joy.)

The 'pop' safety-valve was patented in Britain by T. Adams in 1873 and was first used in 1874. A second patent in 1875 covered an annular pop chamber. In the USA, however, pop safety-valves were used from about 1867.

On the Lancashire & Yorkshire Railway, a pop safety-valve was introduced by Henry Albert Hoy (1855–1910) about 1900.

The Ross pop safety-valve was patented in 1902 and 1904 by fitter R. L. Ross of Coleraine Shed on the Belfast & Northern Counties Railway. It was first used on a locomotive by Bowman Malcolm (1854–1933), then locomotive superintendent of the B & NC, on his 2–4–0 No. 57 in 1908. The first new engine to be fitted was the B & NC 914 mm (3 ft) gauge compound 2–4–2 tank No. 112, also in 1908. It did not achieve extensive use in Great Britain until the 1920s.

The advantage of the 'pop' safety-valve was the small pressure difference, only about 0.07–0.14 kg/cm² (1–2 lb/in²) between opening and closing, compared with 0.35 kg/cm² (5 lb/in²) or more in the Ramsbottom type.

Speed-indicators for locomotives were first used by John Ramsbottom (qv) on the London & North Western Railway in 1861. A superior pattern was devised by William Stroudley (1833–89), locomotive engineer of the London, Brighton & South Coast Railway, in 1874.

Steam reversing gear was first used by James Stirling (1800–76) on the Glasgow & South Western Railway in 1874.

The Davies & Metcalfe exhaust-steam injector, making use of exhaust steam for forcing water into the boiler, was introduced in 1876.

Steel plate frames instead of wrought iron were first used by F. W. Webb on the London & North Western Railway by 1876. The plate frame was peculiar to British and European locomotive practice. American practice used the built-up bar-frame, first used by Edward Bury at Liverpool.

Steam sanding gear, devised by James Gresham and Francis Holt (1825–93), works manager, Midland Railway, Derby, was introduced on the Midland Railway in 1886. By forcing sand beneath the driving-wheels it brought about a revival of the 'single-wheeler' locomotive in Britain where it was built until about 1900 and lasted until the mid-1920s.

The British four-cylinder simple engine was introduced by James Manson (1846–1935) on the Glasgow & South Western Railway in 1897, with the 4–4–0 No. 11.

The smoke-tube superheater was introduced in Germany by Wilhelm Schmidt (1858–1924) in 1897. It was first used in Britain in May 1906 on the Great Western Railway two-cylinder 4–6–0 No. 2901 *Lady Superior* and on the Lancashire & Yorkshire Railway in two 0–6–0s.

A smokebox-type superheater was used by J. A. F. Aspinall (1851–1937), chief mechanical engineer of the

Lancashire & Yorkshire Railway, on his 4–4–2 No. 737 in 1899.

Class 5 4–6–0 No. 44686 fitted with Caprotti valve gear, at Southport, Lancashire, 1 September 1964.

The Lentz poppet-valve gear was first applied in Germany by Hugo Lentz (qv) in 1905. It used the type of valves familiar in internal-combustion engines. In Britain it was applied by H. N. Gresley (qv) to several types of London & North Eastern Railway locomotives.

The Caprotti poppet-valve gear, invented by Arturo Caprotti (qv), was first fitted to an Italian locomotive in 1920. It was first used in Britain on LNWR 'Claughton' 4–6–0 No. 5908 in 1926. It resulted in considerable coal economies, mainly when fitted to engines with poor front-end design.

The first British engine to be fitted with a booster was the Great Northern Railway 4–4–2 No. 1419 in 1923, later No. 4419 on the London & North Eastern Railway. The booster, common in America, was tried only on the LNER in Britain. It consisted of an auxiliary engine on the trailing truck which could be engaged and put into or out of operation as required.

The LNER tried boosters also on two 2–8–2 freight engines, two North Eastern Railway 'Atlantics' and a Great Central Railway 0–8–4 tank. The boosters were removed after a few years' trials.

The Giesl ejector for steam locomotives was developed over a long period by the Austrian engineer Dr Giesl Gieslingen, and was finished in 1951. Multiple exhaust jets along the centre-line of the smokebox exhaust into a chimney of oblong section with a length many times its width. It provides an equal draught through the boiler tubes for less back-pressure in the cylinders compared with the conventional blast-pipe.

It was widely applied in Austria and Czechoslovakia and was tried in Australia (NSW Government Railways 'C36' Class 4–6–0 No. 3616), India and East Africa. On British Railways it was tried on only two engines: standard 2–10–0 No. 92250, and a Southern Railway 4–6–2 No. 34064 *Fighter Command*. The National Coal Board, however, used it quite extensively and it was claimed to be 'worth several more wagons'.

NORTH AMERICAN LOCOMOTIVES

The reason that North American steam-locomotive development was generally anything up to 20 years in advance of British was probably that workers in the USA were better paid. As long as British railways could obtain good coal for a few shillings a ton, or could employ experienced fitters at about £1 a week in well-equipped works, it was of little consequence if the typical British inside valves and motion did take days instead of hours to dismantle and assemble, or if engines were inefficient.

All the biggest advances in steam locomotive development such as superheaters, coned boilers, cylindrical smokeboxes, large bearings, outside valves and motion, long-travel valves, side-window cabs, were well established in the USA many years before they became standard practice in Britain. Inside-cylinder engines were abandoned in the USA in the 1850s and inside valve gear soon after 1905. British Railways were still building them at Swindon in the 1950s.

The first locomotive headlight consisted of a fire of pine knots on a flat car pushed in front of the locomotive on the South Carolina Railroad in 1831. During the 1840s and 1850s candles and whale oil were burned in reflector lamps. Gas and kerosene lamps were introduced in 1859. Electric headlamps first appeared in 1881. The 'figure 8' oscillating headlight was introduced in 1936, and the sealed-beam headlight in 1946.

The first American 'national type' engine was the 4–2–0, originated by John B. Jervis (1795–1885) with the *Experiment* built at West Point Foundry, New York, in 1832 for the Mohawk & Hudson Railroad. It was **the first bogie locomotive in the world**. In its day it was also the fastest in the world, covering 22.5 km (14 miles) in 13 minutes. It was claimed that it reached 128.7 km/h (80 mph) over a 1.6 km (1 mile) stretch. The type was taken up by the Norris Brothers who redesigned it with the firebox behind the driving-axle to give more adhesive weight. Between 1835 and 1842 the 4–2–0 type formed nearly two-thirds of the total locomotives in the USA.

The iron bar frame for locomotives was introduced in the USA in 1833 by the 0–4–0 *Liverpool*, built by Edward Bury of Liverpool in 1830 and, after several rebuildings and changes of ownership, sold to the Petersburg Railroad in 1833. Other Bury locomotives were exported to the USA in the 1830s.

The first recorded American-built iron-frame locomotive was the *Comet*, completed at West Point Foundry, New York, in January 1835 for the Tuscumbia, Courtland & Decatur Railroad, but this was a bolted framing with pedestals for the journals. George E. Sellers claimed to have built the first iron frame, but his first engine was completed in September 1835. Previous American locomotives had wood frames. The Bury-type bar frame was specified for several 4–2–0s built by Stephenson and Tayleur, Newton le Willows, Lancashire, in 1835.

The earliest use of American-built bar frames cannot be established. They are shown on a drawing of the 4–4–0 *Gowan and Marx* built in 1839 by Eastwick & Harrison (Philadelphia 1839–42) but it is not certain if they were actually used on this engine. This firm certainly built them in 1842 for the *Mercury* for the Boston & Worcester Railroad. The bar frame probably became popular in American practice because it could be forged by a blacksmith. The last wooden locomotive frames were made in 1839 by Baldwin.

Cast-iron driving wheel centres were introduced in the USA in 1834. They were replaced by wrought iron in the 1850s.

Bells were first fitted on American locomotives in 1835 when the State of Massachusetts passed a law requiring this warning device.

The first locomotive to be exported from the USA was *Columbus*, built by Ross Winans (1796–1877) of Baltimore for the Leipzig & Dresden Railway in 1837.

The archetypal American 4–4–0 was first patented on 5 February 1836 by Henry R. Campbell (*c.* 1810–*c.* 1870), chief engineer of the Philadelphia, Germantown & Norristown Railroad.

The first American 4–4–0 was completed in Philadelphia on 8 May 1837. The 'classic' American 4–4–0 with 'three-point suspension' first appeared in 1839. It was a direct development of the Norris 4–2–0.

About 1870, 83–85 per cent of locomotives in the USA were this type of 4–4–0. Between 1840 and 1890 about 20 000 were built.

The first American locomotive whistles known to have been fitted were on two engines built at Lowell, Massachusetts, in 1836, appropriately under the supervision of the engineer George Washington Whistler (1800–49). The *Hicksville* entered service at Jamaica, on the Long Island Railroad, and was reported to make 'a shrill, wild, unearthly sound, like drawing a saw flat across a bar of iron'. The *Susquehanna* was tried at Wilmington, Delaware, at 56–64 km/h (35–40 mph), and was said 'to give awful notice of its approach to any point'.

A whistle was also fitted to the first Rogers engine, 4–2–0 *Sandusky*, built in 1837 for the Paterson & Hudson River Railroad (qv). It was the first locomotive in the State of Ohio. During its first trip in 6 October 1837 from Paterson, New York, to New Brunswick, New Jersey, the whistle was used so much that the engine ran short of steam.

Sandboxes were first fitted to American locomotives in 1836, following a plague of grasshoppers in Pennsylvania. On 1 August it was decided to use them on the Tuscumbia, Courtland & Decatur Railroad. The sand was sprinkled on to the rails and it prevented the engines slipping on the squashed insects.

The first 0–6–0 in the USA, named *Nonpareil*, was built in 1838 for the Beaver Meadow Railroad. In the same year the eight-wheeled tender first appeared, on *Uncle Sam* of the New Jersey RR & Transportation Co. By 1838 there were 345 locomotives in the USA; in 1840 there were about 590.

The first iron cab appeared, on *Novelty* of the Pennsylvania & Reading RR, in 1847. In the same year link motion was first used on US locomotives, on the Eastern Railroad.

The steam brake was first used on a locomotive in the USA in 1848 by George S. Griggs (1805–70), master mechanic of the Boston & Providence Railroad. But many years elapsed before it was widely used.

The first variable cut-off valve gear in the USA was produced by Eltham Rogers of the Cuyahoga Steam Furnace Company of Cleveland, Ohio, in 1849 and was first used on the *Cleveland* engine for the Cleveland, Columbus & Cincinnati Railroad in March 1850.

In Canada, as in the USA, **wood was the standard locomotive fuel** for many years. Apart from the three locomotives of the short coal line in Nova Scotia in 1839 (see chapter 1) the first experiments with coal were made about 1858–60; but it was into the 1870s before coal became generally used.

At first engines covered about 58 km (36 miles) on a cord of wood, but by 1859 this had risen to 80 km (50 miles). A 'cord' of wood was a stack 2.44 × 1.22 × 1.22 m (8 × 4 × 4 ft).

The Bissell truck, a short bogie with the pivot behind the rear axle and using inclined planes to support and to centre the front of the locomotive, was patented by Levi Bissell (1800–73) of Newark, New Jersey, on 4 August 1857. It was patented in Britain in May that year but was not used on a British locomotive until 1860. It rapidly replaced the centrally pivoted short truck. Bissell patented a two-wheeled pony truck in 1858. The most familiar application of the Bissell truck was on the 4–4–0 tanks built for the Metropolitan and District railways, London, by Beyer Peacock & Company, Manchester.

Bissell also patented an 'air spring' for locomotive suspension on 11 October 1841.

The early adoption in the USA of large numbers of driving-wheels was to obtain the necessary adhesion without excessive axle loading for the light track then in use.

The first 0–8–0 was built for the Baltimore & Ohio Railroad in 1841 by Ross Winans of Baltimore. He later developed the 'Mud-Digger' type.

One of the earliest 0–8–0s, *Buffalo*, of the Ross Winans 'Mud Digger' type, built in 1844 for the Baltimore & Ohio RR, at the B & O Museum at Baltimore.

Baldwin's first 0–8–0 appeared in 1846, when 17 were built for the Philadelphia & Reading Railroad. The two leading axles were mounted in a flexible truck.

The world's first 4–6–0, 'ten-wheeler', was *Chesapeake*. It was ordered in October 1846 by the Philadelphia & Reading Railroad and was delivered in March 1847 by Norris Brothers. Almost at the same time another, *New Hampshire*, was completed by Holmes Hinkley (1793–1866) for the Boston & Maine Railroad.

The first 2–6–0 was *Pawnee*, built in 1850 by James Millholland for the Philadelphia & Reading Railroad. This was a rigid machine. The proper 'Mogul'-type 2–6–0 followed the invention of the two-wheeled Bissell truck in 1858. The first 'Moguls' were built in 1860 by Baldwin of Philadelphia for the Louisville & Nashville Railroad. The type name probably originated with a 2–6–0 built for the Central Railroad of New Jersey by Taunton Locomotive Works, Massachusetts, in 1866. The name was used for 2–6–0s in a Baldwin Locomotive Works advertisement in *Poor's Manual of Railroads* in 1871–2. The first general use of the name for the type was in the Master Mechanics Association Report for 1872.

Various other locomotive improvements appeared during the 1850s. The 'wagon-top', or partly coned, boiler was introduced by T. Rogers in 1850. The wide firebox was designed by Z. Colburn (1833–70) in 1854 for the Delaware, Lackawanna & Western RR. Fluted side rods were introduced at Rogers, Ketchum & Grosvenor Works, Paterson, New Jersey, also in 1854.

By 1855 the number of locomotives in the USA had grown to about 6000. The firebrick arch, to promote combustion in the firebox, was introduced in the USA in 1856 by George S. Griggs who patented it in December 1857.

By 1855 coal was replacing wood as the fuel for locomotives in the USA. The Reading RR was the first major company to stop using wood, in 1859. Steel piston rods were introduced by Rogers in 1860 and in the same year steel tubes were first used by Baldwin, Philadelphia; the steel firebox was first made by Baldwin and by Taunton Locomotive Works, Massachusetts; and the extended smokebox was patented by J. Thompson. The injector was introduced on US locomotives in 1860.

The first engine in North America to have a boiler made entirely of steel was the inside-cylinder 0–6–0 *Scotia* built at the Hamilton Works of the 1676 mm (5 ft 6 in) gauge Great Western Railway of Canada in 1860. The steel was imported from England and cost 16 cents a pound. The total weight of the boiler was 4652 kg (10 356 lb) without the copper tubes.

The first 12-coupled engine was a 'camel'-type 0–12–0 tank named *Pennsylvania* designed by James Millholland and built at the Philadelphia & Reading Railroad's shops in 1863. It was used for banking coal trains over the summit between the Schuylkill and Delaware rivers. In 1870 it was rebuilt into a 0–10–0 tender engine.

The first regular 2–8–0, named *Consolidation*, in honour of the merging of the Lehigh & Mahanoy and Lehigh Valley railroads, was designed by Alexander Mitchell (1832–1908) in 1865. It gave its name to the type. It was built at Baldwin Locomotive Works, Philadelphia, in 1866 for the Lehigh & Mahanoy Railroad. It soon became the most numerous type in the USA.

In 1867 Mitchell introduced the 2–10–0 type for the Lehigh Valley Railroad.

The first 'pop' safety-valve was patented on 25 September 1866 by George W. Richardson of the Troy & Boston Railroad. (For its introduction and use in Great Britain see p. 108.)

Walschaerts valve gear was first used in the USA on a Mason-Fairlie double-bogie tank engine built in 1874 by William Mason (1808–83) for the Boston, Clinton & Fitchburg Railroad.

The wide Wootten firebox was invented in 1877 by John E. Wootten (1822–98) when general manager of the Philadelphia & Reading Railroad. It was designed to burn waste anthracite, or 'culm', which, because of its slow-burning qualities, required a larger area to give off the same heat as bituminous coal. It was first applied on the P & R 4–6–0 No. 411 in 1880. The grate area was 7.06 m² (76 ft²). The cab was mounted midway along the boiler, ahead of the firebox, so that the engines became known as 'Camelbacks' or 'Mother Hubbards'. The firemen stood on a separate platform at the rear.

The 4–6–2 type engine first appeared on the Lehigh Valley RR in 1886. It was built by the Vulcan Ironworks, Wilkes Barr, Pennsylvania, to a design by George S. Strong. The first 'classic' 4–6–2s, an enlargement of the 4–4–2 'Atlantic' type with wide firebox, were built for New Zealand by Baldwin Locomotive Works in 1901, the NZ 'Q' class. Whether it was these, or some 4–6–2s built in 1902 by Brooks Locomotive Works of Dunkirk, New York, for the Missouri Pacific RR which gave the name 'Pacific' to the type, has never been properly established.

The first 'Atlantic' or 4–4–2 type engine appeared in 1888, also built at the Vulcan Iron Works to a Strong design for the Lehigh Valley Railroad. The type name 'Atlantic' for the 4–4–2 type was suggested in 1894 by J. K. Kenly, general manager of the Atlantic Coast Railroad, for a group of 4–4–2s built by Baldwin.

The last, largest and fastest 'Atlantics' were the four oil-fired, streamlined engines built by the American Locomotive Company (ALCO) in 1935–7 to work the *Hiawatha* between Chicago and the 'Twin Cities' (Minneapolis and St Paul) on the Chicago, Milwaukee, St Paul & Pacific Railroad. They were the first steam locomotives in the world designed specifically to run at 161 km/h (100 mph) on every trip. They recorded speeds of over 193 km/h (120 mph).

The first 2–8–2 engines were built in 1897 by the Baldwin Locomotive Works for the 1067 mm (3 ft 6 in) gauge Japanese Railways. From these derived the type name 'Mikado'. It was introduced in the USA (where examples became affectionately known as 'Mikes') in 1903 on the Bismarck, Washburn & Great Falls Railway.

The Vanderbilt firebox was introduced by Cornelius Vanderbilt (1873–1942) in 1899 on 4–6–0 No. 947 of the New York Central & Hudson River Railroad, the railroad his great-grandfather Cornelius had established. The patent was for a boiler with a tapered barrel and a circular corrugated firebox resembling that introduced by Lentz in Germany in 1888. Although it had no stays, it gave trouble with leaks and breakages, and its limited grate area caused its early abandonment. Similar fireboxes were tried on the London & North Western and Lancashire & Yorkshire railways.

Vanderbilt also designed a tender with a cylindrical tank, first introduced in 1901 on Illinois Central No. 64, a Baldwin 4–6–0. The tender was widely used in the USA and became popular on the Canadian National Railways from 1924 onwards.

Wooden lagging for boilers, to prevent loss of heat, went out of use in the USA soon after 1900. Asbestos was first tried in 1873 on the Fitchburg Railroad, but it was not until about 1900 that, with magnesium lagging, it became widely adopted. Despite known health hazards, asbestos remained in use until the end of steam power in USA, Great Britain and elsewhere.

The 2–6–2 or 'Prairie' type tender engine was introduced by Baldwin Locomotive Works in 1885 with an order for New Zealand. Many of this type were built for passenger and freight work on the Mid-West lines of the USA and so gained the name 'Prairie'.

The last examples in the USA were built in 1910, but the type became popular on some eastern European lines, and in Great Britain with Gresley's famous 'V2' Class introduced on the London & North Eastern Railway in 1936. The first of these, No. 4771 *Green Arrow*, is preserved at the National Railway Museum, York.

The 2–10–2 'Santa Fe' type was introduced by the Atchison, Topeka & Santa Fe Railroad in 1903. These big Baldwin tandem compound machines were designed for helping heavy freight over the Raton Pass. The trailing-wheels assisted in running back down the grade.

The mechanical stoker of the Crawford plunger under-feed type was introduced on Pennsylvania Railroad 2–8–2s in 1905. From about 1915 it was gradually discarded in favour of the steam-jet overfeed system of the Street scatter type introduced about 1910, using a continuous chain belt. The Duplex stoker with screw conveyers was introduced in 1918 and replaced the Street type by 1920.

The Interstate Commerce Commission (qv) ruled that

from 1 July 1938 the mechanical stoker should be used on all coal-burning passenger engines with over 72 570 kg (160 000 lb), and on freight engines with over 79 378 kg (175 000 lb), on the driving-wheels. As a general rule, grates of over 4.6 m² (50 ft²) merited mechanical stokers.

The first superheated locomotive in North America was Canadian Pacific Railway Class SR 4–6–0 No. 548, built in the CPR New Shops at Montreal in September 1891. In 1901 it was equipped with a Schmidt smokebox super-heater. It ran with this until 1911 when a CPT Vaughan & Horsey superheater was fitted. The engine was renumbered 392, Class D3c, in 1907; 7292 Class D4m in 1913; 292 Class D3c in 1922, and was scrapped in May 1929.

The Jacobs-Shupert firebox was introduced in 1908–9 on the Atchison, Topeka & Santa Fe Railroad. It dispensed with stay bolts and gave greater safety, but its numerous joints resulted in leaks and its use was not continued.

The 4–8–2 type was introduced on the mountain section of the Chesapeake & Ohio RR in 1911 and it became known as the 'Mountain' type. The type was extensively used in the USA where about 2400 were built, and in Canada. In Europe the finest examples were the Chapelon 241Ps in France, built 1948–52 and running until 1970.

Boosters were first used in the USA on two-wheeled trailing trucks in 1915 and on four-wheeled trucks after 1925.

Baker valve gear, similar to Walschaert's but using a double bell-crank rocker instead of an expansion link, was introduced in the USA in 1912–13. The gear gives a constant lead; valve travel may be up to 230 mm (9 in).

The cast-steel one-piece engine frame, or bed, was first produced by General Steel Castings Corporation, USA, in 1925. At first the cylinders were separate. Later they were cast integrally with the frame and smokebox saddle, and this became universal from 1930. The whole was a triumph of the foundryman's craft and made possible the Lima 'Super Power' engines.

The tender booster was introduced in 1922 on the Delaware & Hudson Class E3a 2–8–0 No. 901 of 1906 with such success on heavy coal trains that the patent was bought by the Bethlehem Steel Co. and was used on locomotives right across the USA.

The four-wheeled trailing truck to carry increasingly heavy firebox loads was introduced in 1925 and with one-piece cast-steel frames in 1927. The six-wheeled truck first appeared in 1938.

The 2–8–4 'Berkshire' type originated in the USA in 1925, built by Lima Locomotive Works, Ohio. It was the first of the Lima 'Super Power' engines. The first examples went to the Boston & Albany RR which worked through the Berkshire Hills, hence the name.

The 2–10–4 type also originated in 1925 when Lima built some for the Texas & Pacific Railway. These gave the name 'Texas' to the type. The best-known examples were the 'Selkirks' of the Canadian Pacific Railway (see 'Largest and Most Powerful Steam Locomotives', p. 120).

The 4–6–4 tender locomotive appeared in the USA in 1927 when ALCO built the first for the New York Central RR. They were built continuously until 1948. The type became known as the 'Hudson' because the main line of the NYC ran up the Hudson Valley. It gave greater power than the 4–6–2 because of the larger firebox made possible by the trailing bogie.

The popular American 4–8–4 type was introduced in 1927 on the Northern Pacific Railroad. The type represented the maximum power which could be obtained with eight coupled wheels. The type was widely adopted in the USA and Canada.

The first locomotive to be equipped with roller bearings throughout was a 4–8–4, built by ALCO in 1930 for the Timken Roller Bearing Company which numbered it 1111. Its rolling resistance was so small that on level track the 350 ton engine could be kept in motion by three girls. After demonstrations all over the country, it was sold to the Northern Pacific Railroad, which numbered it 2626, in 1933.

The first all-welded boiler was fitted to a Delaware & Hudson Railroad 2–8–0 in 1934, and was given several years of trials before being passed as satisfactory by the Interstate Commerce Commission.

BRITISH AND EUROPEAN LOCOMOTIVE PROGRESS

The first British 4–4–0 was rebuilt from a Norris 4–2–0 of the Birmingham & Gloucester Railway between 1846 and 1850.

Daniel Gooch built 2134 mm (7 ft) gauge 4–4–0s for the Great Western Railway in 1855, but with a rigid wheelbase.

The first British bogie 4–4–0s to be built new were two by Robert Stephenson & Company for the Stockton & Darlington Railway in 1860 to a design by William Bouch (1813–76; brother of Sir Thomas). Next were the London, Chatham & Dover and Great North of Scotland railways. All these engines had outside cylinders.

The first locomotive with the Adams sliding bogie with central pivot was a 4–4–0 tank on the North London Railway. It was designed by William Adams (1823–1904) and was built at the NLR Bow Works in 1865.

The typical British inside-cylinder inside-frame 4–4–0 was introduced by Thomas Wheatley on the North British Railway in June 1871. The first of these, No. 224, went down with the first Tay Bridge in 1879. It was recovered, and after rebuilding it ran until 1919.

The first 2–6–0 or 'Mogul' to be built and to run in Britain appeared on the Great Eastern Railway in 1878. Fifteen were built by Neilson & Company of Glasgow to the design of William Adams. The first of the class, No. 527, carried the name *Mogul* on the sandboxes above the middle coupled wheels. For the origin of the type name see above.

The 2–6–2 tank locomotive first appeared in Britain in 1887 when Beyer Peacock, Manchester, supplied a batch of six outside-cylinder engines to the Mersey Railway.

The first eight-coupled main-line tender engines to run in Britain were two outside-cylinder 0–8–0s built in 1886 by Sharp Stewart in Manchester, originally for the Swedish & Norwegian Railway which, however, was unable to pay for them. In October 1889 they were acquired by the Barry Railway in South Wales where, in 1897, they were joined by two more of the same original order.

The first British inside-cylinder 0–8–0 was built in October 1892 at Crewe on the London & North Western Railway to a design by F. W. Webb. It was Webb's only eight-coupled simple engine.

The 2–8–0 type was introduced in Britain by G. J. Churchward (1857–1933) on the Great Western Railway in 1903, nearly 40 years after the type had become well established in the USA.

The first engine in service in Britain with a Belpaire firebox was the 0–6–2 tank No. 7 designed by Thomas Parker and built by the Manchester, Sheffield & Lincolnshire Railway at its Gorton Works in September 1891. It was renumbered 515 on 24 October 1893; became No. 5515, Class 'N5', on the London & North Eastern Railway in 1923; was renumbered 9250 in 1947 and was withdrawn in 1956 as British Railways No. 69250.

The first 4–6–0 to run on a British railway was Highland Railway No. 103, introduced in 1894 by David Jones (1834–1906). It ran until 1934 and, after a short spell working special trains in the early 1960s, it was placed in the Glasgow Transport Museum. These were not the first 4–6–0s to be built in Britain. The Indian 'L' class, built by Neilson & Co. of Glasgow, appeared in 1880.

The first 4–6–0 passenger engine in Britain was the North Eastern Railway 'S' Class introduced in 1899 by Wilson Worsdell (1850–1920).

Britain's first 'Atlantic'-type locomotive was designed by H. A. Ivatt (1851–1923) and was built at Doncaster in 1898 by the Great Northern Railway. The first, No. 990, was later named *Henry Oakley* after the GNR general manager.

It was closely followed by the inside-cylinder 4–4–2 of the Lancashire & Yorkshire Railway, designed by J. A. F. Aspinall and completed at Horwich Works in February 1899. This was remarkable for its 2210 mm (7 ft 3 in)

coupled wheels and high-pitched boiler.

Ivatt's large-boilered 'Atlantic' with wide firebox first appeared in 1900. Its appearance startled everyone at the time, but its performance was sadly inferior until it was rebuilt with superheater and piston-valves.

The first European railway to operate 'Pacific'-type locomotives was the Paris–Orléans, France. In 1907 the Class 4501 was introduced, later to be rebuilt by Chapelon (1892–1978) into one of the most efficient and powerful steam locomotives in Europe.

The first British 'Pacific' locomotive was built at Swindon in 1908 to a design by G. J. Churchward on the Great Western Railway. No. 111 *The Great Bear* was a large-boilered version of his successful four-cylinder 'Star' Class 4–6–0. Its weight restricted it to Brunel's London–Bristol railway, and the design was not repeated. It was withdrawn in 1923.

The first British 'Pacifics' to be produced as a class were designed by H. N. Gresley (1876–1941) and built by the Great Northern Railway at Doncaster. No. 1470 appeared in April 1922, and was later named *Great Northern*. The most famous, No. 1472, appeared in January 1923 and was the first engine to be completed by the newly formed London & North Eastern Railway. It was renumbered 4472 and named *Flying Scotsman*. It is now preserved.

The first ten-coupled engine in Britain was a three-cylinder 0–10–0 tank designed by James Holden (qv) and built at Stratford Works, London, on the Great Eastern Railway in 1902. Its purpose was to demonstrate that a steam train could accelerate to 48 km/h (30 mph) in 30 s, so defeating a proposal for a competing electric railway. It was the first three-cylinder engine in Britain since 1846. Having fulfilled its purpose, it was rebuilt into a 0–8–0 in 1906.

Britain's other ten-coupled designs were the Midland Railway 0–10–0 of 1919 for banking trains up the Licky Incline south of Birmingham; the Ministry of Supply 2–10–0s of 1943 and the British Railways standard 2–10–0s of 1954. The Midland 0–10–0 was unique in having four cylinders but only two sets of valve gear and valves, using a system of cross-over ports inside the cylinder casting.

France's first ten-coupled locomotives, the 6000 series 2–10–0s, appeared on the Paris–Orleans Railway in 1909. The 2–6–4 tender locomotive, which became known as the 'Adriatic' type, was first built in 1909 for the Austrian State Railway which then extended along the Eastern shore of the Adriatic. The 4–6–4 tender type appeared on the Nord in France in 1910, to the design of Gaston de Bousquet (1839–1910). Two only were built. The second, 3.1102, was sectioned for the 1937 Paris exhibition and is now displayed at the French National Railway Museum, Mulhouse.

The first 12-coupled tender engine in Europe was the 2–12–0 designed by Karl Gölsdorf (1861–1916) for the

Austrian State Railways. It was built in 1911 for the long 1 in 40 or 2.5 per cent grades on the Arlberg route.

Other European systems which used 12-coupled types were the Württemburg State, 1917–24; Bulgarian State, 1931 and 1942; German Reichsbahn, 1941; France, 1947; Yugoslavia (metre gauge), 1947. A 2–12–0 six-cylinder compound (Class 160A) was rebuilt from a 6000 series 2–10–0 by Chapelon for the Paris–Orleans Railway. It first ran in 1940 but the war delayed trials until 1948 by which time the PO was part of the SNCF. French Railways made extensive use of 4–8–2s on heavy express passenger work. The first, four-cylinder compounds, were introduced on the Est system in 1925, followed by the PLM in 1931. A three-cylinder simple type appeared on the Etat in 1933.

Britain's first eight-coupled express passenger engine was the London & North Eastern Railway 2–8–2 No. 2001 *Cock o' the North* designed by H. N. Gresley and built at Doncaster in 1934. It was built with Lentz rotary-cam poppet valve gear and was later rebuilt with Walschaert's valve gear and a streamlined front. With five other 2–8–2s it worked between Edinburgh and Aberdeen. Their tractive effort of 19 714 kg (43 462 lbs) was the highest of any British express locomotives. They had 1880 mm (6 ft 2 in) coupled wheels.

In 1943–4 all six were rebuilt into 4–6–2s by Edward Thompson (1881–1954), Gresley's successor.

Top: Midland Railway 4-cylinder 0–10–0 built at Derby in 1919 for banking trains up the 3.2 km (2 mile) long 1 in 37 Lickey Incline south of Birmingham. Here it is seen as BR No. 58100 banking a freight train on 31 August 1955. It was withdrawn in May 1956.

Above: Cylinder and valve casting of the MR 0–10–0 showing the crossover ports enabling one valve to control steam to and from two cylinders.

STEAM RAILCARS

The first railcar was a four-wheeled vehicle designed by James Samuel (1824–74), while resident engineer of the Eastern Counties Railway. It was built by W. Bridges Adams (1797–1872) at Fairfield Works, Bow, London, and was named *Express*. It first ran on 23 October 1847. It had a vertical boiler. Although it could run at 75.5 km/h (47 mph) and burned only 0.9 kg of coke per km (3.02 lb/ mile), it carried only four passengers and was hardly an economic proposition.

The first large railcar was again by J. Samuel and W. B. Adams, built in 1848 for the 2134 mm (7 ft) gauge Bristol & Exeter Railway. This vertical boilered car, named *Fairfield*, was put to work on the Tiverton Branch.

Their next, *Enfield*, built in 1849 for the Eastern Counties Railway, was the first with a horizontal boiler.

After a quarter of a century the railcar idea was again taken up. In 1873 Alexander McDonnell (1829–1904) of the Great Southern & Western Railway in Ireland produced a 0-4-4 tank with a staff saloon attached to the rear.

Other staff railcars were built as follows:

1. Great Eastern Railway in 1874 by William Adams (1823–1904).
2. London, Brighton & South Coast Railway in 1885 by William Stroudley.
3. London & South Western Railway in 1899 (the famous 'Cab', incorporating a single-drive engine) by Dugald Drummond (1840–1912).

In Belgium the railcar was introduced in 1877 by M. A. Cabany of Malines. A total of 15 were built, some with six and some with eight wheels.

Great Western steam railmotor No. 1 built at Swindon in 1903.

The next railcar phase came in 1903–11, when many railways were trying to economise on branch lines or on urban lines competing with street cars. Most of these cars had a small 0-4-0 locomotive forming one bogie. About 25 companies in Great Britain and Ireland produced about as many different designs. Among the best and longest lived were the Lancashire & Yorkshire Railway cars by George Hughes.

Geared steam railcars appeared in Britain in 1905 and later were developed by the Sentinel Wagon Works at Shrewsbury and by Cammell-Laird Limited in 1923. They had a vertical high-pressure water-tube boiler, and were in use all over the world. The biggest user of these cars in Britain was the London & North Eastern Railway.

ARTICULATED STEAM LOCOMOTIVES

The articulated locomotive with one or two swivelling power bogies was developed to provide great power on lines with severe curvature, or to spread the weight of a large locomotive over many axles to enable it to work on light track. The principal types have been the Fairlie, Meyer, Mallet and Garratt.

The world's first articulated locomotive was a 2-2-2-2 built at West Point Foundry, New York, in 1832 for the South Carolina Railroad, USA. It had a central firebox and four boilers, two at each end. It was designed by Horatio Allen (1802–90) and formed the basis of the Fairlie type. Each engine had one central cylinder. What happened if both stopped in dead centre is not recorded.

The next stage towards the Fairlie design was the 0-4-4-0 built by John Cockerill et Cie of Seraing, Belgium, for trials on the Semmering line in Austria, in 1851.

Robert F. Fairlie (1831–85) patented his double-bogie articulated locomotive design on 12 May 1864 in England

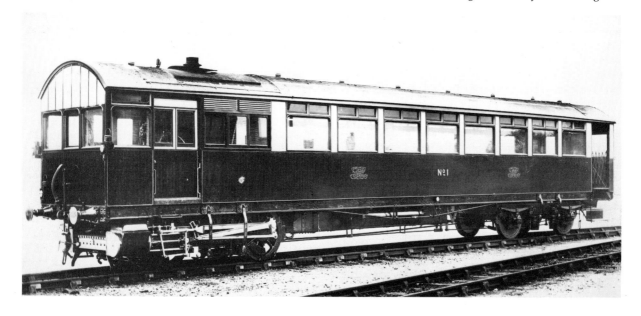

and on 23 November 1864 in France. First to be built was 0–4–4–0 *Progress* in 1865, by Cross & Co., St Helens, Lancashire, for the Neath & Brecon Railway in Wales. It had a double boiler with a common firebox in the centre, and two power bogies. Most Fairlies were 0–4–4–0 and 0–6–6–0, the largest being some 0–6–6–0s built for Mexico in 1911. Fairlie also designed a single-boiler type with one power bogie, and many of these were built. In the USA this design was taken up by William Mason (1808–83), becoming known as the 'Mason-Fairlie' type. From 1871 to 1889, 148 were built for gauges from standard down to 914 mm (3 ft). In 1890 the type was built by the Taunton Locomotive Manufacturing Co., Massachusetts, and later by the Manchester Locomotive Works, New Hampshire. The last were built by the Schenectady Works of ALCO in 1914 for the 914 mm (3 ft) gauge Boston, Revere Beach & Lynn Railroad which used this type exclusively until it was electrified in the 1930s.

On the 600 mm (1 ft 11½ in) gauge Festiniog Railway in Wales, for which the first, *Little Wonder*, was built in 1870, three Fairlies are in operation, built in 1879, 1886 and 1979.

Jean Jacques Meyer (1804–77) and his son Adolphe (1840–91) of Mulhouse, France, patented the Meyer articulated locomotive on 15 March 1861 (French Patent No. 48993). It had the cylinders at the inner ends of the power bogies. The first type, 0–4–4–0, was built by Fives of Lille in 1868. The design restricted the ashpan, but the **Kitson-Meyer** type, developed at Leeds, overcame this by lengthening the frame and placing the firebox between the power bogies, each of which had the cylinders at the rear end.

The Kitson-Meyer was introduced in 1903 when three 0–6–6–0s were built, the first being No. 800 for the 1067 mm (3 ft 6 in) gauge Cape Government Railway, South Africa (Kitson No. 4179).

A later development, introduced in 1908, had the cylinders at the outer ends of the bogies. Some of these show the influence of the Garratt design but differ from this in having a single rigid frame mounted on the power bogies. The Garratt design gained in avoiding this duplication of framing.

The first articulated locomotives in Africa were the 1067 mm (3 ft 6 in) gauge Kitson-Meyer 0–6–6–0s, built by Kitson for Rhodesia in 1903. At the time they were the largest and most powerful engines in southern Africa.

Anatole Mallet (see p. 108) patented the type of articulated locomotive named after him in 1884 as a four-cylinder compound with the low-pressure cylinders on the pivoted front engine frame. The first Mallet was a 600 mm (1 ft 11½ in) gauge 0–4–4–0 tank built in 1887 by Ateliers Métallurgiques at Tubize, Belgium. Its advantage was that it provided high power while adapted to running on light track. In 1890 it was introduced on European main lines and in 1903 in North America where it developed to its greatest extent. The Virginian Railroad

2–10–10–2 of 1918 had low-pressure cylinders 1219 mm (48 in) in diameter, the largest ever used on a locomotive. A triplex type with a third unit under the tender was also produced. These had two high-pressure and four low-pressure cylinders all of equal size. Three 2–8–8–8–2s were built for the Erie Railroad in 1914 and one 2–8–8–8–4 for the Virginian Railroad in 1916.

Mallet opposed the introduction of simple-expansion types, but with the use of superheaters this was a logical development. Mallets grew into the world's biggest engines, examples being the Chesapeake & Ohio Railroad 2–6–6–2s, the Northern Pacific Railroad 2–8–8–4s and the Union Pacific 4–8–8–4 'Big Boys', all over 500 tons.

The largest Mallet tanks (except the Virginian Railroad 2–8–8–8–4) were the 0–8–8–0s built by Maffei in Germany for the Bavarian State Railways in 1913–14 and 1922–3. The first batch weighed 123 147 kg (271 500 lb) or 121 tons.

The first Mallet in North America was a 0–6–6–0 built by ALCO in 1903 for the Baltimore & Ohio Railroad. It was followed by five 2–6–6–2s built by Baldwin in 1906 for the Great Northern Railway.

The first of the Southern Pacific 'cab-in-front' Mallets was built in 1910. They were designed to enable the crews to escape the exhaust fumes in the numerous tunnels and snow-sheds in the Sierra Nevada, USA, in which the line climbs nearly 2133 m (7000 ft) from Sacramento to the summit in 161 km (100 miles) and 610 m (2000 ft) from Reno in 80 km (50 miles). The engines ran 'backwards' with the tender coupled beyond the smoke box. Oil fuel was delivered to the firebox under pressure. They were withdrawn in the 1950s.

The greatest of all Mallets, the Union Pacific 4–8–8–4 'Big Boys' first built by ALCO in 1941, were not compounds. They are described above. To accommodate them, the world's largest turntables, 41.1 m (135 ft) in diameter, were installed at Ogden, Utah, and Green River, Wyoming, in 1945.

The last active simple-expansion Mallets are the 2–6–6–2s built by Baldwin in 1941–9 for the metre-gauge Teresa Cristina Railway in Brazil, Nos. 200–5. Some were still at work in October 1974.

The world's most powerful steam locomotives on a potential horsepower basis were the 2–8–8–4 simple-expansion 'Mallets' of the Northern Pacific Railroad, USA. The first, built by ALCO in 1928, was the first locomotive to weigh over 453 600 kg (1 000 000 lb) with tender. Eleven more were built by Baldwin in 1930. They had a grate area of 16.9 m² (182 ft²), **the largest ever carried by any locomotive**, a heating surface of 712.3 m² (7666 ft²) plus 299 m² (3219 ft²) of superheater and a boiler pressure of 17.6 kg/cm² (250 lb/in²). This gave them the highest potential horsepower of any steam locomotive. The large grate, however, was designed to burn anthracite, so the steaming rate was lower than could have been achieved with bituminous coal. So the maximum potential power of these engines was never fully exploited. They had a tractive effort of 66 193 kg (145 930 lb) with a booster adding 6078 kg (13 400 lb). The ALCO engine was the first Mallet to have a booster.

One of the most interesting articulated locomotive designs was produced by Gaston Du Bousquet. It was a revival of the Wiener-Neustadt 0–4–4–0 tank locomotive built for the Semmering Contest, Austria, in 1851. The Du Bousquet was a four-cylinder compound 0–6–2+2–6–0 with cylinders at the inner ends of the power bogies. The first examples were built in 1905–11 for the French Nord and Est systems and the Peking–Hankow Railway, China, and in 1911 some further engines were built for the 1672 mm (5 ft 6 in) gauge Andalusian Railway, Spain.

GARRATT LOCOMOTIVES

Herbert William Garratt (1864–1913) invented the type of articulated engine named after him, which was developed by Beyer Peacock & Company, Manchester. About 2000 were built.

The first Garratts were two tiny 0–4–0+0–4–0s, built in 1909 for the 610 mm (2 ft) gauge North East Dundas Tramway, Tasmania. They were untypical in that they were compounds and had the cylinders at the inner ends of the engine units. They ran until 1930. In 1947 No. K1 was shipped back to England and after being stored at Beyer Peacock's, Manchester, it was moved to the Festiniog Railway in Wales; but it was much too large. It is now restored for exhibition at the National Railway Museum, York.

The first conventional Garratt with four simple-expan-

sion cylinders at the outer ends of the engines was built in 1911 for the 610 mm (2 ft) gauge Darjeeling Himalayan Railway.

The Tasmanian Government Railway 'M' Class Garratt was a 1067 mm (3 ft 6 in) gauge 4–4–2+2–4–4 and was unique in having eight cylinders and for running at speeds up to 88.5 km/h (55 mph). The coupled wheels were 1524 mm (5 ft) in diameter. Two were built in 1912.

The most powerful locomotives in South Africa are the South African Railways 'GL' Class Garratts—1676 mm (5 ft 6 in) gauge 4–8–2+2–8–4s—first built in 1929 by Beyer Peacock & Company. They weigh 211.1 tons and have a tractive effort of 35 675 kg (78 650 lb).

The world's first express passenger Garratts were six built for the São Paulo Railway, as 2–6–2+2–6–2s, in 1927. In 1932–2 they were rebuilt as 4–6–2+2–6–4s. They regularly ran trains at 96.5 km/h (60 mph).

The world record speed for an articulated steam locomotive was 132 km/h (82 mph) achieved in 1936 during trials of 4–6–2+2–6–4 Garratt No. 377 on the Algerian State Railways. It was built by the Société France Belge at Raismes in Northern France under licence from Beyer Peacock. Coupled wheels were 1.8 m (5 ft 10⅞ in) diameter.

The largest and most powerful locomotive in Great Britain was the 2–8–0+0–8–2 Garratt built at Beyer Peacock in 1925 for the London & North Eastern Railway and used for banking coal trains from Wath up to Penistone in Yorkshire. It was numbered 2395 and classed 'U1'. Its two engine units were standard with H. N. Gresley's three cylinder 2–8–0s.

Britain's last Garratt was a 0–4–0+0–4–0, built in 1937 for the Baddesley Colliery near Atherstone, Warwickshire,

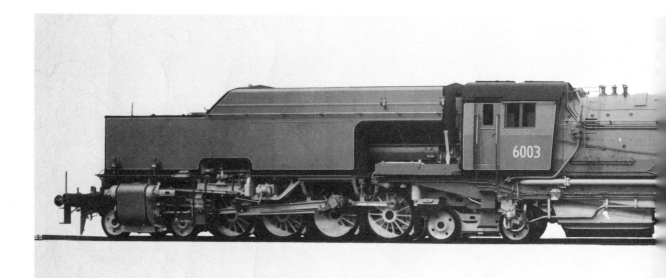

where it worked until 1965. It had a 1524 mm (5 ft) diameter boiler and weighed 61.5 tons. It is now preserved at Bressingham, Norfolk.

The largest locomotives in New Zealand were the three 4–6–2+2–6–4 Garratts built in 1920. They weighed 145.8 tons. These were the only six-cylinder Garratts exported from England and were the first locomotives in New Zealand to have mechanical stokers, exhaust steam injectors, steam reversing gear and grease lubrication to coupled axleboxes.

They were too powerful, however, for the couplings then in use, and loops were too short for the trains they could pull. After transfer from the North to the South Island in 1936, the engine units were built into six 'Pacific'-type tender engines. But their design was faulty and in 1955–6 they became the first New Zealand mainline engines to be replaced by diesels.

The largest, heaviest and most powerful steam locomotives in Australia were the 'AD60' Class 4–8–4+4–8–4 Garratts on the standard-gauge New South Wales Government Railways. They were the first Garratts to have cast-steel engine-bed frames incorporating cylinders. They were introduced in 1952 and weighed 264.7 tons in working order. No. 6042, built by Beyer Peacock in 1952, was the last completed Garratt to be delivered to Australia and was the last steam locomotive in regular service in New South Wales, being withdrawn on 2 March 1973.

The largest Garratt locomotive ever built was completed by Beyer Peacock in 1932 for the USSR railways where it was classed 'Ya-01'. It was a 4–8–2+2–8–4 standing 5.182 m (17 ft) high, with bar-frames and a boiler 2.286 m (7 ft 6 in) in diameter. It weighed 262.5 tons and had a tractive effort of 35 698 kg (78 700 lb).

The smallest Garratts by Beyer Peacock were the two 0–6–0+0–6–0s built in 1913 for the Arakan Flotilla Company of Burma, for 762 mm (2 ft 6 in) gauge, with a wheelbase of 7.32 m (24 ft 2 in). They weighed 23.5 tons.

RUSSIAN STEAM LOCOMOTIVES

The world's tallest locomotives are in Russia where they can be 5.18 m (17 ft) high, 1.22 m (4 ft) higher than in Britain. They can also be up to 3.5 m (11 ft 6 in) wide.

The first Russian steam locomotive was probably a 2–2–0. It was built in 1833 at Nizhni-Tagil in the Urals by M. Cherepanov and it was run on a 0.8 km (½ mile) long 1676 mm (5 ft 6 in) gauge track.

The first locomotive in service in Russia was built by Timothy Hackworth at Shildon, County Durham, for the 1829 mm (6 ft) gauge 22.5 km (14 mile) long line from St Petersburg to Tsarskoe Selo in 1836. The engine cost £1885 including tender which was fitted with brakes. It was accompanied to Russia by T. Hackworth's eldest son John, then not quite 17 years old, and a group of men from Shildon. At Tsarskoe Selo, John Hackworth was introduced to Tsar Nicholas. The engine was then given the blessing of the Greek Church before opening the railway, in November 1836.

In 1837 Hawthorns of Newcastle upon Tyne built a 2–2–0 for the same railway.

The largest steam locomotives built in Russia were the two 'P38' simple expansion 2–8–8–4s, built at Kolomna Works in 1954–5. They each weighed 214.9 tons and were 38.25 m (125 ft 6 in) long. They were the last main-line steam-locomotive type built in Russia.

The only 14-coupled steam locomotive was a 4–14–4, built in Russia in 1934. Its use was severely restricted by its rigidity and it saw little service before it simply 'disappeared'.

AD60 class Garratt No. 6003, the largest and most powerful Australian steam locomotive type.

THE POWER OF STEAM LOCOMOTIVES

Steam locomotive power can be represented in two ways. **Tractive Effort**, when stated in pounds, is obtained by the formula $(D^2 \times S \times P)/W$ where D is cylinder diameter in inches, S is piston stroke in inches, P is steam pressure in lb/in^2 (usually 85 per cent of boiler pressure) and W is driving-wheel diameter in inches. Tractive effort is simply the force exerted at the rim of the driving-wheel, measured in terms of the weight this force could lift vertically. The use the engine can make of it depends entirely on its ability to grip the rails, or its adhesive weight, and the capacity of the boiler to supply the steam.

Horsepower includes a time factor (1 hp=550 ft lb/s =746 Joules/s or 746 Watts; in France 75 kg m/s=736 Joules/s=736 Watts). In a steam-engine this depends on the rate at which fuel can be burnt and water evaporated in the boiler, as well as cylinder efficiency.

With a steam locomotive there are so many variables, for example the strength of the fireman, that a horsepower rating is only approximate and is seldom used.

THE LARGEST AND MOST POWERFUL STEAM LOCOMOTIVES

(See also 'Articulated Steam Locomotives')

The world's largest conventional steam locomotives were the 4–8–8–4 'Big Boys', built by the American Locomotive Company in 1941–4 for the Union Pacific Railroad. Their overall length was 39.852 m (130 ft 9¼ in), they stood 4.941 m (16 ft 2½ in) high and were 3.353 m (11 ft) wide. With tenders they weighed 508 020 kg (1 120 000 lb) and exerted a tractive effort of 61 405 kg (135 375 lb). On test they developed an indicated horsepower of 7000. The grate area was 13.96 m^2 (150.3 ft^2); heating surface was 534.6 m^2 (5755 ft^2) plus 189.8 m^2 (2043 ft^2) of superheater. Working pressure was 21.1 kg/cm^2 (300 lb/in^2). The four cylinders were 603 × 813 mm (23¾ × 32 in) and coupled wheels 1727 mm (68 in).

Twenty-five 'Big Boys' were built for hauling heavy freights on the Sherman Hill section. They could run at speeds up to 129 km/h (80 mph). Seven have been preserved. (See also the C & O steam-turbine-electric locomotives, p. 125.)

The largest locomotives in Canada were the 2–10–4 'Selkirks' of the Canadian Pacific Railway. The 'T1a' Class Nos. 5900–19 were built by the Montreal Locomotive Works in 1929; the 'T1b' Class, Nos. 5920–9 followed in 1938 and the 'T1c' Class Nos. 5930–5 in 1949. They had 1600 mm (5 ft 3 in) coupled wheels, a working pressure of 20 kg/cm^2 (285 lb/in^2) and cylinders 635 × 813 mm (25 × 32 in). They worked passenger and freight trains through the mountain section of the CPR. No. 5934 is preserved at Calgary and No. 5935 at the Canadian Railway Museum near Montreal. **This was the last steam locomotive built for the CPR.**

Canadian National Railways Class T–3–a 2–10–2s Nos. 4100–4 built in 1924 had a higher tractive effort (with and without booster), but the 'Selkirks' were heavier, longer and had greater power.

The largest locomotives in South America were the 216 ton 1676 mm (5 ft 6 in) gauge 4–8–2s supplied by ALCO to the Chilean State Railways in 1940.

The largest metre-gauge engines in South America were the 181 ton 4–8–2+2–8–4 Garratts built by Beyer Peacock & Company, Manchester, in 1950 for the Antofagasta & Bolivia Railway.

Canadian Pacific T1b class 2–10–4 'Selkirk' type locomotive No. 5921. Engines of this type were the largest in Canada. Cylinders were 635 × 813 mm (25 × 32 in), driving wheels 1600 mm (5 ft 3 in). Tractive effort was 35 389 kg (78 000 lb) and the weight 190 tons.

Above: LNER 4–6–2 No. 4472 *Flying Scotsman* crossing Helwith Bridge on the Settle & Carlisle railway.

Right: The Shakespeare Cliff site from which the English end of the Channel Tunnel is being bored.

Top left: 'QJ' 2-10-2 No. 3587 just completed, standing outside the Datong Locomotive Works, China, on 9 June 1981. The author stands beside it. The QJs form the largest class of steam locomotives in the world, with over 4000 in service.

Centre left: The last steam locomotive to be built by British Railways, 2-10-0 No. 92220 *Evening Star*, on the Severn Valley Railway near Bewdley.

Bottom left: War Department 2-10-0 No. 600 from the Longmoor Military Railway, now working on the Severn Valley Railway, at Highley on 16 September 1984.

Top right: The oldest active locomotive in Canada, 4-4-0 'Prairie Dog Central No. 3' preserved by the Winnipeg Locomotive Society, at Winnipeg in 1972. It was built by Dübs at Glasgow in 1882 as Canadian Pacific Railway No. 22.

Centre right: 0-6-0 tank *Bellerophon* at Oxenhope on the Keighley & Worth Valley Railway in Yorkshire on 27 December 1985. The engine, built in 1874, is the oldest with piston valves.

Bottom right: One of the world's oldest steam locomotives in regular service, SP/S class 4-4-0 No. 3078 of Pakistan Railways, built by Beyer Peacock in Manchester in 1904. It was still at work in January 1988 when photographed crossing the Jhelum Canal on the approach to Malakwal.

Top: Britain's last compound locomotive design, No. 10000 of the LNER, designed by H. N. Gresley and built in 1930.

Above: Brush Class 89 CoCo electric locomotive No. 89001 on a Kings Cross to Peterborough train at Hadley Wood on 17 August 1988. From July 1988 it proved its reliability in regular revenue service while the BR Class 91s were having technical problems.

Right: One of several preserved 'Deltic' diesel-electric locomitives, No. 55015 *Tulyar*, shown here at Highley on 9 May 1987 when on a visit to the Severn Valley Railway. The 22 Deltics all ran around 5 million km (3 million miles) on expresses on the East Coast main line out of Kings Cross, London, during 20 years from 1961 to the early 1980s, covering about 4000 miles in a week.

Right: Union Pacific 'Centennial' DoDo diesel-electric locomotive No. 6912 at Salt Lake City in 1977. The 'Centennials' were introduced in 1969 and the class was named and numbered in the '69' series to commemorate the centenary of the completion of the first American transcontinental railway. They were the largest and most powerful diesel locomotives in the world.

Right: Through train from Guangzhou to Kowloon (Hong Kong) behind a Chinese diesel-electric locomotive. The through trains were reintroduced in 1979 after a gap of 30 years. The train is leaving the new Beacon Hill tunnel, 2.3 km (1.4 miles) long, completed in 1981. The entrance to the old single-line tunnel built in 1906–10 is behind the first coach.

Opposite page: BR high speed train from Paddington to the west of England beside the Kennett & Avon Canal at Crofton.

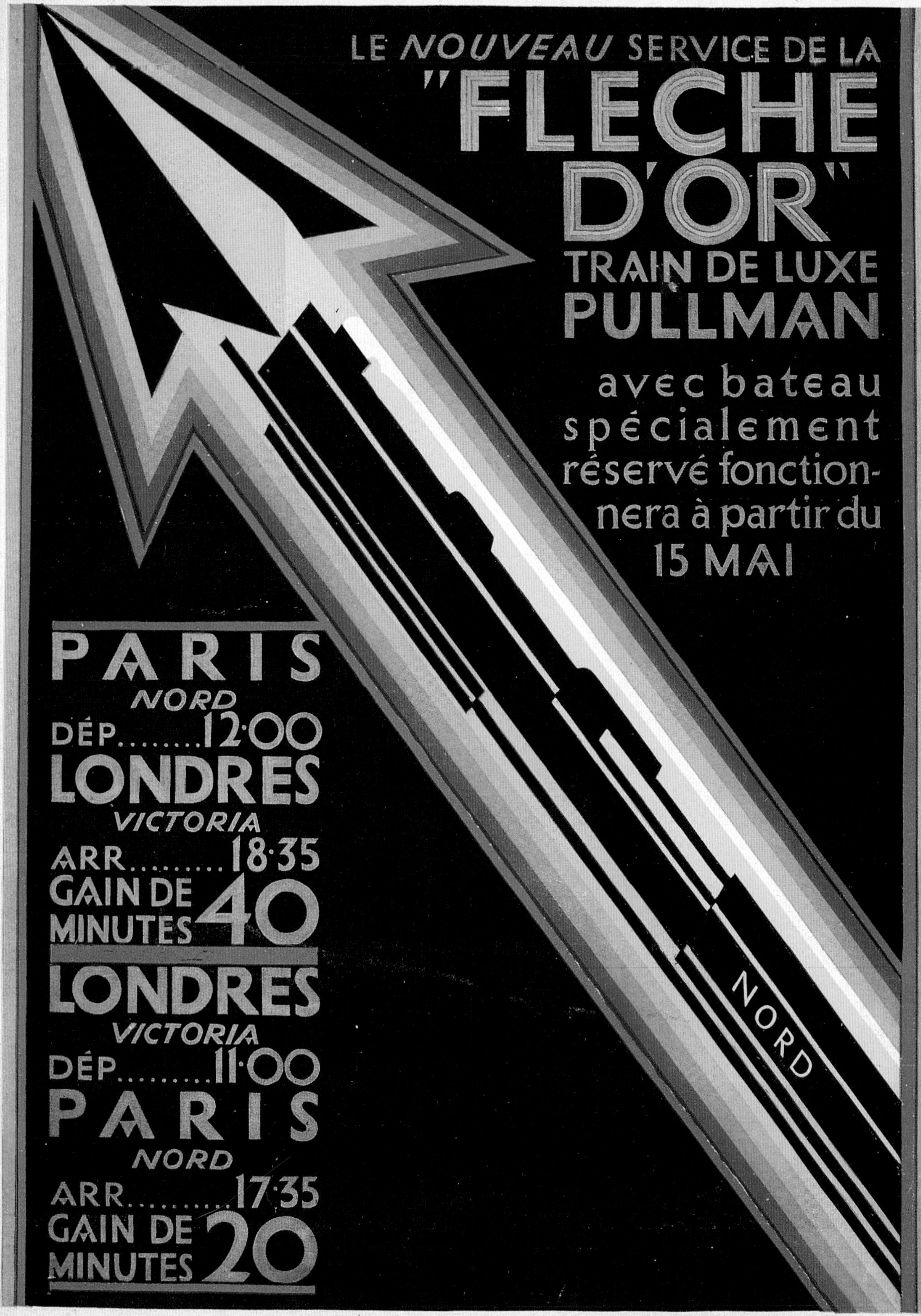
LE NOUVEAU SERVICE DE LA
"FLECHE
D'OR"
TRAIN DE LUXE
PULLMAN
avec bateau
spécialement
réservé fonctionnera à partir du
15 MAI
PARIS
NORD
DÉP.........12·00
LONDRES
VICTORIA
ARR..........18·35
GAIN DE MINUTES 40
LONDRES
VICTORIA
DÉP..........11·00
PARIS
NORD
ARR...........17·35
GAIN DE MINUTES 20
NORD

Announcement of the Southern Railway of England.

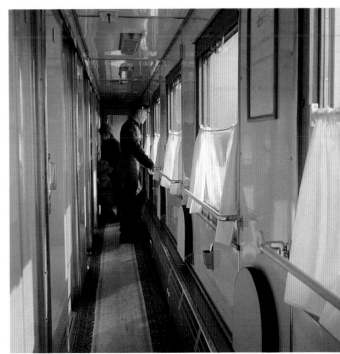

Above: Dining Car and corridor of sleeping car on the Trans Siberian Railway.

Opposite page: An advertisement for the Golden Arrow all-Pullman service, shortly before the service began in 1929.

Below: Privately-preserved LNER A4 class 4–6–2 No. 4498 *Sir Nigel Gresley* on a special train on the Settle & Carlisle railway.

Left: French Railways TGV

Left: The Tokaido Shinkansen, when introduced in 1965, were the first trains to average over 162 km/h (100 mph) start to stop.

The largest non-articulated steam locomotive in Australia was the single 4–8–4 No. H220 built in 1941 by the Victorian Government Railways for freight working on the 1600 mm (5 ft 3 in) gauge. In working order the engine weighed 146.5 tons and with tender 260 tons. Coupled wheels were 1.701 m (5 ft 7 in) in diameter. They had three cylinders 551 × 711 mm (21½ × 28 in). It was withdrawn in 1958 and is preserved in the Australian Railways Historical Society Museum at Newport.

The largest Australian engines built as a class were the ten '500' Class 4–8–4s Nos. 500–9 built in 1926 by Armstrong, Whitworth & Company, Newcastle upon Tyne, for the 1600 mm (5 ft 3 in) gauge South Australian Government Railways. They were 25.653 m (84 ft 2 in) long with tenders and weighed 222.3 tons. The engines alone weighed 143.8 tons. They had 1.6 m (5 ft 3 in) driving-wheels, and two cylinders 660 × 711 mm (26 × 28 in). No. 504, withdrawn on 9 July 1962 with a mileage of 855 029 (1 375 993 km), was placed in the Mile End Railway Museum near Adelaide, maintained by the Australian Railway Historical Society, on 23 July 1965.

The world's most powerful steam locomotive on a tractive effort basis was a triplex articulated 2–8–8–8–4 Mallet compound tank engine built by Baldwin, Philadel-

Union Pacific 3-cylinder 4–12–2 No. 9000 built by ALCO Brooks Works 1926. The Holcroft/Gresley combination gear for driving the middle valve can be clearly seen.
Photographed at Pomona Fairground, Los Angeles, where it is preserved, on 17 October 1983.

phia, in 1916 for the Virginian Railroad—No. 700. It had a tractive effort of 75 434 kg (166 300 lb) working compound and 90 520 kg (199 560 lb) working simple, that is with high-pressure steam to all six cylinders. These were all 864 × 813 mm (34 × 32 in), coupled wheels were 1422 mm (4 ft 8 in), grate area 10.052 m² (108.2 ft²), total heating surface 754 m² (8120 ft²), total weight 377 tons. It was not satisfactory because the engine under the tender section exhausted to the atmosphere and left only half the exhaust steam for the LP cylinders; diminishing fuel and water reduced the weight for adhesion; and the machine was under-boilered. In 1921, following delivery of the ALCO 2–10–10–2s mentioned below, the engine was divided, the rear portion being rebuilt into a 2–8–2 tender engine and the front portion into a 2–8–8–0 Mallet, No. 610. This was later rebuilt into a 2–8–8–2 and was withdrawn in the early 1950s. It was the only Mallet to have existed in three wheel arrangements.

The biggest boilers and biggest cylinders ever used on a locomotive were on the ten 2–10–10–2 Mallets, built by

ALCO in 1918 for the Virginian Railroad, Nos. 800–9. The boilers had a maximum diameter of 3m (9 ft 10½ in). The grate was 2.743 × 3.658 m (9 × 12 ft). Evaporative heating surface was 799 m² (8600 ft²) plus 197 m² (2120 ft²) of superheater. The low-pressure cylinders were 1219 mm diameter × 813 mm stroke (48 × 32 in). The engines stood 5.07 m (16 ft 7½ in) high. Until the railway was electrified in 1926 they banked mile-long coal trains weighing 10 000 tons to over 15 000 tons up to 17.7 km (11 miles) of 2.1 per cent grade at Clark's Gap. They were withdrawn in 1948–9.

Three-cylinder propulsion was introduced in the USA by ALCO in 1922 when New York Central 4–8–2 freight engine No. 2568 was so converted. The Holcroft/Gresley-type combination gear was used for the inside valve. Its success led to the development of the three-cylinder system by ALCO in a series of designs for switching, freight and passenger work, culminating in the giant Union Pacific 4–12–2 described below. Altogether, 250 three-cylinder engines had been built when manufacture ended in 1930.

The largest three-cylinder engines ever built were the Union Pacific 4–12–2s. The first, no. 9000, was completed at Schenectady, New York, in April 1926. A total of 88 were built, the last, No. 9087, in 1930. They were also the only 4–12–2s, and the only 12-coupled engines to exceed 97 km/h (60 mph) in normal service. Apart from the experimental Russian 4–14–4, they had the longest rigid wheelbase in the world, and they were the first non-articulated locomotives to exceed 30.5 m (100 ft) in length over drawbars. They were the first three-cylinder engines to have cast-steel cylinders. The Holcroft/Gresley combination gear was used to drive the middle valve.

In 1956 No. 9000 was presented by the UP to the Southern California Chapter of the Railway and Locomotive Historical Society for preservation.

The largest French express passenger engine was the 242A1 three-cylinder compound 4–8–4 rebuilt by André Chapelon (qv) in 1942–6 from a 4–8–2 three-cylinder simple No. 241.101. In many ways it was the finest steam locomotive ever built. It had the highest power to weight ratio of any steam locomotive. It could maintain a continuous drawbar horsepower of 4000 at 70–100 km/h (44–62 mph), and 3800 hp at 120 k/h (74 mph). The triple Kylchap exhaust gave a high steaming rate at all speeds. The high-pressure cylinder had Trick valves with double admission, and the low-pressure cylinders had Willoteaux valves with double admission and double exhaust. Its coal and water consumption were remarkably low, only about two-thirds of that of a British Stanier Pacific for the same output. Coupled wheels were 1.9 m (6 ft 4¾ in)

diameter and the engine weighed 148 tons. One of the greatest tragedies for locomotive history was that this engine was scrapped in 1960.

The largest tank engines to run on any British railway were the ten 4–6–4 'Baltics' built by the London, Midland & Scottish Railway at the former Lancashire & Yorkshire Railway Works at Horwich to the design of George Hughes (1865–1945), then the chief mechanical engineer. Thirty were to have been built but insufficient suitable work for such large engines led to the last 20 being turned out as 4–6–0 tender engines. They had four cylinders 419 × 660 mm (16½ × 26 in) and 1905 mm (6 ft 3 in) coupled wheels. The last was withdrawn in 1941.

Altogether five British railways used 4–6–4 tanks: the London, Tilbury & Southend in 1912; the London, Brighton & South Coast in 1914; the Furness in 1920; the Glasgow & South Western in 1922; and the LMS in 1924. The type name 'Baltic' probably derived from 4–6–4 tanks built by the Vulcan Works of Stettin, Germany, for the Prussian State Railways in 1912. Numerous examples were built for railways around Europe and all over the world, including the USA and Canada.

The largest locomotives in Ireland were the Great Southern Railway three-cylinder 4–6–0s, of which three were built at Inchicore, Dublin, in 1939–40 to a design prepared under E. C. Bredin, chief mechanical engineer. They were built for the Dublin–Cork expresses.

The first, No. 800 *Maeve* is preserved at the Belfast Transport Museum.

The largest driving-wheels used on any engine in Britain were 3.048 m (10 ft) diameter on the freak Great Western 2–2–2 built by Mather, Dixon & Company of Liverpool to a specification by I. K. Brunel and delivered on 12 December 1838. It 'worked' until June 1840.

The largest driving-wheels in regular use in Britain measured 2.743 m (9 ft) on the eight 4–2–4 tank engines built for the 2134 mm (7 ft) gauge Bristol & Exeter Railway by

The largest steam locomotive type in Ireland, Great Southern Railways 3-cylinder 4–6–0 No. 800 *Maeve* at Cork, August 1948.

Bristol & Exeter Railway 4-2-4T No. 46 built by Peter Rothwell at Bolton, Lancashire, in 1853. The 2743 mm (9 ft) driving wheels were the largest in regular use in Great Britain. In 1854 No. 41 of this type achieved a world speed record of 131.6 km/h (81.8 mph) which remained unbeaten until 1890.

Rothwell & Company of Bolton, Lancashire, to a design by James Pearson in 1854. One of these, No. 41, achieved a record speed of 131.6 km/h (81.8 mph) on Wellington Bank, Somerset, in June 1854, which remained the highest authenticated rail speed until 1890. They were replaced by new B & E engines of the same wheel arrangement in 1868–73.

The largest coupled wheels ever used in Britain were 2.318 m (7 ft 7¼ in) diameter on Wilson Worsdell's 'Q1' Class 4-4-0s Nos. 1869 and 1870 on the North Eastern Railway. Two were built in 1896 for taking part in the railway races to the north.

GEARED STEAM LOCOMOTIVES

Geared locomotives were produced to three basic designs, principally to negotiate light temporary tracks over rough ground with steep gradients.

The 'Shay' geared locomotive was invented by Ephraim Shay (1839–1916) and was produced by the Lima Machine Works, Ohio (from 1901 the Lima Locomotive & Machine Company). The first one appeared in 1880. It had a two- or three-cylinder vertical engine on one side and the bogies were driven by a system of shafts, universal couplings and spur gears. On level track it could reach a speed of 30.6 km/h (19 mph) and on gradients of 1 in 16.7 to 1 in 7 (6 to 14 per cent) it could move loads at 12 to 6.5 km/h (7.5 to 4 mph).

The Climax locomotive was built by the Climax Manufacturing Company of Corry, Pennsylvania. It had two sloping cylinders, one on each side, connected by gearing

and longitudinal shafts to the two bogies. The company operated from 1884 to 1930.

Another type had a two-cylinder high-speed vertical steam-engine driving the bogies through a two-speed gear-box. A similar design was produced by the Baldwin Locomotive Works, Philadelphia.

The Heisler-type locomotive was first built by the Stearns Manufacturing Company, Erie, Pennsylvania, the first being completed on 20 August 1894 for service in Mexico. The Heisler Locomotive Works, Erie, began production of this type in 1898. It had two cylinders arranged like a V beneath the boiler, driving a longitudinal shaft geared to the bogies. This was the neatest and soundest of the three designs, but the Shay was the most popular.

OIL FUEL FOR STEAM LOCOMOTIVES

Some of the earliest experiments with oil fuel were made in the 1870s by a British engineer, Thomas Urquhart. Similar experiments began in France in 1869. The advantage of oil fuel over coal is principally the avoidance of ash, but its use depends largely on the price and availability of fuel. An oil-fired steam-engine is still an inefficient machine, producing only half of the work done by a diesel engine using the same amount of oil.

In the USA early experiments with oil fuel were abandoned because of the cost and it was not taken up again until the 1890s.

The first regular use of oil fuel was on the Russian South Eastern Railway in 1883–4, using the Urquhart system.

In the USA an oil-burning locomotive made successful test runs from Altoona to Pittsburg, Pennsylvania, and back on 17–18 June 1887.

Oil fuel was first used in Britain on the London, Brighton & South Coast Railway in April 1886, when Stroudley 0-4-2 tank No. 27 *Uckfield* was equipped at Brighton Works with Tarbutt's oil-burning apparatus at a cost of £152. It was only moderately successful; complaints about fumes and smoke led to its removal in 1886. Further experiments with oil fuel were made on the LBSCR in 1902–4.

On the Great Eastern Railway in 1887 the locomotive superintendent James Holden (1837–1925) invented an arrangement for burning the waste product from the plant producing oil gas for carriage lighting. It was tried on the Johnson 0-4-4 tank No. 193 and was first regularly used in 1893 on T19 class 2-4-0 No. 760 which was named *Petrolea*. About 60 engines were so fitted, but the apparatus was removed when the price of oil rose to an uneconomic level.

The first oil-burning locomotive in Canada was introduced about 1910, converted from a coal-burner for work in the Rocky Mountains. The first complete class of oil-burners was built by the Canadian Pacific Railway in 1917–19.

In 1947 many British locomotives on the Great Western, Southern and London & North Eastern Railways, and on the Irish railways, were fitted up to burn oil fuel during the acute coal shortage in Britain. However, the increasing cost of oil led to its removal after very little use.

Strange fuels have been used for steam locomotives to keep railways running in difficult times. On a 600 mm (1 ft 11½ in) gauge branch of the Arica–La Paz Railway in Chile, llama dung and dried moss were burned on two 0–4–0 tanks built by Orenstein & Koppel of Berlin. In South America, during a crop surplus, coffee beans were used as fuel.

In 1919, during a coal shortage dried fish was used as locomotive fuel in Russian Turkestan. For this purpose the Soviet Government requisitioned 8000 tons from Aral Sea fishermen.

Electrically fired steam locomotives were tried on Swiss Federal Railways in 1943 during the wartime coal shortage, when two 0–6–0 tanks were converted at Yverdon for shunting at St Gallen and Zollikofen, drawing power from the 15 000 V ac overhead wire. Current consumption was high for the power output compared with an electric locomotive, and the experiment was abandoned about 1948.

STEAM-TURBINE LOCOMOTIVES

The first steam-turbine locomotive to be built was designed by Professor Belluzzo and was built in Milan in 1908 by S. A. Officine Mechaniche. It was a 0–4–0 side-tank engine. The four turbines were single-wheel velocity compound type with the lower part of the blades for forward drive and the upper part for backward.

The idea of an electric locomotive carrying its own power station around with it, as in a diesel-electric, is not new. The Reid-Ramsey steam-turbine-electric machine of 1910 is described below. Heilmann in France produced a steam-electric locomotive in 1893 and two more powerful machines in 1897, using high-speed reciprocating steam engines driving dc generators. In theory the enclosed steam engine, or turbine, required less maintenance than the relatively slow-speed direct-drive engine with its massive heavy parts exposed to dirt and grit, but the experiments failed partly because the ratio of power to weight was too low.

A steam-turbine-electric locomotive was designed by Sir Hugh Reid and W. M. Ramsey. It was built in Glasgow in 1910 by the North British Locomotive Company of which Reid (1860–1935) was chairman and chief managing director. An impulse-type turbine with condenser was coupled to a variable voltage dynamo which supplied four dc traction motors at 200–600 V.

A second Ramsey-type locomotive, a 0–6–6–2 type, was completed in 1922 and was tested by George Hughes at Horwich on the Lancashire & Yorkshire Railway, and on the North Eastern Railway. Turbines and electrical equipment were by Oerlikon, Switzerland. It was built by Armstrong Whitworth & Company, Newcastle upon Tyne.

The Zoelly turbine locomotive was converted from a Swiss Federal Railways 4–6–0 in 1921 by the Swiss Locomotive & Machine Works, Winterthur. It had a 1200 hp impulse turbine across the front of the machine, driving the wheels by gearing and a jack-shaft and side-rods. A surface condenser was positioned beneath the boiler. A similar engine built by Krupp of Essen in 1922 ran on the German State Railways.

The Ljungstrom turbine condensing locomotive was first built in 1921 at the Ljungstrom Locomotive Works near Stockholm. It was rebuilt in 1922 but was withdrawn in 1924.

The second, built at Trollhattan in 1924–5 to the metre gauge for the Argentine State Railway, was capable of travelling 805 km (500 miles) without rewatering.

The third, built by Beyer Peacock & Company at Manchester in 1926, was given extensive trials on the Midland section of the London, Midland & Scottish Railway. It suffered in the numerous tunnels where soot entered the condenser and caused blockages. A fourth, and last, built in 1927, was similar in design and gave good service in Sweden for many years.

In 1932 some non-condensing Ljungstrom locomotives were built in Sweden and they worked iron-ore trains of 1831 tons on the Grängesberg–Oxelösund Railway from the Bergslag to the Baltic coast until displaced by electrification.

The Reid-Macleod turbine locomotive was built by the North British Locomotive Company of Glasgow in 1923–4. It was a 4–4–4–4 with high- and low-pressure turbines and an air-cooled condenser. It had an output of 1000 bhp.

The London, Midland & Scottish Railway turbine 'Pacific' No. 6202 was a non-condensing machine with one turbine for forward running and a smaller one for backward running. It was built at Crewe in 1935 to the design of William Stanier (1876–1965) and ran successfully on the London–Liverpool expresses. In 1952 it was rebuilt into a conventional engine and named *Princess Anne*, but after only a few months' service it was involved in the collision at Harrow & Wealdstone Station on 8 October 1952 and was scrapped. (Photo p. 185.)

The Union Pacific Railroad, USA had a pair of steam-turbine-electric locomotives built by the General Electric Company in 1937–9. They were of the 2–Co–Co–2 type and could work either singly or together under the control of one man. They had a maximum speed of 201 km/h (125 mph). They each had high- and low-pressure turbines and condensers, and together had an output of

5000 hp. The semi-flash-type boiler worked at a pressure of 105.46 kg/cm^2 (1500 lb/in^2).

The first direct-drive turbine locomotive in the USA was the Pennsylvania Railroad No. 6200, a 6–8–6-type non-condensing machine built by Baldwin in 1944 in co-operation with the Westinghouse Company. Like the LMS machine of 1935, described above, it had two turbines, one forward developing 6500 hp at 113 km/h (70 mph) and a reverse developing 1500 hp at 35.5 km/h (22 mph). Wartime restrictions forced Baldwins to use a heavier steel for the boiler shell which resulted in the six-wheeled bogies to distribute the extra weight. Although this handsome locomotive worked 'The Broadway Limited' and other top trains, its excessive steam consumption at low speeds, resulting in boiler troubles, made it uneconomic and it was withdrawn in 1949.

The Chesapeake & Ohio Railroad obtained three giant steam-turbine-electric locomotives built by Baldwin and Westinghouse in 1947–9. They were 47 m (154 ft) long 2–D+2–D–2 type with a starting tractive effort of 4445 kg (98 000 lb) and a continuous of 2177 kg (48 000 lb). They had a short existence because of the closure of the passenger service for which they were obtained, and also because of design faults.

The Norfolk & Western Railroad obtained a 4500 hp turbine-electric non-condensing locomotive in 1954, built by the Baldwin-Lima-Hamilton Corporation with the Westinghouse Company, and a boiler by Babcock & Wilcox. It was 49 m (61 ft 1½ in) long, weighed 525 tons in working order and could run up to 96.5 km/h (60 mph). It

The impressive Pennsylvania RR 6–8–6 non-condensing turbine locomotive No. 6200, built in 1944 and withdrawn in 1949.

was numbered 2300. Although it showed marked economy in coal consumption, it was scrapped in 1958 when displaced by diesels.

LARGE CLASSES OF STEAM LOCOMOTIVES

The world's largest class of locomotives was the Russian 'E' Class 0–10–0 introduced in 1912 and at length numbering about 14 000 engines.

Between 1891 and 1923, 9500 '0' Class 0–8–0s were built in Russia.

The German 'Austerity' 2–10–0, introduced in 1941, numbered more than 8000 by the time the last was built in 1947.

The largest class of steam locomotives now in operation is the 'QJ' ('Quian Jin' or 'Advance Forward') 2–10–2 of the Chinese People's Republic Railways. They are based on the Russian 'LV' design of 1952, with many features of North American practice. The exact number in service is not known but exceeds 4000. The works at Datong have been building hundreds each year since 1960, still about 300 a year in 1981–2.

In 1958–9 about 2000 Russian 'FD' (Felix Dzherzhinsky) 2–10–2s were sold to China where they are still active. About 3200 of these engines were built, from 1931–42.

'QJ' 2–10–2 under construction at Datong Works, about 275 km (170 miles) west of Peking (Beijing), China, on 9 June 1981; the day was the 200th anniversary of the birth of George Stephenson. The QJs are now the world's largest class of steam locomotives.

The largest class of steam locomotives to be built in the British Commonwealth was the Indian 1676 mm (5 ft 6 in) gauge 'WG' Class 2–8–2, first built in 1950. The class eventually numbered 2450.

The largest classes in the USA were the USRA 0–8–0s numbering 1375, and the 'light' 2–8–2s numbering 1266, built 1919–20.

On French National Railways (SNCF) the largest class was the 141R series of 2–8–2s, of which 1340 were built in the USA and Canada between 1944 and 1948. Builders were: Lima (280), ALCO (460), Baldwin (460), Montreal Locomotive Works (100) and Canadian Locomotive Works (40). All but 17 were delivered; Nos. 220–35 were lost at sea on the *Belpamella* and No. 1241 fell into Marseilles harbour while being unloaded.They were designed by Baldwins to French specifications and were similar to a USRA (United States Railroad Administration) type in appearance. More than half were coal burners and 621 were oil fired. No. 141R.73 was the last steam locomotive to work on the SNCF, on 28 March 1974. No. 141R.1158 covered nearly 2.5 million km (over 1.5 million miles). At least 12 examples are still in existence, some preserved and in working order, in Britain, (141R.73 at Bressingham, Norfolk), France and Switzerland.

The largest class of locomotives to be built in Britain was the Ramsbottom 'DX' Class 0–6–0 of the London & North Western Railway, of which 943 were built between 1858 and 1874, including 86 for the Lancashire & Yorkshire Railway in 1871–4.

On the Great Western Railway a total of 863 0–6–0 pannier tanks of the '5700' Class were built between 1929

and 1950. The basic design dated back to the '645' Class of 1872 and the similar '1813', '1854' and '2721' Classes of which a total of 358 were built up to 1901. In 1956–71, 13 were used by London Transport, including several among the dozen or so now preserved on various private railways.

The largest class of modern locomotives in Britain was the London, Midland & Scottish Railway 'Class 5' 4–6–0, designed by William Stanier and first built in 1934. Including several variations in the design, the class eventually numbered 842 engines. A total of 13 has been preserved.

The first locomotive type to be adopted by the British Government for war service was the Great Central '8K' Class 2–8–0 designed by J. G. Robinson (1856–1943) and first built at Gorton, Manchester, in 1911. During the First World War many were built by the GCR and by other locomotive-builders, producing as many as 647 engines. After the war they were dispersed, most going to the London & North Eastern Railway (as successor to the GCR) where they were classed '04' and others to the Great Western Railway and to China, Australia and elsewhere. In 1941–2, 92 were sent to the Lebanon, Palestine, Iraq, Egypt and Tripolitania. These, and five more sent out in 1951–2, never returned to Britain. Many of them put in over 50 years' hard service. They were among the finest British freight engines. One has been preserved in the National Collection, and is being restored at Dinting Railway Centre, Derbyshire.

The Canadian Pacific Railway 'D' Class 4–6–0s totalled over 1000, but there were ten different types and variations within these, built from 1902 to 1915. The 'D10' Class, built 1905–13, numbered 502.

141R 2–8–2 No. 615 at Amiens shed on 5 May 1958. The 141Rs were the largest class of steam locomotives on French Railways, numbering 1340, built in USA and Canada in 1944–8 to help in re-establishing the French Railways after World War II.

DYNAMOMETER CARS

Dynamometer cars for the testing of steam locomotives on the track were used in England by the Great Western, North Eastern and Lancashire and Yorkshire Railways. They were positioned between the locomotive and the train and were equipped to measure and record speed and drawbar pull in the form of graphs which could be used in conjunction with gradient profiles, fuel and water consumption, and indicator diagrams taken at the cylinders, to assess locomotive performance.

The North Eastern car was built at Darlington under Wilson Worsdell in 1906 and was based on the GWR car. It is now preserved at the National Railway Museum, York.

The LYR car was designed by George Hughes at Horwich, Lancashire, in 1911–12 and was based on the Belgian car designed by Jean Baptiste Flamme. It indicated speed and drawbar pull to give drawbar-horse-power-hours. It is being restored at the Midland Railway Centre, Butterley, Ripley, Derbyshire.

The latest dynamometer car is a standard vehicle designed for speeds up to 300 km/h (186 mph) by the Transport Systems Division of Messerschmitt-Bölkow-Blohm GmbH (MBB) in 1976. It is 26.4 m (86 ft 7 in) long, 4 m (13 ft 3 in) high, and it weighs 61.5 tons.

LOCOMOTIVE BUILDING RECORDS

In February 1888 Francis William Webb (1836–1906), locomotive superintendent of the London & North Western Railway, had a 0-6-0 goods engine constructed in Crewe Works in 25½ hours.

The following June this record was reduced to 16¼ h by the Pennsylvania Railroad at the Altoona Works, USA, but we do not know what it was that was built.

The all-time record was achieved by the Great Eastern Railway under James Holden at Stratford, London. On 10 December 1891 0-6-0 No. 930 was completely assembled and given one coat of paint in 9 h 57 min. It was steamed and tested on the line immediately afterwards. As London & North Eastern Railway 'J15' Class No. 7930, this engine ran until 1935.

VETERAN LOCOMOTIVES

The oldest steamable locomotive is *John Bull*, built by Robert Stephenson & Co. of Newcastle upon Tyne in 1831 as a 0-4-0 'Planet' type for the Camden & Amboy RR, USA. It was first steamed on 15 September 1831 by Isaac Dripps (1810–92) who, about 1834, removed the outside cranks and coupling rods and fitted it with two leading wheels and a pilot or 'cowcatcher'. When the C & A was taken over by the Pennsylvania RR in 1871, *John Bull* was hidden away to preserve it from being scrapped. It was exhibited at Philadelphia in 1876 with a new straight chimney and a modified tender, and at Chicago in 1883, before passing to the Smithsonian Museum in Washington where it remained. It was steamed again at the Baltimore & Ohio RR centenary in 1927. In January 1980 work began on a complete restoration to its 1876 condition and in October it was tested under steam. On 15 September 1981, the 150th anniversary of its first steaming in the USA, it was operated on the Georgetown Branch of the B & O, pulling passengers in the old C & A coach of 1836.

The oldest working locomotive in Britain is the 0-4-2 *Lion* of the former Liverpool & Manchester Railway. It was one of two goods engines built by Todd, Kitson & Laird of Leeds in 1838. In 1859 the London & North Western Railway, successor to the L & M, sold it to the Mersey Docks & Harbour Board who used it as a pumping engine at Princes Graving Dock until well into the 1920s. In 1927 it was rescued, thanks to members of the Liverpool Engineering Society, and in 1929 it was restored in Crewe Works in time for the centenary of the L & M in 1930. It was used in three famous films: *Victoria the Great* in 1937; *The Lady with the Lamp* (Florence Nightingale) in 1951; and the *Titfield Thunderbolt* in 1952 in which it played the title role.

In 1965, after long storage in the paint shop at Crewe Works, *Lion* was transferred to the City of Liverpool Museum and, following careful restoration, it was put on display in a new transport gallery from 1967 to 1979. With the approach of the 150th anniversary of the L & M, *Lion* was removed for complete overhaul by Ruston Diesels at Newton-le-Willows, occupiers of the former Vulcan Foundry. Here it was restored to sound mechanical order. About six buckets full of rust, scale and other deposits were removed from the little boiler which is only 2.654 m (8 ft 8½ in) long and 1.03 m (3 ft 4½ in) inside diameter. In January 1980 *Lion* was tested and in May was the star exhibit in the celebration at Rainhill. In August 1980 it was one of the principal exhibits at the exposition at Liverpool Road Station, Manchester, where it was frequently in steam.

The oldest locomotive still active in Britain is *Prince*, No. 2 on the 600 mm (1 ft 11½ in) gauge Festiniog Railway in Wales. It was built by George England, London, in 1863 and was subsequently rebuilt in 1892, 1904, 1920, 1937, 1955–6, and 1974–80.

Another veteran steamable British locomotive is the 0-4-0 well tank *Shannon*, also built by George England in 1857 for the Sandy & Potton Railway, opened on 23 June 1857. In 1862 this became part of the Bedford & Cambridge Railway which in turn was absorbed by the London & North Western Railway in 1865. *Shannon* was used as a works shunter at Crewe until 1878 when it was sold for £365 8s 1d (£365 40½p) to the Wantage Tramway, Berkshire, where it became No. 5. It ran until the tramway closed in 1945 and in April 1946 was bought by the Great Western Railway for £100, renamed *Shannon*, and exhibited on Wantage Road Station. After the station closed, on 7 December 1964, the engine was acquired by the Great

Western Society Limited at Didcot and was so admirably restored that it became the oldest member of the Stockton & Darlington Railway 150th anniversary cavalcade on 31 August 1975, where it travelled under its own steam.

The oldest standard-gauge engine in service in Britain is the former London, Brighton & South Coast Railway 'Terrier' 0–6–0 tank No. 72 *Fenchurch* which entered service in September 1872, one of the first two of its type, designed by William Stroudley (1833–89). It is now at work on the Bluebell Railway in Sussex.

The fame and esteem which this class of 50 tiny engines inspired was out of all proportion to their size. No other locomotive type has gained such warm affection. Several others are preserved in England, and one can even be seen in the Canadian Railroad Historical Association's museum at Delson near Montreal. The design was copied by the New South Wales Railways for working suburban trains in Sydney.

Preserved steam locomotives in Great Britain, including industrial and narrow gauge number about 730. Of these, 375 belonged to the main-line companies and BR, 123 of which belonged to the GWR.

The oldest locomotive to be taken into British Railways stock in 1948 was a 0–4–2 saddle-tank crane locomotive, in use at the Bow Works of the former North London Railway. It was built in 1858 as a 0–4–0 saddle tank and was rebuilt as a crane tank in 1872. It was scrapped in 1951 after 93 years' service.

One of the longest lived locomotives of British Railways was the former Lancashire & Yorkshire Railway 0–6–0 saddle tank, latterly No. 11305. It was built as a 0–6–0 tender locomotive in 1877 to an order of Barton Wright, locomotive superintendent, rebuilt to a saddle tank in 1891 and withdrawn in September 1964, aged 87.

A locomotive of the same class, No. 752 (Beyer Peacock 1881), is preserved on the Keighley & Worth Valley Railway in Yorkshire.

Another long-lived British locomotive was former Midland Railway 2–4–0 No. 158A, built at Derby in 1866 to a design of Matthew Kirtley. After some rebuilding, it was withdrawn in July 1947 as LMS No. 20002, aged 81. It is now preserved in the National Collection and is on loan to the Midland Railway Company at Butterley, Derbyshire.

The longest-lived locomotive in Australia was a 1067 mm (3 ft 6 in) gauge 0–4–2 built in 1865 by Neilson & Company, Glasgow, for the Queensland Railways. In 1896 it was sold to Bingera Sugar Mill and in 1965 was lent to Queensland Railways for its centenary celebrations and was later donated to the QR. It last ran on 20 July 1967, on an Australian Railway Historical Society excursion and was then placed in the locomotive museum at Redbank, Queensland.

The oldest active locomotive in Canada is *Prairie Dog Central No. 3*, a 4–4–0 built by Dübs of Glasgow in 1882 as Canadian Pacific Railway No. 22; in 1918 it was acquired by the City of Winnipeg Hydro where it was renumbered 3. It is now preserved and operated by the Vintage Locomotive Society in Winnipeg. *Credit Valley No. 36*, a 4–4–0 built by Rogers Locomotive Works, Paterson, New Jersey, in 1883 as CPR No. 140, is also regularly operated by the Ontario Rail Association.

THE LAST STEAM LOCOMOTIVES

The last main-line steam locomotives in Britain were the standard types designed under the supervision of R. A. Riddles (1892–1983), then Member of the Railway Executive for Mechanical and Electrical Engineering. They comprised three types of 4–6–2, Classes 6, 7 and 8; a 2–10–0 Class 9; two 4–6–0s, Classes 4 and 5; three 2–6–0s, Classes 2, 3 and 4; a 2–6–4 Class 4; and two 2–6–2 tanks, Classes 2 and 3. The first to appear was Class 7 4–6–2 No. 70000 *Britannia* in January 1951. The 999th and last was the Class 9 2–10–0 No. 92220 *Evening Star* in March 1960.

As a whole, they represented the finest examples of steam-locomotive design on British Railways; but they were about 20 years too late, and they contained few features which were not standard practice in the USA in the 1920s and 1930s. By the 1950s the expense of design and development work on 12 new steam-locomotive types was an extravagance. Further construction of existing types even though, as with the standard engines, some of them may have given only a few years' service, could have kept the railways operating until more modern forms of traction had been developed.

The last French steam locomotives in regular revenue-earning operation were the 2–8–0s Class 140C, which belonged to the private CFTA Company in Franche-Comté. They worked from Gray to Troyes, Châtillon, Vesoul and other towns until 28 September 1975. They were built during World War I for hauling railway artillery, hence the name ALVF (Artilleries Lourdes Voies Ferrées) for the type. Seventy were built by the North British Locomotive Co., Glasgow, and Nasmyth Wilson, Manchester. After the war they were allocated to the Est, Etat and PLM railways and most worked into the 1960s. At least eight are preserved, some at work on French tourist railways.

The last steam locomotives built in Russia were completed in 1956. They were the 'L' Class 2–10–0s, making a class totalling about 4700; the 'LV' Class 2–10–2s and the 'P36' Class 4–8–4s.

The last steam locomotive to be built for service in North America was the Norfolk & Western 'S1a' Class 0–8–0 switcher No. 224, out-shopped from Roanoke Works in December 1953. It worked only until 1960 when steam finally disappeared from the N. & W.

The last steam locomotives built by Baldwin Locomotive Works, USA were 50 'WG' Class 2–8–2s for India, 1676 mm (5 ft 6 in) gauge, in 1955. Their price was about twice that tendered by European and Japanese builders. The last built for domestic use in the USA was a 2–8–0 for the US Army Transportation School at Fort Eustis, Virginia, in 1952.

The last steam locomotive on the Southern Pacific Railroad, USA made its last run, from San Francisco to Reno, in 1958.

The last steam locomotive to be built in Australia was 'BB 18¼', Class 4–6–2 No. 1089 on the 1067 mm (3 ft 6 in) gauge Queensland Government Railways, completed on 13 March 1958 by Walker's Limited of Maryborough (Works No. 557). It was 18.354 m (60 ft 3 in) long and weighed 101.2 tons. It was withdrawn in 1969, one of the last to run, having covered only 398 470 km (247 450 miles), and it is preserved in the Queensland Railways Museum, Redbank, near Brisbane.

The last Australian State Government railway to make regular use of steam locomotives was Tasmania. There, one of the 'H' Class was used on the Hobart–Claremont– Hobart service in 1974 in an emergency following the Tasman Bridge accident.

Steam locomotives in Japan were withdrawn in March 1976.

The last main-line steam locomotive to be built in India was a 'YG' Class metre-gauge 2–8–2 built by Indian Railways at the Chittaranjan Works and completed in February 1972.

The last express passenger steam locomotive to be built for British Railways, No. 71000 *Duke of Gloucester*, built at Crewe in 1954. It was withdrawn in 1962 and partially dismantled, but was rescued and completely rebuilt at Loughborough by the 71000 Duke of Gloucester Steam Locomotive Trust Ltd. It was photographed on the Great Central Railway south of Loughborough in 1986 on one of its first workings.

Indian Railways hope to eliminate steam traction by 1995. The poor quality of the Indian coal and consequent inefficiency, and the vast pilferage of coal throughout the country, make it uneconomic in comparison with electric and diesel traction.

The last express passenger engine built in Britain was the 'Class 8' three-cylinder Caprotti valve-gear 4–6–2 No. 71000 *Duke of Gloucester* completed at Crewe in 1954. It replaced No. 46202 *Princess Anne*. (See Steam Turbine Locomotives, p. 125.) It was the only one of its type. It was withdrawn in 1962 and, after storage with a view towards preservation, the left-hand cylinder and valve gear were removed and were installed in the Science Museum, London. The right-hand cylinder was also removed, but it disappeared. The remainder of the engine was dumped at Woodham's scrapyard at Barry, South Wales. In 1973 it was removed to Loughborough, Leicestershire. Missing parts were manufactured and the engine was completely rebuilt. On 11 November 1986 it was renamed and recommissioned by the Duke of Gloucester, a great enthusiast himself.

The only railway works still manufacturing steam locomotives in 1982 was at Datong, 270 km (168 miles) west of Peking on the Chinese People's Republic Railways. Erection of the works began in 1956 and production of locomotives began in 1959. Besides some modern 2–8–2s of Class JS ('Jang Shan' or 'Construction'), the works has turned out about 300 2–10–2s of Class QJ ('Quian Jin' or 'Advance Forward') each year. The 2–10–2s handle most of the heavy freight traffic in those areas of China where coal is plentiful, and with their 1500 mm (4 ft 11 in) wheels and maximum speed of 80 km/h (50 mph) they also handle heavy passenger trains over difficult routes.

In 1985 270 steam locomotives were built. A new 4–8–4 was completed in that year modelled on the South African Railways 25NC type. Using a gas producer it achieves a power output nearly 50 per cent more than an ordinary steam locomotive with 30 per cent less water and coal consumption and less smoke emission. If success is achieved it may establish the steam locomotive as more economical than the diesel in areas where coal is plentiful and the price of oil is high. Production of steam locomotives at Datong ended in 1988.

LAST STEAM TRAINS

The last steam-worked transcontinental trains on the Canadian Pacific Railway, after 67 years, ran in October 1954.

The last steam locomotive to pull a train on the CPR was 'A–1–e' Class 4–4–0 No. 29, built in 1887. It hauled a special train from Montreal to St Lin and back on 6 November 1960.

The last regularly scheduled steam train in the USA ran on 27 March 1960 on the Grand Trunk Western system, operated by the Canadian National Railways.

Steam locomotives were finally withdrawn on the Canadian National Railways on 25 April 1960.

London Transport passenger trains were hauled by BR steam locomotives (LNER 2–6–4 tanks Class L1) between Rickmansworth and Amersham until 9 September 1961. London Transport continued to use steam locomotives, former GWR 0–6–0 pannier tanks, for internal trip workings until 6 June 1971.

The last steam-worked branch line on British Railways was the Brockenhurst–Lymington Branch in Hampshire. It was opened on 12 July 1858 and was steam-worked until 30 March 1967. Electric trains began on 1 April.

Steam-traction was eliminated from British Railways on 8 August 1968, except for the summer-only service on the Vale of Rheidol narrow-gauge railway in Wales.

A commemorative 'Farewell to Steam' tour was operated by BR on 11 August 1968 from Liverpool to Carlisle and back. The fare was £15 15s (£15.75).

The last express worked by the famous French compound 'Pacifics' ran between Calais and Amiens on 26 May 1971.

The last regular steam passenger train in Australia ran from Newcastle to Singleton, New South Wales, in July 1971. It was hauled by 'C32' Class 4–6–0 No. 3246. (See Greatest Mileages.)

The last steam-powered goods train in Australia ran in NSW on 22 December 1972.

The last steam-hauled expresses in New Zealand ran between Christchurch and Dunedin in October 1971. However, two 'Ab' Class 'Pacifics' were returned to service for use on summer tourist trains between Lumsden and the Kingston railhead on the shore of Lake Wakatipu in Southland.

The last steam passenger train in Japan ran on 14 December 1975 from Muroran to Iwamizawa in Hokkaido, 150 km (87 miles), behind 'C57' Class 4–6–2 No. 135. At its final departure a Japanese National Railways band played 'Auld Lang Syne'.

The last scheduled steam-hauled train in West Germany ran on 22 May 1977.

GREATEST MILEAGES BY STEAM LOCOMOTIVES

The highest recorded mileage for a steam locomotive in Australia was achieved by standard-gauge Class C32 4–6–0 No. 3242 of New South Wales, which ran 3 814 000 km (2 370 000 miles). No. 3246 of the same type, which worked the last regular steam-hauled passenger train in Australia (see above) in July 1971, achieved 3 653 100 km (2 270 000 miles). Both were built in 1893.

In Britain five ex-LNER 'Pacifics' exceeded 2¼ million miles. The highest mileages were achieved by No. 60106 (LNER 4475) *Flying Fox* with 4 253 154 km (2 642 860 miles) in 41 years 8 months, and No. 60059 (LNER 2558) *Tracery* with 4 061 620 km (2 523 843 miles) in 37 years 9 months. The highest daily mileages of any British steam locomotives were achieved by LNER 4–6–2s of Class A1 designed by A. H. Peppercorn. No. 60156 *Great Central* achieved about 154 492 km (96 000 miles) in a year, an average of 423 km (263 miles) per day.

GWR 'Saint' class 4–6–0 No. 2920 *Saint David*, built in 1907, covered 3 348 663 km (2 080 754 miles), and 'Star' class 4–6–0 No. 4021 *The British Monarch* (formerly *King Edward*) of 1909 covered 3 274 987 km (2 034 975 miles). They were withdrawn in 1953 and in 1952 respectively.

The LNWR 'Precedent' class 2–4–0 No. 955 (later 3421) *Charles Dickens*, built in February 1882, ran daily between Manchester and London and by 1902 had covered 2 million miles. At withdrawal in October 1912 its total mileage was 2 345 107 (3 773 981 km).

The French 0–4–2 No. 154 built in 1853 for the Chemin de fer l'Est had covered 3 590 476 km (2 231 014 miles) when withdrawn on 13 July 1933.

At the beginning of this chapter it was noted how the introduction of steam locomotion was stimulated by the cost of using horses. In fact the horse remained in regular use as a form of motive power on British railways from the earliest wagonways at the beginning of the 17th century until 1967.

In 1930 the British railway companies owned 18 429 horses for shunting and road delivery services. By 1940 the number had fallen to 11 163, in 1950 to 4754 and in 1960 to under 100. The last British Railways horse was 24-year-old *Charlie* used, appropriately, for shunting horse boxes at Newmarket, Suffolk, from 1961 until March 1967.

WATER TROUGHS

Water troughs ('track pans' in the USA) were invented by John Ramsbottom (qv) while he was locomotive superintendent of the London & North Western Railway. They were patented in 1860 and were first installed that year at Mochdre on the Chester–Holyhead line. In 1871 they were transferred to Aber on the same line.

Track pans were used in the USA from 1870 to 1956. Water troughs were also used in France on the Etat (later SNCF Région Ouest). One type of tender only, type 30C, was fitted with scoops and this was reserved, almost exclusively, for the TP (Travaux Publics) type Pacifics. A

A1 class 4–6–2 No. 60156 *Great Central* entering Leeds Central Station on 24 September 1960. The A1s achieved the greatest annual mileages of any British steam locomotives. This one, for example, achieved about 154 493 km (96 000 miles) a year.

sectioned tender with a scoop can be seen in the French National Railway Museum at Mulhouse.

The total number of water-troughs in Britain was 141. Some, for example on the Lancashire & Yorkshire Railway, were steam heated in frosty weather.

The highest water-troughs in the world were at Garsdale on the Midland Railway Settle–Carlisle line, at 335 m (1100 ft) above sea-level, installed in 1907. Only 43.5 km (27 miles) away, on the London & North Western Railway at Hest Bank near Lancaster, the water-troughs were almost at sea-level.

The only water-troughs inside a tunnel were in the Diggle end of the three 4888 m (3 mile 66 yd) bores of the Standedge Tunnels on the London & North Western Railway between Manchester and Huddersfield. The tunnels are the only level stretch on the whole route.

9

MOTIVE POWER – ELECTRIC

At the nationalization of British railways on 1 January 1948 there were 20 024 steam locomotives. If, on average, including all passenger, freight and shunting work and those standing idle, each evaporated 22 730 litres (5000 gallons) of water a day then, allowing for engines out of service, British Railways were putting about 400 000 tons of water mixed with waste products of combustion into the atmosphere every day. An express engine on a 644 km (400 mile) run would evaporate about 69 099 litres (15 200 gallons), or nearly 70 tons of water, and burn about 8 tons of coal.

With considerably less fuel consumption, though with fossil fuels still some atmospheric pollution, an equal amount of power is produced in an electric power-station which condenses most of its water and thereby runs at far higher efficiency, besides making more efficient use of fuel in boilers. At high voltages electricity can be transmitted over great distances with negligible power losses. High installation cost is the main obstacle to railway electrification and so it is justified at present only on lines with high traffic density. Future fuel shortages may alter this.

The importance of railway electrification was stressed in the Introduction to this book.

THE PIONEERS

The first electric railway in the world was made by Thomas Davenport, a blacksmith in Vermont, USA, in 1835. It was a small railway powered by a miniature electric motor.

The first serious attempt at electric power on a railway was made by Robert Davidson in 1842 when he tried out a battery locomotive weighing 5 tons on the Edinburgh & Glasgow Railway where it ran at 6.5 km/h (4.5 mph).

The electric dynamo was perfected between 1860 and 1870 but its use as a motor came several years later.

The first practical electric railway was built by the German engineer Werner von Siemens (1816–92) for the Berlin Trades Exhibition—31 May to 30 September 1879. It was an oval about 300 m (328 yd) all round with a gauge of 1 m. The electric locomotive had a 3 hp motor, picking

The opening of Volk's Electric Railway at Brighton on 4 August 1883, Britain's first electric railway.

up current at 150 V from a centre third rail and returning it via the wheels and running rails. It could pull 30 passengers on three cars at 6.5 km/h (4 mph).

The first public electric railway in the world was opened on 12 May 1881 at Lichterfelde near Berlin. It was 2.5 km (1½ mile) long. The car ran on a 100 V supply and carried 26 passengers at 48 km/h (30 mph).

The first public electric railway in Britain was Volk's Electric Railway at Brighton, built by Magnus Volk (qv) and first opened on 4 August 1883 with 610 mm (2 ft) gauge. It was rebuilt to 838 mm (2 ft 9 in) gauge and extended and reopened on 4 April 1884. On 1 April 1940 it was taken over by Brighton Corporation.

The first electric railway to run on hydro-electric power was the 9.5 km (6 mile) long 914 mm (3 ft) gauge Portrush–Giant's Causeway Tramway, Ireland, formally opened on 28 September 1883. It was engineered by William Acheson Traill (1844–1933). Cars could run at 19 km/h (12 mph) on the level. At first an outside conductor rail was used, and the town section was worked by two steam-tram engines from W. Wilkinson & Company of Wigan. In 1899 the entire system was converted to overhead wire collection. It was closed in 1950.

The first electric underground railway in the world was the City & South London, opened on 18 December 1890. At first it used 14 four-wheeled electric locomotives built by Mather & Platt of Salford. By 1901 there were 52 locomotives. They ran until the line was reconstructed in 1924. One is preserved in the Science Museum, London.

The first electric locomotive in the USA for use on standard gauge was designed by Leo Daft for the Saratoga Mount Macgregor Railroad in 1883. It was named *Ampere*, had an output of 12 hp and pulled 10 tons at 9.6–14.5 km/h (6–9 mph).

The first electric train service in the USA began on the 11 km (7 mile) Nantasket Branch of the New York, New Haven & Hartford Railroad (now part of Conrail) on 28 June 1895.

Electric locomotives were introduced on the Baltimore & Ohio Railroad on 4 August 1895, on the Belt line from Henrietta Street, Baltimore (just south of Camden Station), to Waverley Tower—6 km (3¾ miles) through ten tunnels, amounting to 48 per cent of the distance. Passenger traffic began on 1 May 1895, with coke-burning locomotives, and goods traffic began with the electrification. The first trials with electric-traction were on 27 June 1895, originally with an overhead slot pick-up, replaced in March 1902 by a third rail.

The world's first electric elevated city railway was the Liverpool Overhead Railway. The first section opened on 6 March 1893. The line was closed, to avoid massive renewals, on 30 December 1956.

The Chicago Elevated Railway saw its first electric cars in 1895, after the system had been operated for a few years by the 'Forney'-type 0-4-4 tanks.

The Berlin Elevated Railway began as an electric line in 1902.

The first alternating current system was applied on the Burgdorf–Thun railway, Switzerland, which went into operation on 21 July 1899, using a three-phase overhead system at 750 V 16⅔ Hz. The railway, 45 km (28 miles) long, had gradients of 1 in 40. Passenger services were operated by motor coaches and goods trains were hauled by 0-4-0 or B type locomotives of 300 HP. These could haul trains of 100 tons at 32 km/h (20 mph).

The world's first single-phase alternating current locomotive went into service in 1904 on the Seebach–Wettingen Railway, Switzerland. Originally it was built for a 50 Hz supply with direct current traction motors supplied by a motor generator, but in 1904 it was rebuilt for 15 000 V, 15 Hz, with ac motors. The railway was the pioneer of high-voltage single-phase systems. The locomotive remained in service on the Bodensee-Toggenburg Railway until 1958 when it was given a place of honour in the Swiss Transport Museum, Lucerne.

The first revenue-earning single-phase electric railway was the metre-gauge Stubaitalbahn in Austria, 18 km (11 miles) long. In 1904 it was electrified at 2500 V 42 Hz.

The Midland Railway installed a 6600 V 25 Hz system on its 14.5 km (9 mile) section from Lancaster to Morecambe and Heysham in 1908. The power cars had ac commutator motors. In 1953 it was rebuilt to 50 Hz to test this system

Electric train at Heysham, Lancashire, 6 November 1965, on the former Midland Railway line from Lancaster, electrified in 1906 at 6600 V 25 Hz. It was rebuilt by British Railways in 1953 to test a frequency of 50 Hz before the decision was made in 1956 to adopt 25 kV 50 Hz as the standard.

before BR embarked on its 25 kV 50 Hz electrification. The power cars carried mercury-arc rectifiers supplying dc traction motors, thus combining the advantage of high voltage ac with its lighter conductors and fewer sub-stations with the smooth control of a dc motor. Early in 1956 experiments were carried out with germanium recti-fiers which were more compact and efficient than the mercury-arc type.

Railway electrification in North America, apart from sub-urban lines, has never been undertaken extensively because of the nature of the traffic. Electrification pays only if the equipment is used intensively, such as Lon-don–Birmingham and Lancashire, or the St Gotthard route in Switzerland. In North America it is more eco-nomical to assemble the traffic into one enormous train, perhaps over a mile long, which can be handled by a crew of three or four men. In Europe such trains are not pos-sible because the track layouts are not designed for trains of such length.

Electrification was undertaken in North America where there was the difficulty of ventilation in long tunnels such as Hoosac and Cascade, and of handling heavy trains on long climbs in the days of steam locomotives. The intro-duction of diesel power almost eliminated these troubles and consequently the electrical equipment could be dis-mantled and maintenance costs thereby reduced. The increasing cost of oil, however, may change this, and American engineers are watching with interest the devel-opment of the 50 kV system. (See Black Mesa & Lake Powell RR, p. 137.)

The longest electrified line in the USA was on the Chi-cago, Milwaukee, St Paul & Pacific (The Milwaukee Road). It had a total of 1056 km (656 miles) of electrified route out of a total route length of 17 125 km (10 641 miles). The first electrification was carried out in 1915–16 and it was completed in 1927, using a 3000 V dc overhead system.

In 1973 it was decided to abandon the electrification and to convert the entire line to diesel operation.

The Milwaukee is the only system in the USA operating over its own tracks all the way from Chicago to the Pacific Northwest. It was completed to Seattle in 1908.

The first British suburban railway electrification was inaugurated by the North Eastern Railway between New-castle (New Bridge Street) and Benton on 29 March 1904.

The Lancashire & Yorkshire Railway was a close runner-up when it introduced electric trains between Liverpool and Southport on 5 April 1904. In a desperate bid to beat the North Eastern Railway some trains were introduced before this, but the haste resulted in a partial breakdown and steam trains were not completely withdrawn until 13 May.

The first portion of the 'Southern Electric' was the South London line of the London, Brighton & South Coast Rail-way. Electric trains began on 1 December 1909 using ac at

6000 V with overhead collectors. It was later converted to 660 V dc third rail to conform to the other electrified lines south of London.

The first British railway to be electrified at 1500 V dc with overhead catenary was the Shildon–Newport (now Teesside) section of the North Eastern Railway. Electri-cally hauled coal trains with Bo-Bo locomotives designed by Vincent Raven (1858–1934), the chief mechanical engineer, began running on 1 July 1915. It was proposed to adopt this system on the main line between York and Newcastle and a prototype 2–Co–2 express locomotive, No. 13, was built in 1922, but the Grouping into the London & North Eastern Railway and the severe shortage of money following World War I prevented further progress.

With the decline of coal traffic, the Shildon–Newport section reverted to steam-haulage early in 1935. The loco-motives were stored and subsequently scrapped. No. 13 survived World War II but was never used.

The 1500 V dc overhead system was recommended for adoption as a British Standard by the 1921 'Electrification Committee' Report and by the subsequent Pringle (1928) and Weir (1931) Reports.

The first British passenger railway to be electrified at 1500 V dc was the joint LNER and LMS line from Man-chester to Altrincham, where electric multiple-unit trains began running on 8 May 1931. On 3 May 1971 the line was changed to 25 kV ac.

The first mercury-arc rectifier to be installed on a British railway was at Hendon on the Morden–Edgware line of the London Underground in 1930. It marked one of the most important technical improvements in dc electric-traction and made unmanned substations possible. Pre-viously, permanently manned rotary converters had to be used.

The first British main-line electrification was the South-ern Railway London to Brighton and Worthing, brought into use on 1 January 1933. The system is 660 V dc third rail.

The Kando system of 50 Hz electrification, first tried in Hungary in 1923, was installed in 1933 on the Budapest–Hegyeshalom line, 191 km (119 miles), using current at 16 kV converted to three-phase on the Bo–Bo locomo-tives, by using rotary converters.

Further experiments with 50 Hz traction were made in 1936 on the Höllental (Black Forest) section of the Ger-man State Railways, with current at 20 kV. Four experi-mental locomotives were built, two with rectifiers and dc motors, one on the Kando system with rotary converter, and the fourth with 50 Hz motors.

The electrification of the London (Liverpool Street)– Shenfield line, 32 km (20 miles), at 1500 V dc overhead came into operation on 26 September 1949. It was extended to Chelmsford, 15.3 km (9½ miles), on 11 June 1956 and to Southend (Victoria), 25 km (15½ miles), on 31 December 1956. It was converted to 25 kV ac in 1960.

Britain's first 'all-electric' main line (passenger and freight traffic) was the Manchester–Sheffield line of the former Great Central Railway. Through passenger services began on 14 September 1954 following the opening, on 3 June, of the new Woodhead Tunnel. The 'standard' 1500 V dc system was used. The passenger service was withdrawn from 5 January 1970 and transferred to the Midland route, to make way for freight traffic, despite the line's increased capacity. On 18 July 1981 the freight traffic was also withdrawn and the line was abandoned between Hadfield and Penistone, including the new Woodhead Tunnel. The section from Manchester to Hadfield and Glossop remained open for suburban passenger trains and in 1984 was converted to 25 kV, which came into use on 10 December.

On the Netherlands Railways, 1646 km (1023 miles) are electrified at 1500 V dc out of a total route length of 2832 km (1758 miles). Steam-traction was withdrawn on 7 January 1958.

Following withdrawal of the Manchester–Sheffield passenger service in 1970, British Rail sold the seven Co–Co locomotives, Nos. 27000–6, to the Netherlands Railways in 1972.

The 25 kV single phase system at the industrial frequency of 50 Hz was pioneered in France in 1950 as a result of the Höllental line (Black Forest) coming into the French territory after World War II. French Railways decided to install a 50 Hz system using 78 km (48 miles) of track in the French Alps between Aix les Bains, Annemasse and St Gervais for trials. This led to electrification of the main line between Valenciennes and Thionville in 1955. The first locomotives to use this power system were CC 1400 and BB 12 000 'crocodile' types.

The decision to adopt 25 000 V (25 kV) 50 Hz electrification as the future British Standard was made on 6 March 1956.

The first British railway to operate on 25 kV was the 39.5 km (24½ mile) Colchester–Clacton–Walton line, on 16 March 1959.

Semi-conductor rectifiers of the germanium type came into use on locomotives and railcars in 1955, followed a few years later by silicon-diode rectifers. They were used on BR in locomotives of Class 85 and in railcars in 1960–1 and they replaced the mercury-arc rectifiers used on electric locomotives of classes 81 to 84.

The first British main line to operate on 25 kV was the Crewe–Manchester, on 12 September 1960. The Crewe–Liverpool line followed on 1 January 1962.

The first electric trains in Scotland (excluding the Glasgow District Subway) were the Glasgow suburban services—50 km (31 miles) of line at 25 kV. They began on 7 November 1960 but were withdrawn for alteration from 17 December 1960 to 1 October 1961.

The second stage—43.5 km (27 miles) of line south of the Clyde—was inaugurated on 27 May 1962.

The London–Manchester–Liverpool full service began on 18 April 1966. Some trains had run through from 22 November 1965. It was extended to the Birmingham area on 6 March 1967.

The extension of the electrification from London to Glasgow, covering the lines from Weaver Junction, Cheshire, to Motherwell in Lanarkshire, was approved by the Minister of Transport in March 1970. It was opened throughout on 6 May 1974. The total cost was £75 000 000— £30 000 000 for electrification, £38 000 000 for resignalling and £7 000 000 for new electric locomotives.

The '87' class electric locomotives, introduced in 1973 for the Scottish services, have an output of 5000 hp with a total weight of only 80 tons. They have fully suspended traction motors and are designed to run at speeds of over 161 km/h (100 mph) and, unlike the other 25 kV locomotives, can be coupled and driven as multiple-units. With an output of 62½ hp/ton their adhesion at full power on adverse grades is at the mercy of the weather.

The first British Rail electric locomotive with thyristor control was No. 87 101, built at Crewe in 1975. The thyristor gives notchless control at constant tractive effort; tapchanger control produces variations in tractive effort in each notch.

At a ceremony at Piccadilly Station, Manchester, on 12 October 1977, No. 87 101 was named *Stephenson* by Mr A. J. Boston, president of the Stephenson Locomotive Society which provided the nameplates.

Following abandonment of the Advanced Passenger Train project in 1986, BR required a new generation of electric locomotives. For hauling 200 km/h (124 mph) trains on the East Coast main line on which electrification was proceeding, and on the West Coast main line with its heavy climbs to Shap and Beattock, the Class 89 CoCo was designed by Brush Electrical Machines Ltd at Loughborough. The locomotive, whose dimensions in mm are shown in the drawing below, weighs 105 tonnes and has an output of 4350 kW (5833 hp). Traction motors are frame mounted to reduce unsprung weight. Primary rheostatic braking at 200 km/h blends to air braking at 125 km/h. Although the locomotive has proved thoroughly reliable in service, fulfilled all requirements, and rides well on its 6-wheeled bogies (while BR prefers 4-wheeled), BR has decided not to adopt it as a standard type and to go ahead with its own Class 91 BoBo, described below, which has proved less reliable than the Class 89. There is a hope that the 89 may find use on Channel tunnel trains.

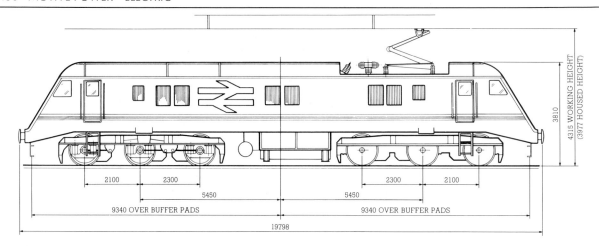

Dimensional drawing of Brush Class 89 electric locomotive.

For working West Coast expresses up to 177 km/h (110 mph) the Class 90 BoBo has been designed. The first of 29 was completed at Crewe in 1987. They are equipped with micro-processor controlled thyristor power circuits which will give smooth performance with trains up to 17 coaches on the steep gradients and sharp curves of the West Coast route. Bogies are the same as those of the Class 87. A second batch of 21 will haul freight and parcels traffic on the electrified East-Coast main line.

For working 200 km/h (124 mph) push-pull expresses mainly on the East Coast main line BR has introduced the Class 91 BoBo locomotive. It is capable of a top speed of 225 km/h (140 mph). The first of 31 left the BREL works at Crewe on 12 February 1988. Electrical equipment is by GEC Traction. The locomotive is 19 560 mm (64 ft 2 in)

The first of the BR Class 90 electric locomotives, designed for working expresses on the London Euston to Lancashire and Scotland lines up to 177km/h (110 mph). It was completed at Crewe in 1987.

long, weighs 81.5 tonnes and has an output of 4530 kW (6075 hp). Because in push-pull working it remains attached to one end of the train it has a streamlined cab at one end only and a square cab at the other, train, end. At the opposite end of the train is a streamlined driving compartment, matching the front of the locomotive.

'The Great Northern Electrics' were introduced on the London (Moorgate)–Hertford/Welwyn Garden City service on 8 November 1976. They operate on 25 kV ac in the open and on 600 V dc on the underground section between Finsbury Park and Moorgate. By a curious misconception in the interior design, the seating is arranged so that no passenger can conveniently see out of a window without twisting his neck through 90 degrees.

The same type of rolling stock has been reproduced for the new London St Pancras–Bedford electrification. This was energized on 12 January 1981 but the trains remained out of use because they were equipped for one-man operation and the unions refused to allow them to be handled. Agreement with the unions on operation was reached on 21 March 1983 and during the year the trains were gradually brought into use.

BR Class 91 electric locomotive, designed for working expresses on the East Coast main line at speeds up to 225 km/h (140 mph), reducing the journey time between London and Edinburgh to 4 hours. Because they will work mainly on push-pull trains, only one end of the locomotive is streamlined.

British Railways Southern Region mainline electrification to Southampton and Bournemouth was completed on 10 July 1967, enabling through trains to run from London, using third rail at 750 V dc. On the same day 145 km/h (90 mph) push-and-pull services were introduced, following successful tests at 161 km/h (100 mph). **The occasion marked the end of steam on BR Southern Region.**

Of the total British Rail network of 16 729 km, 3906 km or 23.35 per cent is electrified with two systems: 2042 km of 25 kV 50 Hz and 1864 km of third rail dc. This can be compared with the French railways which, with a total of 34 541 km, has electrified 11 488 km or 33.26 per cent, at 1500 V dc or 25 kV 50 Hz.

With much of BR's ageing fleet of diesel-electric locomotives requiring renewal in the early 1990s, a decision on future electrification policy is needed soon. If it becomes necessary to renew the diesel-electrics, further electrification could be delayed for 20–30 years. BR urgently needs to electrify at least 52 per cent of its network.

The French TGV or Trains à Grande Vitesse (High Speed Trains) are electric trains consisting of eight coaches and a power unit, or locomotive, at each end. The coaches are articulated on nine bogies to form one unit. The power units are on two four-wheeled power bogies, and another power bogie in the train makes a total of 12 motors normally working at 1070 V 530 A. The motors are body-mounted to reduce unsprung weight. Rheostatic braking on motor bogies supplements electro-pneumatically operated disc brakes. Clasp brakes are also fitted, but these operate only below 200 km/h (124 mph). The trains are designed to operate on both 25 kV 50 Hz and 1500 V dc, and a third type is planned to operate also on 15 kV 16⅔ Hz for use through Switzerland. Thyristors regulate voltage at motor terminals, operating as a mixed bridge on 25 kV and as a chopper on 1500 V dc. On 25 kV they have a continuous power rating of 6450 kW (8649 hp), on 1500 V dc of 3100 kW (4157 hp) and on 15 kV of 2800 kW (3755 hp). Each set has a tare weight of 386 tonnes (first-class-only units 384 tonnes) and a total length of 200.2 m (656 ft 9 in) over couplings. Power units are 22.1 m (72 ft 8 in) long. The trains have seats for 111 first-class and 275 second-class passengers (first-class only trains 287).

The world's first 50 kV railway, the 125.5 km (78 mile) Black Mesa & Lake Powell Railroad in Arizona, began operation in late 1973 and was fully opened on 15 March 1974. Construction began in February 1971. This isolated standard-gauge single-line railway was built at a cost of $75 million to haul coal from the Black Mesa coal mining area, where an 8 km (5 mile) conveyor belt delivers the coal to the railway terminal loop, to the Navaja power station near Page above Lake Powell. With such a high voltage the railway needs only one feed point, which is at the Lake Powell end. The line is operated by six locomotives of about 6000 hp supplied by General Electric Co. at a cost of $750 000 each, and a total of 116 four-door bottom-dump cars, 76 of 122 tons capacity and 40 of 100 tons. Trains carrying 6000 tons of coal are hauled by three locomotives and take 2 h 40 min from the mine to the power station, and under 2 h on the return. Trains consume about 19 000 kWh on a round trip. The line works on the 'merry-go-round' principle at each end; loading takes 1½ h and unloading 20 min. Six round trips daily, six days a week, are needed to feed the power station. Operation is entirely automatic, but an 'attendant' rides at the front of the train to give warnings and to take emergency action if the line is obstructed. The railway is regarded as a test bed for future electrification in the USA.

North of Cape Town a new 846 km (525 miles) 1065 mm (3 ft 6 in) gauge line from Sishen to Saldanha Bay has been electrified at 50 kV as a direct result of the oil shortage. It was built by the South African Iron & Steel Industrial Corporation (ISCOR). Tracklaying started on 11 November 1974 and was completed on 28 April 1976. The first trains ran on 7 May 1976. Ownership was transferred to South African Railways on 1 April 1977. Until electric operation began in mid-1978 trains were hauled by General Electric U26C diesel-electric locomotives in rakes of five. Trains of 204 wagons carrying 17 000 tons of ore (total weight 21 000 tons), are hauled at speeds up to 72 km/h (45 mph) by three GEC locomotives in multiple unit. Seventeen Co–Co electric locomotives of 3780 kW (5069 hp) have been obtained, the world's most powerful locomotives on the 1065 mm gauge, weighing 168 tons each, with a length of 20.1 m (66 ft) over buffer beams. They have thyristor control, and four dynamic brake resistors, capable of dissipating 4210 kW to hold the trains on the long down grades.

The locomotives were built in South Africa by Union Carriage & Wagon Company (Pty) Ltd, with electric equipment by GEC Traction, Manchester.

In Northern Brazil the 1600 mm (5 ft 3 in) gauge single-line Carajás ore railway operates on 50 kV 60 Hz. It is 890 km (553 miles) long and opened in 1984. It handles 60 million tons a year, from Serra dos Carajás through Maraba to the Atlantic port of São Luis on São Marcos Bay.

The most powerful electric locomotive on USSR railways and probably in the world is the WL86, 2 × BoBoBo, built at Novocherkassk works in 1985–6 for the Baikal–Amur Main Line. It has an output of 11 400 kW (15 287 hp) on 25 kV 50 Hz supply. It is 45 m (147 ft 6 in) long overall, weighs 300 tonnes with an axle load of 25 tonnes. The WL86 is similar to the WL85 but is lower geared to give a top speed of 110 km/h (68 mph) compared with 160 km/h (100 mph) in the WL85. The locomotive is designed to operate in temperatures down to −60°C (−76°F).

Chopper circuits, now being used to control some electric locomotives, are solid-state switches capable of rapid closing and opening for controlling the voltage applied to dc traction motors. They consist of thyristors in conjunction with diodes, and capacitors to give continuous current flow. Chopper control results in a 20–25 per cent improvement in energy consumption and also facilitates regenerative braking.

The world's most powerful electric locomotives with chopper control, to be built as a production series, are the 7000 hp Co–Co-type. They are supplied by ACEC (Ateliers de Constructions Electriques de Charleroi Société Anonyme, part of the Westinghouse Electric Group) and La Brugeoise et Nivelles for the 3000 V dc Belgian

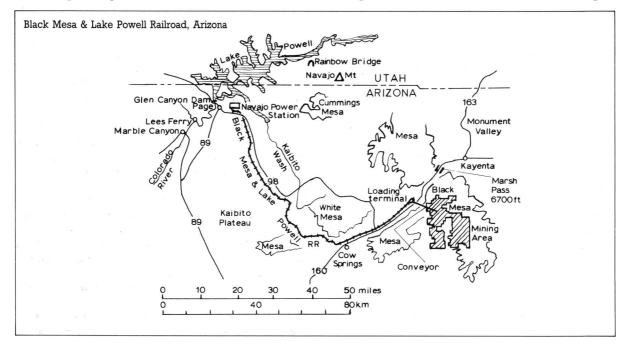

Black Mesa & Lake Powell Railroad, Arizona

National Railways (SNCB) and were first delivered on 9 September 1975. They represented a great advance in the use of semi-conductors for traction-power conversion.

Among the world's most advanced electric locomotives are the ten French four-system Series CC40 100 type built in 1965–6. They are designed to run on 25 kV 50 Hz single-phase, 1500 V dc in France and the Netherlands, 3000 V dc in Belgium, and 15 kV 16⅔ Hz single-phase in Germany and Switzerland. The CC40 100s have a maximum output of 5280 hp and a top speed of 240 km/h (150 mph). They are used on the Trans-Europe Express (TEE) services between Paris and Brussels (314 km (195 miles) non-stop in 2 h 20 min) and Amsterdam. Their full use, however, has been restricted by absurd out-dated frontier practices causing delays by exchange of locomotives, often of the same type.

In 1974 the Belgian National Railways (SNCB) obtained six four-system CC type locomotives of 5870 hp, 'Class 18'. With five three-system Bo-Bos of 'Class 16' they provide a total of 19 Belgian electric locomotives for crossing frontiers.

Electrification of the Trans-Siberian Railway, partly on 3000 V dc, and more recently 25 kV 50 Hz, had reached Karimskaya, 6284 km (3905 miles) from Moscow by 1980. USSR Railways hopes to have electrified the entire Trans-Siberian Railway, 9297 km (5777 miles), by 1990.

The first electric trains in Australia began running at Melbourne, Victoria, in 1919. The first electric locomotive was introduced in the city in 1923. The system is 1500 V dc.

The highest-capacity passenger trains in Australia are the double-deck electric suburban trains at Sydney, NSW, which carry 2500 passengers at speeds up to 96.5 km/h (60 mph). They were introduced on 12 January 1964.

The first electrified trunk railway in China, from Cheng Tu to Paochi in the Province of Szechwan, 676 km (420 miles), was opened on 1 July 1975. The first train was a ChengTu–Peking express hauled by a Chinese-built 5200 hp electric locomotive. The decision to electrify the line, at 25 kV 50 Hz, was made in 1958, and the first 100 km (62 miles) to Fenghsien was completed in 1961, using French equipment. The railway, built in 1953–7, has 304 tunnels and 981 bridges.

In other countries outside Europe electrified railways began operating as follows:

Country	Route	Length		Voltage	Date
		km	miles		
Argentina	Buenos Aires district	24	15	550 V dc OH	1909 (electric tramway vehicles)
General Bartolomé Mitre (former Central Argentine)	Buenos Aires (Retiro)–Tigre (Central)	29	18	800 V dc third rail	24 Aug 1916
Bolivia	Guaqui–La Paz Railway, La Paz–El Alto	9.5	6	550 V dc OH	1908
Brazil	Corcovado Railway, Cosme Velho–Corcovado	3.2	2	750 V 3-phase ac OH	1910
Canada	CNR Montreal			2400 V dc OH	1918
Chile	Bethlehem Chile Iron Mines–Tofo, Cruz Grande	24	15	2400 V dc OH	1916
	Valparaiso–Los Andes and Santiago	232	144	3000 V dc OH	1924
	Chilean Transandine	75.5	47	3000 V dc OH	1927
Costa Rica	Pacific Railroad	124	77	15 kV single-phase ac 20 Hz OH	1929
Cuba	Havana–Mantanzas	145	90	1200 V dc OH	1920
India	Bombay–Poona	192	119	1500 V dc OH	1925
	Bombay–Virar	68	42	1500 V dc OH	1928
Indonesia	Djakarta district	8	5	1500 V dc OH	1925
Japan	Chuo line			1500 V dc OH	1906
New Zealand	Otira–Arthur's Pass	14.5	9	1500 V dc OH	1923
South Africa	Durban area			3000 V dc OH	1926
Turkey	Sirkeci–Halkai			25 kV 50 Hz	1955
USA	Long Island Railroad			700 V dc third rail	1905
	Pennsylvania Railroad			650 V dc third rail	1906
				11 kV single-phase ac 25 Hz OH	1907
	Reading Railroad			11 kV single-phase ac 25 Hz OH	1906

10

MOTIVE POWER – DIESEL

The 'compression ignition' system was invented by Stuart Ackroyd (1864–1927) who developed the idea between 1886 and 1890.

Dr Rudolf Diesel (1858–1913) was born in Paris and became a professor at Munich. He invented his internal-combustion engine, in 1892, to use a fairly crude oil so as to be less costly to run than a petrol engine. It was first demonstrated in 1898.

Oil burned in a diesel engine produces 1.9 times as much work as the same amount burned in an oil-fired steam locomotive. A diesel locomotive will produce less atmospheric pollution than a steam locomotive for the same amount of work.

The major problem of high-power diesel rail-traction is the transmission from engine to wheels. Mechanical and hydraulic transmissions have been used, but electric transmission is now almost universal. It should be borne in mind that a diesel-electric is simply an electric locomotive carrying its own power-station on board. It produces only about a third, and at best less than half, as much power as a modern electric locomotive of equal weight, even though the latter includes a transformer and rectifier.

The first diesel locomotive was a direct-drive 1000 hp Diesel-Klose-Sulzer unit built in Germany in 1912–13, but it ran for only a few months, as an experiment.

The first diesel railway vehicle in revenue service was an Atlas-Deva 75 bhp diesel-electric railcar built in 1913 for the Mellersta & Södermanlands Railway, Sweden. It ran until 1939.

The first 'production' diesels were five 200 hp diesel-electric railcars built by Sulzer in Switzerland in 1914 for the Prussian & Saxon State Railways.

The first diesel-electric switchers (or 'shunters' in English) were three 200 hp units built in the USA by the General Electric Company in 1918.

The first 'commercially successful' diesel-electric locomotive in America was a 300 hp unit built by ALCO in 1923, with an Ingersoll-Rand engine and General Electric Company controls and transmission. It was converted from a GEC demonstration unit of 1917 and from June 1924 to July 1925 it was operated on 13 lines and was then withdrawn. From it came the production design of 60 ton

300 hp units and 100 ton 600 hp units. The first of these, a 300 hp unit, was sold to the Central Railroad of New Jersey on 22 October 1925, becoming No. 1000, and worked until 1957 when it was presented to the Baltimore & Ohio Transportation Museum.

The first experiment with diesel-traction on British railways was in 1924 when the London & North Eastern Railway tried an Austrian-built diesel locomotive for a short period.

One of the most unusual locomotives was the Kitson-Still steam-diesel locomotive built by Kitson & Company of Leeds, and tested on the London & North Eastern Railway in April 1927. It was a 2–6–2 tank engine with eight cylinders operating with internal combustion on one side of the piston and with steam on the other side. The internal-combustion engine helped in raising steam. It attempted to combine the power at slow speed of the steam-engine with the fuel economy of the internal-combustion engine. It gave good performance on freight trains between York and Hull, but was excessively noisy, and the design was not repeated.

The first main-line use of diesel-electric traction was on the Canadian National Railways in 1925 when six railcars were put into service, followed by three more in 1926. They had four- or eight-cylinder engines made by Beardmore of Glasgow, Scotland. One of these (No. 15820) covered 4727 km (2937 miles) on a demonstration run from Montreal to Vancouver in 67 h.

The first main-line diesel-electric locomotives were four 1200 bhp units built for the German State Railways in 1925 to a design by the Russian engineer Professor George V. Lomonossoff (1876–1952).

The Long Island Railroad was the first in the USA to run a diesel-electric locomotive in road service on an 864 km (537 mile) demonstration run in December 1925.

The first successful 'road' or main-line diesel-electric locomotive in North America was introduced by Canadian National Railways in 1928, a twin-unit 2660 hp machine numbered 9000–01. It was withdrawn in 1946. Shortly before its introduction, ALCO completed a 750 hp freight unit and an 880 hp passenger unit for 'road' work on the New York Central, but they were little used.

The German diesel-compressed air 4-6-4 of 1929.

A curious form of transmission was tried in Germany on a 4-6-4 locomotive built in 1929 by Maschinenfabrik Augsburg Nürnberg AG. This was a diesel-compressed air machine. The 1200 bhp diesel engine drove an air compressor. The compressed air was taken through a heater through which the engine exhaust was passed. The drive to the wheels was as on a steam locomotive, with Walschaert's valve gear. The efficiency was stated to be higher than with electric transmission. The cylinders were 700×700 mm ($27\frac{1}{2} \times 27\frac{1}{2}$ in) and with a working pressure of 6.5–7 kg/cm^2 (92.3–99.4 lb/in^2) the tractive effort was 12 000 kg (26 500 lb).

The first British diesel-electric train was adapted by the London, Midland & Scottish Railway in 1928 from an ex-Lancashire & Yorkshire Railway Manchester–Bury electric train, by fitting it with a 500 hp Beardmore engine and English Electric traction equipment. It ran for a time on the Preston–Blackpool service and was later reconverted to an electric train.

The first use of diesel-traction in Ireland was in 1929 when Kerr Stuart & Company of Stoke-on-Trent tried out a 0-6-0 diesel-mechanical locomotive on the Castlederg & Victoria Bridge Tramway in County Tyrone. It ran for about 6 months.

The first regular use of diesel-traction in the British Isles was on the 914 mm (3 ft) gauge County Donegal Railways in Ireland, in September 1931. The diesel railcar No. 7 was powered by a 74 hp Gardner engine. With a second, No. 8, built in November 1931, it was scrapped in 1939.

The first diesel locomotive in regular service in Britain was rebuilt from a Midland Railway 0-6-0 tank engine by the London, Midland & Scottish Railway in 1931. A Paxman engine was used with Haslem & Newton hydro-static transmission.

The first high-speed diesel train, the streamlined *Flying Hamburger,* ran between Berlin and Hamburg and was introduced in the spring of 1932. It was scheduled to run at speeds of over 100 mph (161 km/h). On tests it reached over 198.5 km/h (124 mph).

The first diesel locomotives in main-line service in the USA were used on the Chicago, Burlington & Quincy and Union Pacific railroads in 1934. The first diesels on regular freight work went into service on the Santa Fe in 1940.

The 'Burlington Zephyr' of the Chicago, Burlington & Quincy Railroad entered service in 1934 as the **world's first diesel-electric streamliner.** On 26 May 1934 it travelled the 1633 km (1015 miles) from Denver to Chicago non-stop at an average speed of 125 km/h (77.6 mph). The train is preserved at the Museum of Science and Industry, Chicago, alongside a captured German submarine.

The first lightweight streamlined diesel passenger train went into operation between Lincoln, Nebraska, USA and Kansas City, Missouri, on 11 November 1934.

The first British streamlined diesel train was built by the London, Midland & Scottish Railway in 1938. It consisted of three articulated coaches powered by Leyland diesel engines and hydro-mechanical transmission. After successful service between Oxford and Cambridge, and Nottingham and London, it was stored throughout the war and afterwards was dismantled.

The greatest landmark in the progress of the diesel locomotive was the General Motors 'Electro Motive' No. 103, built in the USA in 1939. It was a four-unit freight machine rated at 5400 hp. In one year's trials it covered 133 572 km (83 000 miles) on 21 roads in 37 States in temperatures from $-40°C$ to $43.3°C$ ($-40°F$ to $110°F$) at altitudes from sea-level to 3109 m (10 200 ft). In $1\frac{1}{2}$ h it hauled 1800 tons up the 40 km (25 miles) of 1 in 40 (2.5 per cent) on the western climb of the Southern Pacific/Santa Fe to Tehachapi Pass, completely outclassing the biggest steam locomotives. From that moment their fate was sealed.

The first diesel-electric locomotive in road freight service in the USA was inaugurated by the Santa Fe Railroad on 4 February 1941.

The 'diesel revolution' in the USA took about 16 years. In 1945 there were 38 853 steam locomotives, 842 electric locomotives and 835 'other types'. In May 1952 diesel locomotives outnumbered steam locomotives with 19 082, as against 18 489. In 1961 there were 110 steam, 480 electric and 28 150 diesel units.

The first British main-line diesel-electric locomotives were built by the London, Midland & Scottish Railway in 1947, Nos. 10000/1. They were Co–Co types with English Electric Company 1600 hp engines and six nose-suspended traction motors, and weighed 128 tons each— a startling contrast to the 'Deltics' (mentioned on p. 144) with a weight of 100 tons and horsepower of 3300, built only eight years later.

DIESEL RAILCARS AND MULTIPLE UNIT TRAINS

A railcar, with its power unit carried on its own chassis, eliminates much of the dead weight of a locomotive and the need to run round at terminals and is thereby more economical to operate.

The first British internal-combustion engine railcar was the 'Petrol-Electric Autocar' built by the North Eastern Railway in 1903. Two worked between Scarborough and Filey in August 1904 and in the winter between Billingham and Port Clarence. In 1908 they were put to work on the Selby–Cawood Branch.

Direct-drive gas (petrol)-engined vehicles were being tried at the same time in North America. In 1904 a Napier car fitted with flanged wheels was tested over 1609 km (1000 miles) of railway in the USA and Canada.

The 'gas-electric' car was introduced in the USA by the General Electric Company in 1906, when a combined passenger and baggage car was built for the Delaware & Hudson Railroad. It was 20.9 m (68 ft 7 in) long and weighed 43.8 tons.

Many railcars for light railways, particularly in Ireland, were adapted from old buses, the first being run on the 914 mm (3 ft) gauge County Donegal Railway in Ireland in 1928.

Pneumatic-tyred railcars were introduced in France by the Michelin Tyre Company in 1931. A similar car was tried on the London, Midland & Scottish and Southern railways in England in 1932. In 1935 the LMS tested the 'Coventry Pneumatic Railcar', a 16-wheeled vehicle by Armstrong Siddeley with Michelin tyres. For about a year two were in regular service around Coventry and Rugby. The tyres had a high rolling resistance and the cars were uneconomic to run but, despite this, pneumatic-tyred railcars have been much used in France.

The first British diesel railbus was produced by Hardy Motors Ltd, a subsidiary of the Associated Equipment Co., who converted an AEC 'Regal' road coach to run on rails in 1933. Thus began the long association of the AEC with railcars.

The first Great Western Railway diesel railcar was built in 1933 by AEC with Park Royal coachwork. It was fully streamlined, was 19.4 m (63 ft 7 in) long and weighed 20 tons. It seated 70 third class passengers and had a top speed of 121 km/h (75 mph). After achieving considerable attention at the International Commercial Motor Exhibition in London it was sold to the GWR, becoming their diesel car No. 1 and entering service in 1934.

Rail Diesel Cars (known as 'RDCs') were introduced in North America by the Budd Company of Philadelphia in 1949. They have two 300 hp General Motors diesel engines mounted under the floor, each driving one axle through a GM hydraulic torque converter and reverse gear. The single cars are 25.9 m (85 ft) long, weigh 51 620 kg (113 800 lb), seat 70 passengers and include a 5.2 m (17 ft) luggage compartment. For multiple-unit operation in trains, passenger-only trailer vehicles are also built with single engines.

By 1973 Budd had built about 500 RDCs. Most are in the USA and Canada. Others are at work in Australia, Saudi Arabia, Cuba and Brazil (Departamento Nacional de Estradas de Ferro—DNEF, and Rède Ferroviaria Federal Sa—RFFSA).

Diesel multiple-unit trains first appeared in Britain in 1954, and were first put to work between Leeds and Bradford via Stanningley on 14 June and between Carlisle and Silloth on 29 November.

Four-wheeled diesel railbuses of various designs were tried on lightly used lines in Britain for several years from 1958. Two are preserved for use on the Keighley & Worth Valley Railway. Another is on the North Yorkshire Moors Railway and two more are at Sheringham, Norfolk. They gave an exceedingly rough ride.

Multiple-unit diesel-electric trains on the Southern Region of British Railways were first used on the London to Hastings via Tunbridge Wells service on 6 May 1957. They are in six-car sets with a 500 bhp English Electric supercharged diesel engine and generator in each end car.

At the end of 1983, BR had 2703 diesel multiple-unit power cars and trailers mostly built between 1957 and 1960. All had achieved high mileages, and by the late 1970s it was clear that they would have to be replaced in a few more years. So, with no hope of sufficient investment to provide for electrification of all suburban services, several new types were evolved.

For inner and outer suburban services with heavy traffic the **Class 210 diesel-electric train** was designed. These are electric trains carrying their own power station around with them. Two prototypes entered service in 1982, one with four cars and one with three. The four-car set accommodates 232 second-class and 22 first-class passengers. It is powered by a six-cylinder in-line diesel engine rated at 839 kW (1124 hp) at 1500 rpm. The three-car set, with seats for 203 second-class passengers, has a 12 cylinder vee engine, rated at 915 kW (1226 hp) at 1500 rpm. In both sets the engine drives a main alternator supplying the traction motors and an auxiliary alternator for other services. The main alternator supplies 650 amps three-phase ac at 1200 V. In both sets, a solid-state rectifier supplies the four traction motors which are similar to those of the Class 317 electric multiple-unit trains, each taking 335 amps at 620 V.

Because the Class 210 trains would be uneconomic for the replacement of all services operated by diesel multi-

The Leyland Experimental Vehicle at Derby in 1985. It was built to test the application of bus bodies to rail use, and was developed into the class 140, 141 and 142 railbuses.

ple units, light-weight diesel trains were designed for routes with less heavy traffic.

The prototype Class 140 is a two-car unit based on the rail-bus known as the Leyland Experimental Vehicle (LEV). This consisted of two Leyland National bus bodies joined back to back and mounted on a four-wheeled underframe carrying engine, transmission and running gear. The railcar was successful in trials in Great Britain and the USA. Each car of the Class 140 unit has an underfloor engine driving one of the axles through a four-speed gearbox. The two cars provide seats for 102 passengers and standing room for about 100 more. The unladen weight of 38 tons is less than 70 per cent of the weight of a conventional two-car train, making it cheaper to run.

This was developed into the **Class 141 two-car diesel railbus**. One car has 44 seats plus a toilet compartment, the other has 50 seats, and each is powered by a Leyland 'TL11' turbo-charged 200 hp diesel engine. Twenty units entered service in West Yorkshire at the beginning of 1984.

Within the basic design a wide range of alternative interiors can be incorporated with a view towards the export market, such as more luxurious seats, toilets, alternative heating and ventilation and air conditioning. A similar but higher capacity design, Class 142, was also introduced in 1984 and 75 two-car sets were ordered on 16 January.

For medium-distance journeys BR introduced the '150' class two-car units seating 149 passengers. Type 150/1 introduced in 1985 has gangways only between the two cars; 150/2, 1987, has additional end gangways. The cars are each 19 740 mm (64 ft 9 in) long and 2816 mm (9 ft 3 in) wide. Though these units give good performance, the seating arrangement, giving no passenger a good lookout, is far from satisfactory. A much better internal arrangement was provided in the Metro-Cammell '151'

Top: Class 142 railbus at Manchester Victoria Station, 2 June 1988.

Above: BR Class 156 two-car diesel train at Derby on 31 May 1988. With a length of 23 m (75 ft 5½ in) these are the longest coaches ever to run on British railways. Their interior arrangement is by far the most pleasant to be found on any British diesel trains.

class units also introduced in 1985, but for various reasons few were built, and the much inferior 150 class was adopted for production.

For longer-distance journeys the Leyland '155' class was introduced in 1987. The two-car units have gangways throughout and seat 160. Because of their great length, 22 640 mm (74 ft 3 in), the cars are only 2690 mm (8 ft 10 in) wide to allow for overhang on curves. The Metro-Cammell '156' class two-car units, also introduced in 1987, seat 163 in a pleasant interior arrangement. These cars are 23 000 mm (75 ft 5½ in), the longest ever to run on British railways, and 2730 mm (8 ft 11½ in) wide. All these classes have underfloor 14 litre diesel engines rated at 285 hp at 2100 rpm and a hydraulic transmission; they have a top speed of 145 km/h (90 mph). Because of their rapid acceleration and high speeds these new diesel trains have been named 'Sprinters'.

A new design, the '158' class, with a speed of up to 160 km/h (100 mph), has been ordered for delivery in 1989.

DIESEL LOCOMOTIVE PROGRESS

Hydraulic transmission was adopted by the Western Region of British Railways, principally because of the greater power/weight ratio. The hydraulic transmission gear weighs considerably less than the generator and motors on a diesel-electric locomotive. For example, the Class '52' 'Westerns' introduced in 1961 had an output of 2700 hp and a maximum tractive force of 32 931 kg (72 600 lb), with a total weight of 109 tons. The Class '46' diesel-electrics, also 1961, had an output of 2500 hp, a maximum tractive force of 31 752 kg (72 000 lb), with a weight of 138 tons, a difference in weight equal to one coach.

The first British main-line diesel-hydraulic locomotive, No. D600, was built by the North British Locomotive Company, Glasgow, and was delivered to the Western Region of British Railways in January 1958. It was an A1A-A1A type, weighed 117.4 tons, and had an output of 2000 hp and a top speed of 145 km/h (90 mph). It was the first of a class of five named, together with the following class of B-B locomotives, after warships, and carried the name *Active*. All five were withdrawn by the end of 1967.

Later in 1958 the first of the 71 B-B type diesel-hydraulic locomotives of Classes '42' and '43' was completed at the Swindon Works, based on the successful German V200 Class, weighing only 78 tons and producing 2100 bhp. The WR version, however, built to the smaller British construction gauge, was not so successful and the entire class had been withdrawn by the end of 1972. Two have not been broken up.

The 58 1000 and 1100 hp B-B type of Class '22', weighing only 65 tons and built by the North British Locomotive Company, were introduced in 1959. They were among the less successful of the WR diesel-hydraulics and their working career was short. The last of the 1000 hp type was withdrawn in 1968, and of the 1100 hp type in 1971.

In 1961 the first of the 74 C-C 'Western' Class '52' locomotives was completed at Swindon. By the end of their career, in 1977, they had become one of the most popular and sought-after diesel classes on BR. Several have been preserved, including one at the National Railway Museum, York, and two on the Severn Valley Railway.

The 101 Beyer Peacock 'Hymek' B-B locomotives of Class '35', introduced in 1961, were more successful than the other B-Bs. With a weight of 74 tons they had an output of 1700 hp. The last of these was withdrawn in 1975. Four have been preserved. The main difficulty with the WR diesel-hydraulics was the expense of maintenance.

Hydraulic transmission was also used on several classes of small 0-4-0 and 0-6-0 shunting locomotives, and some multiple-unit diesel passenger stock.

Fell 2000 hp diesel-mechanical locomotive No. 10100. Built at Derby Works in 1950 to a design by Fell Development Ltd and Ricardo & Co. in conjunction with H. G. Ivatt.

The only successful diesel-mechanical main-line locomotive in Britain was No. 10100, a 2–D–2 machine designed by L. F. R. Fell. The locomotive was powered by four independently-controlled diesel engines, two in each nose end. Transmission was by hydraulic couplers and differential gear boxes. The locomotive was built in the railway works at Derby and it began preliminary tests at the end of 1950. In March 1952 it went into traffic on the Midland route between Manchester and London. The locomotive could match the performance of a Class 7 4–6–2 steam engine, and during service on the West Coast main line it achieved the fastest climb to Shap summit before electrification. The locomotive was unfortunately neglected in favour of the range of standard steam locomotives and was mishandled by some drivers. In the end, after working about 100 000 miles on passenger trains, it was destroyed in Manchester Central station in 1958 when the troublesome carriage heating boiler caught fire.

The prototype British Rail 'Deltic' diesel was built by the English Electric Company at the Dick, Kerr Works, Preston, Lancashire, in 1955. It was then **the most powerful diesel-electric single-unit locomotive in the world**, rated at 3300 bhp with a weight of only 106 tons. After extensive trials on the London Midland Region, an order was placed for 22 units for the East Coast main line between London and Edinburgh and delivery began in 1961. The original locomotive was withdrawn and is now displayed in the Science Museum, London. For the next 20 years the 'Deltics' worked about 6400 km (4000 miles) a week at speeds of 145–161 km/h (90–100 mph) between Edinburgh, London and Leeds. In the week beginning 15 January 1973 No. 9010 (later 55 010) *King's Own Scottish Borderer* exceeded 2 million miles, the **first diesel-electric locomotive in the world to achieve this record in less than 12 years.**

By contrast the record-breaking 'A4' Class 4–6–2 *Mallard*, withdrawn for preservation in 1963, covered only 2 294 943 km (1 426 000 miles) in its 25 years of service. The famous LNWR 2–4–0 *Charles Dickens* took about 20 years to achieve 2 million miles, the GWR 4–6–0 No. 2920 took 46 years for its 3 348 663 km (2 080 754 miles) and No. 4021 took 43 years for a slightly less distance. This illustrates the greater availability of diesel locomotives compared with steam.

The 'Deltics' were withdrawn from service on 31 December 1981, after all had run well over 3 million miles. Nos. 55 002/009/015/016/019/022 have been preserved. No. 55 002 *The King's Own Yorkshire Light Infantry* is in the National Railway Museum at York.

The new numbering system for British Rail diesel and electric locomotives was introduced in 1968. Diesel classes run from 01 to 60 and electric classes from 70 to 91, with many blanks, and gaps where classes have been withdrawn.

The largest class of British diesel locomotives is the 08 0–6–0 type, of which 1193 were built to the same basic design. BR stock at the end of 1976 was 936. The design dates back to 1934.

British Rail's Class 56 Co-Co diesel-electric freight locomotive, introduced in May 1976, included several new design features. Following the Hawker-Siddeley 4000 hp prototype locomotive *Kestrel*, built as a private venture in 1968 and sold to the USSR Railways in 1971, the electric generator is a three-phase alternator, supplying the dc traction motors through a silicon-diode rectifier. Previously only dc generators had been used. With a 16-cylinder engine producing an output of 3250 hp at 900 rpm, the locomotive has a tractive effort of 27 200 kg (60 000 lb). It weighs 128 tonnes and is designed for a service speed of 130 km/h (81 mph). For working 'merry-go-round' coal trains to power stations the locomotive is fitted with slow-speed control. The first 30 were assembled in Romania and the remaining 105 at the Doncaster and Crewe Works of British Rail Engineering Ltd. The Class 56 has a load-bearing body similar to that of several other British diesel-electric locomotives, but the increasing cost of skilled labour needed for this construction led to a demand for a cheaper design.

The Class 58 Co-Co diesel-electric freight locomotive has a non-load-bearing body, supported on a frame of rolled steel joists with a cab at each end. Construction cost of the 58 is 13 to 14 per cent less than the 56. The first was handed over to BR at the BREL Doncaster Works on 9 December 1982. The power unit is a Ruston-Paxman RK3ACT charge air-cooled 12-cylinder engine, developing 2460 kW (3300 hp) at 1000 rpm, driving a three-phase alternator. The weight is 130 tonnes and maximum speed 130 km/h (81 mph). Like the 56, it also has slow-speed control. With a view to future sales abroad, the 58 is designed to enable up to three locomotives to be operated in

The latest BR diesel-electric freight locomotive, the 'Class 58' 3300 hp CoCo first produced in 1982. It has a top speed of 130 km/h (81 mph).

multiple by one driver to produce a maximum of 9900 hp, but this is unlikely to be required on British Railways.

The newest main-line diesel-electric locomotives in Britain are the four Foster Yeoman '59' class Co-Cos built by the Electro-Motive Division of General Motors, USA, and delivered in January 1986. Their origin and work is described on p. 176. They are 21 348 mm (70 ft 0½ in) long, weigh 124 tons, have an output of 3300 bhp and a maximum speed of 100 km/h (62 mph).

British Rail's type 60 diesel-electric freight locomotive is still in the design stage (1988) but is likely to be strongly influenced by the design and performance of the 59s.

The world's most powerful single-unit diesel-electric locomotive is the Union Pacific Railroad 'Centennial' Do-Do type, introduced in 1969, a hundred years after the completion of the first transcontinental railroad. At 29.3 m (96 ft) it is also **the world's longest**. It is rated at 6600 hp and weighs 229 000 kg (504 000 lb). The first was numbered 6900, and a total of 47 were ordered from the Electro-Motive Division of the General Motors Corporation. They have a maximum speed of 115 km/h (71 mph). There are 45 in UP stock, at present out of use because of lack of suitable work.

Canada's most powerful diesel-electric unit is the Canadian Pacific Rail No. 4744, built by Montreal Locomotive Works and delivered in 1971. It is a development of the 'Century' 636 design used in North America and Australia. It is rated at 4000 hp for traction. When introduced, it was the world's most powerful single-engined production unit.

The most powerful diesel-electric locomotives in Europe are the 20 units of 3900 hp, first built by Nydqvist & Holm and Frichs, Denmark, in 1972. They have General Motors

(USA) 16–645–E3 engines, weigh 126 tonnes and have a maximum speed of 165 km/h (103 mph). More are at present on order for Spain.

The first diesel locomotive built in Australia was a 1067 mm (3 ft 6 in) gauge 'DL 1' Class 1 C-type diesel-mechanical shunter. It weighed 17.5 tons and was built by Queensland Government Railways at Ipswich Works, west of Brisbane, in 1939. It had a 153 hp Gardiner six-cylinder engine.

The first diesel-electric locomotive built in Australia was a 49 ton Bo-Bo shunter, No. 350. It was completed in June 1949 for the 1600 mm (5 ft 3 in) gauge South Australian Railways at their Islington Works. Two were built, powered by English Electric 350 hp six-cylinder engines. They were still at work in 1975. SAR built ten A1A-A1A diesel-electric units of Class 900, also at Islington Works. The first went into service on 10 September 1951.

In Tasmania, diesel locomotives went into service in August 1950 when the first of 32 'X' class 600 hp Bo-Bos was delivered from English Electric Co., Preston.

The first diesel-electric locomotive for the Australian Commonwealth (now National) **Railways**, built by Clyde Engineering Co., Sydney, was tested on 24 August 1951 and it went into service in September. It was the first of 11 1500 hp A1A-A1A units weighing 108 tons. New South Wales took delivery of an A1A-A1A hood unit, No. 4001, in November 1951. It was built by Montreal Locomotive Works and was powered by an ALCO 1600 hp 12-cylinder engine. It was withdrawn in November 1971 and is now preserved in the New South Wales Rail Transport Museum.

The most powerful diesel-electric locomotives in Australia are the 'Century' 636 type introduced in June 1968 and owned by the Hammersley Iron Pty Limited on the north coast of Western Australia. They are 180 ton Co-Co ALCO hood units of 3600 hp, built under licence by Goodwins of Sydney. Three units in multiple haul up to 240 cars, each of 100 tons capacity and 120 tons gross weight (total of 28 000 tons), at 64.4 km/h (40 mph).

The standard gauge Hammersley Railway carries greater annual tonnage than any other single track in Australia. On a normal day, six trains carry 90 000 tons of ore one way. It also uses the heaviest track in Australia, 67.5 kg/m (136 lb/yd).

On the 1067 mm (3 ft 6 in) gauge the most powerful diesel-electrics are the '11N' Class on the Western Australian Government Railways. The first was delivered in December 1976, built by Commonwealth Engineering.

The most powerful diesel-electric locomotives on an Australian Government railway are the standard-gauge Western Australian 'L' Class Co-Co type 3000 hp units built in 1968. They measure 19.3 × 2.9 m (63 ft 6 in × 9 ft 8 in) and have a top speed of 134 km/h (83 mph). The Commonwealth Railways 'CL' class introduced in 1970 are of similar power.

Three-phase induction motors for rail traction were first applied in 1965 on the prototype diesel-electric locomotive *Hawk*, built by Brush Electrical Machines,

Two Western Australian 'L' class 3000 hp standard gauge CoCo diesel-electric locomotives on a heavy freight train. These are the most powerful diesel-electrics on an Australian government railway.

Loughborough, Leicestershire. At the time technology was insufficiently advanced and it was not a success. On the German Federal Railways in 1970 experiments were carried out with an 1840 kW (2467 hp) prototype diesel-electric locomotive by Henschel/Brown Boveri. Since then Brown Boveri has applied the technology to locomotives, ranging from 250 kW (335 hp) mining units to the four-axle 5600 kW (7510 hp) E120 multi-purpose electric locomotive. Siemens also has used three-phase traction in shunting locomotives, light rail vehicles and Munich U-Bahn cars. In 1973 Swiss Federal Railways ordered six pioneering 1864 kW (2500 hp) Co-Co diesel-electric locomotives for operating the new Limmattal marshalling yard, about 15 km (9 miles) east of Zürich. The first went into service on 2 November 1976. In 1982 TIBB, Italy, built 20 Class D145 centre-cab Bo-Bo diesel-electric locomotives with three-phase drive for shunting and main-line work on the Italian State Railways. They have a starting tractive effort of 25 000 kg (55 100 lb). Top speed is 100 km/h (62 mph).

The three-phase induction motor is highly efficient and reliable and, having no commutators or brushes, needs almost no maintenance; it is less affected by dust and grit in industrial use, and gives protection against wheel-slip with consequent lower tyre wear. Its low starting losses, good adaptation to the diesel engine, low rolling resistance and its facility for dynamic braking make it highly suitable for shunting locomotives. Orenstein & Koppel and Krupp in Germany, and Brown Boveri in Switzerland, are now producing diesel-electric shunters with three-phase drive.

GAS-TURBINE LOCOMOTIVES

The gas-turbine was first applied to rail-traction in 1941, when a 2140 hp gas-turbine-electric locomotive was built for the Swiss Federal Railways by Brown Boveri & Company of Baden. It was 16.4 m (53 ft 9 in) long, 1 Bo-Bo 1 type and weighed 92 tons.

The Great Western Railway in England ordered a Brown Boveri gas-turbine-electric locomotive with an output of 2500 hp which was delivered in February 1950. It was numbered 18000 by British Railways Western Region. After withdrawal in 1960 it was sold to the International Railways Federation (UIC) and was rebuilt in Switzerland in 1970 for their office of research as a mobile laboratory to test rail adhesion. The turbine drive was replaced by an electric motor bogie from a French BB16500 class. Power was fed to it from another SNCF locomotive of the same class which ran in tandem with it. It operated in several European countries and was unofficially named *Elisabetta*.

The first British-built gas-turbine-electric locomotive was a 3000 hp unit by the Metropolitan-Vickers Electrical Company Limited for the Western Region of British Railways in January 1952 and numbered 18100. It was 20.3 m (66 ft 8 in) long and weighed 130 tons. It was withdrawn in January 1958 and was rebuilt into an electric loco-

motive for the 25 kV electrification for use in training drivers, and was numbered E1000 until withdrawn finally in 1968.

The first gas-turbine-electric locomotive to be built and operated in the USA began track tests on 15 November 1948 on the Union Pacific Railroad. The first unit entered regular pool service on 1 January 1952.

The largest gas-turbine-electric locomotives were the two-unit 8500 hp machines, built by the General Electric Company at Schenectady, NY, for the Union Pacific Railroad. Forty-five were built, from 1957, following the success of the 25 UP 4500 hp gas-turbine-electrics built from 1952, which showed economies over diesels. The 1957 machines were 50.3 m (165 ft) long and weighed 408 tons.

Direct-drive gas-turbine locomotives were built by Renault in France in 1952 (1000 hp), and at Gotaverken in Sweden (1300 hp).

A gas-turbine locomotive with mechanical transmission, known as GT3, was built by English Electric Co. Ltd in 1961 as a private venture. It was on a 4–6–0 chassis with a tender containing fuel. Extensive trials on British Railways proved it was a robust, economical and reliable machine requiring minimal maintenance, but it failed to arouse sufficient interest. It was withdrawn and stored until it was eventually dismantled.

The experimental Advanced Passenger Train (APTE) built by British Railways at Derby in 1975 used four Leyland 300 hp gas-turbine engines driving alternators. On 10 August 1975 it achieved a speed of 244.6 km/h (152 mph) between Swindon and Reading. At the conclusion of tests it was presented to the National Railway Museum at York.

The English Electric gas turbine-mechanical 4–6–0 locomotive 'GT3', built as a private venture in 1961. Despite its success in traffic no one seemed interested and it was withdrawn after a few years. It is seen at an exhibition at Marylebone goods yard, London, to commemorate the golden jubilee of the Institution of Locomotive Engineers in 1961.

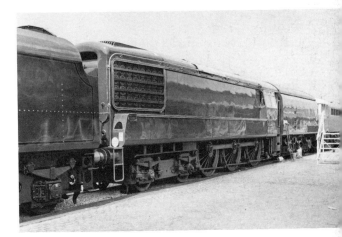

11

PASSENGER TRAFFIC

The first railway passenger carriage was a mere 'garden shed on wheels' pulled by a horse on the Stockton & Darlington Railway in 1825.

The first scheduled passenger service on a railway began on the Stockton & Darlington Railway on 16 October 1826. The first coach, pulled by a horse, was named 'The Unicorn'. It was simply an ordinary horse carriage mounted on railway wheels.

In the USA the first passenger car to make a regular scheduled run was another 'shed on wheels' pulled by a horse, on the Baltimore & Ohio Railroad in 1829.

On the Liverpool & Manchester Railway in 1830, passenger carriages were similar to horse road carriages mounted on a railway-wagon chassis on four wheels.

The last horse-drawn passenger service on an English railway was the 'Port Carlisle Dandy' on the North British Railway branch to Port Carlisle on the Solway Firth, Cumbria, built along the bed of the old Carlisle Canal and opened on 23 January 1854. Dandy No. 1 was built at the NBR works at St Margaret's, Edinburgh, and after brief service on the North Leith and North Berwick Branches it replaced the first horse-drawn car on the Port Carlisle Branch in 1859. It accommodated 12 first and second class passengers inside and 15 third class passengers on the outside benches. It ran until the horse-drawn service ended on 4 April 1914. After being used for many years as a pavilion on a sports field it was rescued by the London & North Eastern Railway and restored for the Stockton & Darlington Centenary in 1925. After that it was displayed on Edinburgh's Waverley Station until 1939, when it was moved to Carlisle Station. It was beautifully restored again in 1975 for display in the National Railway Museum, York.

The last such service in Great Britain was on the Inchture branch of the Caledonian Railway between Perth and Dundee which continued until 1 January 1917. The last in the British Isles was the Fintona Tram on the 1.2 km (¾ mile) branch to Fintona from the Londonderry to Enniskillen line in Ireland. The double-deck car, built in 1883, provided first and second class 'inside' and third on the open upper deck. As the journey lasted only 6 minutes (at about 9.6 km/h (6 mph)) few passengers troubled to go upstairs. The branch was closed on 30 September 1957.

Bogie carriages were introduced in the USA as early as 1831 by Ross Winans, engineer, on the Baltimore & Ohio Railroad and by 1835 they were being generally adopted. The reason was primarily the light track to which they adapted themselves more readily than a four-wheeled vehicle. A bogie carriage built about 1836 for the Camden & Amboy Railroad, and now preserved in the Smithsonian Institution, Washington, DC, is the **oldest eight-wheeled passenger car in existence.**

The first compartment coach was built by Nathaniel Worsdell (1809–86) for the Liverpool & Manchester Railway in 1834. It was named *Experiment* and consisted of three horse-carriage bodies on a four-wheeled truck. From this developed the standard compartment carriage used in Britain and throughout most of Europe.

The compartment carriage was never adopted in North America, because passengers liked to move around and meet each other. Therefore the 'open' type of car was used. Through the influence of the Pullman Car Company this reached Europe in the 1870s and, a century later, became the standard type in Britain.

Carriage heating by stoves at the ends of the open cars was well established in the USA by the 1850s. In Great Britain and in most of Europe carriages were unheated.

The introduction of hot water cans, or 'foot warmers', was claimed by the Great Northern Railway, England, soon after the opening of its main line in 1852. The cans could be hired by passengers at various main stations. For many years they were the only form of carriage heating and their use continued until the early 20th century.

The first bogie carriages in regular service in Great Britain were built by the 600 mm (1 ft 11⅝ in) gauge Festiniog Railway, Wales, in 1871. They were designed by C. E Spooner (1818–89) and were 10.9 m (35 ft 9 in) long.

The first vestibule connections were provided in Connecticut, in June 1853, when a passenger train was fitted with covered and enclosed passageways between the cars.

Gas lighting was introduced on North London Railway trains in 1863, after being used experimentally on the Great Northern Railway.

Oil-lamps were first used on USA trains in 1850; gas-lighting came in 1860; Pintsch gas in 1883; electric light in 1885 and fluorescent light in 1938.

Steam-heating was introduced in the USA in 1881 and on the Caledonian Railway in Scotland in 1884. On other British railways it gradually came into use after 1890.

The Milwaukee Road (Chicago, Milwaukee, St Paul & Pacific Railroad) was the first railway in the USA to equip all its passenger cars with steam heating in 1887.

Electric lighting was introduced on British trains in 1881.

The first trains in the USA to be fully equipped with electric lights ran between New York and Chicago, Boston and New York, New York and Florida and from Springfield to Northampton, Massachusetts in 1887.

Corridor trains appeared in Britain on the Great Western Railway on 7 March 1892. Corridor connections were at the side, which was inconvenient if a coach became turned when returning by a different route. The connections between the coaches were at first locked and used only by the guards. Corridor trains next appeared on the northern lines out of London and then, in 1900, on the London & South Western Railway. These had centre connections, which became universally used.

Buck-eye couplings of the American Gould pattern were introduced by the Great Northern Railway in England on East Coast Joint Stock in 1896.

Vista-dome cars were invented and patented by T. J. McBride of Winnipeg, Canada, in 1891. The idea was simply a development of the roof-top cupola first fitted to freight train cabooses on the Chicago & North Western Railroad in 1863.

A vista-dome car was introduced on the Canadian Pacific Railway in 1902 and three more in 1906. They had a cupola at each end and a glazed centre portion with clerestory. They were withdrawn in 1914–18.

The first cast-steel bogie truck frame with integrally cast journal boxes was patented in the USA by William P. Bettendorf in 1903. Its use became standard throughout the USA.

All-steel passenger cars were first placed in service in the USA on the Long Island Railroad in 1905. The LIRR was also the first to operate an all-steel-car passenger fleet, in 1927.

Stainless steel in car construction was introduced by the Budd Car Co. of USA in the pioneer 'Zephyr' of 1934. By 1980 not one of the 5000 stainless steel passenger cars built by Budd had been scrapped because of corrosion or structural failure.

Articulated coaches were introduced in Britain by H. N. Gresley (qv) in 1907. He mounted the bodies of two old Great Northern six-wheelers on three bogies, thus improving the riding and reducing the weight and length. Four- and five-coach sets were made up. The later 'quad-arts', four-coach sets on five bogies, were familiar to a generation of long-suffering commuters in north London.

Roller bearings were first successfully used on rolling stock in 1926 on the Chicago, Milwaukee, St Paul & Pacific Railroad passenger stock because of the increased weight of the Chicago–Twin Cities (Minneapolis/St Paul) trains.

The Metropolitan Railway experimented with roller bearings in 1924 and approved them for general use in 1929. Several earlier trials on various railways were unsatisfactory.

Air-conditioned cars first appeared in the USA as an experiment in 1927 and were first put into regular service in 1930. The world's first completely air-conditioned passenger train went into service on the Baltimore & Ohio Railroad between Washington and New York on 24 May 1931. In Canada, air-conditioning came into regular use in 1935 when the sleeping car *Sturgeon Falls* was so equipped.

The first air-conditioned coach in Australia went into service on the Melbourne–Albury run in Victoria on 23 December 1935. The coach was built in 1910 but was rebuilt with air conditioning in 1935.

The first air-conditioned train in Australia was the light-weight diesel-mechanical railcar named *Silver City Comet*. It was introduced in 1937 in New South Wales, between Parkes and Broken Hill, 676.5 km (421 miles). Times were 9 h 45 min in the down direction and 9 h 35 min in the up.

Air conditioning was introduced in England by the Great Western Railway which installed an apparatus in two dining cars, completing the work on 21 December 1935.

British Rail's first air-conditioned coaches in regular service were introduced on 12 July 1971, when the Mark II coaches went into service between London (King's Cross) and Newcastle and in August between King's Cross and the West Riding of Yorkshire and Scotland. They followed trials with an experimental train introduced on 15 June 1964. The Mark IIE coaches were introduced on the London to Birmingham, Wolverhampton and Manchester services in 1972. They provide wider entrances and better luggage storage. By the end of 1972, 450 were in service. The Mark III coaches, designed for 200 km/h (124 mph), went into ordinary service in 1973. Their running is remarkably smooth and, for the passenger, silent. A regrettable feature of the Mark III design is that the second class seating does not fit the window openings which are designed for the first-class, and the passenger can find himself in a seat with no view out.

British Rail's Prototype 'High Speed Train' consists of seven Mark III air-conditioned passenger cars between two Bo-Bo power-cars, and is designed to run at 200 km/h (124 mph). It carries 96 first class and 276 second class passengers. Each power-car has one Paxman 12RP200L 'Valenta' 12-cylinder pressure-charged and intercooled diesel engine, developing 2250 bhp, driving a Brush Electrical three-phase 1430 kW alternator. This supplies the four 450 hp dc traction motors through the rectifier and control equipment. The two traction motors in each bogie are frame-mounted to reduce unsprung weight.

Features include double-glazed windows, air-conditioning, interior doors automatically operated by treadmats, colourful upholstery, and a public address system. Catering consists of a trolley service to all seats, and a full range of meals cooked in modern micro-wave ovens.

On 12 June 1973 the train reached a world record speed for diesel-traction of 230 km/h (143 mph) between Thirsk and Tollerton while on test on the York–Darlington section. (For details of 'Inter City 125' service see chapter 12.)

Vista-dome cars were introduced in the USA on 23 July 1945 between Chicago and Minneapolis on the Chicago, Burlington & Quincy Railroad (now part of Burlington Northern).

The **Canadian** transcontinental trains on Canadian Pacific Rail, running between Montreal/Toronto and Vancouver, consisting of new stainless-steel cars, were inaugurated on 24 April 1955. It was the longest vista-dome train ride in the world, 4675 km (2904.8 miles) from Montreal to Vancouver. It required the purchase of 173 new cars from the Budd Company, Philadelphia. Under VIA Rail Canada Inc., 'The Canadian' has run only from Toronto to Vancouver since October 1978.

The lightest passenger cars in the USA are the air-conditioned 'Pioneer III' first produced by the Budd Company in July 1956. They are 25.9 m (85 ft) long, seat 88 passengers and weigh 23.4 long tons or only 269.9 kg (595 lb) per passenger. In July 1958 the 'Pioneer III MU' (multiple-unit) cars were introduced on the Pennsylvania Railroad.

The 'Tightlock' automatic coupler for passenger cars was adopted as standard in the USA in 1946.

Gallery cars, with seats on two levels, were introduced by the Chicago, Burlington & Quincy Railroad on its Chicago suburban services in 1950. Each car accommodates 148 passengers, 96 on the main (lower) floor and 52 in the single seats in the galleries.

The first 'double-decked' train in Britain, with seats on two levels, designed by O. V. Bulleid (1882–1970), went into service on the Southern Region of British Railways on 2 November 1949. Its higher capacity made longer station stops necessary and so its advantage was lost. It was withdrawn on 1 October 1971.

Double-deck coaches at Čerčany, Czechoslovakia, in May 1988. These high-capacity coaches are much used on suburban trains on the Czech and East German railways.

Canada's first gallery-car train, comprising nine air-conditioned cars built by Canadian Vickers Limited, went into operation on 27 April 1970 on the Montreal Lakeshore suburban service.

The most luxurious train in the world is 'The Blue Train' in South Africa. It was introduced on 4 September 1972 to replace the 33-year-old former 'Blue Train' on the Pretoria–Johannesburg–Cape Town service. It carries 108 passengers in 16 coaches and runs beautifully on air-cushioned bogies on 1065 mm (3 ft 6 in) gauge at speeds of 64.5–80.5 km/h (40–50 mph). It makes the journey in 26 h. Accommodation is entirely in private rooms, three of them with private bathrooms; it is fully air-conditioned and sound-proofed, and ranks as a five-star hotel. Passengers normally dress for dinner.

'The Indian Pacific' in Australia, introduced in 1970, is probably the second most luxurious train in the world, crossing from Perth to Sydney in 65 h on standard gauge throughout. The streamlined, stainless-steel, air-conditioned train provides sleeping accommodation for all passengers, with showers and private toilets, a cocktail lounge, drawing-room and music-room with piano. Early morning and afternoon tea are wheeled round to everybody.

The new Australian XPT (Express Passenger Train) sets are based on the British High Speed Train, but with lower gearing, larger coolers, and seating similar to that of the French Corail coaches. There are 24 sets each with seven to nine vehicles, comprising a power car at each end and trailers seating 72 second-class or 48 first-class passengers, a guard's compartment and a 30-seat first-class galley. The trains went into regular service in New South Wales during 1982, first on the hilly 'Mid West' and 'Mid North Coast' routes and the third, from 23 August, on the

'South Line', covering the 642 km (399 miles) Sydney to Albury in 7 h 20 min southbound and 7 h 25 min northbound. The fastest average speeds of 113.6 km/h (70.6 mph) are achieved between Albury and Wagga Wagga, 124.9 km (77.6 miles) covered in 66 min. This is probably the fastest train in the Southern Hemisphere. (See chapter 12.)

The first through passenger service between Kowloon (Hong Kong) and Guangzhou (Canton) in 30 years began on 4 April 1979. One train runs each way daily. The Canton–Kowloon Railway was built by British engineers and opened on 5 August 1911. (See colour photo.)

BRAKES

The energy stored in a train travelling at 100 km/h (61 mph) is sufficient to lift the entire train vertically through nearly 40 m (130 ft). The function of brakes is to absorb this energy as rapidly and as efficiently as possible. The two most common methods are friction, and the regeneration of electrical power against a load which may consist of a resistance unit, or another train if on an electrified railway.

Braking may be assisted by a rising gradient, as at the approaches to stations on the London Underground system.

Early trains had no continuous brakes. The only brake power was on the engine tender and the guard's van. From a speed of 48 km/h (30 mph) it might take 800 m (½ mile) to stop a train. Hence the great height of early signals, to be seen from a distance.

The earliest practical continuous brakes were mechanical systems such as those patented by George Newall of the East Lancashire Railway in 1852 and by Charles Fay (1812–1900), carriage and wagon superintendent of the Lancashire & Yorkshire Railway, in 1856.

The compressed-air brake was first used by the Caledonian Railway, Scotland, by Steel and McInnes in 1871.

George Westinghouse (qv) applied for an air brake patent on 23 January 1869.

The Westinghouse continuous automatic air brake was introduced in 1872–3. 'Automatic' means that the brake applies itself on both halves of a train if it breaks apart.

The non-automatic vacuum brake was introduced by J. Y. Smith on the North Eastern Railway, England, in 1874.

The Gresham automatic vacuum brake was introduced in Britain in 1878, but it was about 1890 before all passenger trains were equipped.

Continuous automatic brakes became compulsory in Britain under the Regulation of Railways Act of 1889. (See 'Runaways', p. 186.)

Most of the world's railway systems use the air brake. Countries using the vacuum brake:
Europe — British Isles (except new British Rail stock); Austrian minor railways; Spain; Portugal
Australia — Western Australia; Tasmania
Africa — South Africa; Zimbabwe; United Arab Republic
Asia — most railways in India and Pakistan; Malaysia; Thailand (Siam); Burma
South America — most railways except the Transandine; Antofagasta & Bolivia; high-altitude lines in the Andes; Central of Brazil.

The communication cord, on British railways, was first recommended by Capt. Tyler, inspector for the Board of Trade, in 1865. Various electrical communication systems were tried, in May 1865 on the London & South Western Railway, and in 1866 on the Dover mail trains of the South Eastern Railway and also on the Great Western. The last two caused a bell to ring in the guard's van and a disc to show outside the compartment.

The Regulation of Railways Act of 1868 compelled railway companies to provide communication between passengers and guards on trains running 20 miles (32 km) or more non-stop. The systems introduced on the various railways were all designed to ring a bell in the guard's van, and on some at the engine.

The modern system, now in universal use, enabling the passenger to open the brake pipe and so apply the brakes on the whole train, was introduced on the GWR. It received provisional Board of Trade approval in 1890 and this was confirmed in 1893. Pulling the 'communication cord', besides applying the brakes, causes a disc to appear outside the coach concerned. The point at which the cord was pulled can quickly be found because the chain sags and cannot be pushed back.

Railway companies have always imposed fines for wilful misuse of the alarm signal. On British railways the penalty was initially £5. It is now £50.

SLEEPING AND DINING CARS

The world's first sleeping car was designed by Philip Berlin, manager of the Cumberland Valley Railroad, now part of Penn Central, USA. It operated between Harrisburg and Chambersburg, Pennsylvania, in 1837. Sleeping arrangements were adapted from the seating.

Similar cars were also operated between Philadelphia and Baltimore in 1838, and on the Richmond & Fredericksburg Railroad (now Richmond, Fredericksburg & Potomac), Virginia, in 1839.

The first provision for sleeping on British trains was made in 1838, when a makeshift bed was introduced. It consisted of two poles with strips of webbing between them which were laid across the compartment.

The New York & Erie Railroad (now Erie & Lackawanna) operated experimental sleeping cars in 1843 and a regular sleeping-car service in 1856.

The Illinois Central introduced six state room sleeping cars, known as 'Gothic cars', in June 1856. Each one measured nearly 15.2 × 3.1 m (50 × 10 ft).

Night-seat coaches, with luxurious adjustable reclining seats, were put into service between Philadelphia and Baltimore in 1854.

The first sleeping-car patents were issued to T. T. Woodruff in the USA on 2 December 1856.

The world's first proper sleeping cars were designed by Samuel Sharp and built at Hamilton, Ontario, by the Great Western Railway of Canada in 1857. The design was adopted by the Wagner and Pullman companies. The first Pullman sleeping car appeared in 1859. (See also 'Pullman cars and trains'.)

'Parlour cars' first appeared in Canada in 1860 on the Grand Trunk, Great Western and Buffalo & Huron railways. They were fitted out with every possible luxury; the Grand Trunk even had a form of air-conditioning.

The first railway to serve meals on a train was the Baltimore & Ohio, USA. On 10 January 1853 it ran two special trains from Baltimore to Wheeling and back to mark the completion of the railway to that point. A caterer was engaged to provide food.

The world's first dining cars were operated by the Philadelphia, Wilmington & Baltimore (now part of Conrail) between Philadelphia and Baltimore in 1863. Two such cars, rebuilt from day coaches 15.2 m (50 ft) long, were fitted with an eating bar, steam-box and 'everything found in a first class restaurant'.

Canada's first dining cars, or 'hotel cars', appeared in regular service on the Great Western Railway in 1876.

A first class sleeping car was introduced in Britain by the North British Railway on the Glasgow–Edinburgh–London trains on 2 April 1873. It ran alternate nights each way, leaving Glasgow at 21.00 h and arriving in London at 9.40 h via the North Eastern and Great Northern railways. There was a supplementary charge of ten shillings (50p).

On 31 July 1873 the Great Northern Railway introduced a similar service so that it could operate every night.

The London & North Western and Caledonian railways first used sleeping-car trains on the 'West Coast Route' between London and Scotland on 1 October 1873.

The Great Western Railway introduced sleeping-car trains in December 1877. In 1881 it built the forerunner of the modern sleeping car, with six double-berth compartments, three lavatories and an attendant's pantry. Passengers provided their own bedding. In 1890 the GWR used the first sleeping car, equipped entirely with lateral berths in compartments.

The prototype British first class sleeping car was built by the North Eastern Railway in 1894. It had four compartments with single berths, two with double berths, a smoking compartment which could be adapted to sleep two, and an attendant's pantry with gas cooker.

Dining cars were first used on the London–Leeds trains by the Great Northern Railway on 1 November 1879.

The 'Flying Scotsman' was provided with corridor stock throughout and with dining cars on 1 August 1900. The 20-min lunch stop at York was ended.

The first restaurant cars in Europe with electric cooking were put into service on the metre-gauge Rhaetian Railway in Switzerland in 1929 by the Mitropa Company (Mitteleuropäische Schlafwagen und Speisewagen Aktiengesellschaft) of Berlin.

Third class sleeping cars were introduced in Britain by the London, Midland & Scottish, the London & North Eastern and the Great Western railways on 24 September 1928. For daytime use they had ordinary third class compartments which could be converted to four berths. Only a pillow and a rug were provided.

The first shower compartment in a British train was installed in a first class twin sleeping-car set by the London & North Eastern Railway in 1930.

PULLMAN CARS AND TRAINS

George Mortimer Pullman (1831–1897) converted two passenger coaches on the Chicago & Alton Railroad (now part of the Gulf, Mobile & Ohio Railroad) into sleeping cars at the railway company's shops at Bloomington, Illinois, in 1859. The first ran from Bloomington to Chicago on 1 September 1859. The first Pullman Car conductor was Jonathan L. Barnes. Pullman regarded these merely as experiments and in 1864 began building the first real Pullman sleeping car, named *Pioneer*, which went into service in 1865. Pullman sleeping cars were soon in common use throughout the USA.

Most sleeping-car services in the USA were operated by the Pullman Company until 1 January 1969. Since then they have been taken over by the individual railroads.

Pullman 'Hotel Cars' were introduced in 1867. They were sleeping cars equipped with kitchen and dining facilities. The first Pullman-built car providing only restaurant facilities, the *Delmonico*, was operated on the Chicago & Alton Railroad in 1868.

Pullman sleeping cars were in use on Canadian railways from 1870. The Grand Trunk Railway cars were among the best appointed of their time. The convenience could be enjoyed for an extra $1.

Pullman cars were first used in Britain on 1 June 1874

Top: A train at South Quay Station on the Docklands Light Railway in East London, opened on 31 August 1987. The driverless trains are operated automatically by computer, a method which can be used only when the tracks are isolated from all other forms of transport.

Above: Train on the Wuppertal 'Schwebebahn' or suspended railway over the River Wupper in Germany in 1982. It is near the Zoo-Stadion 'turntable' where a movable section of track enables trains to be turned in mid-route.

Opposite page, top: Train on the Tokyo–Haneda monorail leaving Tokyo. The railway was built in 1964 to connect Tokyo with the Haneda airport. The trains trundle to and fro covering the 13km (8 miles) in 15 minutes.

Opposite page, bottom: Solna Centium station on the Stockholm underground railway.

Right: Class 59 diesel-electric freight locomotive No. 59001 *Yeoman Endeavour* with the bell presented by the builders, General Motors, with a train of hopper wagons at Acton, West London, on 12 September 1986. The four 59s are the only privately-owned locomotives in regular service on British Railways tracks.

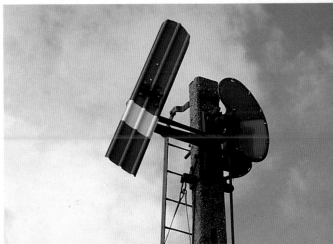

Right: One of the last Great Northern somersault signals, at Havenhouse, Lincolnshire, in September 1988. The GNR pioneered the use of concrete for signal posts, as in this one.

Bottom: Shrewsbury Severn Bridge Junction signal box, built by the LNWR in 1903. With 180 levers, it is now the largest in Britain (1988), but it may soon be demolished.

THE RAILWAY BELLE(E)
& RAILWAY GUARD.

I try to be merry but it is no use
My Case is very hard
She left me as silly as a farm-yard Goose,
When she married that railway Guard.

WRITTEN & SUNG WITH THE GREATEST SUCCESS BY

HARRY CLIFTON.

NT. STA. HALL

LONDON HOPWOOD & CREW 42 NEW BOND STREET W

Above: A scene from the film *Murder on the Orient Express*.

Right: Charles Dickens who survived the Staplehurst accident on the South Eastern Railway in 1865, was fascinated by railways. He died 10 years to the day after the accident.

Opposite page: A mid-Victorian railway scene depicted on the cover of a light-hearted song.

Above: An example of American railway art by Currier and Ives.

Below: The hall of Grand Central Station, New York City, USA.

Above: St Pancras Station Hotel, London.

Below: Bombay Victoria Station, a fine example of Victorian Gothic architecture.

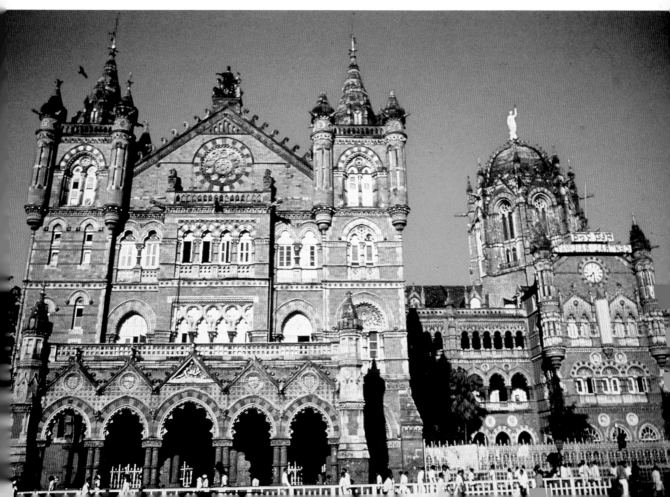

Top left: Moscow metro, Novoslobodskaya Station.

Below left: Moscow metro, Zhdanovskaya Station.

Below right: The frontage of the main station at Bangkok, Thailand, terminus of the northern lines from about 1900, showing another mixture of eastern and western styles.

Bottom: Traditional Chinese architecture applied to a modern station at Beijing (Peking).

on the Midland Railway between London and Bradford. The earliest cars were pre-fabricated in Chicago and assembled at the MR Works at Derby. They were so popular that by the end of 1874 the MR had 36 in operation, including 11 sleeping cars. In 1876 the services were extended to Edinburgh and Glasgow over the new Settle & Carlisle line and the Glasgow & South Western and North British railways.

The first 'restaurant car' in Britain was a Pullman named *Prince of Wales*. It was in operation from 1 November 1879 on the Great Northern Railway between London (King's Cross) and Leeds.

The first all-Pullman train in Britain was on the London, Brighton & South Coast Railway in December 1881. It was also the first train in Britain to be electrically lit throughout. The London–Brighton 60-min Limited Pullmans (Sundays only) began running on 2 October 1898.

The Pullman Company Limited was registered in England from 1882 to 1907. It was then purchased by Mr Davison Dalziel (1854–1928), an English newspaper proprietor. In 1915 the Pullman Car Company Limited was formed under his chairmanship to acquire the British cars.

Dalziel also controlled the International Sleeping Car Company from 1927 and negotiated purchase by this company of Thomas Cook & Son in 1928.

Pullman introduced the first vestibule train, in the USA, in 1887.

The Pullman Car Company introduced the first two all-steel trains in England in May 1928. They formed 'The Queen of Scots' on the London & North Eastern Railway and ran between London, Leeds, Harrogate and Edinburgh.

The all-Pullman 'Southern Belle' was put into service by the London, Brighton & South Coast Railway on 1 November 1908. At the same time Buckeye couplings and drawgear were first used in Great Britain by the Pullman Company. 'The Southern Belle' was renamed 'The Brighton Belle' on 29 June 1934, having become an electric train on 1 January 1933. It made its last run on 30 April 1972.

The first air-conditioned Pullman car went into operation between Chicago and Los Angeles on 9 September 1929, following experiments began in 1927.

The most famous all-Pullman train, the *Golden Arrow* service between London and Paris, began on 12 September 1926 with Pullman cars between Calais and Paris. From 15 May 1929 it became all-Pullman throughout the journey.

From September 1939 to 15 October 1946 the service was withdrawn. Second class Pullmans were introduced in October 1949, but these were replaced by ordinary coaches in May 1965. The *Golden Arrow* made its last run on 30 September 1972. The 4000 ton cross-Channel steamer *Invicta*, which carried 'Golden Arrow' passengers to their connection with the Calais–Paris 'Flèche d'Or' from 1946, was withdrawn at the same time.

The first diesel multiple-unit Pullman train was the six-car first-class-only 'Midland Pullman', inaugurated on 4 July 1960. It ran between London (St Pancras) and Manchester (Central). The 'Midland Pullman' was withdrawn in 1966 with the introduction, on 18 April, of the electrically hauled London to Manchester and Liverpool Pullman trains.

SLIP CARRIAGES

The earliest slip carriages were on the London & Blackwall Railway during cable operation from 1840 to 1849, when coaches were detached from the moving ropes at all intermediate stations between Minories and Blackwall.

The first coaches to be slipped from moving trains were on the London, Brighton & South Coast Railway in February 1858, when a portion for Eastbourne was slipped at Hayward's Heath from the 16.00 London Bridge–Brighton express.

Three months later the South Eastern Railway slipped a portion for Canterbury off the 12.30 express from London Bridge to Ramsgate and Margate.

The first Great Western Railway slip carriages were introduced in December 1858 at Slough and Banbury.

In 1914 there were 200 slip-coach services, operated by most of the main-line companies in Great Britain and Ireland, of which the Great Western Railway operated 72. By 1918 the GWR total was down to 17.

The last slip working in Britain was at Bicester, off the 17.10 Paddington–Wolverhampton train on 9 September 1960, at the end of the summer service.

Slip coaches were operated on the French Etat Railway between 1933 and 1935 on the Paris–Le Havre non-stop services. The coaches travelled to St Valéry-en-Caux, Beauté, Fécamp and Etretat after being slipped at Motteville.

EXTRAORDINARY RAILWAYS

For conveying passengers around the Empire Exhibition at Wembley, London, in 1924–5 an ingenious **'Never-Stop-Railway'** was constructed. Cars were propelled around the endless track by a rotating worm formed of a coiled steel bar. At stations the coils were close together so that the cars almost stopped. Between stations the pitch was increased to give higher speed.

The car on the Brighton & Rottingdean Seashore Electric Tramroad. At high tide it travelled through about 3 m (15 ft) of water for which it had to be equipped like a ship, with a lifeboat and lifebelts.

The saloon of the Brighton & Rottingdean car.

The world's most extraordinary railcar ran on the Brighton & Rottingdean Seashore Electric Tramroad in Sussex. The line was 4.42 km (2.75 miles) long and was built by Magnus Volk (qv) on the seashore, with a total gauge of 5486 mm (18 ft). At high water the four rails were covered by about 4.5 m (15 ft) of water. The car stood on legs about 7 m (23 ft) high and had a cabin like a ship. It was the only railcar that carried a lifeboat and lifebelts as normal equipment. The railway opened on 28 November 1896 and ran until January 1901. The car was built by the Gloucester Railway Carriage & Wagon Co. Ltd.

RAILWAY ROAD SERVICES

The first railway-operated motor buses in Britain were inaugurated by the Great Western Railway between Helston and the Lizard in Cornwall on 17 August 1903. They were Milnes Daimler buses which had originally been used in connection with the Lynton & Barnstaple narrow-gauge railway, where they were owned and operated by the railway chairman, Sir George Newnes.

Another service began on 31 October between Penzance and Marazion; meanwhile the North Eastern Railway introduced buses on 7 September 1903.

The London & South Western Railway began operating buses on 1 June 1904.

The first railway buses in Scotland were operated by the Great North of Scotland Railway between Ballater and Braemar on 2 May 1904. By 1911 the company offered six services.

By 1928 the Great Western Railway operated 330 buses on 154 routes. In the early 1930s, however, along with other railway companies, the road interests were sold to other bus companies in the area and a great opportunity for developing a unified transport system was lost,

although the railways maintained a financial interest in the bus companies.

ROAD-RAIL VEHICLES

A road-rail bus was placed in service by the London, Midland & Scottish Railway in 1931. Designed by J. Shearman of the LMS, it was a Karrier chassis with a Craven body and could be quickly adapted for rail or road use. It was used between Blisworth and Stratford-upon-Avon, being used on the road in Stratford. It could run at 113 km/h (70 mph) on rails and at 96.5 km/h (60 mph) on roads. After only a few years it was scrapped.

PASSENGER CLASSES

Third class passengers were first carried in Britain in 1838, in open wagons without seats.

Gladstone's Railway Act of 1844 ruled that railways must carry third class passengers in closed carriages with seats at one (old) penny a mile on at least one train a day. 'Parliamentary' trains as they were known were often run at the most inconvenient times and at the slowest speeds.

The first British railway to carry third class passengers by all trains was the Midland Railway, on 1 April 1872. The Great Eastern Railway followed in the same year.

The Midland Railway and its joint services with the Glasgow & South Western were the first on which second class was abolished, on 1 January 1875.

Bogie carriages for first and third class were introduced in Britain by the Midland Railway in 1875.

The use of third class carriages by 'wearers of kid gloves and kid shoes' was strongly condemned by Thomas Barnes, chairman of the Lancashire & Yorkshire Railway in 1880, because of the danger of 'Americanizing our institutions'!

Third class passengers were carried on all trains of the Great Western Railway from 1 October 1890.

First class was abolished on the Metropolitan and District railways, London, from 1 February 1940. From that date only one class operated on all London Transport services.

Third class was redesignated second class on British Railways on 3 June 1956 and by the Ulster Transport Authority (which had retained three classes) on 1 October 1956. Following the example of the Irish Railways it was renamed 'Standard Class' in 1987.

Greece and Turkey adopted two classes only from 1 January 1957, leaving only Spain and Portugal in Europe with three classes.

In Australia, on all systems, the second class was renamed 'economy' in 1971. Only the first class is now marked.

The last 'early-morning' (workmen's) tickets on British Railways were issued at the end of 1961.

The first modern trains with 'No Smoking' accommodation throughout began running on the Boston & Maine Railroad, USA, on 1 June 1970. They carry commuters only, 90 per cent of the journeys lasting under half an hour.

The only surface trains in the British Isles to be 'No Smoking' throughout are the electric trains on the Howth–Dublin–Bray service in Ireland.

Smoking was not permitted at stations on the London, Brighton & South Coast Railway. This rule continued until 1923, when the company became part of the Southern Railway.

London Regional Transport, one of the few authorities to allow smoking in underground trains and stations, **introduced a total ban on smoking** in all its trains from 9 July 1984, largely in the interests of safety following a fire at Goodge Street in 1981. Following a request from London Transport Passengers' Committee, smoking at stations partly or wholly underground was prohibited from 17 February 1985.

After the disastrous fire at Kings Cross underground station on 18 November 1987 smoking was banned at BR deep-level underground stations in London and Liverpool and on trains serving them.

Car-sleeper services, or trains of sleeping cars carrying motor cars on special wagons, were introduced on British Railways between London (Kings Cross) and Perth from 15 June to 18 September 1955. Trains ran northwards on Wednesday and Sunday evenings and southwards on Tuesday and Saturday evenings. Its success led to another service between London (Paddington) and St Austell, Cornwall, from 7 May to 27 October 1956.

The idea was not new. Passengers on the Liverpool & Manchester Railway could travel in their own horse carriages on flat wagons in the 1830s.

The Trans-Europ-Express (TEE) service was first proposed in 1954 by Den Hollender, then president of the Netherlands Railways. Services began on 2 June 1957, and they now cover nine countries: Austria, Belgium, France, Germany, Italy, Luxembourg, Netherlands, Spain and Switzerland, by 35 trains operating over 27 routes and serving 125 stations, and carrying 500 000 passengers a year in first-class accommodation with all seats reserved. The offices of TEE are at the headquarters of the Netherlands Railway at Utrecht. Trains are all painted red and cream.

Motive power and rolling stock is owned by the various administrations. The first trains were diesel multiple units. In 1961 Swiss Federal Railways introduced four five-coach multi-current electric trains. In 1972 only 7 out of 35 trains were diesels.

TEE services operate: Paris–Lille–Tourcoing; Paris– Brussels; *The Rheingold,* Amsterdam–Mainz–Salzburg/ Chur; *Kleber,* Paris–Strasburg; *Jules Verne,* Paris–Nantes; *Gottardo,* Zürich–Milan; *Adriatico,* Milan–Bari; Milan– Rome–Naples.

The first passenger train into Turkey left Vienna for Istanbul (then Constantinople) on 12 August 1888. On 1 June 1889 a through train was inaugurated between Paris and Constantinople, taking 67 h 35 min. This became the famous *Orient Express*. It stopped running in August 1914. On 11 April 1919 the *Simplon Orient Express* began running from Calais to Istanbul via Paris, Milan, Vinkovci, Belgrade and Nis, and also Vinkovci to Bucharest. The *Direct Orient Express* with coaches for Istanbul and Athens left the Gare de Lyon, Paris, for the last time at midnight on 19 May 1977. There are no longer through coaches between Paris and Istanbul and no sleeping cars east of Belgrade.

Excursion trains, or special trains not in the regular timetable and generally with reduced fares, organized either by the railway company or privately, have been a feature of railway operation since the earliest days. Special trains at reduced fares were operated by the Liverpool & Manchester Railway in 1830. The Newcastle & Carlisle ran a special train from Blaydon to Hexham in 1835, and on 7 and 8 August 1839 the Whitby & Pickering Railway ran excursions between Whitby and Grosmont in Yorkshire. On the Newcastle & Carlisle again a special excursion at half fare was run from Newcastle to Carlisle and back on 14 June 1840 for employees of R & W Hawthorn, locomotive builders of Newcastle.

A privately organized excursion train was arranged by the Nottingham Mechanics Institute to Leicester and back on 20 July 1840. Another, from Leicester to Nottingham on 24 August 1840, carried 2400 passengers. Thomas Cook (1808–92), founder of the famous firm of travel agents, organized his first excursion on the Midland Counties Railway from Leicester to Loughborough on 5 July 1841. Its success led to many more similar ventures.

Special reduced fares on specified timetabled trains are in a different category. On 13 May 1840 the Newcastle & Carlisle Railway offered cheap fares by certain trains from Carlisle to the Polytechnic Exhibition in Newcastle. Today, reduced fares are commonly used as a means of selling spare seating capacity on certain specified trains.

The first royal railway journey was made by Prince Albert and his brother Ernest from Slough to London (Paddington) on the Great Western Railway on 14 November 1839. Queen Victoria's first railway journey, also from Slough to Paddington, was on 13 June 1842. The first reigning monarch to travel by train was Frederick William IV of Prussia on 24 January 1842.

The first royal railway carriage was built by the London & Birmingham Railway in 1842 for Queen Adelaide.

The first 'railway enthusiasts' rail tour in Britain was

organized by the Railway Correspondence & Travel Society on 11 September 1938, when the Great Northern Railway Stirling 2438 mm (8 ft) single-wheeler No. 1 took a train of old six-wheeled carriages from London (King's Cross) to Peterborough and back. The fare was five shillings (25p). The excursion was a repeat of a similar working by the same engine and train, organized by the LNER, on 24 August.

The longest passenger trains ever to run in Australia were of 42 carriages. One ran between Perth, Western Australia, and Port Pirie, South Australia on 27 December 1974. It was a combination of one 'Indian Pacific' and two 'Trans Australian' trains, because of delays caused by floods. Another ran over the same route on 11 February 1975, again because of serious delays. Both were operated by Commonwealth Railways.

The only steam train to cross the Australian continent from Sydney to Perth and back was 'The Western Endeavour' which covered the 3991 km (2480 miles) each way on standard gauge throughout from 22 August to 12 September 1970. One steam locomotive, C38 class Pacific No. 3801, covered the entire return journey, assisted for part of the way by 3813 of the same class and some diesel electrics.

The bedroom used by King George VI in the royal train built at the LNWR works at Wolverton, originally for King George V and Queen Mary.

The last passenger trains in Tasmania ran between Hobart and Wynyard on 28 July 1978.

The world's longest journey in one train is from Moscow to Vladivostok, 9297 km (5777 miles). (See chapter 5.)

The only person to have travelled over every section of railway in the British Isles which carried a passenger service, including sections used only occasionally, was Thomas Richard Perkins (1872–1952). He began the task of exploring the entire British railway network in 1893 and he completed his achievement in 1932, after travelling over 35 400 km (22 000 miles) of individual lines and also making detailed notes on all his journeys.

STATIONS

The world's oldest station building is at Cuautla, Mexico. It was built in 1657 as a convent until 1812. It became part of the railway station about 1860.

The world's oldest railway station is at Liverpool Road, Manchester, the original terminus of the Liverpool & Manchester Railway, opened on 15 September 1830. Its passenger services ended, however, when Manchester (Victoria) was connected to the L & M on 5 May 1844 and it was used as a goods station until it was finally closed on 30 September 1975. It was subsequently sold to Greater Manchester Council, for £1, and it is now part of the Greater Manchester Museum of Science and Industry. It has been beautifully restored.

The first station refreshment room was established in 1838 at Curzon Street Station, Birmingham. The station was the terminus of the then uncompleted London & Birmingham Railway from 9 April and of the Grand Junction from 19 November 1838. The refreshment room was reported in *The Times* on 18 September, the day after the London & Birmingham was fully opened. The station was closed to passengers on 1 July 1854 on the opening of New Street station.

The world's highest railway station is at Condor, Bolivia, on the metre-gauge line from Rio Mulato to Potosí, at an altitude of 4787 m (15 705 ft). The railway was completed in 1908.

The highest station on standard gauge is Galera on the Peru Central, 4777 m (15 673 ft). It was opened on 14 November 1893.

The highest station on British Rail is Corrour on the West Highland line from Glasgow to Fort William, 153 km (94¾ miles) from Glasgow. It is 411 m (1347 ft) above sea-level. The line was opened on 7 August 1894.

Until closure on 3 May 1965 the highest station was

The world's oldest railway station at Manchester Liverpool Road, terminus of the Liverpool & Manchester Railway from 1830 to 1844. It is now fully restored and it forms a part of the Greater Manchester Museum of Science and Industry. Photographed in June 1988.

Dalnaspidal on the former Highland Railway main line from Perth to Inverness, 82 km (51 miles) from Perth, 433 m (1420 ft) above sea-level.

The highest station in England is Doveholes, Derbyshire, between Buxton and Whaley Bridge, about 330 m (1083 ft).

The lowest railway station in the world was at Samakh, now in Israel, at the south end of the Sea of Galilee, 186.9 m (613 ft) below sea level. The 1042 mm (3 ft 5¼ in) gauge railway from Haifa to Derraa was opened on 31 August 1908 and was closed in 1949.

The world's largest station is the Grand Central Terminal, New York. It has 44 platforms, all below ground, on two levels, with 41 tracks on the upper and 26 on the lower level, and covers 19.4 ha (48 acres). It was built in 1903–13. It is used by 550 trains and 180 000 people daily. On 3 July 1947 it handled a record number of 252 288 people.

Other large stations are:

Pennsylvania Terminal, New York	32 platforms
Union Station, Washington	32 platforms
Saint-Lazare, Paris	27 platforms

Clapham Junction, besides being Britain's largest station, in area, is also the busiest junction, with an average of 2200 trains passing through every 24 h, in May 1983.

The world's busiest rail interchange is at Châtelot, Paris. In the peak hour 144 trains pass through the junctions at each end.

Carlisle Station was used by more railway companies than any other British station. Until the Grouping on 1 January 1923 it was used by the North British, North Eastern, Midland, London & North Western, Maryport & Carlisle, Glasgow & South Western, and Caledonian railways. Carlisle Station was administered by the Carlisle Citadel Station Joint Committee, established under an Act of 22 July 1861.

The largest span station roof ever built was the 91.4 m (300 ft) span of the second Broad Street Station, Philadelphia, built in 1892 by the Philadelphia & Reading Railroad. The engineer was William Henry Brown (1836–1910).

The Pennsylvania Railroad Station at Jersey City, built in 1888, had a roof span of 76.8 m (252 ft).

The largest station roof in Great Britain is St Pancras, London, built by the Midland Railway, with a span of 73.1 (240 ft) and 30.5 (100 ft) high above rail-level. The engineer was William Henry Barlow (qv). The station was opened on 1 October 1868.

Top: Britain's largest span station roof, at London St Pancras, erected in 1867–8.

Above: A rare old photograph by James Gregory, foreman on the site, showing the erection of the first girder of St Pancras station roof from a great travelling timber gantry, in 1867.

Milan Central Station, designed by Ulisse Stacchini and completed in 1930, has a central roof span of 70.3 m (236 ft). The main building is one of the most grandiose in existence.

The largest station roof in South America is at the Retiro terminal in Buenos Aires. It is 250 m (820 ft) long with two spans totalling 100 m (328 ft) wide and each 25 m (82 ft) high. It was designed and constructed at Hamilton Iron Works, Garston, Liverpool, and was erected by J. H. & W. Bell of Liverpool for the former Central Argentine Railway and inaugurated on 2 August 1915.

The present trend to utilize the space above stations for car parking, business or shopping centres, by covering the entire area with a vast concrete slab as is happening at London Victoria, lends support to the idea that money matters more than the passengers. Other examples are London Euston (where the area above the slab has not been used), Birmingham New Street (see p. 194) and Kowloon (Hong Kong).

The station at Dartmouth, Devon, never had any trains. It was opened on 16 August 1864 and was connected by a ferry with Kingswear Station across the Dart Estuary. Since 30 October 1972 the section from Paignton to Kingswear has been owned by the Dart Valley Railway and operated by the Torbay Steam Railway.

A similar arrangement existed at Hull Corporation Pier where the Great Central Railway had a booking office connected by the Humber Ferry with New Holland Pier Station. (See 'Last paddle-steamers of BR', p. 178.)

Largest British stations

	Platforms	Total length		Area	
		m	ft	hectares	acres
Clapham Junction	17	3409	11 185	11.23	27¾
Waterloo, London	23[1]	4679	15 352	9.81	24½
Victoria, London	17	5611	18 412	8.8	21¾
Crewe	16	3473	11 394	9.31	23
Waverley, Edinburgh	19	4360	14 305	7.28	18
London Bridge	21	4157	13 574	4.65	11½
Liverpool Street, London	18	3478	11 410	6.47	16
Paddington, London	16	4580	15 025	5.97	14¾

[1] Including two Waterloo & City Railway platforms below ground.

Longest railway station platforms

	m	ft
Chicago, Illinois (State Street Centre subway)	1066	3500
Khargpur, Bihar, India (formerly Bengal–Nagpur Railway)	833	2733
Perth, Western Australia (standard gauge)	762	2500
Sonepur, India (formerly Bengal & North Western Railway)	736	2415
Bulawayo, Zimbabwe	702	2302
New Lucknow, India (formerly East India Railway)	685	2250
Bezwada, India (formerly Madras & Southern Mahratta Railway)	640	2100
Jhansi, India (formerly Great Indian Peninsula Railway)	617	2025
Gloucester, England	602.6	1977
Colchester, England	585	1920[1]
Kotri, Pakistan (formerly North Western Railway)	578	1896
Mandalay, Burma	545	1788
Bournemouth, England	533	1748
Perth, Scotland	522	1714
York, England	516 and 480	1692 and 1575
Storvik, Sweden	c. 500	c. 1640
Edinburgh (Waverley), Scotland	486	1596
Trichinopoly, India (former South India Railway)	471	1546
Ranaghat, India (formerly Eastern Bengal Railway)	464	1522
Crewe, England	460	1509
London (Victoria), England	457	1500
Dakor, India (formerly Bombay, Baroda & Central India Railway)	448	1470
Newcastle upon Tyne, England	423	1389
Cambridge, England	382	1254

[1] Colchester is not one platform, but has a horizontal step in it and serves two tracks. The longest platform in Britain was Manchester Victoria No. 11—Exchange No. 3 measuring 682 m (2238 ft), but Exchange station was closed on 5 May 1969. The platform still exists along a running line.

At Chester Station trains to London via the former London & North Western Railway and Great Western Railway routes left in opposite directions.

Similar situations could be seen at Plymouth (North Road), Exeter (St David's), Nottingham (Midland), and Trent now demolished, between Nottingham and Derby. Also at Trent, trains to and from London could call at the same platform going in the same direction. At Wakefield Kirkgate in South Yorkshire trains between Sheffield and Leeds can pass through the station either way.

The first station escalator was installed at Seaforth Sands Station on the Liverpool Overhead Railway in 1901.

RAILWAY HOTELS

British railways were pioneers in the establishment of railway-owned hotels. The earliest was the Victoria Hotel at Euston, London, built by the London & Birmingham Railway and opened in the last week of September 1839, about a year after the opening of the railway. Euston Hotel opened in November 1839, and the two were leased to a subsidiary, the London & Birmingham Railway Hotels Company. In 1831 the Victoria Hotel became the west wing of the enlarged Euston Hotel. The building was demolished in 1962 during reconstruction of Euston station.

By the mid-1930s the four British railway companies owned, or managed for other proprietors, 79 hotels including eight at London termini. It was then the largest chain of hotels in the world. The hotels came under the control of British Transport Hotels Ltd. In 1983, 21 of the 23 remaining railway hotels were sold. Only the Great Eastern Hotel at Liverpool Street Station and the Great Northern Hotel at Kings Cross, both in London, were retained as part of station reconstruction schemes.

CP Hotels, formerly a department of the Canadian Pacific Railway, operates 28 hotels in Canada, Mexico and Germany.

Sixteen-car Shinkansen train entering Tokyo, September 1985.

12

SPEED

RAILWAY RACES

In the Great Locomotive Chase on the Nashville Chattanooga & St Louis Railroad on 12 April 1862, during the American Civil War, Capt. James J. Andrews and his Yankee raiders seized the Confederate Rogers 4-4-0 *General* at Kennesaw about 40.2 km (25 miles) north of Atlanta, Georgia. They drove it 140 km (87 miles) to within 32 km (20 miles) of Chattanooga, where it ran out of fuel and was caught by the Confederates in another 4-4-0, *Texas*. The chase was over light unballasted track at speeds of over 96.5 km/h (60 mph). For 80.5 km (50 miles) the *Texas* was running tender first.

Both engines are preserved; the *General* at Kennesaw Museum, Georgia, and the *Texas* at Grant Park, Atlanta.

In the race from London to Edinburgh in 1888 the West Coast companies (London & North Western and Caledonian) on 13 August covered the 643.2 km (399.7 miles) in 7 h 6 min at an average speed of 90.4 km/h (56.2 mph).

On 31 August the East Coast companies (Great Northern, North Eastern and North British) set up a record over their 632.8 km (393.2 mile) route, taking 6 h 48 min at an average speed of 92.9 km/h (57.7 mph).

In the subsequent race from London to Aberdeen the West Coast companies set up a world speed record on 22 August 1895 by covering the 870.7 km (541 miles) in 512 min at an average speed of 101.9 km/h (63.3 mph) including three stops and the climbs over Shap and Beattock, but with only a 70 ton train.

The best East Coast time was 518 min for the 842.5 km (523.5 miles) on 21 August 1895, but they had reached Edinburgh in 6 h 18 min, averaging 100 km/h (62.3 mph) with three stops and with a 120 ton train, thereby beating their record of 1888.

When the Atlantic liners called at Plymouth, there was great rivalry between the Great Western and the London & South Western railways in getting passengers and mail to London.

On 9 May 1904 the GWR 'Ocean Mail' ran the 205.7 km (127.8 miles) from Millbay Crossing, Plymouth, to Pylle Hill Junction, Bristol, in 123 min 19 s with the 4-4-0 locomotive *City of Truro*. Down Wellington Bank it reached a very high speed, but the reputed maximum of 164.6 km/h (102.3 mph) has since been seriously questioned and is no longer accepted. From the recorded data, however, there is now little doubt that a speed of about 160 km/h (100 mph) was reached.

The same train, behind 4-2-2 *Duke of Connaught*, covered the 191 km (118.7 miles) from Pylle Hill Junction to Paddington, London, in 99 min 46 s, with an average speed of 128.7 km/h (80 mph) over the 113.1 km (70.3 miles) from Shrivenham to Westbourne Park, a record for sustained high speed which stood in Britain until broken by the 'Cheltenham Flyer' in 1929. The disastrous derailment at Salisbury at 13.57 on 1 July 1906 brought the racing to an end. The London & South Western Railway boat express was wrecked taking a sharp curve at excessive speed. Twenty-four passengers and four railwaymen were killed.

LONGEST NON-STOP RUNS

The world's longest non-stop run was established by the London & North Eastern Railway in the summer timetable of 1927 with the 431.8 km (268.3 miles) between London and Newcastle.

Not to be outdone, the London, Midland & Scottish Railway immediately cut out the crew-changing stop at Carnforth in the run of the 10.00 train out of London (Euston), which had just been named 'The Royal Scot', and ran the 484.4 km (301 miles) non-stop to Carlisle (Kingmoor) shed where engines were changed.

On 1 May 1928 the LNER decided to run the 10.00 from London (King's Cross), the 'Flying Scotsman', non-stop between London and Edinburgh, 632.5 km (393 miles), thereby establishing another world record. For this purpose, H. N. Gresley designed his famous corridor tender, enabling the engine crew to be changed during the journey.

On the Friday before this, however, the LMS stole the glory by dividing the 'Royal Scot' and running the two halves non-stop between London and Edinburgh and Glasgow.

The Edinburgh portion of six coaches was taken by the 4-4-0 compound No. 1054 whose run of 643.2 km (399.7 miles) was certainly a British record for a 4-4-0, and probably a world record.

'Royal Scot'-type 4-6-0 No. 6113 *Cameronian* with the Glasgow portion, achieved a world record with any locomotive by running the 646 km (401.4 miles) non-stop.

On 16 November 1936 the LMS crowned this achievement by running a special 230 ton train non-stop from London to Glasgow in 5 h 53 min 38 s at an average speed of 109.6 km/h (68.1 mph) behind the Stanier 'Pacific' No.

6201 *Princess Elizabeth*. The following day it returned with 260 tons in 5 h 44 min 15 s, at an average speed of 112.6 km/h (70 mph).

The result of this exercise was the inauguration of the LMS 'Coronation Scot' streamlined train, which ran between London and Glasgow in 6½ h on 5 July 1937 stopping, however, at Carlisle for change of crew.

On the same day the LNER introduced the 'Coronation' between London and Edinburgh, streamlined from the front of the 'A4' Class 'Pacific' to the tail of the rear observation car. It called at York and Newcastle going north and at Newcastle going south. The journey took 6 h.

In late August 1948 disastrous floods in south-east Scotland forced the diversion of main-line trains via Kelso and St Boswells. On 17 days the 'Flying Scotsman' made the run of 657.6 km (408.6 miles) non-stop.

Today the 'Flying Scotsman' runs non-stop between King's Cross and Newcastle, 432.1 km (268.5 miles). This is now the **longest non-stop run** by an ordinary passenger train.

The longest distance in Britain without an advertised stop is by the night Motorail service from Inverness to London (Euston), 913.7 km (567.7 miles), in 11 h 4 min.

The longest non-stop steam-hauled service in France was the Paris–Saumur Rapide, 285 km (177 miles). The Paris–Brussels express was, at 312 km (194 miles), claimed to be the longest non-stop steam service in Europe, not requiring a water pick-up. Tenders holding 38 m³ (8360 gallons) of water were used with the Chapelon Pacifics and Nord Super Pacifics on this route.

RAILWAY SPEED RECORDS

The train that arrived seven years late left Beaumont, Texas, on the Gulf & Interstate Railway, at 11.30 on 8 September 1900 for Port Bolivar, about 112.6 km (70 miles). At High Island, 53.1 km (33 miles) on, it was caught in a tremendous flood which washed away miles of track. The passengers and crew were saved, but the train remained isolated until after the impoverished railway company had been taken over by the Atchison, Topeka & Santa Fe Railroad which relaid the track. In September 1907 the train was overhauled and the engine steamed up and the journey, which should have taken 2 h 25 min, was completed. Some of the original passengers were there to greet the train on its arrival.

Several early rail speed records were claimed by the USA but most of these are unauthenticated and are not internationally accepted.

The earliest rail speed record worthy of mention was achieved by the Stephensons' *Rocket* at the Rainhill Trials on the Liverpool & Manchester Railway on 8 October 1829 when it ran at 46.8 km/h (29.1 mph).

On the opening day of the Liverpool & Manchester Railway, on 15 September 1830, the Stephenson 0–2–2 *Northumbrian* reached 58 km/h (36 mph), while conveying the fatally injured William Huskisson from Parkside to Eccles. (See chapter 16.)

A record speed of 91.3 km/h (56¾ mph) was achieved down Madeley Bank in Staffordshire on the Grand Junction Railway by the 2–2–2 engine *Lucifer* on 13 November 1839.

The next three speed records were achieved on the Great Western Railway. In June 1845 the broad-gauge 2–2–2 *Ixion* reached 98.2 km/h (61 mph) between Didcot and London. On 1 June 1846 the 2–2–2 *Great Western* ran at 119.5 km/h (74½ mph) near Wootton Bassett, Wiltshire and in the same place on 11 May 1848 the 4–2–2 *Great Britain* reached 125.5 km/h (78 mph).

The Bristol & Exeter Railway 4–2–4 tank No. 41 achieved a record speed of 131.6 km/h (81.8 mph) down Wellington Bank in Somerset in June 1854. It was one of the class with 2743 mm (9 ft) diameter driving-wheels designed by James Pearson and built by Rothwell & Company of Bolton in 1853 (see chapter 8).

The next speed record was made in France in 1889 when a Crampton 4–2–0 No. 604 reached a speed of 144 km/h (89½ mph) between Montereau and Sens on the Paris–Dijon line.

Britain re-established its claim to the world speed record in March 1897, when Midland Railway 2362 mm (7 ft 9 in) 4–2–2 No. 117 was timed by Charles Rous-Marten at 144.8 km/h (90 mph) between Melton Mowbray and Nottingham. The engine was then still new.

The record by *City of Truro* on 9 May 1904 was mentioned earlier.

On 15 June 1902 the New York Central & Hudson River Railroad inaugurated 'The Twentieth Century Limited' between New York and Chicago, covering the 1547 km (961 miles) in 20 h. On the same day the Pennsylvania Railroad introduced the 'Pennsylvania Special' between the same places, taking 20 h for the 1443.5 km (897 miles).

The NYC & HR route included a 24 km/h (15 mph) journey of 1.6 km (1 mile) through the main street of Syracuse which was replaced by a viaduct on 24 September 1936. The Pennsylvania Railroad route included 644 km (400 miles) through the Allegheny Mountains, round the famous Horseshoe Curve, and over a summit of 668.7 m (2194 ft).

'The Twentieth Century Limited' was accelerated to 18 h in 1908, but was later restored to 20 h until reduced to 18 h again in April 1932. On 15 June 1938 the new streamlined trains reduced the time to 16 h. In 1929 the route had been shortened from 1547 to 1543 km (961 to 958.7 miles) by the Cleveland by-pass. Steam traction with the famous

New York Central 'Hudson'-type 4–6–4s ended in March 1945. 'The Twentieth Century Limited' made its last run on 13 March 1967.

The earliest speed record with electric-traction was 162 km/h (101 mph) attained by a German double-bogie locomotive built by Siemens & Halske in 1901 and operating on 1500 V dc, but it severely damaged the track.

On 6 October 1903 a 12-wheeled electric railcar with motors by Siemens & Halske reached a speed of 203 km/h (126 mph) on the military railway between Marienfeld and Berlin. A similar car with AEG (Allgemeine Elektrizitäts-Gesellschaft, Berlin) equipment reached 210.2 km/h (130.5 mph) on 23 October 1903.

This record stood in Germany until 1974, when one of the prototype luxury four-car train sets of the German Federal Railways Class 'TE403' reached a speed of 215 km/h (133.6 mph) between Bielefeld and Hamm. These trains are designed for speeds of 200 km/h (124.3 mph) in public service and for experimental running up to 230 km/h (142.9 mph).

A new world speed record was established in Germany on 21 June 1931, when a petrol railcar driven by an airscrew maintained 230 km/h (143 mph) for 10 km (6.2 miles) between Karstädt and Dergenthin. The car was designed by Dr F. Kruckenburg.

'The world's fastest train' was the claim made by the Great Western Railway on 6 June 1932, when the 'Cheltenham Spa Express' behind 'Castle' Class 4–6–0 No. 5006 *Tregenna Castle* ran the 124 km (77.3 miles) from Swindon to London (Paddington) in 56 min 47s at an average speed of 131.3 km/h (81.6 mph). The maximum speed was 148.5 km/h (92.3 mph). The train became known as 'The Cheltenham Flyer', but the record was held only until 1935. For a brief period it was then held by the Canadian Pacific Toronto–Montreal service.

Germany established a record speed for steam-traction in May 1935, when the streamlined 4–6–4 No. 05.001 reached 200.4 km/h (124½ mph) on a test run between Berlin and Hamburg. The engine was built by the Borsig Locomotive Works, Berlin, in June 1935.

The fastest speed with a steam locomotive in Canada was made on the Canadian Pacific on 18 September 1937 during a test of air brakes by the Canadian Westinghouse Company on a train of new lightweight stock. Eastbound from Smith's Falls to Montreal the train reached 180 km/h (112½ mph) before making an emergency test stop at St Telesphore. The locomotive was No. 3003, one of the five 'Jubilee' class F2a 4–4–4s built by Montreal Locomotive Works in 1936.

A record speed with diesel-electric traction was achieved in Germany on 23 June 1939, when 265.5 km/h (133.5 mph) was reached.

The diesel-electric 'Zephyr' of the Chicago, Burlington & Quincy Railroad covered the 1637 km (1017 miles) from Denver to Chicago at an average speed of 124.8 km/h (77.6 mph) throughout on 26 May 1934.

On 23 October 1936 it ran from Chicago to Denver in 12 h 12 min at an average speed of 147.4 km/h (91.6 mph); 1270 km (750 miles) were covered at 144.8 km/h

Canadian Pacific Railway 'Jubilee' class 4–4–4. One of this type reached 180 km/h (112 mph) in 1936, the fastest speed with steam in Canada.

One of the four streamlined 'Atlantics' built by ALCO in 1935 for the 'Hiawatha' service between Chicago and the 'Twin Cities', Minneapolis/St Paul, on the Milwaukee Road. These were the first steam locomotives designed to run at speeds of over 160 km/h (100 mph).

(90 mph), 42.8 km (26.6 miles) at 169 km/h (105 mph) and a maximum speed of 186.7 km/h (116 mph) was reached.

The first American transcontinental speed record was made in June 1876 by the 'Jarrett and Palmer Special' when it ran the 5330 km (3312 miles) from Jersey City to San Francisco in 84 h 20 min, or about 3½ days.

The Union Pacific Railroad achieved a record for diesel-traction with the first American streamlined diesel-electric express, the M10000. In October 1934, during tests, it covered 96.5 km (60 miles) at 165.4 km/h (102.8 mph) and reached 193 km/h (120 mph). It crossed the continent from Los Angeles to New York, 5245 km (3259 miles), in 56 h 56 min, at an average speed of 99.8 km/h (62 mph). In service it ran the 3657 km (2272 miles) between Chicago and Portland in 39¼ h. It was scrapped in 1942.

The Chicago, Milwaukee, St Paul & Pacific began experiments with high speeds in the early 1930s, and on 29 July 1934 'F6' Class 4–6–4 No. 6402, built in 1930, with a train of five roller-bearing steel cars, reached a speed of 166.5 km/h (103.5 mph) at Oakwood, Wisconsin, and averaged 149 km/h (92.6 mph) for 98.8 km (61.4 miles) between Edgebrook, Illinois and Oakwood. The average over the 137.9 km (85.7 mile) Chicago–Milwaukee run

was 122.4 km/h (76.1 mph). This was the first authentic 161 km/h (100 mph) run in the USA.

The famous 'Hiawatha' service began on 29 May 1935, covering the 660 km (410 miles) Chicago–St Paul in 6 h 30 min. The Chicago–Milwaukee section was covered in 75 min at a speed of 161 km/h (100 mph). The loco-motives were the four 'Atlantics', described in Chapter 8 which could run up to 193 km/h (120 mph).

The success of the 'Hiawatha' created heavier loadings which led to the introduction in 1938, of the six 'F7' Class streamlined 4–6–4s. These shared the workings with the 'Atlantics', and from 21 January 1939 worked two additional Chicago–Twin Cities trains known as the 'Morning Hiawathas'. Later that year one of them averaged 193 km/h (120 mph) for 8 km (5 miles) and maintained over 161 km/h (100 mph) for 30.5 km (19 miles).

Today badly maintained track has forced Amtrak (National Railroad Passenger Corporation) to slow down the Chicago–Minneapolis service to over 10 h, about 3½ h longer than with steam in 1940.

In the course of a trial run from London to Leeds and back on 30 November 1934 the London & North Eastern Railway 'Pacific' No. 4472 *Flying Scotsman* with a load of 145 tons covered the 299 km (185.8 miles) outwards in 151 min 56 s. On the return, with 208 tons, it took 157 min 17 s. Down Stoke Bank between Grantham and Peterborough the dynamometer-car speed recorder gave a maximum of 161 km/h (100 mph) for 548.6 m (600 yd). However, this was disputed by the most experienced of all train-timers, Cecil J. Allen, who was on the train and who would accept nothing higher than 157.7 km/h (98 mph).

The first petrol-driven Bugatti 'Presidential' type railcar (autorail in French) achieved a world record speed at 173 km/h (107 mph) in 1933, which was increased to 196 km/h (122 mph) in 1934. In all, 88 Bugatti autorails were built. In passenger service they could travel at speeds of up to 140 km/h (87 mph). The last finished as a circuit test vehicle for checking point and signal operation. One is preserved at the French National Railway Museum at Mulhouse.

A world speed record for steam was achieved by the London & North Eastern Railway on 5 March 1935, when the 'Pacific' No. 2750 *Papyrus* reached 173.8 km/h (108 mph) down Stoke Bank during a round trip of 863 km (536 miles) from London to Newcastle and back at an overall average speed of 112.6 km/h (70 mph). The outcome of this test was a new 4-h service between London and Newcastle in October 1935.

The first of the Gresley 'A4' Class 'Pacifics', No. 2509 *Silver Link*, broke the record the same year, on 27 September 1935, when it twice reached 181 km/h (112½ mph) and averaged 173 km/h (107½ mph) for 40 km (25 miles), 161 km/h (100 mph) for 69 km (43 miles) and 147.7 km/h (91.8 mph) for 113 km (70 miles) continuously, with a 230 ton train.

An attempt to break this record was made by the London, Midland & Scottish Railway during a trial of the 'Coronation Scot' with 'Pacific' No. 6220 *Coronation*. Four reliable train-timers (Cecil J. Allen, D. S. M. Barrie, S. P. W. Corbett and O. S. Nock) independently recorded a speed of 181 km/h (112½ mph) at a point only 3.2 km (2 miles) south of Crewe Station. The LMS, eager to beat the LNER record, officially claimed a speed of 183.5 km/h (114 mph), but this is seriously doubted. It was followed by a hazardous entry into Crewe Station over crossovers, resulting in a heap of smashed crockery in the restaurant car.

The all-time record for steam-traction was achieved by the LNER on 3 July 1938 when the 'A4' Class No. 4468 *Mallard* with a seven-coach train weighing 240 tons reached 201 km/h (125 mph) on Stoke Bank between Grantham and Peterborough. Five miles (8 km) (mileposts 94–89) were covered at an average speed of 193.8 km/h (120.4 mph). The overrunning of the middle valve spindle (a fault of the Holcroft/Gresley combination gear) at a cut-off of over 40 per cent, resulted in destruction of the bearing metal in the middle big end.

The driver, Joseph Duddington, retired in 1944 and died in 1953, aged 76. The fireman was Thomas Bray. *Mallard* is preserved in the National Railway Museum, York.

New records were achieved in Italy by three-car electric units. On 27 July 1938 the 213.9 km (132.9 miles) from Rome to Naples were covered in 83 min at an average speed of 154.7 km/h (96.1 mph) and with a maximum of 201 km/h (125 mph).

On 20 July 1939 the 315 km (195.8 miles) from Florence to Milan were covered in 115.2 min at an average speed, start to stop, of 164 km/h (102 mph) with a maximum of 202.8 km/h (126 mph).

In Germany a record for a diesel train was made on 23 June 1939 with a speed of 214.8 km/h (133.5 mph).

The highest speed on sub-standard gauge was achieved on the 1067 mm (3 ft 6 in) gauge South African Railways on 11 November 1976, when a test coach hauled by a specially geared electric locomotive exceeded 200 km/h (124 mph). The purpose was to test the stability of the Scheffel cross-anchor bogie with its self-steering wheelsets widely used on the SAR.

New records were achieved in France on 21 February 1953 when Series CC 7100 type electric locomotive No. 7121, with a three-coach train of 102.5 tonnes, averaged 239.8 km/h (149 mph) for 4.8 km (3 miles) on the 1500 V dc line between Dax and Beaune. It reached a maximum speed of 242.8 km/h (150.9 mph). The 4300 hp locomotive weighed 106 tons.

On 28 March 1955 No. 7107 of the same type reached 330.9 km/h (205.6 mph) with a three-coach train of 100 tonnes for 1.24 miles (2 km) between Facture and Morcenx on the Bordeaux–Hendaye line. The following day this speed was equalled by the 81 tonne 4000 hp Series BB 9000 type locomotive No. 9004, also 1500 V dc. The drivers were H. Braghet and J. Brocca.

A rail speed record of 378 km/h (235 mph) was achieved in France on 4 December 1967 between Gometz-le-Châtel and Limours by 'L'Aérotrain', powered by jet aero engines.

French Railways created a new record on 26 February 1981, when TGV (Train à Grande Vitesse) electric set No. 23016 attained a top speed of 380 km/h (236 mph) near Tonnerre in central France during a test run on the new track between St Florentin and Sathonay.

On 27 September 1981 TGVs began a regular hourly service between Paris and Lyon, covering the 510 km (317 miles) in 2 h 40 min, to be reduced later to 2 h. Maximum speeds will be 260 km/h (162 mph). Speeds up to 300 km/h (186 mph) are planned.

The world's highest speed for a flanged-wheel vehicle on rails of 410 km/h (254.8 mph) was achieved on 14 August 1974 by the Linear Induction Motor Test Vehicle of the United States Department of Transportation at its 10 km (6.2 mile) standard-gauge test track at Pueblo, Colorado.

A special Budd car fitted with two turbo-jet 'J–47' aircraft engines mounted on the forward end reached a speed of 296 km/h (183.85 mph) in July 1966 on the New York Central Railroad near Bryan, Ohio, between mileposts 350 and 345. The 8 km (5 miles) were covered in 1 min 39.75 s at an average speed of 291 km/h (181 mph). The record was achieved near milepost 347 over a length of 91.5 (300 ft).

The fastest train speed in the USA was 251 km/h (156 mph), recorded at Princeton Junction, New Jersey, on 24 May 1967 by a test train built as part of the Northeast Corridor Project.

The first regular scheduled service at over 161 km/h (100 mph) was introduced in Japan on 1 November 1965 on the then new standard-gauge Shinkansen line when trains began running between Tokyo and Osaka (516 km, 321 miles) in 3 h 10 min at an average speed of 163 km/h (103.3 mph) with a maximum of 210 km/h (130 mph). They covered the 342 km (212.4 miles) between Tokyo and Nagoya in 120 min at an average speed of 171 km/h (106.2 mph). The trains, then 12 cars weighing 720 tons, are now 16 cars weighing 950 tons.

The new service between Tokyo and Hakata, inaugurated on 10 March 1975, covers the 1069.1 km (664.3 miles) in 6 h 56 min at an average speed of 154.2 km/h (95.8 mph). On the 515.4 km (320.2 mile) Tokyo–Shin–Osaka section the average scheduled speed is 162.8 km/h (101 mph).

During trials with a Series 961 train set on 7 December 1979 on the Shinkansen test track, Oyama, a speed of 319 km/h (198 mph) was reached. On 23 January 1980 JNR announced that trains on the Tohoko and Joetsu Shinkansen lines will operate at a maximum speed of 260 km/h (162 mph). In December 1980 JNR took delivery of a prototype Series 262 train set, designed to operate at an average speed of 210 km/h (130 mph).

The number of passengers carried on the Shinkansen system reached 1000 million on 25 May 1976. The record number of passengers carried in one day was 807 875 on 6 April 1975.

British Rail's 'Inter City 125' High-Speed Trains gained a Design Council Award in 1978. The design work was mostly carried out at the BR Technical Centre at Derby.

The last HST power cars, Nos. 43197/8, were handed over at Crewe on 26 August 1982. In eight years, 199 were built.

The 'Inter-City 125' trains, using the first 27 'production' HST (High Speed Train) sets, went into operation between London (Paddington) and Bristol and South

Wales on 4 October 1976. They were introduced on the East Coast main line on 8 May 1978, cutting the London–Edinburgh time from 5 h 27 m (by 'Deltic'-hauled express) to 4 hr 52 min for the 632 km (392.7 miles). London–York, 302 km (187.6 miles), was reduced from 2 h 31 min to 2 h 10 min.

On the same day the London–Bristol and Cardiff times were cut by a further 3 min, giving average speeds of 158.7 km/h (98.6 mph) between Paddington and Bristol Parkway.

The fastest run achieved by an HST set was on 27 September 1985 when the *Tees-Tyne Pullman* made the 432.5 km (268.7 mile) journey from Newcastle to London in 2 h 19 min 37 sec at an average speed of 185.7 km/h (115.4 mph).

BR established a new world speed record for diesel traction on 1 November 1987 when a special train testing the prototype SIG (Swiss Industries Company) bogies for the Mk IV Inter City coaches reached 283.9 km/h (176.4 mph) between Darlington and York.

The British Advanced Passenger Train, developed at vast expense from 1967 and finally abandoned in 1986. One of its main, and most troublesome, features was the tilting mechanism designed to enable it to take curves super-elevated for 160 km/h (100 mph) at much higher speeds. This photograph shows an APT on such a curve. The inclined sides of the train were necessary to keep within the loading gauge when it was tilted.

The fastest recorded speed by an electric multiple unit train using a third-rail pick-up was 177 km/h (110 mph) on 14 April 1988 by a five-coach '442' class Wessex express unit on the London (Waterloo)–Southampton line.

The world's first 300 km/h (186 mph) train left the Alsthom works at Belfort, France, on 14 April 1988, the first of 95 sets. They will run up to 300 km/h (186 mph) on the new 65 km (40 miles) Auneau–Courtalain section energized in October 1988. High-speed trials up to 350 km/h (217 miles) are regularly carried out on the Paris South East line.

West Germany's new Intercity High-Speed Train set achieved a world speed record of 405 km/h (252 mph) on the new line between Würzburg and Fulden on 1 May 1988.

On USSR Railways (SZD), following track improvements, the Moscow–Helsinki service was accelerated to 160 km/h (100 mph) from 9 November 1987, reducing the journey time by 1 hour.

The fastest metre-gauge train in Europe is operated by the Rhaetian Railway in Switzerland. The 07.12 from St Moritz to Chur covers the 89.3 km (55½ miles) in 2 h, over a difficult mountain route with innumerable curves and long gradients of 1 in 28.6 (3½ per cent).

The highest recorded rail speed in New Zealand, 125.5 km/h (78 mph), was achieved on test by one of the 250 hp diesel railcars, built by Vulcan Foundry Limited, Lancashire, in 1940. Only nine were delivered; one was lost at sea in a submarine attack. They have three-axle motor bogies and two-axle trailing bogies. Unofficial speeds over 145 km/h (over 90 mph) have been claimed.

The fastest steam locomotives in New Zealand were the 'Ja' Class 4–8–2s with a top speed of 120.8 km/h (75 mph).

In Australia the State Rail Authority of NSW introduced the XPT services in 1982. The design of the Australian Express Passenger Train is based on the British HST, but there are many detail differences. Dimensionally the XPT is 230 mm (9 in) wider and 200 mm (8 in) higher than the HST and the power cars are 450 mm (nearly 1 ft 6 in) shorter, with lighter construction to reduce the axle load. The power car has a 12-cylinder turbocharged diesel engine rated at 1492 kW (2000 hp). On trial on the Southern Line on 6 September 1981, an XPT set with power car No. XP 2000 achieved 183 km/h (113.7 mph) between Table Top and Gregory. This is more than 50 km/h (31 mph) faster than the existing NSW record speed.

The fastest speed achieved by a medium-gauged steam locomotive was 130 km/h (81 mph) on the 1067 mm (3 ft 6 in) gauge Japanese National Railways, by a C62 Class 4–6–4 of 1948 design. The JNR has the highest speed limit of 120 km/h (75 mph) on the 1067 mm gauge.

The highest speed on sub-standard gauge has been attained on the 1067 mm (3 ft 6 in) gauge South African Railways. In December 1978 a Class 6E electric locomotive fitted with a bullet nose and modified gear ratio, hauling one coach, reached a speed of 245 km/h (152 mph) over a distance of 3 km between Midway and Westonaria near Johannesburg.

Japanese National Railways is developing 130 km/h (80 mph) trains for 1067 mm gauge routes. The present speed limit is 95–120 km/h (59–74.5 mph). The new trains, to be introduced in 1986, will reduce the Osaka–Kanazawa journey time by 22 min, to 2 h 50 min, and Shinjuko–Matsumoto by 44 min, to 2 h 55 min.

A record for 'minimum gauge' is claimed by the 381 mm (15 in) gauge Romney, Hythe & Dymchurch Railway in Kent. A 14-coach train of about 37 tons pulled by 4–6–2 No. 10 *Dr Syn* and driven by ex-BR driver Eric Copping ran non-stop over the 43.2 km (26.8 miles) from Hythe, round the loop at Dungeness and back to Hythe in 73 min 22 s at an average speed of 35.4 km/h (22 mph), on 2 October 1982.

A new Canadian speed record was made on 10 March 1976 during a test of a new LRC (Light Rapid Comfortable) train which achieved 207.6 km/h (129 mph) on the Canadian Pacific Railway Adirondack sub-division east of Montreal. It established another Canadian record by maintaining an average speed of 200 km/h (124½ mph) over a distance of 1 mile.

FASTEST SCHEDULED TRAINS IN THE USA AND CANADA

Amtrak has now reduced the New York–Washington time to 2 h 30 min for the 361 km (224 miles) with one stop, an average speed of 144 km/h (89.5 mph).

The 'North Coast Hiawatha' is Amtrak's name for the former Northern Pacific 'North Coast Limited'. This streamlined train runs three times weekly, taking 50 h 29 min over the 3586 km (2228 miles) between Chicago and Seattle. In the reverse direction, the time is 54 h 25 min. These times give average speeds of 71 km/h (44 mph) and 66 km/h (41 mph). The route crosses the Rockies at Momestake Pass and the Cascades at Stampede Tunnel, 2997 m (3278 yd) long.

The fastest scheduled services in Canada operate between Montreal and Toronto. The Canadian National 'Turbo' trains cover the 539 km (335 miles) in 4½ h with three stops, at an average speed of 120 km/h (74.4 mph); and the 'Rapido' trains take 4 hr 55 min with the same three stops, at an average speed of 109.6 km/h (68.1 mph), in both directions. Between Guildwood, Ontario, and Dorval, Quebec, the 'Turbo' covers 500 km (310.9 miles) in 208 min at an average of 144.8 km/h (90 mph).

13

LIGHT RAIL TRANSIT

Light Rail Transit includes street and inter-urban tramways, underground railways, metros, 'U-Bahnen', 'S-Bahnen', rapid and mass-transit railways, designed to carry large numbers of passengers on short or medium distance journeys.

UNDERGROUND RAILWAYS

The first underground passenger railway in the world was the Metropolitan Railway, London, built on the 'cut and cover' principle. It was opened, with mixed 2134 mm (7 ft) and standard gauge, from Bishop's Road to Farringdon Street on 10 January 1863 and extended to Moorgate on 23 December 1865. The broad-gauge outer rails were removed in March 1869 following a dispute with the GWR. Trains were lit by gas.

With the Metropolitan District Railway, the first section of which was opened from Kensington to Westminster on 24 December 1868, the Metropolitan formed a circular route known as the 'Inner Circle' which was completed on 6 October 1884, together with the opening of the connection with the East London Railway through Marc Brunel's Thames Tunnel. It was electrified from 12 September 1905 and the last steam trains ran on 23 September.

The world's first 'tube' railway was the Tower Subway beneath the River Thames in London. It was opened, using cable-traction, on 2 August 1870, though it had worked experimentally since April. From 24 December 1870 it closed as a railway and was used as a footway until March 1896. It then carried a water main, now abandoned.

The shortest underground railway is probably the Istanbul Metropolitan, 650 m (711 yd) long. It has a 'gauge'

An early 2134 m (7 ft) gauge train at Bellmouth, Praed Street, London, on the Metropolitan Railway in 1863, with outside-cylinder 2-4-0 tank engine. The last broad-gauge trains ran in March 1869.

of 1510 mm (4 ft 11½ in) with cable haulage on a steep gradient. It was opened on 17 January 1875 and was operated from 26 November 1971. It now has a concrete track and two pneumatic-tyred cars.

The Mersey Railway between Liverpool and Birkenhead was opened on 1 February 1886. It includes 1 in 27 (3.7 per cent) gradients under the River Mersey, and at its lowest point it is 39.2 m (128.6 ft) below Ordnance Datum. At first it was worked by steam locomotives, one of which, Beyer Peacock 0–6–4 tank No. 5 *Cecil Raikes* (1885), is preserved at Southport, awaiting restoration.

On 3 May 1903 the Mersey Railway became the first steam underground railway to be electrified. It now forms part of the *Merseyrail System* (see below).

The first electric underground railway in the world was the City & South London, opened on 18 December 1890.

London Transport's oldest tube coach, known as the 'padded cell' because of its high upholstered seat backs, ran on the City & South London Railway from Stockwell to the City in 1890. For 35 years it was on display at the old Queen Street Railway Museum at York. It now forms part of the London Transport collection at Covent Garden, London.

The Glasgow District Subway was opened on 14 December 1896. It was 1219 mm (4 ft) gauge, cable operated, and consisted of two parallel tunnels, for either direction, forming a loop round the city centre, twice crossing beneath the River Clyde. The railway was electrified at 600 V dc in 1935, the 'inner circle' coming into operation on 28 March and the 'outer circle' on 5 December. It was the first electric passenger railway in Scotland. It was modernized in 1982.

The first section of the Paris Underground (the Métro) from Port de Vincennes to Porte Maillot was opened on 10 July 1900.

The first driverless underground railway was built in 1910 by the Post Office in Munich. It was a 360 mm (14.17 in) gauge double-track and ran from the Post Office in Hofenstrasse to the Starnberger railway station, about 800 m (½ mile). The tunnel was 2.3 m (7 ft 8 in) wide and 1.2 m (4 ft) high. Trains used a 160 V overhead system and ran at 12–14 km/h (7–8 mph). It had to be rerouted before construction of the Munich Olympic Underground line, which was opened on 8 May 1972.

The first driverless underground railway in Britain was the Post Office Subway in London. It was begun in 1914 and fully opened in December 1927. It is 610 mm (2 ft) gauge and 10.5 km (6.5 miles long) from Paddington Station to the Eastern District Post Office. The main double-track tunnels are 2.7 m (9 ft) in diameter. It carries about 30 000 mail-bags a day.

London Underground Railways have a total route length of 410 km (255 miles) of which 383 km (238 miles) are administered by London Regional Transport and the remainder by British Rail. A total of 167 km (104 miles) is underground of which 135 km (84 miles) is in small-diameter deep-level tube tunnels and 32 km (20 miles) in sub-surface, mostly 'cut and cover' tunnels. The greatest depth below the surface is 67.3 m (221 ft) below Hampstead Heath, 579 m (1900 ft) north of Hampstead station on the Northern Line. There are 273 stations of which 250 are managed by LRT. Ventilation is provided by 93 fans moving nearly 2400³ (84 755 ft³) of air per second, excluding the Victoria Line which has 16 fans moving 531 m³ (18 752 ft³) per second. At 31 stations on the older system and at all stations on the Victoria Line draught relief shafts are provided to cope with the air moved by the trains. London Underground Limited owns 2475 motor cars, 1400 trailer cars and 330 other rail vehicles. Electric supply is by third rail at 600 V dc. In 1986–7 the system handled 769 million passengers in a year. LU Ltd employs a staff of 20 600.

Of 1 250 000 journeys to work in Central London, London Regional Transport carries 34 per cent by Underground and 14 per cent by bus. British Rail carries 460 000, or nearly 40 per cent, and two-thirds of this on the Southern Region. Thus the private cars which choke London's streets represent less than 12 per cent of the people travelling.

The maximum number of passengers passing over one track in 1 h on the London Underground system is as high as 28 000 on the Central Line.

The most frequent service is on the southbound Bakerloo Line between Baker Street and Waterloo at the morning peak; 33 trains in 1 h, 18 in one peak ½ h.

The Victoria Line was completed throughout from Walthamstow Central to Brixton on 23 July 1971.

London Underground Ltd's Piccadilly Line extension to Heathrow Central for the Airport, was opened by the Queen on 16 December 1977. It was further extended by a loop line serving the newly opened Terminal 4 in April 1986.

The Jubilee Line was opened from Baker Street to Charing Cross on 1 May 1979.

The first London Transport train with automatic driving equipment entered experimental service on the District Line on 8 April 1963. Full-scale trials on the 6.5 km (4 mile) Woodford-Hainault shuttle service on the Central Line began on 5 April 1964. The entire service on the Victoria Line is operated by automatic trains.

The deepest lift shaft on the London Underground is at Hampstead Station, 55 m (181 ft) below ground. The lift operates at maximum speed of 243.8 m (800 ft) a minute. Hampstead is the deepest station on LT, 58.5 m (192 ft) below ground.

The first escalators on the London Underground were at Earl's Court, between the District and Piccadilly line platforms, brought into operation on 4 October 1911. The last lifts, or elevators, on the London Underground were installed at Broad Street, Central London Railway, in 1913.

The longest escalator on the London Underground is that serving the Piccadilly Line at Leicester Square Station. The shaft is 49.3 m (161 ft 6 in) long with a vertical rise of 24.6 m (80 ft 9 in).

The newest British Underground railway system is the **Merseyrail** Loop and Link, designed to ease traffic congestion in Liverpool and Birkenhead. The central portion consists of the original Mersey Railway. This has been extended under Liverpool to form the Loop and another line, the Link, connects the former Lancashire & Yorkshire lines to Southport, Ormskirk and Kirkby with the Loop and with the former Cheshire Lines Railway to Garston. (See map.) Under Birkenhead a new burrowing junction greatly increases the traffic capacity of the junction between the Rock Ferry and West Kirby/New Brighton lines. Parliamentary powers for the Loop and burrowing junction were obtained in 1968 and after grants for construction had been arranged, work began on the Loop in March 1972. Powers for the Link line were obtained in 1971 and construction began in spring 1973. On 2 May 1977 the Link line was opened from the north to Moorfields and Central and electric trains were extended up the Wigan line as far as Kirkby. The Link line was com-pleted on 3 January 1978 when trains began running through to Garston. On 9 May 1977 the Loop was opened, with James Street and Central stations only, and the burrowing junction. Lime Street was opened on 30 October 1977 leaving Moorfields to be opened later. Trains use the 600 V dc third rail system as on the former LYR, Mersey and Wirral lines.

The Tyne & Wear Metro in north-east England was conceived in 1970. It combines former North Eastern Railway lines on the north and south of the Tyne, with new underground sections and a bridge over the Tyne at Newcastle. The first section, from Tynemouth to Haymarket, Newcastle, was opened on 11 August 1980. The remainder of the system opened in stages in 1981 and 1982 and the final section, Heworth to South Shields, opened on 24 March 1984. The 56 km (35 mile) system forms part of an integrated transport organization serving a wide area.

The first un-manned métro line, at Lille, France, was opened on 16 April 1983. Trains of rubber-tyred cars operate for 20 h a day. Lille, with a population of only about 180 000, is one of the smallest towns to have a métro. Normally a million is regarded as the minimum. Pneumatic-tyred trains were introduced on the Paris Métro on 8 November 1956.

The world's longest station escalator is on the Leningrad Underground with a vertical rise of 59.5 m (195 ft). On the Moscow Underground is one with a rise of 50 m (164 ft).

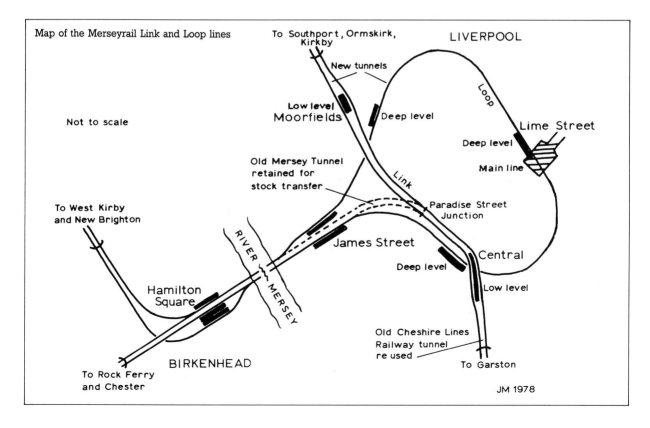

Underground Railways were first opened in other towns as follows: Budapest 1896; Boston, USA 1898; New York, 1900; Berlin, 1902; Philadelphia, 1908; Hamburg, 1912; Buenos Aires, 1914; Madrid, 1919; Barcelona, 1924; Sydney, 1926; Tokyo, 1927; Moscow, 1933; Osaka, 1933; Chicago, 1943; Stockholm, 1950; Toronto, 1954; Rome, 1954; Leningrad, 1955; Cleveland, Ohio, 1956; Nagoya, 1957; Lisbon, 1959; Haifa, 1959; Kiev, 1960; Milan, 1964; Montreal, 1966; Rotterdam, 1968; Munich, 1971; San Francisco, 1972; Bucharest, 1979; Hong Kong, 1979.

LIGHT RAPID TRANSIT RAILWAYS

The latest development in urban mass transport, commonly referred to as Light Rail Transit (LRT), is simply a modern electric tramway. One such line has existed in Britain for many years, along the sea front at Blackpool in Lancashire. The first section was opened in October 1884, using a conduit system. It was the first electric tramway. It was converted to overhead trolley collection in 1898–9.

The pioneer electric tramways, or street-car systems, dated mostly from the first decade of this century. The single or double-deck cars, grinding and lurching along the middle of a road at a top speed of about 32 km/h (20 mph), certainly moved masses of people, but with standards of comfort and convenience which left much to be desired. Those wishing to discover, or rediscover, what they were like should visit the Tramway Museum at Crich in Derbyshire. Various cities in Britain attempted to modernize their tramways; Leeds set an example with its

short-lived light railway to Middleton, but a completely redesigned system was needed.

New schemes are now being prepared for West Midlands, centred on Birmingham, and around Manchester.

The most exciting development in London Transport in recent years is the **Docklands Light Railway**. It was formally opened by Queen Elizabeth II on 30 July 1987, but public services were delayed until 31 August because of technical problems. The two-car driverless trains are controlled by computer. It is operated jointly by LRT and London Docklands Development Corporation.

In Europe numerous towns are developing LRT systems with both surface and sub-surface sections, and fast, quiet, smooth-running articulated cars. In German-speaking countries these systems are known as S-Bahnen (Stadt, or Town, railways) to distinguish them from the U-Bahnen (Underground railways). Many areas operate fast inter-urban lines. The most common gauges are metre and standard, 1435 mm. Readers requiring detailed information about LRT systems throughout the world should refer to Jane's *World Railways* (which includes rapid transit systems) and Jane's *Urban Transport Systems*, both published annually and available at large libraries.

Electric trams on the outskirts of Prague; an example of Light Rail Transit. Modern systems are proposed for Manchester and Birmingham in England.

MONO RAILWAYS OR MONORAILS

The first recorded mono railway was opened about 1810 and patented by Henry Palmer in 1821 for transporting foodstuffs at the Royal Military Yard, Deptford, London. It consisted of boards supported on posts straddled by the cars which were pulled by horses. A similar line at Cheshunt, Hertfordshire, had a passenger carriage for occasional use.

The first passenger-carrying monorail was built in 1876 by General Roy Stone in Fairmont Park, Philadelphia, as part of the city centenary exhibition.

The first commercial monorail was also American, built in 1880 to connect Brooklyn and Coney Island, New York. It ran for a few months but failed for lack of revenue.

Three types of monorail have been used. The type invented by Charles Lartigue in 1883 was used for the Listowel & Ballybunion Railway in County Kerry. This 14.5 km (9 mile) line was opened on 1 March 1888. The twin-boilered locomotives and cars straddled the rail which was supported on trestles. The most comical pieces of the equipment were the mobile steps which were marshalled into the train to enable passengers to cross the line. Loads had to be balanced. The railway was closed in October 1924.

Lartigue-type monorails were also built in North Africa, central France, Russia, Guatemala and Peru.

The Tokyo–Haneda Monorail in Japan is a modern version of the Lartigue system. It was opened in October 1964, to connect Tokyo with the international airport at Haneda. Trains cover the 13 km (8 miles) in 15 min.

A similar monorail was opened in Seattle, in 1962 in connection with the World's Fair. It is about 1.6 km (1 mile) long.

Another, also about 1.6 km long, was opened at Rhyl in North Wales on 1 August 1980.

The second type of monorail, still in operation, is the 13 km (8 mile) long Wuppertalbahn from Elberfeld to Barmen in Germany. This is the Langen suspended type, much of it straddling the Wupper River. The first section was opened on 1 March 1901. By 1960 it had carried 1 000 000 000 passengers. It was this system which inspired the Swiss engineer Feldmann to build the first mountain aerial ropeway, up the Wetterhorn, opened in July 1908 and closed in 1914. It is electrically operated, and stock now consists of 28 articulated carriages.

The Ewing monorail system, which used an 'outrigger' wheel for balancing, was used by C. W. Bowles when State Engineer for the Patiala Government in India. He laid down a system totalling about 96 km (60 miles), known as the **Patiala State Monorail Trainway**. The single rail was laid along the edge of a road and the balancing wheels ran on the road. About 95 per cent of the load was carried on the rail and 5 per cent on the sprung road wheel. The rail wheels had double flanges.

In March 1909 four 0–3–0 steam locomotives were built for this monorail by Orenstein & Koppel, Berlin. One of these engines has been restored and it operates at the Indian Railway Museum, New Delhi.

The Listowel & Ballybunion Railway, Ireland.

14
FREIGHT TRAFFIC

The earliest railways were built primarily for the carriage of minerals. General goods, or freight, though carried, was largely a by-product of the passenger carrying railways from the 1820s onwards.

Containers were first used in the USA on the Camden & Amboy Railroad in 1849 and on the Pennsylvania Railroad in 1869.

The first recorded use of refrigerators on an American railroad was on 1 July 1851, when 8 tons of butter were carried from Ogdensburg, New York, to Boston, in a wooden box car stocked with ice and insulated with sawdust.

In 1857 box cars with ice compartments at each end were used for carrying fresh meat from Chicago eastwards over the Michigan Central Railroad (now Conrail).

The 'caboose' at the rear of an American freight train was originally known as a 'cabin car', 'conductor's van', 'brakeman's cab', 'accommodation car', 'train car' and 'way car'. The first recorded use of the term 'caboose' was in 1855 on the Buffalo, Corning & New York Railroad (now part of the Erie Lackawanna). The roof-top cupola appears to have been introduced in 1863 by T. B. Watson, a freight conductor of the Chicago & North Western Railway, Iowa. In parts of Canada, particularly on the Canadian Pacific, they are known simply as 'vans'.

The Railway Express Agency in the USA was established on 4 March 1839 by William F. Harnden (1812–45), formerly a passenger train conductor on the Boston & Worcester Railroad (now part of Conrail). Harnden contracted with the Boston & Providence (also now part of Conrail) and a steamship company operating between Providence and New York for the carriage of his business.

The business grew rapidly and was extended to Philadelphia and elsewhere. The Railway Express Agency Company, established on 7 December 1928, was owned and operated by US railroads until 1960 when its name became 'REA Express'. It was purchased by a group of its executives in 1969. The handling of its business brings the railroads an annual income of over $40 000 000.

The first tank car especially built for transporting bulk oil in the USA went into service at Titusville, Pennsylvania, on 1 November 1865.

The first code of rules to govern the interchange of freight cars in the USA was adopted at a meeting of officials of six freight lines at Buffalo, New York, on 20 April 1866.

The Master Car Builders' Association was formed in the USA in 1867 to conduct tests and experiments towards the standardizing of freight cars, brakes, couplers, etc. It subsequently became the Mechanical Division of the Association of American Railroads. (See chapter 4.)

Containers were introduced in Britain and Europe during the early 1920s. These large boxes could be transferred from train to truck or ship, so avoiding much loading and unloading.

First tests with automatic couplers in the USA were carried out by the Master Car Builders' Association, beginning in 1869 and continuing for many years. Further tests from September 1885 led to the approval in 1887, by the MCBA, of an automatic coupler working in a vertical plane. It was invented by Major Eli Hamilton Janney (1831–1912) and patented on 21 April 1868. A second patent was issued on 29 April 1873 for the basic car-coupler design in general use today. Standard, interchangeable, automatic car couplers were introduced in 1887. The Janney automatic coupler was adopted as standard on Pennsylvania Railroad passenger cars in 1884. Link-and-pin couplers on passenger cars continued until about 1888. The fitting of automatic couplers and automatic air brakes became statutory in 1893. The 'Type F' interlocking coupler for freight cars was adopted as standard in 1953.

Automatic couplers were adopted on the Imperial Japanese Government Railway on 17 July 1925, after eight years of preparation. The conversion was completed in 24 h.

Roller bearings were first applied to rail freight vehicles by the Timken Company of USA in 1923. Progress was slow because the interchange of freight cars between railroads prevented proper evaluation by the owning company. A large-scale experiment in 1930 on 100 70-ton hopper cars on the Pennsylvania Railroad with roller-bearing bogies designed and supplied by Timken proved the advantages, not only in freer running, but in avoidance of delays and derailments resulting from overheated plain bearings. Also in 1930, ALCO built a demonstration 4–8–4 with roller bearings on all axles. It is described in chapter 8.

Today in the USA about 63 per cent of the cars operating under The Association of American Railroads have roller bearings. Roller bearings are now in almost universal use on new passenger and freight vehicles.

The first 'Piggy-back' service in North America was introduced in September 1855 in Nova Scotia, with horse and buggy flat-car services for farmers. Farmers' truck-wagon trains were introduced on the Long Island Railroad, New York, in 1884.

'Piggy-backing' was reintroduced on USA railroads in the early 1950s. It is the transport of containers and motor-truck trailers on specially equipped flat-cars. Technically it is known as 'Trailer-on-Flatcar' (TOFC) or 'Container-on-Flatcar' (COFC). Its success resulted in an eightfold increase from 1955 to 1970 and in 1972 it handled a record number of 2 253 207 trailers.

Freight cars on USA railroads on 31 December 1986 totalled 1 339 453. This included 125 962 box cars; 267 153 hoppers; 151 859 gondolas (open wagons); 177 923 tank cars; 291 489 covered hoppers; 135 653 flat cars and 56 756 refrigerator cars. The average freight car capacity is now 85.8 tons.

The average length of an American freight train over a recent ten-year period was about 70 freight cars and a caboose. In 1929 the average was only 48 cars. Experimental trains have been run with as many as 500 cars. Freight cars vary in length from 7.6 to 38.1 m (25 to 125 ft) and average about 13.7 m (45 ft).

Plans for an Automatic Car Identification (ACI) systems in the USA to facilitate prompt location of freight cars were announced in October 1967. It began in 1970 in conjunction with Tele Rail Automated Information Network (TRAIN) with a central computer at the headquarters of the Association of American Railroads in Washington.

Freightliner services on British Railways were introduced between London and Glasgow on 15 November 1965; London and Manchester on 28 February 1966; London and Liverpool on 13 June 1966; Liverpool and Glasgow on 5 September 1966; Manchester and Glasgow on 12 September 1966; London and Aberdeen on 31 October 1966. By the end of 1966 about 27 000 loaded freightliner containers had been carried.

From 1 January 1969, under provisions in the Transport Act of 1968, Freightliner Services were taken over by Freightliners Limited of which 51 per cent is owned by the National Freight Corporation (see below) and 49 per cent by British Railways Board.

The National Freight Corporation was established under the Transport Act of 1968 to promote and to provide integrated freight services by road and rail in Great Britain and to ensure that goods go by rail where this is efficient and economic. Users of British motorways may well wonder if the Corporation is having any effect.

The British Railways service for carrying new cars between Dagenham, Essex, and Halewood near Liverpool using two-tier 'Cartic' (articulated car carrier) units began on 13 July 1966.

The Self-Discharging Train, developed by Standard Railway Wagon Co. at Heywood, Lancashire, in conjunction with Redland Aggregates in 1988. On straight track, a system of conveyor belts carries the contents of the wagons to the Transfer Car which can discharge the entire payload on either side of the line, with no requirement for expensive permanent unloading facilities. The conveyors are driven by hydraulic motors powered by a series of air-cooled diesel engines.

The first British 100-ton bogie tank wagon for Shell Oil Products was completed on 21 February 1967.

The Harwich-Zeebrugge container service between England and Belgium was introduced on 18 March 1968 using special cellular container ships and wide-span transporter cranes.

In 1988 French Railways changed the name of its freight services from 'SNCF Marchandises' to 'Fret SNCF' to coincide with the introduction of 160 km/h (100 mph) freight trains. During development of the new fleet of 160 km/h freight wagons for these services a train achieved 203.8 km/h (127.4 mph), a world record speed for railway freight vehicles.

The first container shipped from Japan over the Trans-Siberian Railway arrived at Harwich, England, in May 1969 after a journey of 12 231 km (7600 miles).

The heaviest train ever hauled by a single locomotive was probably one of 15 300 tons made up of 250 freight cars stretching for 2.6 km (1.6 miles) at 21 km/h (13.5 mph), by the world's then largest locomotive, Erie Railroad 2-8-8-8-2 No. 5014 *Matt H. Shay*. It was the first of three built in 1914–18 for banking freight trains up the 1 in 67 Susquehanna Incline in Pennsylvania. The engines were withdrawn in 1929.

The longest and heaviest freight train on record was run on 15 November 1967 over the 253 km (157 miles) of the Norfolk & Western RR, between Iaeger, West Virginia, and Portsmouth, Ohio. The 500 coal cars weighed 42 000 tons and stretched about 6.5 km (4 miles). The load was moved by three 3600 hp diesels in front and three in the middle of the train.

The heaviest single piece of freight ever carried by rail was a 32 m (106 ft) tall hydrocracker reactor weighing 549.2 tons, from Birmingham, Alabama, to Toledo, Ohio, on 12 November 1965.

The largest rail-carrying vehicle is a 36-axle 'Schnabel' built by Krupp of West Germany in 1978 for the USA. It is 86.3 m (283 ft 1½ in) long and has a capacity of 850 tonnes. A similar vehicle built by Krupp in March 1981, also for the USA, is 92 m (301 ft 10 in) long, weighs 336 tonnes and has a capacity of 807 tonnes.

The heaviest load carried by British Railways was a 37.2 m (122 ft) long boiler drum weighing 275 tons from Immingham Dock to Killingholme, Humberside, in September 1968.

The heaviest freight trains on British Railways began regular running from Foster Yeoman's Merehead quarry in Somerset to Acton in West London on 16 September 1983. They carried 3300 tonnes of limestone in 43 wagons and were hauled by two '56' class Co-Co diesel-electric

locomotives. The unreliability of the 56s and the later '58' class led Foster Yeoman to order four locomotives from the Electro-Motive Division of General Motors, USA.

The '59' class as they are known were delivered in January 1986 (see p. 145). During trials on 16 February No. 59001 started a 4639 tonne train, **the heaviest on record in Britain**, on wet rails up the 1 in 136 of Savernake bank in Wiltshire. The train included No. 59004 as a dead load, just in case it would not start.

BR is responsible for maintenance and provision of drivers of the locomotives which are the first in private ownership to run on BR in regular service. Already the reliability of the 59s has been proved in their regular haulage of 43 wagons loaded to 102 tonnes each totalling 4386 tonnes.

The record run by a 'Super C' freight in the USA was made in January 1968 on the Atchison, Topeka & Santa Fe Railroad between Corwith and Hobart yards. The 3544 km (2202.1 miles) were covered in 34 h 35 min 40 s at an average speed of 102.4 km/h (63.6 mph).

A 'Super C' freight on the Santa Fe is booked over the 202.5 km (127.2 miles) between Winslow and Gallup in 105 min at an average speed of 117 km/h (72.7 mph). Another takes 175 min over the 330 km (205.2 miles) between Waynoka and Amarillo at an average speed of 113.2 km/h (70.3 mph).

Ton-miles on USA railroads reached a world record of 921 542 000 000 in 1984 and 867 722 000 000 at the end of 1986.

Canada's first remote-controlled mid-train diesel locomotives in regular freight service, using the new 'Robot' radio-command system were first tested on the Canadian Pacific on 16 November 1967. The system is now in regular use in North America.

The longest freight train on record in Canada was Canadian Pacific train of 250 loaded grain cars, powered by seven diesel-electric locomotives, about 4 km (2.5 miles) long. It ran on 22 October 1974 from west of Moose Jaw, Saskatchewan, to Thunder Bay, Ontario, where it had to be divided into three sections to be handled in the yards. It was part of experiments to increase trans-continental line capacity.

The heaviest trains in Australia are the ore trains in northern Western Australia, on the private railway of the Hammersley Iron Pty Ltd. Trains of 210 wagons each carrying 100 tons of ore and weighing a total of 26 000 tons are hauled by three 3000 hp diesel-electric locomotives. The Mount Newman Railway runs trains of 180 wagons weighing 22 000 tons.

In January 1974 the State Rail Authority of New South Wales introduced fast container trains, the first in an interstate network. They carry 40 6 m (20 ft) long containers, and run between Sydney and Brisbane in 17 h.

(The Limited passenger trains take 15 h 20 min.) The new wagons have a maximum speed of 112 km/h (70 mph).

The largest 1067 mm (3 ft 6 in) gauge trains in Australia are in Queensland, Central Division, where 100-wagon coal trains operate regularly. They are equipped with remote control and consist of two diesel-electric locomotives, 50 wagons, three more locomotives, plus 'locotrol' wagon, 50 wagons and brake van. The average overall length is 1609 m (5279 ft); gross weight 7153 tonnes. It is planned to run 120-wagon trains.

The Trans-Europ-Express Marchandises (TEEM) services were introduced in May 1961 to provide fast international goods services at speeds of 85–100 km/h (53–62 mph) on similar lines to the TEE passenger trains. They now operate 114 connections between 20 countries.

MAIL TRAINS

Mail was first carried by train on the Liverpool & Manchester Railway on 11 November 1830.

The carriage of mails by rail in Britain was authorized by Act of Parliament in 1838.

The first travelling post office was an adapted horse-box operated by the Grand Junction Railway between Birmingham and Liverpool on 6 January 1838. Its success led to a decision, on 19 June, to establish the Travelling Post Office (TPO) permanently.

An apparatus for picking up and depositing mail bags from a moving train was invented by Nathaniel Worsdell and patented on 4 January 1838. He tried to sell it to the British Post Office, first for £3500 and later for £1500, but the offers were declined. On 13 March 1838 he refused an offer of £500 for its use.

At the same time Frederick Karstadt, son of a Post Office surveyor, suggested an idea for a similar apparatus. It was designed by John Ramsay, an officer in the 'Missing Letter Branch', and it was tried successfully at Boxmoor on the London & Birmingham Railway on 30 May 1838. The Postmaster General gave instructions for mail exchange standards to be erected between London and Liverpool. Complications in Ramsay's apparatus resulted in an improved device designed by John Dicker, an inspector of mail coaches, in January 1848, but its general use was delayed until Worsdell's patent expired on 4 January 1852. Dicker received £500 for his improvements.

The first special postal train in the world was inaugurated by the Great Western Railway between London and Bristol on 1 February 1855. Passengers were carried from June 1869 when one first class carriage was attached.

The first mail train between London and Aberdeen was inaugurated by the London & North Western and Caledonian railways on 1 July 1885. It did not carry passengers.

Travelling sorting offices and exchange apparatus were discontinued in Britain from 22 September 1940 until 1 October 1945.

Apparatus for exchanging mail-bags on British Railways was last used on 4 October 1971, just north of Penrith.

Today British Rail carries 25 million letters a day, involving 144 travelling post office vehicles operating in 42 daily trains, as well as about 400 vans and 4000 service trains to carry individual bags.

The oldest named train in the world is 'The Irish Mail' running between London and Holyhead in Anglesey, North Wales, where it connects with the sailings to Dun Laoghaire. It began on 31 July 1848 and still runs, though the nameboards have been carried only since 1927. Until the completion of the Britannia Tubular Bridge over the Menai Strait on 18 March 1850, the train ran to Bangor and passengers made part of the journey by coach.

The first railway mail traffic in the USA was on the South Carolina Railroad (now part of the Southern Railway) in November 1831 and on the Baltimore & Ohio in January 1832. Soon after the B & O opened between Baltimore and Washington in 1835 a car was fitted up for carrying mail between the two cities.

From 1855 the Terre Haute & Richmond Railroad (now part of Conrail) west of Indianapolis operated Post Office cars in which mail was sorted and distributed on the journey.

A car equipped for handling overland mail for places west of St Joseph, Missouri, was introduced by the Hannibal & St Joseph Railroad (now part of Burlington Northern) on 28 July 1862.

Mail was first carried by rail in Canada on the Great Western Railway between Niagara and London in 1854, letters being sorted on the train under the supervision of P. Pardon, pioneer mail clerk of North America.

The first North American railway to use regular mail cars was the Grand Trunk Railway of Canada. In 1854 the baggage cars were replaced by specially fitted-up mail cars, at least ten years before such cars appeared elsewhere in North America.

The first permanent railway Post Office car in the USA for picking up, sorting and distributing mail on the journey was put into operation by the Chicago & North Western Railroad on 28 August 1864, between Chicago and Clinton, Iowa.

US railroads carry about 50 per cent of all domestic first class mail and about 80 per cent of all domestic bulk mail.

TRAIN FERRIES

The first wagon ferry was operated by the Monkland & Kirkintilloch Railway, Scotland, on the Forth & Clyde Canal in 1833. A barge was fitted with rails and turnplate.

The first railroad car ferry in the USA, the *Susquehanna*, went into operation on the Susquehanna River between Havre de Grace and Perryville, Maryland, in April 1836. In the winter of 1854 the river froze so solidly that rails were laid on the ice, and between 15 January and 24 February 1378 freight and other cars were hauled across.

The world's first 'train ferry' was designed by Thomas Grainger and was built in 1849 by Robert Napier & Sons on the Clyde. Named *Leviathan*, it ferried goods wagons across the Firth of Forth, Scotland, between Granton and Burntisland.

In 1858 a similar vessel, named *Carrier*, was put on the Tayport–Broughty Ferry crossing near Dundee.

Thomas Bouch is sometimes credited with the designs of these; actually he designed only the loading mechanism.

The Harwich–Zeebrugge train ferry, 150 km (93 miles) between England and Belgium, began operating under Great Eastern Train Ferries Limited on 24 April 1924.

The Dover–Dunkirk train ferry was inaugurated on 14 October 1936. Through trains between London and Paris were operated by the Southern Railway of England, the Northern Railway of France, the Société Anonyme de Navigation Angleterre-Lorraine-Alsace, and the International Sleeping Car Company.

One of the most famous train ferries was the *Baikal* which operated across Lake Baikal in Siberia as a link in the Trans-Siberian Railway. It was launched on 29 July 1899 and entered service in April 1900, combining the duties of train ferry and ice-breaker. It remained in use as a ferry until the Circum–Baikal Railway round the south of the lake was completed in 1904, and it was destroyed in the civil war of 1918–20.

The largest fleet of train and automobile ferries is operated by Danish State Railways (Danske Statsbaner). There are six train ferries and three car ferries, and in addition train ferries operated jointly with the German Federal Railway, German State Railway and Swedish State Railways. The total distance covered is 208 km (129 miles). The speed with which the Danes handle the trains on to and off the ferries is almost unbelievable.

The world's longest train ferry is operated by Italian State Railways from Civitavecchia, 81 km (51 miles) north of Rome, to Golfo Aranci in north-east Sardinia, a distance of 222 km (138 miles). The ferry, established in 1961, carries only railway freight wagons, with passengers and motor cars.

DOCKS AND SHIPS

The earliest railway-owned docks and harbours were:

Carmarthenshire Dock, Llanelli, South Wales, opened in 1806 and owned by the Carmarthenshire Railway, authorized in 1802;

Lydney Dock, Gloucestershire, opened in 1813 by the Severn & Wye Railway Company;

Porthcawl Harbour, South Wales, opened about 1830 by the Duffryn, Llynvi & Porthcawl Railway.

Whitstable Harbour, Kent, opened in 1832 by the Canterbury & Whitstable Railway, was the first built and operated by a railway company using locomotive haulage and providing a passenger and freight service.

The first steamships to be owned by a British railway company appear to be three acquired in 1842 by the London & Blackwall Railway (opened 1841) for operating between Blackwall and Gravesend on the Thames. The ferry was later taken over by private owners.

The first British railway company to operate a sea-crossing service was the Chester & Holyhead Railway which, under the Act of 22 July 1848, operated ships from 1 August 1848 between Holyhead and Kingstown. The service was taken over by the London & North Western Railway from 18 March 1859. Also in 1848 the Hartlepool Dock & Railway Company purchased three steamships to trade between West Hartlepool, Hamburg, Rotterdam and Cronstadt.

The first three Canadian Pacific ships, *Empress of India*, *Empress of Japan* and *Empress of China*, built at Barrow-in-Furness in 1889–90, began operations in spring 1891. The CPR then advertised tours 'Around the World in 80 days', for $610! The name 'Canadian Pacific Steamships Limited' was adopted on 8 September 1921, and on 17 June 1968 it became 'CP Ships' (see chapter 4).

The Lancashire & Yorkshire Railway operated more ships than any other British railway. Twenty-nine (including some owned jointly with the London & North Western Railway) were handed over to the London, Midland & Scottish Railway at the Grouping on 1 January 1923.

The last paddle-steamers operated by British Rail were engaged on the New Holland Pier-Hull ferry across the Humber. *Wingfield Castle*, withdrawn on 15 March 1974, was built by W. Gray & Company of West Hartlepool in 1934, and was 61 m (200 ft) long. It had coal-fired boilers and a triple-expansion three-cylinder engine. *Tattershall Castle* (Gray 1934) was withdrawn in June 1973. *Lincoln Castle* is similar, built by A. & J. Inglis of Glasgow in 1940. These coal-fired steamers had a draught of only 1.4 m (4 ft 6 in) to clear sandbanks at low tide. The service ended when the Humber Bridge was opened in 1981.

The world's highest railway-owned ships are operated by the Southern Railway of Peru, now part of the National Railways of Peru, on Lake Titicaca in the Andes at a height of 3810 m (12 500 ft). The first ship, *Yavari* of 170 tons, was built in 1861 and was carried up from the coastal port of Mollendo in sections on the backs of mules and Indians to Puno on the lake. With the original steam-engine replaced by a diesel it is still in use.

Another ship, the 650 ton *Inca*—69 m (228 ft) long, and 15.2 m (50 ft) beam—was built at Hull, in 1905, sailed out round Cape Horn to Mollendo, was dismantled and transported up the Southern Railway (completed to Puno in 1876) and reassembled on the lake. The flagship of the Titicaca fleet is the *Ollanta* of 850 tons, built in 1929. There are five ships at work on an itinerary of 2173 km (1350 miles). The longest voyage, Puno to Guaqui, takes 12 h for the 193 km (120 miles). Lake Titicaca is the highest navigable water in the world.

For supplying emergency electric power to devastated European cities, during the allied invasion in 1944, the Westinghouse Co. of USA built a number of mobile power stations for running on railways. This photograph shows the first, installed on pedestals to relieve the bogies and track, with eight roof-mounted exhaust stacks for the condensers. Each of these passed 2832 m³ (100 000 ft³) of air per minute. The eight-car power station had an output of 5000 kW.

15

SIGNALLING

On the earliest railways, during the 1830s, traffic was regulated on a time-interval basis. 'Kite' or 'ball' signals were used to indicate when a train should leave a station. The 'kite' consisted of a canvas screen mounted on rings. When spread out it indicated 'danger', and when furled, 'proceed'. The 'ball' signal showed 'line clear' when hoisted to the top of a post. Hence the North American railroad term 'highball' for a clear line. For the opening of the Great Western Railway to Reading, on 30 March 1840, Daniel Gooch (1816–89), the locomotive superintendent, issued an instruction that if the ball at the entrance to Reading station was not visible then the train must not pass it.

Disc-and-crossbar signals were introduced on the GWR in 1840. The disc and crossbar were at right angles to each other. If the crossbar faced the train it indicated 'stop'; turned through 90 degrees the disc showed 'line clear', so giving a positive indication in both positions.

The electric telegraph was first used on a railway on the GWR in 1839. William Fothergill Cooke (qv) and Charles Wheatstone (1802–75), both later knighted, experimented on the London & Birmingham Railway, and they installed it between London (Paddington) and West Drayton. It was extended to Slough in 1843. In 1845 it was instrumental in the arrest at Paddington Station of a murderer, John Tawell, who had boarded a train at Slough.

The telegraph was introduced in the USA by the Baltimore & Ohio Railroad on 24 May 1844. The first use of the telegraph for train dispatching in the USA was at Turner (now Harriman), New York, on 22 September 1851.

The block system with Cooke and Wheatstone's electric telegraph was first used at Clay Cross Tunnel on the North Midland near Chesterfield in Derbyshire in 1841. In the USA it was introduced by Ashbel Welch in 1865.

Detonators were invented by E. A. Cowper in 1841, for giving audible warning in fog or emergency. Clipped to the rail head, they explode with a loud report when a wheel passes over them.

The first record of a semaphore signal appears to be of one erected in 1841 by Charles Hatton Gregory (1817–98) at New Cross on the London & Croydon Railway. From that time its use spread throughout the railways of Britain. It was a three-position signal: horizontal for 'stop',

inclined at 45° for 'caution', and vertical, hidden inside a slot in the post, for 'line clear' when a signal was considered unnecessary. For use at night a rotating lamp showed a red light for 'stop', green for 'caution' and white for 'line clear'. Three-position semaphore signals continued to be in use until 1871. Three-position upper-quadrant semaphore signals appeared in Britain in 1914 and 1924, as described below.

Gregory was also responsible for the construction of a central lever frame with rudimentary interlocking at Bricklayers' Arms Junction, South London, in 1843.

The first railway to use the block system from opening was the Norwich & Yarmouth, opened on 1 May 1844.

Staff working on single lines, to prevent two trains being on a section at once, was introduced on the London & North Western Railway in 1853.

Interlocking of points and signals was developed in France by Vignier who first installed it on the former Western Railway in 1855. The system used wooden wedges which simply jammed the mechanisms of certain lever combinations.

Interlocking was patented in England in 1856 by John Saxby (qv) and it was first installed in that year at Bricklayers' Arms. He installed the first interlocking frame on the London, Brighton & South Coast Railway near Haywards Heath.

The modern form of interlocking, which necessitates the completion of one lever movement before a dependent movement can be begun, was introduced by Austin Chambers at Kentish Town Junction (North London and London & North Western Railways) at Camden Town, north London, in 1859.

The facing point lock and locking bar came into use in the late 1860s, to prevent points being changed while a train was passing over. The locking bar, 15 m (50 ft) long, is held down by the wheels. Interlocking ensures that the points are locked before the appropriate signal can be cleared. The points cannot be changed again until the signal is restored to danger.

Automatic block signals appeared in the USA in 1866.

Track circuiting, in which trains complete an electrical circuit via the rails, was first used in the USA by William

Robinson in 1870. In connection with this, three-position lower-quadrant signals were introduced. Later upper-quadrant arms were used. This type of signal is still in use in the USA.

Somersault signals, pivoted in the centre, were adopted by the Great Northern Railway in 1876 after the collision at Abbott's Ripton on 21 January 1876 caused by a signal being put out of order by frozen snow. They were also used on the Barry, Brecon & Merthyr, Taff Vale and Rhymney railways in Wales and on the Belfast & Northern Counties in Ireland. The signalling firm of Mackenzie & Holland introduced them in Australia and New Zealand and on the East Indian Railway.

Many early signals were very tall so as to be visible against the sky from a great distance to allow for the time taken to stop the train with hand brakes only. Signal arms were always painted red on the fronts and white on the backs. Later a white stripe was added on the front and a black stripe on the back.

Signal lamps were at a lower level to be seen easier at night and to be more accessible. Early lamps burned rape oil and later petroleum, about 91 litres (20 gal) a year. Longer-burning lamps appeared in 1906 and by 1919 oil consumption had been reduced to 36 litres (8 gal) a year.

The distant signal was introduced on the LB & SCR in 1872. It was distinguished by a 'fish tail', or 'V' shaped notch in the end. When horizontal, it indicated 'proceed with caution' to the next stop signal. At 45° it indicated that the entire section ahead was clear. Like the stop signal it was painted red and had the same red and white lights. With the introduction of distant signals three-position signals went out of use.

From 1893 a green light was used to indicate 'line clear' because the white light could be confused with ordinary lights which were then becoming common.

In Britain distant signals showed a red light when horizontal. Yellow lights were in use on distant signals in Italy before 1895 and in 1903 on the Central South African Railways. The Great Central was the first British railway to use yellow lights for distant signals, between London Marylebone and Neasden, in 1917, and during the 1920s they were adopted by other railways. The GN was the first British railway to paint the fronts of distant arms yellow. This too became universal in Britain during the 1920s.

Three-position semaphore signals reappeared and were tried experimentally on the GWR at London Paddington in 1914 and at Wolverhampton in 1923. In 1920 it installed three-position automatic signals on the Ealing and Shepherds Bush line used by Central London trains. They were also tried on the Great Central, Great Northern and South Eastern & Chatham Railways. At night these signals showed a red light for 'stop', yellow for 'caution' and green for 'line clear'. In 1924 the Institution of Railway Signal Engineers recommended yellow as the standard colour for 'caution'. While approving the use of three-aspect colour-light signals, they advised against three-position semaphores, and these were later taken out of use.

'Upper-Quadrant' signal arms were introduced on British railways in the late 1920s, except on the GWR which continued to use lower-quadrant arms. These are still found on the Western Region of BR. Lower-quadrant signals of other companies could still be seen in the 1980s. Upper-quadrant signals were in use in Europe and North America long before they were introduced in Britain.

The first use of telephone communication on USA railroads followed tests on 21 May 1877 at Altoona, Pa.

The electric tablet instrument for operation of single lines was invented in 1878 by Edward Tyer (1830–1912), following the Norwich Thorpe accident on 10 September 1874, in which 25 were killed in a single-line head-on collision on the Great Eastern Railway.

The Regulation of Railways Act enforcing the block system, interlocking of signals and points, and the provision of continuous automatic brakes on passenger trains on British railways, came into operation on 30 August 1889.

The first automatic track-circuit-controlled signalling system on a British main line was installed on the London & South Western Railway between Andover and Grateley, Hampshire, and was brought into use on 20 April 1902. This was a 'normally clear' system. Another system, using 'normally danger' was first used on the North Eastern Railway in 1904 on the main line between Alne and Thirsk Junction.

The first practical application of electro-pneumatic operation of points and signals in Britain was at Bishopsgate, London, on the Great Eastern Railway early in 1899. The first complete electro-pneumatic installation was on the Lancashire & Yorkshire Railway at Bolton in 1904.

Audible cab signalling was introduced by the Great Western Railway, on the double-track Henley Branch on 1 January 1906 and on the single-line Fairford Branch on 1 December when the ordinary distant signals were removed.

The Great Western Railway audible cab signalling was introduced on a main line in 1908, on the four-track section between Slough and Reading, Berkshire, and was extended to London (Paddington) in 1912. About this time the automatic brake application was added, becoming known then as the 'Automatic Train Control' (ATC). Between 1931 and 1937, 4587 km (2850 miles) of route were equipped.

The last GWR ATC equipment was removed from the Birmingham–Stratford-on-Avon line early in 1979 after replacement by BR AWS equipment (mentioned below).

The Hudd Intermittent Inductive ATC Apparatus was installed at 112 distant signal locations on the London–Southend line in 1938. On the L & NER Edinburgh–Glasgow line the system came into use on 13 August 1939.

Electric colour-light signals of the two-aspect type were first used in Britain on the Liverpool Overhead Railway in 1920. Their first use on a main line was in 1923 when three-aspect colour-light signals were installed by the London & North Eastern Railway between London (Marylebone) and Neasden. Four-aspect signals were introduced in 1926 by the Southern Railway between Holborn and Elephant & Castle, London.

Electric interlocking, instead of mechanical, was installed by the Southern Railway at North Kent East Junction in 1929.

The Panel type of power interlocking, now extensively used, was first installed by the London & North Eastern Railway at Thirsk on the main line between York and Darlington in 1933.

Centralized Traffic Control (CTC) was introduced in the USA on a 64 km (40 mile) route at Berwick, Ohio, on 15 July 1927. It has since been used on over 64 300 km (40 000 miles) of track.

First experiments with a train-to-land telephone were made on 20 April 1911 on the Stratford-on-Avon & Midland Junction Railway. The 'wireless inductive' system was known as the 'Railophone'. Although claimed to be a success, it was not developed except, in 1912, as a train control device.

Train-to-land radio telephones were first used on the Canadian National Railways in 1930.

Radio channels exclusively for railways were allocated by the Federal Communications Commission, USA, on 17 May 1945 and the first construction permit was granted on 27 February 1946.

The first train-to-land telephones in the USA were installed in 1947 on the Baltimore & Ohio *Royal Blue*, New York Central *Twentieth-Century Limited* and the Pennsylvania *Congressional*, *Potomac* and *Legislator*.

In Europe, telephones are installed on many trains used by business executives in France and Germany.

The first passenger train in Great Britain with train radio was inaugurated on the 381 mm (15 in) gauge Ravenglass & Eskdale Railway on 28 May 1977, when a special train was run to mark the event. Previously train radio had been used in Great Britain only on private industrial lines. The R & E equipment is similar to that used on the Zillertalbahn in Austria.

Two-way radio communication between drivers and central control was extended throughout the London Transport Bakerloo line in 1977.

The first push-button route-selecting signalling control system in Britain was brought into operation by London Transport at Ealing Broadway on 29 November 1952.

London Transport's last electro-pneumatic semaphore signal was removed from service on 21 November 1953.

The largest and busiest signalling centres in Great Britain are at Motherwell, London Bridge, Trent, Clapham Junction and Victoria, London.

Motherwell Signalling Centre near Glasgow was completed in 1973. It replaced 67 mechanical signal-boxes and one power box (Newton) and now controls 200 km (124 miles) of route with 555 signals and 329 point machines, the largest control area in Britain. This includes 137 km (85 miles) of the main London–Glasgow line extending from Kirkpatrick, 19 km (12 miles) north of Carlisle to Cambuslang, 8 km (5 miles) south of Glasgow. An average of 500 trains pass through Motherwell station every 24 h.

London Bridge Signalling Centre, although controlling only 75.6 km (47 miles) of route, handles over four times the volume of traffic handled by Motherwell.

Trent Signalling Centre between Nottingham and Derby controlling 119 km (74 miles) of route, 336 km (209 miles) of track, with 613 signalled routes, handles the most traffic of any in Great Britain. At any time there are at least 40 trains displayed on the console. About 250 passenger and 300 through freight trains pass through daily in addition to freight workings north of Toton and trip workings to many collieries.

Clapham Junction Signalling Centre south of London was completed in 1983. It controls 430 km (267 miles) of track on the approaches to Holborn Viaduct, Blackfriars and Victoria stations from as far out as Epsom, Croydon, Sevenoaks and Longfield. It replaces 36 manual boxes at a cost of £35 000 000 with two signal panels, each 22 m (72 ft) long. Its area includes 70 stations.

Victoria Signalling Centre, London, commissioned in 1984, covers the widest range on BR. It replaces 37 manual signal boxes and covers a complex network of 180 route-km (112 miles) and 434 track-km (270 miles). There are nearly 1400 individual route settings.

It is planned to control most Inter-City and important freight routes of BR from about 75 signalling centres.

British Rail's Automatic Warning System (AWS) for use with non-electric traction was approved by the Minister of Transport on 30 November 1956. It now covers 8500 route-km (5280 miles).

The first automatic level-crossing barriers on British Railways were installed at Spath Level Crossing near Uttoxeter, Staffordshire, on the now-abandoned Churnet Valley line, and came into use on 6 February 1961. Following a further 130 installations in 1982–3 there were 640 automated level crossings on BR. Also 182 were remotely controlled by closed-circuit television.

Railway accidents and failures are classified under four headings:

1 Train accidents on or affecting passenger lines;
2 Movement accidents, to people injured by moving railway vehicles, excluding those in train accidents;
3 Non-movement accidents, to people on railway premises, not caused by movement of railway vehicles;
4 Failures of rolling stock, track and structures which could, but which may not, cause train accidents.

Under the Regulation of Railways Act, 1871, and the **Railway Employment (Prevention of Accidents) Act, 1900**, all train accidents on passenger railways in Britain and all accidents on railway premises resulting in injury or death must be reported to the Minister of Transport in accordance with the **Railways (Notice of Accidents) Order, 1965**. Under these Acts the Minister is empowered to order an inquiry into any of the reported accidents. The 1871 Act requires that all reports of accident inquiries are published.

No passengers were killed in train accidents on British Railways in 1949, 1954, 1956, 1966, 1976, 1977, 1980, 1982 and 1985. In 1986 accidents on BR caused the following deaths and injuries:

	Train accidents	Movement accidents
Passengers killed	8	24
Passengers injured	342	2346
Railway staff killed	5	8
Railway staff injured	137	80
Others killed	14	9
Others injured	32	17
Trespassers and suicides killed		325

Death rates per billion travel-km, 1986

Rail	0.54
Bus/Coach passenger	0.57
Car occupant	5.50
Two-wheel motor vehicle user	130.00

Although the number of rail passengers represents only a small portion of the population, almost the whole of which uses the roads, it is salutary to make some comparisons. The cost of a fatal accident on the roads in 1986 was £299 840 and of a serious injury £18 182. The total cost to the taxpayer of road accidents in Great Britain in 1986 was £3 800 000 000. There were 14 773 accidents involving heavy goods vehicles causing 883 deaths. In most of these accidents the drivers of the goods vehicles escaped uninjured, or with minor injuries. An average of about three railway underbridges are damaged every day by lorries carrying high loads. Many of these are unreported and the damage has to be repaired by BR. Much of this traffic could be carried by rail with greatly reduced cost to the nation.

Many accidents on BR are caused each year by malicious acts by the public. In 1980, for example, one major derailment of a sleeping car train and two minor derailments were caused by obstructions placed on the track.

The earliest recorded fatal railway movement accident occurred on Wednesday, 5 December 1821, when a carpenter, David Brook, was walking home from Leeds along the Middleton Railway in a blinding sleet storm. He failed to see or hear an approaching train of coal wagons drawn by one of the Blenkinsop/Murray engines and he was run over and fatally injured.

On the opening day of the Liverpool & Manchester Railway, on 15 September 1830, William Huskisson, Member of Parliament for Liverpool, was run over by the Stephensons' *Rocket* at Parkside near Newton le Willows. His thigh was fractured and he died later at Eccles near Manchester. He was taken there on the engine *Northumbrian*, driven by George Stephenson who, on the journey, established a world speed record of 58 km/h (36 mph).

The first passenger-train accident in the USA occurred on 9 November 1833 on the Camden & Amboy Railroad between Spotswood and Hightown, New Jersey. One carriage overturned and 12 of its 24 passengers were seriously injured.

The first British railway accident to be investigated by an inspecting officer of the Board of Trade was at Howden on the Hull & Selby Railway on 7 August 1840, when a casting fell from a wagon and derailed a mixed passenger/ goods train, causing six deaths.

The first large railway accident was in France on 8 May 1842. A 15-coach express from Versailles to Paris crashed when the axle of one of the two engines broke and several coaches piled on top of it. Locked compartment doors prevented people from escaping and 48 were burned to death. This ended the locking of train doors in France.

Canada's first major railway collision occurred on the Great Western Railway, west of Chatham, in 1854 when a train of ballast for the track collided with a passenger train, killing 47 people.

The worst railway accident in Canada was on the Grand Trunk Railway at Beloeil, Quebec, on 29 June 1864 when 99 people were killed. This stimulated safety-consciousness and led to the introduction of standard operating procedures on Canadian railways.

The first fatal railway accident in Australia was at Lidcombe, a suburb of Sydney, on 10 July 1858. A train took a curve too fast and was derailed, killing two and injuring 13.

Charles Dickens escaped with a shaking when he was involved in the derailment at Staplehurst, Kent, on the South Eastern Railway, on 9 June 1865. Ten people were killed when the train ran on to a viaduct where repairs were being carried out. He never fully recovered and he died on 9 June 1870, exactly 5 years later.

The only British railway disaster in which there were no survivors was on 28 December 1879 when the Tay Bridge collapsed in a gale while a train was crossing. All 73 passengers and crew of five were drowned. Some bodies were never recovered. (See 'Tay Bridge', chapter 6.)

'The Great Train Wreck' in Texas on 15 September 1896 was deliberately contrived as a public entertainment by William G. Crush, general passenger agent of the Missouri, Kansas & Texas Railway, or the 'Katy' as the MK & T was known. The event was widely advertised and drew a crowd of about 30 000 to witness the event, greatly enhancing Katy passenger receipts. At the appointed time two old empty trains were dispatched towards each other from a distance, but the collision and boiler explosions hurled debris into the crowds of spectators lining the valley on both sides, causing a sad toll of dead and injured.

Britain's worst rail disaster occurred at Quintinshill near Gretna Green, just north of Carlisle, on 22 May 1915. Signalling irregularities led to the overlooking of a train standing on the wrong line. A military special was accepted and it collided with the stationary train. The 195 m (213 yd) long train was telescoped to 61 m (67 yd). Fifty-three seconds later an express from the other direction ploughed into the wreckage. Fire added to the horror and destruction in which 227 lives were lost.

The worst fully recorded railway disaster occurred at Saint-Michel-de-Maurienne in France on 12 December 1917. A packed troop train carrying 1025 soldiers in 19 Italian carriages weighing 526 tons behind a single locomotive, PLM 4-6-0 No. 2592, was ordered away from Modane at the north end of the Mont Cenis Tunnel at about 22.00. The maximum permitted load for this locomotive was 144 tons. Only the first three coaches had Westinghouse continuous brakes and the rest had only hand brakes. Driver Louis Girard was unwilling to proceed but was unable to act against military commands. On the 10 miles of 1 in 33 (15 km of 3 per cent) falling grade the train ran out of control, brakes became red-hot and set fire to the coaches, the engine became derailed, breaking the coupling with the train, and finally the entire train was wrecked at 150 km/h (91 mph) on a curve at Saint-Michel-de-Maurienne. Of the 543 dead which could be accounted for in the wreckage, 135 could not be identified. The driver miraculously survived and was freed of all blame.

The most recent serious railway accident occurred in Ethiopia on the night of 14 January 1985, near Awash on the metre-gauge single-track main line about 190 km (120 miles) east of Addis Ababa. According to reports, a train from Djibuti to Addis Ababa carrying about 1000 passengers ran on to a curving bridge at too high a speed and was derailed. Part of it fell into a ravine causing 392 deaths and 370 serious injuries.

This caused more deaths than any railway accident since 2 March 1944, when 509 people were killed by fumes and 60 suffered from smoke poisoning while stealing a ride on a freight train which stalled in Armi tunnel near Salerno, Italy.

In the collision at Pompone, France, on 23 December 1933, 230 were killed and over 500 injured. Because of fog the Paris–Strasbourg express, behind 4–8–2 No. 241.017, was running about an hour late. The train over-ran signals and crashed into the rear of the Paris–Nancy express which was about 2 hours late. The failure of an automatic device emphasized the importance of an alert observance of signals at all times.

The first serious accident to an electric train in Britain was at Hall Road on the Liverpool–Southport line of the Lancashire & Yorkshire Railway on 27 July 1905. A signalman's error led to a collision in which 21 people were killed.

England's worst railway disaster was at Harrow & Wealdstone Station on the London Midland Region on 8 October 1952. An express from Perth, running 80 min late in patchy fog, failed to stop at signals and ran at 90–95 km/h (56–59 mph) into the rear of a crowded local train at the platform. Almost immediately a double-headed express travelling northwards at the same speed crashed into the wreckage. The death toll was 112.

This accident almost certainly would have been prevented by automatic train control such as was in use on the Western Region or the Automatic Warning System (AWS) now installed on most British main lines.

At Lewisham in South London, on the evening of 4 December 1957, an express hauled by a 4–6–2 steam locomotive ran past a red signal in dense fog and crashed into a stationary electric suburban train. The accident demolished the pier of an overbridge which fell onto the train

before it had stopped. Eighty-eight people were killed and 109 injured. Although the blame was placed on the driver, the design of the Bulleid 4–6–2 with its wide, flat boiler casing and narrow cab was considered a contributory cause, by restricting the driver's vision.

The worst accident on a London 'tube' railway occurred on Friday, 28 February 1975 when the 08.37 train from Drayton Park ran unbraked through Moorgate Station on the Highbury Branch and crashed into the end of a blind tunnel. The front 14 seats were compressed into a space of 61 cm (2 ft). A total of 43 died and 77 were seriously injured. The rescue operation was the most difficult ever undertaken on a British railway, in temperatures often exceeding 49°C (120°F). The last of the bodies was not recovered until late on Tuesday, 4 March.

The cause of the accident was the failure of Motorman Newson to stop the train. The reason for this could not be discovered. The station is now used by the new Great Northern Electric trains and is protected by a severe speed restriction and an automatic trip device.

The oddest collision on record occurred in February 1913 on the Memphis Branch of the Louisville & Nashville Railroad, USA, during a flood. A freight train collided in the dark with the shallow-draught packet-boat *Lochie S* which

England's worst railway accident; the double collision at Harrow & Wealdstone station on 8 October 1952. The Perth to London express on the far tracks over-ran signals and crashed into the rear of a suburban train standing in the station. Almost immediately a London to Liverpool express, hauled by 4–6–0 No. 45637 *Windward Islands* and 4–6–2 No. 46202 *Princess Anne*, ploughed into the wreckage. These two engines can be seen overturned. This accident would almost certainly have been prevented by the Automatic Warning System now used on all principal routes. It was the loss of No. 46202 which led to the construction of No. 71000 *Duke of Gloucester*, Britain's last express steam locomotive.

was sailing above the tracks at Cumberland, Texas. No one was injured, but the responsibility for damage was never properly settled.

A locomotive that disappeared was 0–6–0 No. 115 of the Furness Railway, built by Sharp Stewart & Company in 1881. On 22 October 1892 at about 08.16 it was shunting at Lindal, Cumbria, an area of extensive iron-ore mines, when the ground gave way beneath it and the engine began to sink in. The crew, Driver Postlethwaite and Fireman Robinson, jumped clear and by 14.15 the engine had disappeared completely. It fell to a depth of 61 m (200 ft), beyond recovery, and the hole was filled in.

One of Britain's most curious railway disasters was at Swinton near Manchester on 28 April 1953 when the roof of Clifton Hall (Black Harry) Tunnel collapsed under a filled-in shaft. A pair of semi-detached houses above collapsed into the crater, causing five deaths. The tunnel was on the Patricroft–Clifton branch of the London & North Western Railway and was opened on 2 February 1850. The accident led to a review of all old tunnel records.

Grade crossing collisions cause the largest number of deaths on railroads in the USA, amounting to about two-thirds of the total. There are about 180 000 unguarded grade, or level, crossings in the USA where about 1500 are killed and 3700 injured annually.

The worst level (grade) crossing accident in Britain was at Hixton, Staffordshire, on the Colwich–Stone section of the electrified main line from London to Manchester, on 6 January 1968. A transporter loaded with a 120 ton transformer was crossing at 3.2 km/h (2 mph) when the automatic barriers closed. The 11.30 Manchester–Euston express behind electric locomotive E3009 arrived at 113 km/h (70 mph) before the crossing was cleared and struck the transformer, hurling it 6 m (20 ft). There were 11 deaths and 45 serious injuries. The transporter was being escorted by the police who had failed to telephone the Colwich signalman for permission to cross with an exceptional load.

The 140-page report published by the Ministry of Transport made it clear that the designers of the barrier crossings, British Railways management, the police, and everyone else concerned were heavily to blame for this appalling accident. The result was a complete review of the operation of all half-barrier level crossings, but their safety still depends on the care and alertness of the road user.

On the New South Wales Government Railways, during a period of 14 years there was not one fatal passenger accident on any part of the system. Unfortunately, in 1977 they had **the worst railway accident in Australia**. On 17 January a crowded commuter train from Blue Mountain to Sydney crashed into a bridge support at Granville near Sydney and a concrete span collapsed on to the train, resulting in 80 people being killed and 81 injured.

USA statistics show that railway travel is the safest of all. In terms of fatalities per 100 000 000 passenger miles (161 000 000 km) the rate for the railroads is 0.1; for internal air services 0.3; for buses 0.24; and for cars and taxis 2.39.

RUNAWAYS

The first serious passenger-train runaway in Britain was on the Oxford, Worcester & Wolverhampton Railway at Round Oak near Wolverhampton on 23 August 1858, when part of a heavy passenger train broke away and ran back into the following passenger train. Fourteen lives were lost.

A similar accident occurred at Helmshore, Lancashire, on the Lancashire & Yorkshire Railway on 4 September 1860 when 11 people died.

These led to experiments with continuous brakes, and the eventual adoption by law of automatic continuous brakes. (See 'Brakes', chapter 11.)

The most serious runaway in British railway history occurred on the Great Northern Railway of Ireland at Armagh on 12 June 1889, when the rear half of an overloaded excursion train, which had failed on a gradient and had been divided, ran back and collided with a following train, killing 80 passengers. The train had continuous but non-automatic brakes.

This accident led to the **Regulation of Railways Act** of 1889 (see chapter 4) which gave power to the Board of Trade to order absolute block working on passenger lines (only one train in a section at one time), automatic continuous brakes on passenger trains, and the interlocking of points and signals.

The British unbraked freight train was the cause of many runaways. The worst was at Abergele on the London & North Western Railway in North Wales on 20 August 1868, when some wagons being irregularly shunted on the main line ran away and collided with a passenger train, causing 33 deaths.

On 12 December 1870, at Stairfoot near Barnsley on the Manchester, Sheffield & Lincolnshire Railway, a similar runaway killed 15 passengers.

These accidents led to the installation of trap points to derail runaways on falling gradients.

A record run of 100 miles (161 km) was made on the Chicago, Burlington & Quincy Railroad east of Denver on 26 March 1884 when a wind of tremendous force ripped off the roundhouse roof at Akron and set eight coal cars on the move. They ran on to the main line where the wind drove them along at speeds up to 64 km/h (40 mph). One downgrade stretch of 32 km (20 miles) was covered in 18 min. At Benkelman, 153 km (95 miles) from Akron, a freight engine gave chase and in a few miles was coupled to the cars and they were brought under control after covering 100 miles in less than 3 h.

BREAKDOWN, OR WRECKING, CRANES

'Accident cranes', known in North America as 'wrecking cranes' and more commonly as 'big hooks', and on the Canadian Pacific as 'auxiliary cranes', were originally hand-powered machines with a lifting capacity of 5–10 tons. As the weight of locomotives and rolling stock increased, steam-power became necessary, but many British companies were unwilling to lay out capital on such equipment. The London & North Western, one of

Britain's biggest railways and the largest joint stock corporation in the world, had no steam accident cranes until 1910.

The first steam accident cranes on a British railway were self-propelling machines of 5 tons capacity on four-wheeled trucks built for the Midland Railway by Appleby Brothers, London, in 1874–5.

Five years later the same firm built some of 10 tons capacity for the London & South Western Railway.

For many years the world's most powerful railway crane was one built for the Norfolk & Western Railroad, USA, by Industrial Works (later Industrial Brownhoist) of Bay City, Michigan, in 1912. It could lift a load of 134 tons (150 short tons) at a radius of 5.2 m (17 ft).

The most powerful British steam breakdown cranes are ten of 75 tons capacity built by Cowans Sheldon & Company Limited, Carlisle, and completed in 1962. Two more were built with diesel-power.

The world's most powerful railway breakdown crane has a lifting capacity of 226 800 kg (223.2 tons) (500 000 lb), at a radius of 5.3 m (17 ft 6 in). It was built by Cowans Sheldon & Company Limited, Carlisle, in 1960 for the Quebec Cartier Mining Company of Canada. It is powered by a Rolls-Royce 225 bhp super-charged oil engine through a hydraulic torque converter. It is carried on two three-axle trucks on standard gauge, and is designed to operate in temperatures as low as −51°C (−60°F).

In 1961 Cowans Sheldon supplied the same Canadian company with a wrecking crane of 136 080 kg (300 000 lb) or 134 tons capacity at 5.3 m (17 ft 6 in) radius. Both cranes can negotiate curves of 45.7 m (150 ft) radius.

Cranes of similar, though not greater, capacity have been built in the USA.

SNOW-PLOUGHS

The rotary snow-plough was invented by J. W. Elliott, a dentist of Toronto, Canada, who patented a 'compound revolving snow shovel' in 1869. The idea was not taken up, however.

The first rotary snow-plough was built by Leslie Brothers of Orangeville, Otario, Canada, in 1883–4 and was tested by the Canadian Pacific Railway. Its success led to an improved design constructed in 1887 by the Danforth Cooke Company (which became part of the American Locomotive Company in 1901) and which was put into operation on the Union Pacific Railroad.

Timber trestle in the River Kwai, from a Nam Tok–Bangkok train, Thailand. The pillar on the left, dated 1945, is a grim reminder of the thousands of British and Australian prisoners who died in the construction of the Burma–Siam Railway under the Japanese. Photographed in September 1985.

RAILWAYS AND THE ARTS

RAILWAYS IN LITERATURE

The first railway to be mentioned in English literature was Ralph Allen's wagonway at Bath (see p. 2). **M. Chandler** in his poem 'A Description of Bath' (1733) writes of:

> 'The new-made Road, and wonderful Machine,
> Self moving downward from the Mountain's Height,
> A Rock it's Burden of a Mountain's Weight!'

Many later English poets have been inspired by railways. The earliest poem by an important writer is 'Steamboats, Viaducts and Railways' by **William Wordsworth** (1770–1850), No. 42 of his *Itinerary Poems* (1833). Two of his poems are anti-railway: 'On the projected Kendal and Windermere Railway', and 'Proud were ye, Mountains', Nos. 45 and 46 of his *Miscellaneous Sonnets* (1844).

No fears were entertained by **Charles Mackay** (1814–89) whose poem 'Railways' (1836) begins:

> 'No poetry in railways!' foolish thought
> Of a dull brain, to no fine music wrought.

The second verse is positively triumphant:

> Lay down your rails, ye nations, near and far –
> Yoke your full trains to steam's triumphal car;
> Link town to town; unite in iron bands
> The long-estranged and oft embattled lands.

Robert Louis Stevenson (1850–94) wrote two railway poems, 'From a Railway Carriage' from *A Child's Garden of Verses*, and 'The Iron Steed'. In conjunction with his stepson, **Lloyd Osbourne**, he wrote a novel *The Wrong Box* in which a railway accident and a joker changing the labels on packages in a guard's van result in some exquisite situations.

Thomas Hardy (1840–1928) left us two railway poems: 'Midnight on the Great Western' and 'Faintheart in a Railway Train', as also did **Siegfried Sassoon** (1886–1967), 'A Local Train of Thought', a homely picture of a branch-line train, and 'Morning Express', a vivid account of a train's arrival and departure.

This poem, and 'From a Railway Carriage' by R. L. Stevenson, was set to music by Arthur Butterworth as part of his *Trains in the Distance*, performed at the NRM, York, on 13 June 1976.

In the course of a journey from Oxford to Worcester on 23 June 1914 the train in which **Edward Thomas** (1878–1917) was a passenger stopped at Adlestrop, Gloucestershire. The outcome was his famous poem:

Adlestrop

Adlestrop Station.

> Yes. I remember Adlestrop –
> The name, because one afternoon
> Of heat the express-train drew up there
> Unwontedly. It was late June.
>
> The steam hissed. Some one cleared his throat.
> No one left and no one came
> On the bare platform. What I saw
> Was Adlestrop – only the name
>
> And willows, willow-herb, and grass,
> And meadowsweet, and haycocks dry,
> No whit less still and lonely fair
> Than the high cloudlets in the sky.
>
> And for that minute a blackbird sang
> Close by, and round him, mistier,
> Farther and farther, all the birds
> Of Oxfordshire and Gloucestershire.

Thomas was killed in World War I, as was **Rupert Brooke** (1867–1915) whose two poems 'Dawn (from the train between Bologna and Milan, second class)' and 'The Night Journey', both describe train journeys through the night, the first in a hot and humid compartment with two Germans who 'sweat and snore', the second forward-looking and purposeful.

'Railway Note' by **Edmund Blunden** (1896–1974) gives a vivid picture of a journey in mid-winter. 'Night Mail' by **Wystan Hugh Auden** (1907–73) was written to accompany a Post Office documentary film of that name. Its galloping rhythm and energy speed us along while pointing to the all-embracing range of the postal freight. These poets portrayed the railway journey simply as part of life's experience. **John Betjeman** (1906–84) loved railways; for him they were a part of life itself. One of his poems, 'Great Central' describes in verse a journey from Sheffield to Banbury. His book *London's Historic Railway Stations* (1972) should be compulsory reading for all those concerned with stations and their design.

Hans Christian Andersen (1805–75), the Danish fairy-tale author, wrote a remarkable piece in *Le Figaro* describing trains and train journeys. This was in 1840, seven years before the first railway was opened in Denmark, and was one of the earliest pieces of railway writing by a fiction author.

Railway fiction is mainly in the form of the short story. In 1845 'Tilbury Tramp' (C. J. Lever) (1806–72) published *Tales of the Trains*, five short stories based on train journeys.

William Makepeace Thackeray (1811–63) has left us *Jeames on the Gauge Question*, a short story or a journey from London to Cheltenham with changes of carriage at Swindon and Gloucester and the confusion arising from the transfer of 93 packages and a baby.

Arthur Quiller Couch (1863–1944) produced several works containing references to railways: *Delectable Duchy* (1893) in his native Cornwall, *The Destruction of Didcot* (1908) and *Pipes in Arcady* on a Cornish branch line, reprinted in *Sixteen On* edited by Charles Irving (1957).
One of the 'Reginald' stories, *The Mouse* (1930) by **H. H. Munro** (Saki) (1870–1916), takes place in a railway carriage. D. H. Lawrence (1885–1930) wrote a short story called *Tickets please*, based on a journey on the Nottingham–Ripley street tramway, and L. A. G. Strong (1896–1958) wrote two, *Departure* (1929) at a country station, and *The Gates* (1931) about a crossing keeper.

Railways and crime have often been linked in author's minds. Although railway journeys are frequently mentioned in the 'Sherlock Holmes' stories of **Arthur Conan Doyle** (1859–1930), in only one, *The Adventures of the Bruce Partington Plans* (1924), do railways feature. In this the Metropolitan Railway forms an important part of the story. 'The Lost Special' from his *Round the Fire Stories* (1908) describes the events leading to the total disappearance of a train.
Three of the 'Dr Thorndike' stories by **R. Austin Freeman** (1862–1943) have railway settings, or railway incidents form an essential part of the plot: *The Moabite Cipher*, *The Blue Sequin* and *The Case of Arthur Brodski* (1928).

The Mysterious Death on the Underground Railway by **Baroness Orczy** (1865–1947) is another example of a crime story where the railway setting is an important ingredient. **F. W. Crofts** (1879–1957) wrote several crime stories with railway settings: *Crime on the Footplate, Death of a Train, Death on the Way, The Level Crossing, The Mystery of the Sleeping Car Express* and *Sir John Magill's Last Journey*.

Three of the well-known crime books by Dame Agatha Christie (1890–1976) have railway settings: *Mystery of the Blue Train* (1928); *Murder on the Orient Express* (1934) and *4.50 from Paddington* (1957). *Murder on the Orient Express* was filmed by EMI Films in 1974, using French National Railways '230G' Class 4–6–0 No. 353 and four coaches restored by the Wagons Lits Company to conform to the 1930s period.

Novels with railway settings tend to be written mainly by authors with particular interest in railways. However, in his novel of the 'Hungry Forties', *Sybil* (1845), **Benjamin Disraeli** (1804–81) makes considerable references to railways.

Charles Dickens (1812–70) was fascinated by railways and they figure prominently in many of his works. In *Dombey and Son* (1848) Chapters 6 and 15 contain accounts of the London & Birmingham Railway; *Our Mutual Friend* (1864–5) refers to the London & Greenwich and the Great Western railways and Paddington Station, not entirely accurately, and in a postscript Dickens describes his experiences in the Staplehurst accident in 1865 (see 'Accidents'). *The Uncommercial Traveller* refers to railways in Kent. *The Mystery of Edwin Drood* (unfinished at his death in 1870) makes reference to the South Eastern Railway. Of his other works, his story *A Flight* is based on a journey from London Bridge to Folkestone. Four of the 'Mugby Junction' stories (1866) are by Dickens: *Barbox Brothers; Barbox Brothers & Co.; Main Line: the Boy at Mugby;* and *No. 1 Branch Line: the Signalman*. These stories came to be written as a result of an enforced stop at Rugby Junction on the London & North Western Railway, following a fire in the coach in which Dickens was travelling. Finally, *Lazy Tour of Two Idle Apprentices* contains references to the LNWR in the Chester district.
Besides his terrible experience in the Staplehurst disaster, Dickens had other railway adventures. During a journey to Holyhead, *en route* for Ireland, his train was snowed up near Bangor for four hours, with no train heating. On one of his American journeys, between Rochester and Albany, he was caught in one of the worst floods on record when nearly 482 km (300 miles) of line were inundated. After he had spent an enforced night at Utica the railway company got him to Albany through floods and floating blocks of ice, taking ten hours for a journey normally taking three.

The great American writer of Western thrillers, Zane Grey (1872–1939) gave a vivid picture of the construction of the Union Pacific Railroad in *The Roaring UP Trail*

(1918) describing the experiences of a young engineer and a girl.

An even better story on the same subject is *The Mountain Divide* (1912) by **Frank Hamilton Spearman** (1859–1937). Another UP book is *Building the Pacific Railway* (1919) by **Edwin L. Sabin**.

Probably the most successful railroad novel written in the USA is *The Big Ivy* (1955) by **James McCague**.

Edith Nesbit (Bland) (1858–1924) produced one of the best loved of all railway stories, *The Railway Children* (1906) in which three children prevent a train from running into a landslip. A successful film version was made on the Keighley & Worth Valley Railway in Yorkshire. In *Hatter's Castle* (1931) by **A. J. Cronin** (1896–1981) the villain, Denis, perishes in the Tay Bridge disaster. This made a dramatic sequence in the film version, in which the deceived heroine had left the train at a signal stop.

'**Somerville & Ross**' (Edith OEnone Somerville, 1858–1949, and Violet Florence Martin, 1862–1915) gave us a delightfully humorous short story, *Poisson d'Avril*, in *Further Experiences of an Irish R.M.* (Resident Magistrate), published in 1908, describing an Irish cross-country train journey.

Bhowani Junction (1954) by **John Masters** (1914–83) is a vivid portrayal of the Indian railway scene and of the Anglo-Indian community during World War II. Some readers, however, may find the sensuous aspect somewhat overdrawn. This has also been made into a film.

Hamilton Ellis (1909–87), the well-known railway writer and artist, produced two novels about railways: *The Grey Men* (1939), a mystery story on the West Highland Railway, and *Dandy Hart* (1947) set in southern England in the period 1830–60. In *The Engineer Corporal* (1940) he gives a vivid account of 'The Great Locomotive Chase' during the American Civil War. This story is also told in 'The Railway Raid in Georgia' from *A Book of Escapes and Hurried Journeys* (1925) by **John Buchan** (1875–1940).

L. T. C. Rolt (1910–74), best known for his biographies of Telford, the Stephensons and Brunel, wrote a novel *Winterstoke* (1954) set in an imaginary Midlands town in the nineteenth century during the financing and construction of rival railway projects.

The first, and probably only, novel to be dedicated to a railway was *Blue Eyes and Grey* (1928) by Baroness Orczy. It was dedicated 'To the President, Directors and all connected with that marvellous organization the Canadian Pacific Railway'. The romance was based on the author's CPR journey in 1925.

It is in the form of the essay that railway literature achieves its greatest profusion. Many, written as articles for periodicals, of an amusing, light-hearted or ephemeral nature, can hardly be classed as 'literature', but there are some by **Paul Jennings** (b 1918), **Hamilton Ellis** and others which can be read repeatedly with enjoyment. Among well-known writers who have given the railway consideration in essays are **Robert Lynd** (1879–1949)

who wrote three: *In the Train, Railway Stations I have loved,* and *Trains*; **A. A. Milne** (1882–1956) who gave us *A Train of Thought* (1921); and **J. B. Priestley** (1894–1984), *Man Underground* (1932) in which he philosophizes on travelling beneath London.

An example of factual literature on railways is *Across the Plains* (1892) by Robert Louis Stevenson. **Pierre Berton** of Canada (b 1920) has written two volumes on the building of the Canadian Pacific Railway which contain fine historical writing and deserve consideration as literature: *The National Dream, The Great Railway, 1871–1881* (1970) and *The Last Spike, The Great Railway 1881–1885* (1971).

The railway does not figure prominently in drama. John Galsworthy (1867–1933) wrote a one-act comedy in three scenes, *The Little Man* (1915) set on railway platforms and in a railway carriage compartment. Perhaps the best-known play is *The Ghost Train* (1925) by **Arnold Ridley** (1896–1984) which has been made into a film on several occasions. He also wrote *The Wrecker* (1927). In *Brief Encounter* by **Noël Coward** (1899–1973) part of the action is set in a railway station. The most completely 'railway' play is probably *The Knotty*, first produced by the Victoria Theatre, Stoke-on-Trent, in 1966, a musical documentary outlining the history of the North Staffordshire Railway.

RAILWAYS AND ART

The earliest railway pictures of any value are those produced as series of prints made during the construction or soon after the opening of some of England's earliest main lines. Chief among these are:

The Liverpool & Manchester Railway, a series of coloured aquatints by **Thomas Talbot Bury** (1811–77), published by Ackermann & Company in 1830. Rudolf Ackermann lived from 1764 to 1834.

The Newcastle & Carlisle Railway, a series of drawings by **James Wilson Carmichael**, a marine artist (1800–68), published in Newcastle in 1837 and reprinted in 1970.

The London & Birmingham Railway and **The Great Western Railway**, two series of hand-coloured lithographs by **John Cooke Bourne** (1814–96), produced in 1837–9. The GWR pictures were reprinted in 1969 and the L & B in 1970. Bourne's view of Camden Shed, shown here, illustrates the use of stub points.

The Manchester & Leeds Railway, a series of lithographs by **Arthur Fitzwilliam Tait** (1819–1905), published in both black and white and colour in 1845 and reprinted in 1972. Tait was primarily a landscape and animal painter. He emigrated to the USA in 1850.

All these pictures, besides being works of art in themselves, possessed the additional advantage of technical accuracy and are valuable historical documents.

The first great artist to be inspired by the railway was **Joseph Mallord William Turner** (1775–1851) whose famous painting *Rain, Steam and Speed, the Great Western Railway* (1844) shows a 'Firefly' class locomotive on a train crossing Brunel's Maidenhead Bridge towards Reading. It is in oil on canvas 908 × 1219 mm (35¾ × 48 in). (National Gallery, London.)

David Cox (1783–1859), an English landscape-painter and one of the greatest English water-colourists, was inspired by Turner's painting to paint his *Wind, Rain and Sunshine* (1845) which recaptures some of the atmospheric effects but is really a landscape with a small train in the background. He also painted *The Night Train* about 1857, another landscape with a small train motif. (Both Birmingham City Art Gallery.)

Adolf Friedrich Erdmann von Menzel (1815–1905), a German historical and genre painter and illustrator, produced *Die Berlin–Potsdamer Bahn* in 1847. The curve of the railway is an important element in the composition, and a train is shown. (Berling Nationalgalerie.)

Gustave Doré (1832–83) in his sketches of London published in 1872 (reprinted 1971) included two showing railways. *Ludgate Hill* shows a street scene which makes modern traffic appear insignificant. Over the bridge above a train of the London, Chatham & Dover Railway is entering the Ludgate Hill Station. In *Over London by Rail* we look through an arch of a railway viaduct along a row of cramped, overcrowded tenements to another viaduct over which a train is passing.

In 1871 the French landscape painter **Camille Pissarro** (1830–1903), on a visit to London with Claude Monet (see below), by way of escaping from the Franco-Prussian War, produced the painting which has been known as *Penge Station, Upper Norwood* (Courtauld Institute Galleries, University of London). The picture shows an early signal and a train approaching through a cutting in a bright, spring-like setting.

Actually the station was Lordship Lane on the branch of the London, Chatham & Dover Railway from Peckham Rye to Crystal Palace High Level, opened on 1 August 1865, quite close to Penge, and looking towards Nunhead. It was closed on 20 September 1954 and is now a housing estate.

The Dutch landscape-painter **Paul J. C. Gabriel** (1828–1903) of Amsterdam painted his *Train in Landscape* about 1887. (Kröller-Müller Museum, Otterloo near Arnhem.) It shows a train approaching beside a canal in a typically flat Dutch landscape.

Claude Monet (1840–1926), French landscape artist and one of the greatest of the Impressionists, was greatly inspired by Turner's work during his London visit in 1871. His earliest known railway picture is *Train dans la Champagne*, probably before 1870 (Louvre, Paris). In 1875 he painted his *Le Train dans la Neige* (Marmottan Museum,

Paris) and *Railway Bridge at Argenteuil* with a train passing over (Philadelphia Museum of Art). His best-known railway paintings are his series of ten of the Gare Saint-Lazare, Paris, in 1877. At the time he was still an unknown and impecunious artist. He put on his best clothes and introduced himself to the station superintendent as 'Claude Monet, the painter'. The superintendent, knowing nothing of art, believed he was a world-famous artist and had trains stopped and arranged specially for his benefit, and when Monet had finished he was graciously bowed out by uniformed officials. Today the series is scattered. One is in New York, one in Harvard University, and one in the Marmottan Museum, Paris.

Perhaps the best loved of all railway pictures is *The Railway Station* (1862) by **William Powell Frith** (1819–1909) showing a bustling scene at Paddington Station, London, with one of Gooch's broad-gauge engines, *Great Britain* of 1847, on the left, and on the right the arrest of a criminal. Above all are the leaping arches of Brunel's great station roof. The original canvas, 2.6 × 1.2 m (8 ft 5 in × 3 ft 10 in), hangs in the Art Gallery of Royal Holloway College Egham, Surrey. It was commissioned by L. V. Flatow, an art-dealer in Haymarket, London, and Frith was paid £4500 plus £750 for waiving his right to exhibit it at the Royal Academy and for allowing it to be exhibited at Flatow's Gallery where 21 150 people paid to see it in 7 weeks. It was exhibited at the International Exhibition, Paris, in 1878, and at the British Empire Exhibition, Wembley, London, in 1924.

The railway carriage compartment was a popular setting for some mid-Victorian paintings. **Abraham Solomon** (1824–62) produced a pair of paintings in 1854 entitled *First Class—The Meeting* and *Second Class—The Parting*. In the first a girl is fascinated by a young officer while her father talks animatedly between them. (In the original version the father was asleep in the corner, but this did not accord with Victorian decorum!) The second shows the sad parting of a mother and her son who is emigrating.

Honoré Daumier (1808–79) produced a vivid impression of travelling conditions in the mid-19th century in *The Third Class Carriage* about 1862 (Metropolitan Museum, New York).

August Leopold Egg (1816–63) left us *The Travelling Companions* (1862), now in Birmingham City Art Gallery, showing two extravagantly attired women, one asleep and the other reading, in a first class compartment, totally oblivious of the beautiful coastal scenery near Menton on the French Riviera.

To Brighton and back for 3s 6d by **Charles Rossiter** (1827–97) is a colourful painting of a group of mid-19th century excursionists, in a third class carriage with wooden seats and roof but no windows and with the rain driving in from the left (Birmingham Museum and Art Gallery).

The oldest known photograph of a locomotive, taken in 1851 at the Great Exhibition at the Crystal Palace, London. It shows Crampton 4-2-0 No. 134 *Folkstone* (sic) of the South Eastern Railway, built by Robert Stephenson & Co. in 1850.

London, where the photograph was taken. The Calotype process was patented in 1841 by William Henry Fox Talbot (1800–77).

Most of the increasing number of railway artists today are ardent railway enthusiasts. **Hamilton Ellis** is mentioned in 'Railways and Literature'. His numerous paintings are distinguished for their technical accuracy. The paintings of **Terence Cuneo** (b 1907) are remarkable for their animated life and energy. An outstanding example is his reconstruction of the opening of the Stockton & Darlington Railway.

Nathaniel Currier (1813–88) and **James Ives (1824–95)** formed a partnership in the USA in 1857 and for over 50 years mass produced about three lithographs every week, hand-coloured by one girl per colour. They depicted accurately every aspect of American life, and a great many were pictures of railways.

The earliest known photograph of a locomotive is a Calotype of the Crampton 4-2-0 No. 134 *Folkstone* [sic] built by Robert Stephenson & Company for the South Eastern Railway in 1851. It was exhibited at the Great Exhibition of 1851 in the Crystal Palace in Hyde Park,

RAILWAY ARCHITECTURE

In Victorian England the railway was almost alone in maintaining a high standard of architectural design. The most outstanding examples of fine design were the great viaducts and tunnel entrances, displaying a simplicity of form unique at the time. Some of the leading architects applied their skills to railway stations, but for these they often chose exotic and extravagant styles.
Famous examples were:
London, Euston Station, the Doric Arch and Great Hall designed by Philip Charles Hardwick. Both were demolished in 1962.
Newcastle upon Tyne Station built in 1846–55 in the Classical style, by John Dobson (1787–1865).
London King's Cross Station, 1851–2, in a style of the utmost dignity and simplicity by Lewis Cubitt (1799–1883).
Huddersfield Station designed by J. P. Pritchett & Son has a magnificent central edifice flanked by Corinthian colonnades. It was built in 1847–8.
London St Pancras Station, 1866–75, is one of the greatest pieces of Victorian Gothic, by Sir George Gilbert Scott

(1811–78). To pass through this building and to emerge beneath Barlow's tremendous arched roof is a startling experience.

York Station on the former North Eastern Railway is one of the finest examples in England, constructed in 1871–7, with three great arched roofs laid out in a long curve. The architects were Thomas Prosser, Benjamin Burley and William Peachy.

The great Doric Arch at Euston Station, London, erected in 1838 as the gateway to the London & Birmingham Railway. It was demolished in 1962 by British Railways who, bent on creating a 'new image', refused to have it re-erected close to Euston Road, even when the contractors offered to do this at their own expense. It might have survived had not one of the greatest protest demonstrations ever seen in Britain been opposed by the Prime Minister, then Harold Macmillan.

Outstanding examples in Europe and America are:

Paris, Gare du Nord, 1861–5, by Jacques Ignace Hittorf (1793–1867), and **Gare de l'Est**, 1847–52, by François Duquesney (1800–49).

Boston, Massachusetts, Kneeland Street Station, by Gridley J. F. Bryant (1816–97), completed in 1847.

Philadelphia, Broad Street Station on the Reading Railroad, designed by F. H. Kimball (1849–1919) and built in 1891–3, has a distinguished building displaying Renaissance features, and the greatest of all arched roofs, of 91.4 m (300 ft) span, by Wilson Brothers & Company, Engineers.

Helsinki Station, designed in 1905 by the Finnish architect Eliel Saarinen (1873–1950), was not completed until 1914. It is one of the finest in Europe.

Stuttgart Station, the work of the German architect Paul Bonats (1877–1951), is a pioneering example of modern station architecture. It was built in 1928.

Some of the best examples of modern station design are to be found on the London Underground system, mostly built in the 1920s and 1930s by Adams, Holden and Pearson, largely inspired by Frank Pick (1878–1941).

The ugliest, most depressing and inhuman station in Britain must surely be Birmingham New Street. It marks the depths to which British architecture descended in the 1960s. It can be entered or left only through a swirling car and taxi parking area or through a bustling shopping centre. Stairs and escalators to the platforms are too narrow to cope with crowds of commuters. The concrete raft over the platforms is oppressively low; in the middle of the station it is eternal night. On wild winter days it becomes a freezing wind tunnel, a result of the restricted headroom and the high buildings above forcing the air through beneath, though the wind does clear the diesel fumes. Only at the ends of the platforms, where there are no seats, can the wretched passenger enjoy the daylight and the English climate.

Fortunately the new station at Birmingham Snow Hill, opened on 5 October 1987, shows a commendable recovery in quality of design.

RAILWAYS AND MUSIC

One of the earliest composers to be influenced by the railway was the Dane, **Hans Christian Lumbye** (1810–74), whose *Københavns Jernbane Damp-Galop* or *Jernbane Galop* (Railway Galop) is an exhilarating orchestral item.

Hector Berlioz (1803–69) composed his *Chant des chemins de fer* (Railway Song) for tenor, chorus and orchestra in 1846. It was a setting of a poem by the French journalist, novelist and critic Jules Gabriel Janin (1804–74), commissioned to celebrate the opening of the Chemins de fer du Nord and first perfrmed at Lille on 14 June 1846. In Britain the first performance of the full score was given by the Royal Philharmonic Orchestra and John Aldis Choir at a concert in the Royal Albert Hall, London, to celebrate the 150th anniversary of the Stockton & Darlington Railway, in September 1975. It was performed again, by the Huddersfield Philharmonic Orchestra, College of Ripon and York St John Choir and Saddleworth Musical Society, at a promenade concert of railway music

Monkwearmouth Station, Sunderland, designed by Thomas Moore and opened in 1848 by the Newcastle & South Shields Railway. It became a through station in 1879 when the railway was extended to Sunderland. It was closed on 6 March 1967 and is now a railway museum.

conducted by Arthur Butterworth (see below) in the National Railway Museum, York, on 13 June 1976 as part of the York Festival.

Johann Strauss junior (1825–99) wrote a fast polka *Vergnügungszug* (Excursion Train), opus 281, in 1864.

His brother Eduard Strauss (1835–1916) composed an entertaining polka, *Bahn Frei*, opus 45, a musical train ride complete with guard's whistle and engine hooter, and followed it by *Mit Dampf* (With Steam), opus 70.

The Czech composer Antonin Dvořák (1841–1904) was a keen railway enthusiast and made daily visits to the Franz Josefs Station in Prague where he was friendly with many engine crews. On one occasion he was too busy to go, so he asked his future son-in-law, Josef Suk, to go and note the number of the engine on a particular train. The young man returned with the number of the tender by mistake, and Dvořák remarked to his daughter 'So this is the sort of man you intend to marry!'

The Swiss composer Arthur Honegger (1892–1955) was fascinated by the steam locomotive and in 1924 wrote his famous symphonic movement for orchestra *Pacific 231*. The figures 231 refer to the French axle notation. In the White system a 'Pacific' is a 4–6–2.

The Brazilian composer Hector Villa-Lobos (1877–1959) gave us a delightful musical picture of a Brazilian narrow-gauge train in 'The Little Train of the Caipira' which forms the final toccata section of his second *Bachianas Brasilieras* (Brazilian Bach pieces), composed in 1930.

The British composer **Arthur Butterworth** (b 1923) composed *Trains in the Distance* to a commission for the Saddleworth Festival, Yorkshire, in 1971. It is scored for orator, tape recording, chorus and orchestra, and is a setting of poems about trains by Gilbert Thomas, Charles Armstrong Fox, Thomas Wolfe, Siegfried Sassoon, Robert Louis Stevenson, Vivian de Sola Pinto, Alfred Noyes, Lawrence Durrell and Horatio Browne. It formed the first part of the concert in the National Railway Museum on 13 June 1976 (see above).

The British composer and conductor **Eugene Goossens** (1893–1962) was a knowledgeable railway enthusiast, as was **Constant Lambert** (1905–51). There have been many other organists, conductors, composers and performers with a keen interest in railways.

The spontaneous musical tendencies of the Italians received severe discouragement by Italian State Railways under a new law on 1 December 1980. For singing or playing musical instruments in trains soloists may be fined 30 000 to 90 000 lire, choral singers 500 000 lire, while orchestras and pop groups may receive two-month prison sentences.

Andrew Smith Halli
1836 - 1900
Inventor of the Cable Street F

irst Cable Street Railway in the World
Andrew S. Hallidie's Patent Endless-rope Street Railroad installed in San Francisco in 1873
View on Clay Street Hill, showing propelling or grip car and trailer

INDEX